WORLD POS in the TWENTIETH CENTURY

Second Edition

Harriet Ward
Formerly Lecturer in History
Kingsway — Princeton College
London

British Broadcasting C........emann Educational Books, London

Published by

BBC Publications
35 Marylebone High Street
London W1M 4AA

ISBN 0 563 21114 8

and

Heinemann Educational Books Ltd
22 Bedford Square
London WC1B 3HH

London   Edinburgh   Melbourne   Auckland
Hong Kong   Singapore   Kuala Lumpur   New Delhi
Ibadan   Nairobi   Johannesburg
Portsmouth (NH)   Kingston   Port of Spain

ISBN 0 435 31911 6

Printed by Butler & Tanner Ltd
Frome and London

Contents

Acknowledgements

The author and publishers wish to thank the following for permission to reproduce illustrations:

Associated Press Ltd., front cover
BBC Hulton Picture Library, Figures 2 and 3, 2.1, 2.3, 3.1, 9.1, 10.3, 11.3, 14.2, 15.1, 23.3
British Library, 10.4, 11.2
Brown Bros., 1.2
Camera Press, Title page (ii) 4.2, 15.3, 16.2, 16.3, 17.2, 18.1, 18.2, 19.1, 19.2, 19.3, Part IV title page, 23.5, 25.2, 26.3, 26.5
Fox Photos, 5.1
R. and S. Greenhill, Title page (i), ST11.1, 19.4, 20.2, 20.3
John Hillelson Agency, 7.1
Imperial War Museum, ST8.1, ST9.1
Keystone Press Agency, back cover, 5.2, 6.1, 7.2, 13.1, 15.2, 21.5
Library of Congress, Part I title page, 1.1
London Express News and Features Service, 12.2, 22.3
Museum of the City of New York, ST2.2
Novosti Press Agency, Title page (iii), Part II title page, 8.2, 9.2, ST5.1, 12.3
The Observer, 25.1
Popperfoto, 7.3, 13.2, 20.1, 25.5, 26.4, 26.6, 27.4

All artwork has been drawn by Reg Piggott.

Acknowledgement is made to:

Brian Catchpole, author of the *Map History* series, whose work is the basis of Figs. 4.1, 10.1, 10.2, 15.4, 16.1, 21.1, 21.2, 21.3, 21.4, 21.6, 22.1, 22.4, 23.4, 23.6, 24.4

Daniel Snowman, for permission to reproduce Figs. 3.2, 3.3 and 3.4 from his book, *America Since 1920* (Heinemann Educational Books, 1978).

Acknowledgement is also due to the following for permission to reproduce copyright material:

Victor Gollancz Ltd., for the extract from Edgar Snow, *Red Star Over China* (1937), p. 173.
B. T. Batsford Ltd., for extracts from Jack Miller, *Life in Russia Today* (1969), pp. 138–9.

BBC Radio Programmes:

'World Powers in the Twentieth Century'

'World Powers in the Twentieth Century' was launched in 1978–9 as a course of study, a book – and a 26-part series of radio programmes.

When starting to prepare the 'World Powers' programmes I wrote to a distinguished American asking if I might record an interview with him. He wrote back to say 'yes', but added that, since everything he had to say on the relevant subject was in his book, he wondered why I wanted him to say the same things all over again. He ended: 'I shall never understand the electronic media.'

His letter was friendly, but tongue-in-cheek. I wrote back in the same vein: 'I happen to have in my office the only copy of a dialogue recorded in ancient Greece between Socrates and Plato, which I plan to wipe soon so as to be able to re-use the tape. It contains nothing that Plato did not write in his philosophy books, so I take it that you would not be interested in hearing it ...'

*　　*　　*　　*

The best way of learning history, or philosophy for that matter, is from books. However, by using to the full the resources of the BBC's unique sound archives and the capacity of the tape-recorder, radio – particularly where the recent past is concerned – can authenticate the story by adding the sound of the drama and excitement of events and the voices of actual participants. It can both recreate the sense of historic occasions and put them into a perspective.

The programmes in the 'World Powers' series made no attempt to be comprehensive in themselves (for the 'story-line' of the series listeners were referred to this textbook), but they concentrated instead upon some of the more significant and colourful personalities, events and episodes in the history of the world powers. Listeners heard Lenin speaking in 1919; Huey Long and his corny campaign song; the death of Stalin and the impact of the Chinese Cultural Revolution vividly evoked by some who were there at the time; and so on. In this way it was hoped to *realize* the key events of the immediate past that may have been unexperienced or partially forgotten by the present-day listener.

The programme plan was as follows:

Programme 1 Introductory
  1 Versailles and the world in 1919

Programmes 2–6 America since 1920
  2 Al Smith and the presidential election of 1928
  3 Huey Long of Louisiana
  4 US attitudes towards the Spanish Civil War
  5 McCarthyism
  6 Civil Rights

Programmes 7–11 Russia since 1917
  7 The 1917 Revolution
  8 Stalin – the Twenties and Thirties
  9 The Siege of Leningrad
  10 Russia and the nationalities
  11 The quality of life in modern Russia

Programmes 12–16 China since 1911
  12 The Long March
  13 The war against Japan
  14 Village life in the Fifties
  15 The Cultural Revolution
  16 An assessment of Mao – the man and the myth

Programmes 17–22 The World Powers
  17 How the World Powers entered World War II
  18 Berlin, 1945-9
  19 De-Stalinization
  20 The Cuba Missile Crisis, 1962
  21 The Vietnam War
  22 Nixon's China visit, 1972

Programme 23 The world today

Programmes 24–26 Update USA, USSR and China

Throughout production of the radio series I kept closely in touch with the author of this book and initiator of the course, Harriet Ward, and tried to make radio programmes that, while entertaining radio in their own right, would complement class-room teaching and home study. For three years, all these elements ran alongside each other. But after 1981 the demands of programme planning and scheduling dictated that the 'World Powers' radio series would not be given further repeats. Furthermore, it was also felt that it would prove uneconomic to issue the programmes commercially on cassette.

As producer of the programmes I naturally regretted these decisions but as an historian I still believe that there is no substitute for a good book. The radio programmes were, perhaps, the icing on the cake, an enjoyable (I hope) and instructive confectionery for those trying to tackle the course and entertaining radio in their own right, but not in themselves the stuff of historical instruction. For this, the student must turn to more substantial fare, and for the purposes of the 'World Powers' course few text-books have been more carefully tailored than this excellent work by Harriet Ward. I am delighted that the book has been revised and updated, and I wish the new edition every success!

DANIEL SNOWMAN
BBC
April 1984

Preface to the Teacher

This book was written as the text of a Mode 3 GCE 'O' level history course devised by a group of teachers at Kingsway–Princeton College under the auspices of the Associated Examining Board. The needs of further education students were not well suited by the Mode 1 syllabus 'World Affairs from 1919 to the Present Day' which we had previously taught. Both teachers and students resented the fragmentary treatment made necessary by such a wide syllabus, which in any case could not be adequately covered in one year by part-time students. Like many others in the profession we also disliked having to fossilize the events of the past fifty years in the dry old memory game played out for examination purposes. History is not a glacier of unquestioned facts, after all. It is more like a jelly that never quite jells, prevented from setting by continuous research and reappraisal. A syllabus in recent political history is admirably suited to demonstrate this: for example, by looking at conflicting interpretations of the Cold War. It can also lead the student to an informed understanding of current events which are updating history every day.

In designing our own course we chose to study three countries in some depth while still covering a good part of the world affairs spectrum through the interrelations of these three 'world powers' since 1945. The Mode 3 system, giving teachers a say in what is taught and in the assessment of students' work, also allowed us to make links with other social sciences and with the literature and art of the period. We hoped that these sideways references would help to break down, in the student's mind at least, the boundaries between related subjects. The recent history of these countries gave ample scope for this treatment, and for another of our aims. By examining in turn their different political and economic systems we intended to explore the ideological issues underlying major world conflicts and thus to develop the political understanding of students who are almost (if not already) of voting age. This is an important 'life skill' for citizens of a democracy, and one which seems often to be neglected in schools.

The course was launched in 1972 at Kingsway–Princeton College and City and East London College. As there were no books in simple language to suit our purposes, we produced our own handouts as a basic text. During the first three years we were able to revise the syllabus and handout material in the light of classroom experience. Deficient language skills were a serious handicap for many students, and since most historical information is found in books and their own progress is mainly assessed through written work, we had to undertake some responsibility in this area. The AEB were commendably flexible in allowing us to develop the course in our own way while keeping a watchful eye on the interests of students, a function most tactfully performed by Mr. John Lloyd and the Board's Moderator for the course, Mr. Derek Culley.

In the next few years the Kingsway/City consortium was enlarged to include several other further education colleges and schools in the London area. It was at this stage that I undertook to write a full text for the course — the first edition of this book, published in 1978, which at once gained a wider circulation through the BBC Further Education radio course launched in 1978 in co-operation with the AEB (see page vii). During its three-year run the radio course built up a clientele of schools and colleges throughout the country where a modified version of our original Mode 3 course is still offered (AEB Syllabus 181), in some cases on a flexistudy basis with the additional help of a study guide produced by the National Extension College.

To take account of the wide variation in the age and educational background of the students taking the World Powers course, *language* was a prime concern in writing a common text for their use. Important terms and concepts had to be carefully defined, while at the same time we hoped that older or more able students could use a self-contained text with minimal help from a teacher. The questions at the end of each chapter can be used as a self-checking device or by a teacher working with a class; beyond this, teachers may wish to set their own follow-up work using other resources.

New readers may feel reassured to know that the book has already been well tried out with students of varying age and ability. The account of its origins is also a humble admission that it is not all my own work! To a large extent its scope and emphasis is the formula worked out at the experimental stage of our course by the four teachers who pioneered it—hence the editorial 'we' throughout the text. Certain sections are so closely based on the original handouts prepared by my colleagues that their contribution must be explicitly acknowledged here. Ian Macwhinnie, now Vice-Principal of North London College, produced the original material for Part I on the United States and offered the useful device of an appendix or Study Topic to develop more difficult or supplementary themes beyond the basic text. Hugh Higgins, now Vice-Principal of Kingsway–Princeton College, prepared our handouts for Part II on the USSR; three of his own books will be found on the Further Reading list for Parts III and IV of this book. The subject matter of Part IV, the World Powers' relations since 1945, was the most difficult to organize and condense; it was re-cast and re-worked more than once and we all had a hand in it. Chapters 21, 23, 24 and 25 of this volume incorporate material produced by Dr. Andrew Caplan, now Senior Lecturer for Multi-ethnic Education at North London College. To all these friends I am grateful for permission to crib their homework. Since I have worked over every passage, however, I must absolve them from blame for any errors of fact or slanted interpretation which may have crept in.

Preface to the Second Edition

A comparison of the first and second editions of this book underlines my point above about the fluidity of contemporary history. To maintain the topicality of the World Powers course and other syllabuses for which the book is now used, for several years now teachers have had to supplement and reassess certain sections of the text. The new edition will lighten their task for a few years at least. Three new chapters have been added, and one considerably extended, to update the chronicle of events. Other sections have been revised in the light of recent developments—for example to reflect the different picture of the Cultural Revolution in China which emerged after the death of Mao Tse-tung, and to give a fuller account of the world powers' earlier involvement in current areas of crisis such as the Middle East and Central America. As always it was the kaleidoscope of global politics which presented the most tricky problems of selection and emphasis; here again I must record my grateful thanks to my friends in the London Colleges Consortium, and especially to Andrew Caplan and Frank Nieto, for their helpful advice in planning the revisions.

To keep the book to a manageable size and price, non-essential Study Topics have been omitted or condensed while still retaining enough of this supplementary material to suggest further lines of enquiry for the keen reader. And when the new chapters in turn begin to seem like the yellowing pages of an old newspaper I hope students will eagerly turn to libraries and current news reports to find out what happened next.

HARRIET WARD
April 1984

Notes on Resources

Although originally devised with further education students in mind, the World Powers course has been well received in schools. Naturally younger pupils will need a slower pace and more illustrative material to cope with certain topics, but given these conditions, the text is quite within their reach. I am greatly indebted to Keith Wilkinson and his colleagues at Hendon School, who are using it with fourth- and fifth-year groups, for advice on other suitable books and additional resources for younger students; and to the library staff at Kingsway–Princeton College for invaluable help in tracking down information.

In the interests of younger readers particularly, I have separated into two sections the lists for Further Reading which will be found at the end of each Part of the book. Books listed as Supplementary Reading are those either written for, or with content and language easily accessible to, 'O' level students. Fiction and other illustrative material is included here, although some 15-year-olds will obviously find some of it too difficult. Books in the More Advanced category are those written for 'A' level studies or for the general reader. These usually contain more difficult language and few or no illustrations, but many younger students will be able to use them as resources for written work if they are encouraged to follow the advice on page xv and to ask for help if they need it.

Is it too much to expect a 15-year-old to read a chapter from Isaac Deutscher's *Stalin* for an essay on 'The Purges'? Some teachers will think so – and certainly the student will usually prefer to paraphrase a simple predigested text into his exercise book. In practice the teacher is best able to judge whether a particular student can tackle a more difficult book. But in principle surely we should begin to introduce 'adult books' at a stage which is close to the end of formal education for the majority of students, and for others a step towards the taxing requirements of 'A' level. Some at least may be successfully weaned on to the solid reading we hope they will pursue later on.

BOOKS

Once upon a time every school subject was encapsulated in one or two books whose antiquated type face and the list of reprints on the fly-leaf testified to at least twenty years in the schoolrooms of Britain and the Empire. Not so today! No teacher can keep up with the stream of overlapping books in his subject area, some already out of print by the time he hears about them, and never given a second lease of life. This is especially true in the field of contemporary history, perhaps because a book is thought to be useless if its concluding paragraphs have been outdated by later events. On the contrary it is very instructive to read a 1968 assessment of the Vietnam War, for example, and to compare it with a later one – always provided that students are warned to note the publication date of any book they consult. I have therefore *not* excluded from the Further Reading lists an 'old' book or a useful one which is currently out of print, since it may still be found in libraries and in any case may be reprinted. Nor should the book lists be regarded as definitive; there may be other equally good books on that area of the syllabus which I have not come across. In keeping with the broad view of history taken in this book, many of those recommended for further study are not specifically history books. On the other hand, I have not included (except by mentioning a few below) some well-known world history textbooks which, although they are useful to place the subject matter of this book in a wider context, usually do not take the reader deeper into a topic than the treatment it gets here.

Generally useful

Alan Palmer, *The Penguin Dictionary of Twentieth Century History, 1900–1978* (Penguin, 1979).

Martin Simons, *Three Giant Powers* (Oxford Social Geographies, Book 2), OUP, 1974. Useful comparisons of population, farming, industries, etc., in America, Russia and China. Simple text for younger students.

Maps are essential for certain topics. There are two useful series of map histories:

Martin Gilbert, *Recent History Atlas* (1966), *American History Atlas* (1968), and *Russian History Atlas* (1972), all published by Weidenfeld and Nicolson.

Brian Catchpole, *A Map History of the Modern World* (2nd ed. 1982), *A Map History of the United States* (1972, updated 1981), *A Map History of Russia* (1974, updated 1982), *A Map History of Modern China* (1976, updated 1982), *A Map History of Our Own Times: From the 1950s to the Present Day* (1983), all published by Heinemann Educational Books. This latter series has the extra advantage of a brief but informative accompanying text.

Teachers in the London area will already be aware of the material produced by the ILEA World History Curriculum Project, some of which is useful as illustration for this book or as a lead-up to it. Among the World History Topics for 14–16-year-olds are *Social Change* in India, China and the United States, and *Communist Societies* (the Soviet Union, Eastern Europe and China).

Two of the modern world studies promoted by the Schools Council History 13–16 Project are also relevant: *The Rise of Communist China* and *Arab–Israeli Conflict*. For each of these topics the Project team has produced a textbook (including much primary source material), a teacher's guide, a film-strip with notes, and an audio tape. Details from the publishers: Holmes McDougall Ltd, Allander House, 137–141 Leith Walk, Edinburgh EH6 8NS.

The magazine series *History of the Twentieth Century*, edited by A. J. P. Taylor and originally issued in 1968–70 (BPC Publishing Ltd/Phoebus Publishing Co.), is a valuable reference. Most of the articles must be classed as advanced reading for 'O' level students, but the excellent graphic material is accessible to all. The Further Reading lists indicate issues particularly relevant to certain chapters of this book. Although the publishers do not intend to reprint the series, many public and educational libraries will have a complete set, at least for reference.

Keesings Contemporary Archives, updated weekly, is invaluable for information about very recent events. If the school or college library doesn't have it, the public library will.

'O' Level textbooks

Most educational publishers include at least one modern world history textbook in their lists. Here are a few up-to-date and comprehensive ones:

Christopher Culpin, *Making History – World History in The Twentieth Century* (Collins, 1984). Written for CSE and 'O' level. Makes good use of primary source material.

Tony Howarth, *Twentieth Century History – The World Since 1900* (Longman, 1979). Linked to the BBC TV series mentioned below.

Peter Neville, *World History 1914–80* (Heinemann Educational Books, 1982).

Richard Poulton, *A History of the Modern World* (OUP, 1981).

J. B. Watson, *Success in Twentieth Century World Affairs* (John Murray, 3rd ed., 1984).

FILMS AND OTHER AUDIO-VISUAL AIDS

Most education authorities have their own libraries of films and other audio-visual material; consult the librarian or Media

Resources Officer for details of what is available, and the conditions on which educational radio and TV programmes may be recorded off-air for classroom use. For teachers or students without access to these services I give below a short list of addresses from which catalogues or further information can be obtained.

Audio Learning Ltd, Unit 1, 105A Torriano Avenue, London NW5 2RX. Audio-cassettes for 'O' and 'A' level.

Audio Visual Library Service, Pegasus House, Golden Lane, London EC1Y 0UD.

BBC Enterprises Hire Library, Guild House, Oundle Road, Peterborough PE2 9PZ. Video-cassettes of the educational series on twentieth century history made in 1977 (14 20-minute programmes) can be hired from here. Write to BBC School Radio, Broadcasting House, London W1A 1AA, for details of relevant audio-cassettes which may be purchased.

British Film Institute Distribution Library, 9 Chapone Place, Dean Street, London W1V 6AA.

Concord Films Council Ltd, 201 Felixstowe Road, Ipswich IP3 9BJ. Full catalogue £2.50.

Contemporary Films Ltd, 55 Greek Street, London W1V 6DB.

Educational and Television Films Ltd, 247 Upper Street, London N1 1RU.

Most of the independent television companies also transmit educational broadcasts, some of which may be useful for this course. Contact your regional ITV company for details of transmissions in your area. Some companies have also made good historical documentaries; look for these in film catalogues, or write direct to the company concerned if you are trying to track down a particular programme.

The well-known series of *Sussex Tapes* (30-minute audio-cassettes for purchase) includes many on relevant topics and personalities. These are rather academic for classroom use but may be useful for teachers'

preparation or as resources for students' written work. Details from Sussex Publications, 62 Queen's Grove, London NW8.

Films which we have used successfully include *The Promise Fulfilled and the Promise Broken* (1920s to 1941) and others in the Alistair Cooke BBC-TV series *America* (from BBC Enterprises); *I Have a Dream...*, the life of Martin Luther King (from Concord); the excellent Yorkshire TV documentary *Struggle for China* (from the British Film Institute); and *The War Game*, Peter Watkins' fictional documentary of a nuclear attack (also from the BFI)—but use it with care: it may horrify some in the audience. We have also used two well-made Soviet feature films about the Second World War to illustrate the Russian view of that traumatic event: *The Cranes are Flying* (made in 1957) and *Ballad of a Soldier* (made in 1959), both from Contemporary.

When it comes to the United States a whole history course could be devised from feature films! As a special supplement to Part I, Jack Babuscio, Lecturer in American History and Film Studies at Kingsway–Princeton College, has contributed a selected list of these.

NEWSPAPERS, TV AND RADIO PROGRAMMES, FAMILY SOUVENIRS

Encourage the library to collect news cuttings if it doesn't already do so. The death of an important person or any other dramatic event always produces a rash of survey articles: the files will quickly grow fat. Similarly there is a steady stream of retrospective TV and radio programmes, with or without the excuse of an anniversary to celebrate. Note – students need help to distinguish between fact and fiction in the historical TV programmes they watch!

Finally, it is worth remembering the fund of family possessions, your own or students', which can be used to personalize history.

How to use this book

This book was written as the text of a course which you may follow under the direction of a teacher or by working through it on your own. Its aim is to teach you new *facts*, new *ideas* and new *words*.

Facts

History is about the past – not only *what* happened in the past, but *why* it happened in the way it did. So you might think that history is just *facts*, and studying history is just learning them. But of course there are far too many facts! So in practice every writer of a history book, and every history teacher, makes his own choice of what to include and what to leave out; what to emphasize and what to skim over. Look at any two history books about the same period and you will see different versions of the same story.

We have made our own selection of facts and topics to include in this book. We preferred to explore a few themes thoroughly rather than describe everything sketchily. In the history of each World Power we have chosen themes which best explain that country as it is today – so that, for example, fifty years of earth-shaking events in China since 1900 are crowded into two chapters in order to examine more fully the Communist society which has developed there since 1949. In the case of the United States we have tried to give you an insight into British as well as American twentieth-century problems by deliberately emphasizing features which are common to other Western democratic countries. Throughout the book we have been less concerned to list every small fact of *what* happened (which you can look up in any library) than to help you understand *why* it happened. This is where the ideas come in.

Ideas

Why did Stalin in the 1930s force Russian farmers, often against their will, into large collective farms? Why were American soldiers fighting in Vietnam in the 1960s, 10,000 miles from home? Both these policies were shaped by the ideas behind them. Stalin in the 1930s was putting into practice the collectivist ideas of Communism; the American Government in the 1960s believed that if Communism was not stopped in Vietnam, it would spread to other countries – even to America. Both Stalin and the American Government held to these ideas so strongly that they were ready to disregard the opposition to what they were doing. Such is the power of ideas!

Some of the facts and ideas of history come from other social sciences:

Every nation's history and the life of its people is influenced by *geography* – its size, natural resources and neighbours.

The way a nation is governed is based on ideas from *political science* – the ideas of Democracy or Communism, for example. To understand the Great Depression in the United States you must learn something about the way wealth is created and shared out in America, and the way Americans *think* it should be shared out. These are facts and ideas from *economics*.

In studying political movements against 'Reds' and racial discrimination against blacks in America, research from *sociology* (the study of human society) is particularly useful.

So this book includes facts and ideas from these subjects as well as the record of dates and events which most people think of as 'history'.

Words

Some of you will be more competent than others in the use of language – the passport to knowledge in all the social sciences. We have tried to cater for these differences by using words carefully, and by giving special attention to important terms which are central to the course. These are marked (*k*) for *keyword* and explained at the end of the chapter in which they occur. Make sure you fully understand their meaning; they often describe the ideas which are such an important motivating force in history. Certain other words and phrases essential to understanding, and which may not be adequately explained in a dictionary, are marked with an asterisk (*) and briefly defined at the end of the chapter. If there are any other words unfamiliar to you, consult your teacher or a dictionary before going on.

Your own work

If you are working within a structured course it will always help to read each chapter *before* the lesson on that topic. If you are working on your own it is also wise to read slowly and carefully: digest one chapter thoroughly before moving on to the next.

At the end of the chapter there may be a Study Topic. This will sometimes contain more difficult ideas or language than the chapter itself; for example, it may be a document or speech from the period you are studying. If you find it *too* difficult, don't worry. A Study Topic is usually an 'optional extra' for students who have time and interest to go beyond the basic text, or can do so with additional help from a teacher.

Most chapters have questions at the end which will help you to learn as you go along. Exercises under the heading 'Did you notice?' will test your memory and understanding of what you have read. 'Can you explain?' questions cover main points in the chapter; you should now be able to answer them verbally or in writing in your own words (if you can't, look back to see what you missed!). Questions headed 'What's your view?' may be used

by teachers in different ways – but at least read and think about them before moving on.

If you are working under a teacher's direction you will probably have longer pieces of written work to do as well. In addition to any special instructions you are given, here is some general advice which will help you to write good essays for history and for other subjects.

WRITING A HISTORY ESSAY

How to use resources

History is largely a factual subject, so your essays will contain *information*. Naturally this information comes from books and other resources, but your essay must present it *in your own words*. You must not merely copy the words of books or handouts you have consulted. If you wish to make a point with a brief word-for-word quotation from someone else, you must put quotation marks round the borrowed phrase(s) and state the source in brackets or a footnote, like this: Horowitz, *From Yalta to Vietnam*, p. 32.

At the end of each Part of this book you will find a list of books and other resources on that section of the course. You may find other useful books in your school or college library, or your local public library. Ask the librarian to help you find books on the topic you are writing about.

Remember, you don't have to read a book right through to get the information you need. Scan the table of contents and the index to find the relevant chapters or pages. But *don't* write your essay straight from books: first make notes from all your sources and *then* write the essay from your notes.

Follow the rules

Two of the most common faults in essays are copying from books and handouts, and straying from the point. A fluent style and the ability to *answer the question* are also vitally important in written examinations, so it is wise to develop these skills in your essays. Here are the general rules which apply in history and other social sciences:

1. Use your own words.

2. Make sure you fully understand what is meant by the title you have been given, and write *only* about that. For example, an essay on 'What were Lenin's achievements between 1917 and 1924?' should not be just an account of events in Russia between those dates but should emphasize Lenin's part in them.

3. Support all general statements with facts. If you say 'The New Deal benefited the unemployed', give some examples of New Deal laws which did so.

4. Similarly, if the question asks for your own opinion, support it with facts. Historians do have opinions about what happened in the past and why, but these opinions must be based on evidence. Your wording should always make a clear difference between fact and opinion. For example: 'Khrushchev ordered missiles to be placed in Cuba in 1962' (fact). 'I think Khrushchev was to blame for the Cuba crisis of 1962 because he ordered missiles to be placed in Cuba' (opinion).

5. Don't forget these simple points of style which apply in any subject:

Organize what you have to say into clear paragraphs, gathering all the information on one point in one place.

Arrange the material into some overall 'shape': first an *introduction*, then the *development* of your ideas and information, and finally a *conclusion*. In history it is often helpful to write in chronological order: start with 1920, finish with 1970.

Make your points as clearly and briefly as possible.

Write clearly and as carefully as you can. And please *read over* your work before you hand it in! The student who wrote this paragraph evidently didn't:

'Firstly they can't afford to go and live anywhere else as they can't afford it, and secondly they couldn't afford it if they did have the money as it would cost far too much.' There's not a comma out of place here, but what's wrong with it?

6. Finally, note your teacher's comments on marked essays and discuss any queries you may have. Try not to make the same mistakes next time!

Note (with special reference to Part III)

In 1978 the Government of the People's Republic of China adopted a different form of spelling, the Pinyin romanization, for languages using the Roman alphabet. Since that date, publications from China in these languages use the new spelling, so that, for example, Peking becomes Beijing and Mao Tse-tung becomes Mao Zedong.

Throughout this book the old spellings have been retained for Chinese names already familiar in the West, while names which became prominent after 1978, such as Deng Xiaoping, are spelt in the new way. See page 221 for a glossary of some important names in both forms of spelling.

Figure 1   Europe before the First World War (1914).

Figure 2   Europe after the First World War (1919).

Starting Point:

The First World War, 1914–18

In this book we begin the history of each World Power at a point which suits its own story. For the United States this is 1920; for the Soviet Union, October 1917; for China, 1911. The purpose of this section is to set the scene; it will serve as a starting point for the first three Parts of the book.

Both the USA and the USSR became involved in the First World War, that terrible blood-bath which killed 10 million men and wounded 20 million more. America was herself little affected by the war, although it was her strength that saved the Allies from defeat in 1918. By 1920 she had returned to her pre-war policy of *isolationism* (k), as you will see in Part I. For Russia, as she was then called, the suffering caused by the war led directly to the event which begins Part II of the book: the Bolshevik (Communist) Revolution of October 1917. China was not involved in the fighting, but the Peace Settlement of 1919 had important results for her too, as you will see in Part III.

Europe in 1914 (Figure 1) looked very different from Europe in 1919 (Figure 2). Some of the smaller countries in Eastern Europe, such as Poland and Hungary, did not even exist as separate states. Poles, Hungarians and other *national groups* (k) were unwilling subjects of three huge empires which dominated the European continent: Germany, Austria-Hungary and Russia. Great Britain's strength was greater than her size because she had a huge overseas empire. Germany and France, the fifth large European power, also had colonies overseas.

These states were the main opponents in the war. Here is the full line-up:

The Allies	*The Central Powers*
Russia	Austria-Hungary
France	Germany
Great Britain	Turkey
Serbia (now part of Yugoslavia)	Bulgaria (joined 1915)
Rumania	
Japan	
Italy (joined 1915)	
USA (joined 1917)	
China (joined 1917)	

Some of these states were connected with others by treaty, and when war broke out between Austria-Hungary and Serbia in July 1914, one by one the other states were drawn into a general conflict. But the underlying cause of the war was the rivalry of the great powers, which had been developing for a decade before 1914. In particular, Germany had been trying to tilt the balance of power in her favour, and was well prepared by the militaristic policies of Kaiser Wilhelm II (Figure 3) to do so by warfare. In August 1914

Figure 3   Kaiser Wilhelm II in his military finery.

the German attack on Belgium and France opened the Western Front of the war, where its result was eventually decided. Here German troops fought British and French soldiers in the awful trench warfare which devastated the countryside of France. As late as mid-1918 the outcome of the war was still not certain. Russia had dropped out in 1917 (the reasons for this are explained on pages 3–4), and after three and a half years of war all the states taking part were nearly exhausted.

HOW AMERICA BECAME INVOLVED

In 1914 America had been determined to stay out of the war, which she regarded as a European affair. Many Americans were immigrants, or descendants of immigrants, who had fled to the 'New World' to escape European quarrels and persecution. During the nineteenth century America's foreign policy had been firmly isolationist – that is, 'minding her own business' and not getting involved in the affairs of other countries (though this didn't apply to near neighbours whose affairs America thought *were* her business).

In the words of one American President, 'the business of America is business'. During the World War it was her right as a neutral, so Americans thought, to sell arms and other supplies to the warring states – but in practice this trade was only with the Allies because the British Navy totally blockaded German ports. The German Navy's reply was to sink ships en route* to her enemies. In May 1915 a German U-boat (submarine) sank the British liner *Lusitania* with the loss of over 1,000 lives, including 128 Americans. The American Government protested, and Germany promised not to attack civilian or neutral ships in future.

But the British blockade was a stranglehold on Germany. In January 1917 Germany announced that she would once again sink *any* ships on sight. This, and the growing sympathy in America for the Allied cause, led

President Wilson to declare war on Germany in April 1917. But America was not prepared for war and she took some time to get a trained army to the battlefield in France.

In March 1918 the German army began a strong offensive which had great success at first, but in July the Allies counter-attacked. By that time the French and British forces were reinforced with 2 million American troops. One by one Germany's allies surrendered, and in November 1918 Germany herself gave in.

Once in the war, America (characteristically) took a high-minded view of it. President Wilson saw it as a crusade for freedom. In January 1918 he set out the Fourteen Points he thought necessary as a basis for a peace settlement. The peace treaties, he said, must 'make the world safe for democracy' and ensure 'a future free from war'.

THE EFFECT OF THE WAR ON RUSSIA

In 1914 Russia was ruled by a Tsar (Emperor) who had absolute power. This means that although he had advisers – even a parliament of sorts, called the Duma – he did not have to take their advice (and the ruling Tsar, Nicholas II, usually did not).

Even before 1914, Russia was a simmering kettle of discontent. For decades there had been demands for improvements in the living conditions of the people, and protests against the Tsar's one-man rule. Many political groups (some working 'underground' to escape the Tsar's secret police) had campaigned for reforms, but they achieved little. The Tsar obstinately held down the lid of the kettle – until in 1917 it boiled over.

When the war began, there was a surge of patriotic feeling in support of it. In 1914 Russian troops were successful against Austria-Hungary, but a counter-attack in 1915 brought heavy losses for Russia. The war soon caused disaster in the economy: supplies of arms ran out and the effort to make more slowed down the production of other goods.

Figure 4   Two would-be deserters from the Russian trenches are stopped by a comrade with raised rifle.

By the end of 1916, 14 million men had been called to fight in the war. Food became short, strikes and demonstrations broke out. Two million Russians had already been killed, 2 million taken prisoner, and 4 million wounded. How much more could the Russian people bear?

The events of 1917

The Tsar was so incompetent in running the war effort and dealing with problems at home that he gradually lost all support. In March 1917 he was forced to abdicate*. This was Russia's *first revolution* of 1917.

A Provisional Government was set up, led by members of the Duma, who mainly represented the interests of the middle class. At the same time, Soviets (councils) of workers and soldiers were formed, and these had the support of the working-class in the cities. The next few months are sometimes called the period of Dual Power because there were two centres of power: the 'official' Provisional Government and the Soviets.

At first the Soviets co-operated with the Provisional Government headed by Kerensky. But this government made serious mistakes. First, it tried to continue the war: another offensive was launched in July, but it failed, and more Russian soldiers were added to the heap of dead. Secondly, the new government did nothing about *the land*. For years the millions of peasants (the vast majority of Russia's population) had wanted a chance to own the land they worked, but which still belonged to a few rich men. Now, tired of waiting, the peasants began to seize the land for themselves. Thousands of soldiers left the trenches (Figure 4) and returned to their villages to join in the land-grab.

In the cities, living conditions grew desperate, and the Provisional Government seemed unable to cope. Gradually the real power of government transferred to the Soviets: they issued orders and people obeyed them. Now the Bolsheviks – one of the many political groups which had been active in Russia for years – began to take control of the situation. In April their leader Lenin had arrived home from exile in Switzerland, and after that, events moved swiftly. Lenin called for 'All power to the Soviets!' and campaigned against the Provisional Government under the slogan 'Peace! Bread! Land!' – which exactly expressed the people's desires. The Bolsheviks' popularity increased and by September they had control of the Moscow and Petrograd Soviets. Lenin was forced into hiding in July but he continued to direct his party, and now began to plan a Bolshevik take-over of power.

With remarkably little bloodshed (that was to come later) the Bolsheviks took control of Russia on 7 November 1917 (25 October by the old Russian calendar†). Their Red

†At that time Russia was still using the Julian calendar, 13 days behind the one in use in Europe. When the new government changed to the European calendar, 25 October became 7 November.

Guards seized the main government buildings in Petrograd, the capital, and dismissed the Provisional Government. This October Revolution was the *second revolution* of 1917, and the government that took power then still rules the USSR today.

In Part II you will learn more about Lenin and the ideas of Marxist Communism that the Bolshevik Party, under his leadership, now began to put into practice in Russia. One of the first acts of the new government was to sign an armistice with Germany, which ended Russia's part in the First World War.

THE VERSAILLES PEACE SETTLEMENT

In 1919 a Peace Conference was held at Versailles, near Paris. In due course, peace treaties were signed with all the defeated powers and the 1919 Treaty of Versailles with Germany gave its name to the whole peace settlement.

New states

America's President Wilson took a leading part at the Peace Conference. He tried to put into practice American ideals of self-government and democracy (we shall fully discuss these ideals later, in Part I). Austria's empire was stripped away from her and Germany too was reduced in size (Figures 1 and 2). Vast areas of former Tsarist Russia were also put into the 'pool' of land which was formed into six new states: Finland, Estonia, Latvia, Lithuania, Poland and Czechoslovakia. Serbia was greatly enlarged and became Yugoslavia.

Russia's new government was disappointed by the peace settlement. The Bolsheviks had accepted harsh terms from Germany in the Treaty of Brest-Litovsk in March 1918, expecting that it would be cancelled by Germany's eventual defeat at Allied hands. But most of Russia's lost territories became independent states and it was left to a later Soviet leader, Josef Stalin, to recover them (see Part II).

China too had cause for complaint at Versailles. She had little interest in the European war but had been persuaded by the Allies to declare war on Germany in 1917, and hoped to be rewarded by getting back areas of China which Germany had 'owned' for many years. But she did not know that the Allies had secretly promised these to Japan, China's strong and aggressive neighbour. In disgust, Chinese delegates at Versailles refused to sign a treaty which gave away parts of China to another state. But there was nothing more they could do about it.

However, the most aggrieved victim of the 1919 settlement was defeated Germany.

Germany's fate

Germany lost one-eighth of her land area in Europe, including valuable mineral resources and $6\frac{1}{2}$ million people. Her overseas colonies were also confiscated, but the victorious colonial powers (Britain and France) did not give up theirs. In fact they and other states were given Germany's to run! Germany was also forced to say that she alone was 'guilty' for the war, to accept the limitation of her army and navy to token forces, and the demilitarization of the Rhineland, bordering on France. Finally she was expected to pay huge sums in reparations to the victors, which would place a crippling burden on her already shattered economy.

Germany's emperor, the Kaiser, had fled to Holland to escape the consequences of his country's defeat. The new democratic government of the Weimar Republic* therefore had to suffer the shame of signing a treaty which nearly all Germans thought was very unfair. This enabled Adolf Hitler later to accuse the ruling Social Democratic party of 'stabbing Germany in the back' and to rally support for his own aggressive policies of 'revenge' (see Chapter 12).

Despite the genuine effort of President Wilson to draw up a 'fair' settlement, the Treaty of Versailles left many grievances burning in European hearts which would erupt into another world war only twenty years later.

But at the time no one dreamt that such a thing could happen, for any new arguments between states would be dealt with by the League of Nations – or so they thought.

The League of Nations and collective security

President Wilson was especially keen on the League of Nations; indeed it was largely his creation. Like the United Nations (set up after the Second World War), the League was supposed to keep peace in the world on the principle of *collective security*. The idea of this is that if one state attacks another, all the others will act 'collectively' to defend the victim. So far, at any rate, the idea has never worked properly in practice. For one thing it is often difficult to decide, when two nations start fighting, which is the aggressor and which is the victim. But the main reason why collective security has not stopped wars is that governments – whatever they may say at international meetings – are still mainly interested in the welfare of their *own* people. Only if a state sees its own interests at stake will it sacrifice its men by going to war, or upset its economy by breaking trade relations with another state.

America returns to isolationism

Another reason for the weakness of the League of Nations was that several important states were not members. Germany was not allowed in until 1926 and the USSR joined only in 1934. But the most important absentee was the United States. To President Wilson's bitter disappointment, a mood of renewed isolationism swept America as soon as the war was over. He could not persuade Congress (the American parliament) to accept his view that America should, in the twentieth century, play a continuing role in international affairs.

So the United States, by this time already the strongest nation in the world, refused to join the League of Nations or take part in enforcing the peace treaties which its own President had partly written. In 1920 America returned to 'minding her own business', and it was not until after the Second World War that she took up her present position in the centre of the world stage.

*GLOSSARY

abdicate, usually means (as it does here) to give up a throne and therefore the right to rule.

en route, a French term meaning 'on the way' (to somewhere).

republic, a state without a monarch, usually ruled by an elected government.

KEYWORDS

isolationism, a policy of not becoming involved in disputes with other countries, and not signing treaties or joining international organizations. This is the foreign policy which the United States followed until 1941 except for her participation in the First World War. The policy arose out of her own history (see Part I). America was forced into the Second World War when Japan attacked her in 1941, and this ended her policy of isolationism. Since then her government has not returned to it.

national groups (nationality), 'nationality' can be a legal term: you need to be a 'national' or citizen of a state to get a passport. But it really means the common bonds of history, language, race, culture, religion which make people *feel* they belong together. This list of bonds is not the same for every nationality – for example, the English are not all of the same race or religion, while the word 'British' includes more than one nationality: English, Scots, Welsh, etc.

National groups don't always have a nation they can call their own! This often leads them to a policy of *nationalism*, trying to unite together and (often) to push out foreign rulers. We shall come across important examples of nationalism later.

Questions

Did you notice?

1. In 1914, Poland was (a) a separate state, (b) part of other empires, (c) a British colony
2. The Western front was in (a) France, (b) Russia, (c) Britain
3. A blockade is (a) a fortress, (b) a submarine, (c) a method of warfare
4. Before 1917 the United States (a) declared war on Russia, (b) sold arms to the Allies, (c) sank the *Lusitania*
5. The Duma was (a) a Russian emperor, (b) a kind of parliament, (c) the Russian secret police
6. True or false?
   In the Versailles peace settlement:
   (i) Czechoslovakia became a separate state
   (ii) Germany was allowed to keep her colonies
   (iii) Japan gained territory in China
   (iv) the United Nations was set up
   (v) the United States lost territory
7. Which statement is *more* accurate?
   (i) The Bolsheviks became popular in 1917 because
   (a) they offered what the Russian people wanted
   (b) they won the war against Germany
   (ii) Most Germans felt bitter about the Versailles Treaty because
   (a) they thought it was unfair
   (b) they wanted to continue the war
   (iii) One weakness of the League of Nations was that
   (a) it did not allow the United States to join
   (b) the United States decided not to join

Can you explain?

8. What made the United States declare war on Germany in 1917? Why had she not done so earlier?
9. What were the most urgent needs of the Russian people in 1917? How did they show what they wanted?
10. President Wilson believed in the right of nations to govern themselves. How was this shown in the post-war settlement of Europe?
11. Give two examples of 'unfair' provisions in the 1919 settlement.
12. What is meant by the term 'collective security'?

What's your view?

13. For what reasons might one state sign a treaty with another?
14. Should people of one nationality *always* have the right to rule themselves? Can you think of any examples of:
    (a) states (such as Britain) which contain more than one nationality?
    (b) states which contain only *part* of one nationality?
15. Read again the paragraph about the League of Nations (page 5). Do you think that 'collective security' can ever work? Do you know of any cases where the League of Nations or the United Nations has tried to 'punish' any state? Do you think national governments should just 'mind their own business' or try through international action to make each other behave peacefully and fairly?

Billboard on a Californian highway (about 1936), part of a national advertising campaign to help business out of the depression.

1

America: Ideals and Reality

America's economic strength

The land of America is large and rich. On the whole it has a good climate and plentiful resources, especially such vital ones for industry as coal, oil and water. No part of the United States is totally uninhabited, although there are desert areas (and Alaska) which are thinly populated. But of the total population of 224 million, most live in the eastern part of the country around big industrial cities and along the eastern seaboard. It was from this area that American pioneers pushed westwards in the nineteenth century, adding states to the Union one by one until there were forty-eight. Alaska and Hawaii became states in 1959, making fifty 'united states' today.

Even more important than her natural riches is the fact that America's economy is *developed*. Her oil is driving the wheels of industry; water is dammed to make electricity; an efficient transport network spans the country. This is the main reason why, although smaller both in area and population, the USA is so much more powerful than her rival World Powers, the USSR and China. By now America has nearly used up some of her resources (iron ore, for example, which is needed for making steel) but for the time being, at any rate, she is rich enough to buy what she lacks from other countries. With less than 6 per cent of the world's population, America uses 30 per cent of the world's annual output of resources. Her standard of living – the 'comforts of life' that most of her people have – is among the highest in the world. Even the poorest Americans are better off in this way, at least, than most other people.

Her system of government

The United States of America was founded in 1789 as a democratic republic with a federal system of government. Each of the fifty states is to some extent self-governing, but the federal government in Washington has wide powers over the whole nation, and of course it is also responsible for foreign policy. Congress, like our Parliament, is the law-making body, but two important features are different from our system: (1) the special role of the Supreme Court, and (2) the independence of the President from Congress (see Study Topic 1). In the twentieth century there have been strong and weak Presidents, but undoubtedly the one who brought the greatest change to America, and to her foreign policy, was President Franklin D. Roosevelt (FDR).

America has two main political parties. For historical reasons both parties encompass a wide range of interests and attitudes: they cannot be simply labelled Left and Right. Nowadays, however, the Republican Party is usually more conservative than the Democratic Party: it tends to favour the interests of business and richer Americans, whereas the more progressive or reforming policies of the twentieth century (for example, trying to help blacks and poorer people) have come from the Democrats.

America in the twentieth century

America has changed less in the twentieth century than either the USSR or China. In 1900 she already had a developed economy, while both those powers were still industrially 'underdeveloped' (as China still is today). Nevertheless, there have been important changes in America in this period. One is the growing wealth of her people and the demand from poorer Americans, especially blacks, for a greater share in it. Another is the greatly increased power and activity of the federal government. In foreign policy the main theme is America's change from an isolationist policy of 'minding her own business' to an interventionist policy of getting involved in everyone else's!

These developments resulted from the events which are described in this book. But as we suggested earlier, the course of history is influenced not only by impersonal facts but by the *ideas* of the people concerned. To understand American history in the twentieth century we therefore need to know something about Americans. What sort of people are they, and what do they believe in?

AMERICAN IDEALS

The 'American way of life' that her citizens value so highly is much more than hot dogs and efficient plumbing. Apart from these material comforts – which they do enjoy and cherish – Americans hold strong beliefs about the way human society should be organized. The source of these ideas is American history itself: they are expressed in the words of the Founding Fathers of the eighteenth century and in the deeds of more humble Americans who lived before and after them.

Origins of 'the American creed'

Personal freedom was the magnet which drew the first English settlers to America: freedom to own land and perhaps get rich, freedom to believe and practise any religious faith. One of the earliest colonies was established in New England, where the Puritans landed from the *Mayflower* in 1620. But these refugees from religious persecution in England were themselves so intolerant of other beliefs that anyone who could not accept their narrow creed had to go elsewhere. Later Rhode Island and Connecticut were founded by more broad-minded Protestants, Maryland by a Catholic, and Pennsylvania by Quakers. Thus America has always contained groups holding different religious views, although most – like the Puritan faith – were varieties of Protestantism*. One important Protestant belief is the idea that everyone has a personal duty to God, and must earn a place in Heaven by 'good works' during his life on earth.

Alongside freedom of thought, equally important to these early Americans was the economic freedom to enrich themselves through trade or farming. In that wide-open, fertile land, many did so. A new upper class of gentlemen farmers and merchants developed which eventually came to resent the controls and taxes of London. In 1776 $2\frac{1}{2}$ million Americans declared their independence from Britain with these famous words of Thomas Jefferson:

> We hold these truths to be self-evident, that all men are created equal, that they are endowed by their Creator with certain unalienable* rights. Among these are Life, Liberty and the Pursuit of Happiness. To secure these rights Governments are instituted among Men, deriving their just powers from the consent of the governed. Whenever any form of government becomes destructive of these ends, it is the Right of the People to alter or abolish it . . .

This classic statement of democratic principles has inspired other revolutionaries and democrats the world over. But the Founding Fathers did not mean those words to be taken in quite the way that later generations interpreted them. They were asserting the *political* right of overseas colonies to self-government but they did not intend a *social* revolution. They expected that men like themselves – men of property, education and refinement – would 'naturally' become the leaders of a free society, and that others would 'naturally' look up to them. Only in the course of later history did other Americans – and eventually blacks, and Indians, and women! – rise up to claim that they too were 'created equal' and therefore entitled to a share in government and a chance to compete for wealth and status on equal terms.

These later developments were made possible by the loose-fitting Constitution of the United States drawn up in 1787. It left considerable powers in the hands of the separate states and was carefully designed to prevent any branch of government from becoming too powerful. It embodied Jefferson's belief that 'the best government is the least government' – yet when the need arose through changing circumstances, it could be stretched to give the government in Washington far-reaching powers over the whole nation. The Founding Fathers wrote a document so durable and flexible that a system of government devised for a small nation of farmers is still in use today for a vast, industrialized continent of over 200 million people.

The American Constitution clearly states those *individual rights* which Americans believe are man's 'birthright' – not only to life and liberty, but to the protection of property. It is the framework for the political system of *Democracy* (k) and the economic system of *Capitalism* (k) practised in the United States. Before you read further, look at the definitions of these words on page 14. You will see that they also apply to Britain and other countries in the West, which developed their own democratic systems more slowly from the same belief in individual liberty.

Pride in their revolutionary origins and a reverence for the Constitution are often called 'the American creed'. It is not quite a religion, but many Americans have an almost religious faith in it. They see the proof of their system in the remarkable success of America as a nation and the 'rags to riches' life stories of some of her citizens.

Rugged individualism

By 1920 the United States was already the richest and strongest nation in the world. Americans attributed this success to the spirit of 'rugged individualism' which they believed gave their forefathers a special moral strength. They looked back admiringly at the self-reliant, hard-working individuals, both famous and anonymous, who 'made America what she is today': first the trapper, the lone cowboy, the pioneer farmer who pushed the frontier of the United States westwards to the Pacific (Figure 1.1); then the great inventors who gave us the electric light-bulb, the telephone, the sewing-machine and many other useful devices of modern life; and in their footsteps the industrial tycoons who planted oil derricks and factory chimneys across the land – and made a personal million or two on the way.

Here you may notice a connection with the 'Protestant ethic' we mentioned earlier: the idea that everyone has a *duty* to work hard throughout his life. Rugged individualism was not only the route to success but the *right* way to live. This belief made it 'okay' to deprive the Indian tribes of their land because they were not developing it as God intended man to develop His gifts. Americans assumed that 'their way' was the best way and therefore felt no guilt about sweeping aside more primitive peoples who followed a different way of life.

The American Dream

These adventurous Americans had a try-anything, go-anywhere attitude to life. With plenty of rich land to develop and no heavy old traditions to weigh them down, they could make up the rules of the American way of life as they went along. How different from the cramped and class-ridden society of the 'old world'!

The United States was founded by immi-

Figure 1.1 A pioneer family's sodhouse in the Dakotas, 1885.

grants and peopled by later waves of new-
comers. Towards the end of the nineteenth
century the steady stream became a flood:
between 1880 and 1920, over 23 million
poured into the American 'melting-pot'
(Figure 1.2). The new arrivals at once caught
the infectious optimism of a country in which
anyone could achieve anything if he tried
hard enough. For you didn't have to be born
in America to join in the American Dream –
you could arrive barefoot and penniless and
in one short life-time perhaps become a millionaire or a Supreme Court judge!

But was it really like that? Well no, not
quite. Real American history was of course
more complicated and often more cruel than
this simplified picture.

AMERICAN REALITY

One serious violation of the American creed
was the fact that many Americans were not

considered to be 'created equal' at all. Blacks
and other racial minorities were not given
equal chances even *after* they had been
granted legal equality, and this situation was
not effectively challenged until the liberation
movements of the mid-twentieth century.

Nativist movements

Rugged individualism on the frontier had its
bad side too – for example the vigilante
groups of 'respectable citizens' who would
lynch a presumed law-breaker on the excuse
that the sheriff was fifty miles away – or perhaps without any excuse. Similar groups
sometimes savagely terrorized unpopular
local minorities: Catholics, Jews, Negroes or
dark-skinned immigrants. This intolerance of
minorities was not merely local or temporary:
it gave wide national support to *nativist*
movements like the Know-Nothing political
party in the 1850s, the American Protective
Association of the late 1880s and the

11

Figure 1.2   Immigrants arriving in America.

notorious Ku Klux Klan. The motive was not only racism but the Protestant majority's fear of religious 'contamination', especially by Catholics. From 1807 to 1920 the Catholic population increased from 9 million to 18 million, mainly through the immigration of poor Irish and Italians to eastern cities.

As for the American Dream, there was always enough truth in it to make it more than a myth. But we might remember that 'history is written by those who survive', as a wise man once remarked, while 'those who go under have the experience'! For every Andrew Carnegie or Judge Felix Frankfurter there was an abandoned patch of barren land in Kansas, a thousand illiterate immigrants whose 'Dream' ended in the sweatshops of New York City at 8 cents an hour. Bullies and cheats were quick to exploit the 'free for all' to their own advantage: votes and influence in government could be bought, and even more useful were the deals and sharp practices agreed upon in saloon bars and social clubs, outside politics altogether.

How to succeed in America

New arrivals, however, soon copied the example of other Americans by forming or joining social and economic groups whose aim was not to overthrow the big boys but to find a place in the sun for themselves. Henry Clay Frick, an industrialist who shamelessly exploited cheap immigrant labour, sourly complained, 'The immigrant, however illiterate or ignorant he may be, always learns too soon.' Poles, Russian Jews, Italians all hurried to 'Americanize' themselves, for only when they were '100 per cent American' could they meet the scornful stare of older-established WASP Americans (White Anglo-Saxon Protestants) who took pride in tracing their ancestry back to the earliest white settlers.

This is an important feature of American history – and her twentieth-century society – which is different from the European experience. Social and economic conflicts in America have been not so much between the 'working class' and the 'upper class' as a competition for influence and priority between interest groups: Western frontiersman versus Eastern merchant, homesteader versus cattle rancher, farmer versus railroad interests. Hostility was increased when other issues were combined with economic interest: 'free' industrial north versus slave-owning agricultural south, Protestant small town versus Catholic cities, richer 'old Americans' versus poorer 'new Americans'.

There have been Socialist political parties in American history, but the collectivist* ideas of Socialism and Communism could never match the powerful appeal of individual success in the American Dream. However poor and exploited he was, the American working man hoped rather for a lucky break which would catapult *him* to the top than for a re-ordering of society to provide 'fair shares for all'. He was often just as ready to join a hue and cry against 'Commies' and other left-wing radicals* as the propertied classes who were directly threatened by their propaganda*.

Populism and reformism

Yet concern for the underdog and a hatred of exploitation is also part of the American character. We can see something like a class struggle in the occasional outbursts of populist feeling when the 'plain man' of the rural West would launch a candidate in state or national politics to expose the dirty deals of Big Business (often hand-in-glove with Big Government) which fleeced the honest small farmer or businessman. Moral outrage at corruption and exploitation also spurred numerous social reformers and a group of 'muck-raking' writers in the early 1900s – an episode which has a modern parallel in the

'investigative journalism' which laid bare the trickery of the Nixon Government in the 1970s. Americans have never been shy to 'demand an explanation' from their high-ranking public servants and businessmen. The Investigating Committees of Congress are another channel for this aspect of American democracy.

Americans want to 'do right'

Often the motive in campaigns for 'clean government' and 'clean living' was strong religious sentiment. One example of this is the important Puritan influence handed down from the early settlers of New England. America has always been a breeding-ground of Protestant fundamentalist* sects, from Shakers, Mormons and Holy Rollers to the Jesus Freaks of the 1960s. These groups tried to live their own lives exactly as the Bible said, and shouted loud warnings to other 'sinners' about the hell-fire and damnation awaiting them. They deeply distrusted the loose-living cities and in the early twentieth century tried their best – but in vain – to put a brake on the inevitable development of permissive modern America. Most Americans happily disregarded their 'old-fashioned' views, but to others they sometimes sounded like the voice of their own half-forgotten Protestant conscience.

It will be clear by now that Americans are a very moralistic people. They are self-confident, but also self-critical. They are ready to admit defects in their own system and to try to correct them, for they do sincerely *want* to live up to their own ideals. But the ideals themselves are beyond question, for are they not 'obviously' right? Like other people with a strong faith, Americans expected that everyone else would eagerly adopt it if they had the chance. When they set out to spread the American way of life around the world they therefore found it hard to accept that people with a different historical experience, and different views about the 'right' way to organize human society, might reject American ideals altogether.

These were the challenges America had to meet in the twentieth century. She has had to recognize dramatic failures of the American Dream at home, and try to repair the damage. In the outside world she faced a head-on collision with Communism, an ideology with moral strength – and in due course military strength – to match her own. How she has coped with these problems you will see in the course of this book.

*GLOSSARY

collectivist, a word applied to political beliefs such as Communism or Socialism which emphasize the *collective* interests of the whole community (see the full discussion of these ideas in Part II, pages 88–9).

fundamentalist, a term for religious sects which insist that the 'fundamentals' of the Bible are literally true.

left-wing radicals, in general 'left-wing' means a view leaning towards Socialism and 'right-wing' towards Capitalism. 'Radical' means extreme, and 'a radical' usually means an extreme left-winger; but there is also a 'radical right-wing' view (see Chapter 5).

propaganda, publicity or information about a cause or doctrine which is designed to gain support for it. It has been called 'the art of persuasion'.

Protestantism, the branch of Christianity which broke from the Catholic Church in the sixteenth century; early leaders were Luther and Calvin.

unalienable (nowadays *in*alienable), cannot be taken away.

KEYWORDS

Capitalism, the *economic* system that America practises. It is based on the private ownership of property, including industry and land. An individual can invest his money (capital) in land or a business, where its value may increase and make him richer than others. This is thought to be a good thing because the chance of becoming rich will make him work hard to save up capital, and (in theory) everyone has the opportunity to do this. Capitalists believe in a *laissez-faire* system (see Chapter 2) because it encourages effort of this kind.

Democracy, the *political* system of America, i.e. the way it is governed. The word means 'government by the people' and therefore any state with an elected government (including Communist states) may be called a democracy. The special features of American or Western Democracy (sometimes termed Liberal Democracy) are these:

1. *An elected government* which serves for a limited term. All adult citizens may vote at elections. Any number of political parties may be formed and may put forward candidates, but in practice America (and Britain) has a 'two-party system' in which there are only two main parties.

2. *Individual rights* are considered very important. They were written into the American Constitution and are protected by law. They include the right to free speech, free assembly (i.e. to meet and form organizations), free movement, freedom from arrest without charge, a free press, etc.

3. *The role of government is limited.* Americans believe that the government should do only what is necessary, and no more. As Thomas Jefferson put it, 'that government is best which governs least'.

The American Constitution put these principles into practice in what many people consider to be, at least on paper, the most democratic system of government ever devised. Some knowledge of how the system works is essential to an understanding of American history, so you should read Study Topic 1 before you go on to the next chapter.

The American System of Government

There are fifty separate states in the United States: California, Idaho and so on. The government of each state is a smaller version of the national government: each system has a *legislature* (Congress) to pass laws; an *executive* (the President, or a state Governor) to initiate policy and carry out the wishes of Congress; and a *judiciary* (the Supreme Court) to decide legal disputes. A state law applies only in the state where it was passed; a federal law applies throughout the land.

The federal Congress consists of a Senate to which each state sends two Senators, and the House of Representatives in which Congressmen are elected by proportional representation (so that a populous state like New York will have more seats than a thinly-populated one like Alaska). Congressmen are elected every two years, the President every four years, and Senators every six years.

Limited powers of government

When the original thirteen colonies (now states) banded together in 1787 to form the United States of America, they wanted to remain as self-governing as possible. So they gave their national or federal government in Washington only limited powers. A rough list of what it was allowed to do was written into the Constitution, and all the other powers of government were kept by the states.

The Constitution also separated the powers of government and built in a system of 'checks and balances'. The President acts independently of Congress and he and his Cabinet are not members of it; he cannot be

questioned by Congress in the way that our Prime Minister is 'accountable' to Parliament. The system was supposed to prevent either the President or Congress from becoming too powerful. Thus Congress can reject a proposal from the President, or refuse to vote the money he requests for some purpose; and equally, the President can veto a law passed by Congress. Congress can override the President's veto by passing the law again with a two-thirds majority, but Congress itself can be overruled by the Supreme Court.

The role of the Supreme Court

If at any time there is a dispute about whether a state or federal law is allowed by the Constitution, the Supreme Court decides the matter. In other words the Supreme Court can *cancel* any state or federal law by declaring it 'unconstitutional'. So it plays an important part in government. By taking a narrow or 'states' rights' view of the Constitution, the Court can *check* the federal government's activities. By taking a broad or national view of what the Constitution allows, it can *enlarge* the powers of Washington. In the twentieth century most of the Court's decisions have had the latter effect.

Amending the Constitution

The Constitution was not meant to be final for all time. New powers could be given to the federal government, or taken away, by passing a Constitutional Amendment. But this is a long and difficult process. First the amendment must be passed by both Houses of the federal Congress, and then considered by the state governments. When three-quarters of these have accepted it, the amendment becomes law. The first ten Amendments came into force in 1791 as the Bill of Rights, embodying the basic personal liberties which Americans value so highly.

The system in practice

On the whole the American Constitution has proved remarkably adaptable to changing needs and circumstances over 200 years. When necessary the Supreme Court has bent with the wind of change, for example by deciding that the practice of racial segregation which had been found 'constitutional' in the nineteenth century was *not* constitutional in 1954 (see pages 65–6). Similarly a mistake like the 18th Amendment, which brought in an unworkable law prohibiting alcohol throughout the nation, could be cor-

rected with another Amendment to cancel it (see pages 22 and 23).

Nevertheless some criticism of the system has been made. The frequency of elections sometimes paralyses the White House at a moment of domestic or international crisis. And when it happens that a President of one party has to work with a Congress dominated by the other party, their 'checks' on each other can cause deadlock. This has happened frequently in recent years, and under President Nixon (1968–74) it led to such an abuse of Presidential power that special laws were passed to reassert the rights of Congress. This episode (see page 74) also demonstrated a dangerous inflexibility in the American system: the President, even if he becomes unfit for office through illness or corrupt behaviour, can only be removed by death or the long and complicated process of impeachment. Some people think that at least these aspects of the Constitution–the inviolability of the President and his relationship to Congress–now need to be reformed.

2

The Roaring Twenties

Figure 2.1 Liberated young women of 1925. Older people were deeply shocked by sights like this.

You may already have a mental picture of America in 'the roaring twenties' from the many books and films about those years. The usual theme is one of gaiety – of jazz, flappers* (Figure 2.1) and wild parties in America while Europe licked her wounds after the slaughter of the First World War. And the picture is not untrue. Social life certainly was 'roaring'. In 1920 women got the vote, in recognition of the part they had played in the war effort. Equally important, new ideas had freed them from their long skirts and long hair, and from old rules about how they should behave. The movies showed small-town girls what city girls were up to, and the

radio piped wild jazz music into many homes. You will see later that the generation gap between these bright young things and their parents helped to make the twenties a period of deep social strain as well as gaiety.

THE ECONOMIC BOOM

But the most important thing that was 'roaring' in America in the 1920s was the economy. America had got off lightly in the war: her country was intact, most of her sons came home, and everyone owed her money. During the war the Allied governments had borrowed

17

huge sums to pay for their war effort, and in the 1920s America began to lend money to Germany so that she could pay her war debts to Britain, France and Belgium, so that they could pay their debts to America! In fact there was so much 'spare' money in America that businessmen were looking for ways to invest money overseas. In this period big American companies like Ford and Woolworth began to set up branches in other countries – a process which has continued ever since.

How could Americans afford to lend money so freely? As we said earlier, America is blessed with many natural resources and a good climate. During the nineteenth century she had been busy developing these riches – sinking oil wells, laying railways, building factories, cultivating the vast fertile plains of her land. By the early twentieth century the United States had overtaken Germany and Britain in industrial output, partly thanks to the inventive genius and business sense of men like Thomas Edison and Henry Ford, who were quick to adapt new inventions to the mass market that was just developing.

The war gave America a further advantage. German and British industry turned to producing guns, and French wheat fields became trenches. To fill the gaps American factories and farmers greatly increased their production, helped by new machines and methods. By 1920 the American economy was like a racing car which has reached top gear and a straight road ahead: just put your foot down and there seems no limit to the speed and distance you can travel.

The straight road continued in the 1920s. Factories turned out more and more goods, and could sell all they made. Businesses made good profits, so they expanded. In the decade 1919–29 total industrial production doubled, and average production per man increased by 53 per cent. In 1929 the national income of the United States (the total earnings of all her citizens) was greater than that of Britain, Germany, Japan, France and eighteen other countries put together!

What did this mean for Americans?

Many people got richer

Greater production of course meant higher profits for the owners of businesses (the shareholders). Between 1923 and 1929, dividends rose by 65 per cent. With all this cash jingling in their pockets, many people speculated on the stock exchange. Share prices were going up so fast that fortunes could be made almost overnight. In 1914 there were 4,500 American millionaires and in 1929 – 11,000! This bonanza of speculation was to come to a sudden end in 1929, but for the time being no one worried.

The factory worker also benefited to some extent from the boom. In the period 1923–9 the average hourly wage rose by 8 per cent, and the average working week fell from 47.3 hours to 45.7 hours. And while prosperity lasted, there was no shortage of jobs for trained men or those able to learn an industrial skill.

So a few people had a *lot* more money to spend and many people had a *little* more. What did they buy?

New industries

We were now in the age of electricity. The wiring-up of factories, offices and homes created a vast expanding market for electrical appliances, and stimulated the invention of new ones. Domestic consumer goods that we now take for granted were just appearing – radios, vacuum cleaners, refrigerators. In 1921 5,000 fridges were produced and in 1929 – 900,000!

The movies was another boom industry – though not yet the 'talkies'. Many people would make a weekly visit to the cinema to idolize their favourite stars, a habit that was not broken until the rapid spread of television after the Second World War.

But by far the most important new consumer product was the motor car, which also created a huge 'spin-off' demand for steel, rubber, oil, glass, garages, roads. This was the heyday of Henry Ford's famous Model T. Ford's aim was to make a cheap car which the ordinary man could afford, and he succeeded. In 1908 a Model T cost $850, by 1917 $360, and in 1925 $290. Ford achieved this reduction in cost by standardizing the product ('You can have any colour so long as it's black') and the production process. The Ford assembly line, by 1925 turning out one car every 10 seconds, was the first step in automation. It was as important in the 1920s as the computer revolution in our own time.

American materialism

It is often said that 'money can't buy happiness'. But many Americans in the 1920s certainly thought it could! They would scrimp and save to buy the things which seemed to lead to 'the good life'. At the top end of society, this is where the wild parties came in. Mr. A had to show Mr. B his superiority not by anything he did, or the quality of his conversation or the shape of his ears, but by the number and size of cars in his garage, the splendour of his house, the fur coat on his wife's shoulders. This obsession with acquiring things, the *materialism* (k) of American life, disgusted some Americans. Many intellectuals and artists went to live in Europe, where they felt the 'true values' of life – creativity and intellectual achievement – were still appreciated. These people were called America's 'Lost Generation'.

But most Americans regarded the comforts of life as a reward for virtuous hard work, as their Protestant religion taught. President Coolidge, who came from a puritanical New England background, summed up this typically American blend of business and religion with a famous saying: 'The man who builds a factory builds a temple. The man who works there worships there.'

Some were left out of prosperity

Unfortunately, however, not everyone could afford the goods produced in those factories. As the economic racing car gathered speed, some Americans were left standing at the roadside. All they got was the dust in their faces.

One such group were farmers and farm workers. As European agriculture revived after the war, and new American machines like the combine harvester increased output, there was a world surplus of farm products. This meant lower prices and therefore declining incomes for American farmers in the 1920s. In farming areas the *per capita* income (the average annual income per person) was always below that in other regions. For example in 1929 it was $921 in the booming far west, $881 in the industrial north-east and $365 in the agricultural south-east. Within the state of South Carolina, farmers earned $129 per year against $412 for citizens who made their living in other ways.

Another group left out of prosperity was America's black population. Farmers in the south (where most Negroes lived) had to fire their hired men, and this forced Negroes to look for work in the cities. But if they got a job it had low pay and poor conditions of work, and the only housing they could get was in the slums. The arrival of large numbers of southern Negroes in northern American cities established the ghetto* conditions which we look at in Chapter 6.

You may also have noticed that the increase in profits for the owners of industry was far greater than the increase in wages for their workers. An important point about the prosperity of the 1920s was that the increased wealth was unevenly distributed in the population: 78 per cent of the profits of industry went to a tiny minority (0·3 per cent) of Americans. A survey in 1929 showed that the top 5 per cent of rich Americans were receiving one-third of all personal income in the country, while 60 per cent of families were earning only enough to pay for the bare necessities of life. In the long run this was bad for the whole national economy because not enough people could afford to buy the products of industry. Sooner or later there would be a log-jam of unsold goods.

In Britain or America today, trade unions would have made sure that working men got a bigger share of the profits of industry by bargaining for higher wages. But in America in the 1920s, trade unions were weak. The reason for their weakness is explained below and in more detail in Study Topic 3, page 28.

Why didn't the government act?

You might think that the government should have noticed the unfairness of this situation, or at least realized that it would lead to trouble later, and should have done something about it. The government could have raised taxes for the rich (who could easily afford them), or made very low wages illegal so that working men could earn more and therefore buy more. But American governments of the 1920s did not do this, and there are important reasons why not.

For one thing, governments at this time were all Republican, and the Republican Party always tends to favour big business because it gets much of its support in votes and money from businessmen. But there was a more important reason than that. By not interfering in the economy, governments of the 1920s were carrying out the general American belief in *laissez-faire* – a French term meaning 'let things alone'.

Laissez-faire has a special meaning as a theory of how the economy should run. According to this idea no one should interfere with free competition by trying to control prices or wages. Free competition (a) between one firm and another, (b) between the employer and his workers, and (c) between the producer and the consumer of goods, should always ensure low prices, fair wages and good profits. Left to itself the economy would run itself, and it was not part of the government's job to get mixed up in it. Nor should any other organized group upset free competition in their own interests. Exactly how this theory was supposed to work is more fully explained in Study Topic 2.

You can see how a *laissez-faire* economy fits the American belief in individual freedom. In the 1920s most Americans accepted the idea without question, and the governments of those years carried it out to the letter.

The growth of monopolies

In the 1920s businessmen cleverly used *laissez-faire* to their own advantage. Many employers banned or hindered the formation of trade unions on the grounds that they would interfere with the free running of the economy by bargaining for higher wages. The employers' attitude was that if a man wasn't satisfied with his wage-packet, he could go and work elsewhere. But businessmen did not apply the rules about not interfering to themselves! In many parts of the economy they had organized monopolies. A monopoly is formed when one company buys or drives out of business all its rivals, until it is the only firm making and selling its own product. Once it has got rid of all competition, a monopoly firm can fix high prices and low wages. Profits for the owners of the business will then be very high.

In America in the 1920s monopolies had become very powerful. For example, the whole steel industry was dominated by one huge corporation, US Steel. In many steel manufacturing towns a man had no choice but to work for US Steel, which banned trade unions and paid very low wages. The consumer also had no choice but to pay the high prices the company fixed.

Laissez-faire was out of date

You can see that if monopolies are not controlled they give unfair advantage to big business. But so far no one else – neither government nor trade unions – had interfered enough in the American economy to limit the power of big business. In reality, by this time the whole *laissez-faire* theory was out of date. It had been thought up in the eighteenth century for a much simpler economy, with many small firms competing on equal terms. It simply did not fit the big business system that had developed in America by the 1920s. But so long as prosperity lasted, people still believed in the theory because it seemed to be working well. Only when the theory had obvi-

Figure 2.2 A painting by Ben Shahn of a Women's Christian Temperance Union parade. Their campaign against alcoholic drink was eventually successful (or was it?–see page 23).

ously failed did Americans begin to question it, as you will see in Chapter 3.

SOCIAL CONFLICTS IN AMERICA

One by-product of our twentieth-century machine age is the accelerating pace of social change. Galloping technology leads to what is now sometimes called 'future shock', and *shock* is the right word for it. Before we have half-adjusted to one momentous development, let's say air travel faster than sound, we have to accept another – men on the moon! Having just got used to frozen food, we are fed 'meat' made of soya beans, and are promised in a few years' time a three-course dinner in pills! 'Future shock' is a continuous theme of the twentieth century, and one which affects us all.

Like the economic trends we have already described, the permissive social life we know today began in America in the 1920s. It led to bewilderment and fear among people who had grown up in the quieter, rural, religious America of the nineteenth century. The growth of cities, the swelling proportion of dark-skinned immigrants in America's popu-

lation, the shift of Negroes from the south into areas which up to then had scarcely seen a black face, made the 'original Americans' (as they liked to call themselves) very uneasy. They saw the old ways passing and their own influence declining. They were outraged by the beer-swilling, free and easy city-dwellers who by 1920, for the first time, outnumbered the inhabitants of rural America. They were horrified by lipstick, night clubs, short skirts, jazz – by everything in the new, swinging life which was sweeping away their sons and daughters to an unimaginable future. The very soil of *their* America was shaken by the buzz-saws clearing woodland for a suburban housing development, by the Model T whizzing by at 30 miles an hour and scaring the buggy-horse half to death.

Some of the older generation gladly adapted to the new social trends. We can imagine many a Grandma living out her life in a corner of her daughter's all-electric kitchen, looking back without regret to the dim and dirty scullery of her own youth. But others saw the new age of leisure and gadgetry as a threat to traditional Protestant values of hard work, thrift and self-denial. These people were the main supporters of reac-

Figure 2.3   A Ku Klux Klan initiation ceremony, 1922.

tionary movements which blotted the progressive landscape of America in the 1920s.
There was a clash of cultures*, the old against
the new, which was almost social civil war.

Prohibition and fundamentalism

In 1920 the sale and manufacture of alcoholic
liquor was banned throughout the United
States. Nation-wide Prohibition was the
result of a long campaign by a self-righteous
minority who tried to force on all Americans
their own belief in the evil influence of drink
(Figure 2.2). Eventually their efforts were
rewarded by the 18th Amendment to the
Constitution, allowing Congress to regulate
an area of life hitherto reserved to the states.
This it did with the Volstead Act of 1920.

Encouraged by the success of the Prohibition movement, a huge Bible conference
launched a campaign in 1919 against the
teaching in American schools of Darwin's
long-accepted theory that men and monkeys
are descended from a common ancestor. By
1929 six states in the 'Bible belt' of the Deep
South had passed 'anti-evolution' laws. It
seemed that some American children would
grow up ignorant of scientific facts which
were common knowledge throughout the
civilized world.

The Ku Klux Klan

Another outlet for narrow-minded conservatism was the sinister Ku Klux Klan. By fan-
ning the flames of prejudice against Negroes,
Catholics and Jews, and with the help of new

22

techniques in advertising and public relations, the white-hooded Klansmen expanded their membership to an all-time peak of around 5 million in 1924 (Figure 2.3). For a few years in certain rural states the Klan was a political force which could not be publicly challenged. Anyone who did so might attend the next torch-light lynching or branding as a victim rather than a bystander. And the Klan's enemies were numerous! They included, in the words of a leaflet, 'every criminal, every gambler, every thug, every libertine*, every girl-ruiner, every home-wrecker, every wife-beater, every dope-peddler, every moonshiner*, every crooked politician, every pagan Papist priest, every shyster lawyer ... every black spider.'

These moralistic, reactionary* forces certainly had an influence in political life. While many state politicians dared not offend the Klan or the local stalwarts of the Anti-Saloon League, so the smear propaganda against the Democrat Al Smith, the urban, Irish Catholic, 'wet' Presidential candidate of 1928, persuaded many upright citizens not to vote for him. But in retrospect this contribution to Smith's defeat can be seen as a desperate rearguard action by the self-appointed protectors of 'dry', rural, white, Protestant America whose voice has been drowned by the more liberal urban vote ever since the 1920s. Their racism and bigotry were firmly resisted by liberal politicians and more broad-minded religious leaders who pleaded for tolerance and brotherly love. And their views were simply ignored by millions of happy-go-lucky citizens who were going to drink, smoke and dance all night no matter *what* Grandma said!

The liberal counter-attack

After 1920 any American who wanted to drink alcohol could easily evade the Prohibition law. By 1929 New York City had 2,000 illegal bars or 'speak-easies', as they were called, against 1,000 legal bars in that city before Prohibition came in. Huge fortunes were made by Al Capone in Chicago and other gang bosses who provided the 'bootleg'

liquor that people wanted. What a hollow victory for the movement which had tried so hard to Do Good to America! Prohibition did nothing but bad. It led to gang warfare in the streets, widespread police corruption, blindness and death from 'bathtub gin', and a reputation for lawlessness which America has never lived down.†

Similarly the Old Time Religion of the fundamentalists and the political power of the Klan were soon checked by the scorn and ridicule of more liberal Americans. In 1925 a test case was taken against Tennessee's anti-evolution law in order to make fun of it. Sophisticated Americans and Europeans had a good laugh at the proceedings of the 'monkey trial' where two famous lawyers debated such questions as whether Joshua made the sun stand still, as the Bible said he did. In the mid-1920s the Klan was publicly shamed, and 'respectable' support withdrew from it, when Klan leaders were convicted of murder and embezzlement.

The political legacy of reactionary movements

Nevertheless the dark forces of racism and religious bigotry had left their mark. In 1937 a survey among American teachers showed that more than a third of them were still afraid to admit openly their acceptance of Darwin's theory. Nor did they dare to criticize the Klan or the saintly heroes of American history. The state of Arkansas abolished its anti-evolution law only in 1968, and Mississippi still has one!

No anti-evolution law has been used since 1925, but in one important sphere the law of the United States was permanently changed by the extreme right-wing temper of the early twenties. The view of a Klan leader that the 'dangerous influx of foreign immigration' was 'threatening to crush and overwhelm Anglo-Saxon civilization' helped to rally support for a series of immigration laws after 1921 which

†The failure of Prohibition was eventually acknowledged by the 21st Amendment passed in 1933, which repealed the 18th Amendment of 1919. Today the laws about alcohol vary from state to state, or even from district to district by local option.

ended for ever America's traditional policy of an 'open door' to all comers. These laws limited the yearly intake and set up a national quota system designed to maintain a white Anglo-Saxon majority in the United States. This discriminatory principle remained in American immigration law until 1965.

Another reason why the open door must be spiked and guarded in future was the nightmare fear of many Americans that Reds were trickling through it to provoke a Communist revolution in America. The political hysteria of the Big Red Scare was shorter lived than Prohibition and not so terrifying as the Klan's activities, but here we shall give it special attention because of its relevance to a later theme of this book: the Cold War between Capitalist America and Communist Russia.

THE BIG RED SCARE

The ideological grounds for Russian–American conflict are obvious, for the collectivist ideas of Communism are exactly opposite to the American philosophy of life. While Democracy and Capitalism stress the rights of the individual, Communism holds that the interests of society as a whole are more important. Communists also believe that so far as possible everyone should be equal and remain equal. No one should be able to get richer than others or think himself better than others. So the resources of a community – including the work of its members – should belong to the whole community. No one should exploit them for personal gain.

The Russian Revolution

Americans were understandably alarmed when the Bolshevik revolution of October 1917 brought a Communist government to power in Russia. They had strongly disapproved of Tsarist oppression, but the new government looked even worse. It confiscated private fortunes, took industry into state ownership and proposed to do the same with the land. The Bolsheviks seemed to confirm

the worst fears of people who had dreaded Communism ever since Karl Marx announced its birth in 1848.

Worst of all, Communism was an *international* doctrine. According to Marxist ideas the Communist revolution would be worldwide, and it was the duty of Communist parties everywhere to make this happen. In 1919 Lenin set up an agency – the Communist International or Comintern – to form Communist parties in other countries and help them to achieve their revolutionary aim. No wonder people in the Capitalist West were scared!

The Palmer raids

In 1919 sudden unemployment after the war caused several violent strikes and a few bomb outrages in America. These incidents struck terror in the hearts of nervous Americans; was this the predicted Communist revolution already? In the jittery mood of the moment there was little protest when Attorney-General† A. Mitchell Palmer swiftly arrested 6,000 suspects, mainly from the immigrant community, and held them in prison without charge. Some hundreds were deported. In the same mood, five democratically-elected members of the New York State Assembly were deprived of their seats because they were Socialists.

The Palmer raids were an overkill reaction to a largely imaginary threat. Many recent immigrants were Jews who had fled terrible persecution in Tsarist Russia. Some, it is true, were people with left-wing views who were also refugees from the Tsar's secret police and probably were active in strikes and protests in 'the land of the free'. But most immigrants were peaceable folk who had come to America for a chance to climb the tree of success, not to chop it down. If some of them listened to radical propaganda it was hardly surprising at a time when the economic system (and the American Government) was

†The highest law officer of the United States Government.

so heavily biased in favour of those already at the top.

Fortunately there were American voices to champion the rights of free speech and immunity from unlawful arrest. Eminent lawyers reminded a panicky populace that the American Constitution was based on the 'free trade of ideas' and that essential liberty should not be sacrificed for 'a little temporary safety'. The detained suspects were released and the Red Scare subsided. In the Presidential election of 1920 the Socialist candidate Eugene Debs received 1 million votes. Once again you can see the contradictions in democratic America: even at a time when many Americans wanted all Socialists locked up, others were voting for one to be President!

Yet again there is an unhappy tail-piece to the story. Left-wing ideas have never been popular in the United States, and there was to be an even worse Red Scare after the Second World War, as we shall see. In the 1920s two unlucky Italian immigrants served as a convenient scapegoat for political intolerance long after the release of other Red Scare victims.

The Sacco and Vanzetti case

Nicola Sacco and Bartolomeo Vanzetti were professed anarchists* who did their best to spread their ideas. In 1920 they were arrested and charged with robbery and murder. To this day no one knows for sure whether they were actually guilty of these crimes, but what *is* certain is that their trial was unfair. Some of the evidence against them was doubtful, and outside the court the judge in their case made clear his own attitude to 'those anarchistic bastards'. Regardless of the evidence about the robbery, they were presumed to be guilty of it by the press and many of the public who disliked their political beliefs. The court's verdict of guilty, although insufficiently proved, was a foregone conclusion.

Despite several appeals to higher courts, and liberal protest in America and abroad, Sacco and Vanzetti were executed in 1927. To the end both men protested their innocence of the crimes. Vanzetti had said in a speech to the court, 'I am suffering because I am a radical, and indeed I am a radical; I have suffered because I was an Italian, and indeed I am an Italian.'

Vanzetti was certainly right that it was uncomfortable to be radical or Italian in America at that time. And in spite of the obvious injustice, it took officialdom fifty years to apologize. In 1977 the State Governor of Massachusetts, in the presence of Sacco's grandson, acknowledged that there had been a mistrial and proclaimed 23 August, the day of their death, a Memorial Day for Sacco and Vanzetti. The exact truth about the robbery is still a matter of dispute among historians.

Cross-currents in the twenties

America in the twenties was a land of contrasts and contradictions. Americans were boastfully self-confident, but at the same time fearful and insecure. Permissiveness and Prohibition co-existed uneasily in one society. And while some people became very rich, others continued to live in poverty.

But as the decade wore on, the zoom-zoom of the roaring economy drowned out everything else. Even those standing at the roadside cheerfully waved on the 'racing car', hoping that it would soon be their turn to climb on board. No one suspected that the engine of the car had serious faults; and in the age of *laissez-faire* there were no controls – no brakes, no speed-cops! – to guide its course. When the Great Crash came in 1929 there was not even anyone standing by to pick up the casualties.

Study Topic 2

The Theory of *laissez-faire*

A *laissez-faire* economy is one in which no one – and especially not the government – interferes with the freedom of individuals. It is a system of private enterprise where anyone has the opportunity, and the right, to start a business and make a profit from it – or go broke!

The early Capitalist economies of nations like Britain and America did develop in this private enterprise way. No government arranged or planned to dig a tin mine, set up a shipping company, invent a new machine. These enterprises were started by private individuals. British economists like Adam Smith in the eighteenth century made a 'theory' out of what they saw happening around them. They argued that *laissez-faire* not only gave the maximum freedom to individuals (which they thought was a good thing) but that it was the most efficient way for an economy to run.

How *laissez-faire* is supposed to work

Competition between many traders and manufacturers is the basis of *laissez-faire*. Competition would have three main effects:

1. It should ensure low prices

When there are many buyers and sellers, the prices of goods will drop to the level of the lowest prices offered. If some manufacturers produce goods more efficiently (i.e. more cheaply) then the price of their goods can be reduced. Rival manufacturers must then reduce their prices or nobody will buy their goods.

2. It should ensure that producers supply what consumers want

Products which consumers do not want will not be sold, or their price will have to be very low to attract buyers. So a manufacturer will get little or no profit unless he produces goods that people want. When he makes what people want, then he can employ more workers and also increase his profit. In this way his desire for profit will benefit everybody – workman, manufacturer and consumer.

3. It should ensure full employment

If the demand for goods falls, workers may lose their jobs. When that happens, they will be ready to work for lower wages. This will reduce the costs of production and then manufacturers will lower the prices of goods. When prices come down, more goods will be sold. As the demand for goods increases, so there will be more jobs until all willing workers are again employed. So no one will be unemployed for long.

A *laissez-faire* economy is one which regulates itself. It does not need a government to run it; in fact any interference by government or any organized group will upset the smooth running of the system. Governments should not discourage businessmen by high taxes; trade unions should not interfere to make wages artificially high; nor should manufacturers co-operate to fix high prices. And of course there should be no monopolies which can charge unfairly high prices and pay unfairly low wages. If any of these things happens, free competition is interrupted.

Changes in the American economy

You can see that this system will work well only when there are a large number of small companies competing on equal terms. It also expects that workers will be ready to take lower wages, change their jobs and perhaps move elsewhere if the law of supply and demand puts them out of work. On the whole this was the situation in the early economic development of America.

But from the 1860s on, much larger industrial units were formed. Many small companies could not compete with these giants and so went out of business. The government did try to control the huge corporations for the sake of fair competition, but with little success. New industries like steel, railways and oil had to be organized on a very big scale. Monopoly companies like US Steel and Standard Oil (the Rockefeller empire) seemed to be an unavoidable feature of the advanced economy which America had reached by the late nineteenth century.

On the other side of industry, workers were no longer willing to be just obedient cogs in the system. They felt that the labour they contributed to the production of goods entitled them to a share of the profits from selling them, just as much as the employer's investment of capital entitled him to his share. But the employer was not likely to reduce his own profits just to be fair to his workers! So the only way for workers to get their share was by forming trade unions to bargain with the employer.

For all these reasons, *laissez-faire* did not fit the American economy of the 1920s. But Republican governments of the period clung to it stubbornly. President Hoover, elected in 1928, would not admit the need for government action even when the economy had totally collapsed in the Great Depression after 1929. It took another man, with a different view of the role of government, to break away from *laissez-faire*.

Study Topic 3

Trade Unionism in America

As you might expect in a country so deeply committed to individualist values, trade unionism has had less influence in shaping American society than in West European democracies (even today only 20 per cent of the American workforce is unionized, compared to about 50 per cent in Britain). Nevertheless, since the mid-nineteenth century, workers had been trying to establish their right to form trade unions, though with limited success.

The American Federation of Labour–a loose alliance of separate unions, formed in 1881–covered only 10 per cent of the industrial workforce by 1914. Its members were mainly skilled craftsmen; the AFL was little concerned with unskilled workers (who included most of the immigrant and black workers) or with the growing labour force of women–8 million by 1910. In 1905 a more radical organization–the Industrial Workers of the World, nicknamed the Wobblies–had begun to organize these most vulnerable groups. The IWW had some success, notably in Lawrence, Massachusetts in 1912, where a bitter three-month strike won a small pay increase for 10,000 immigrant textile workers. But more often, strikes were defeated by a formidable combination of employers, state governments and the hostility of 'respectable' citizens. A shocking but not untypical example was the Colorado coal strike of 1913–14, when the coal owners (the Rockefeller family) followed the common custom of hiring gunmen to break the strike. When this did not succeed, the Governor called out state troops (their wages being paid by the employers), who ferried in strike-breakers, machine-gunned the miners'

tent camp and then set fire to it, killing eleven children and two women. This little 'war' was eventually ended by federal troops sent in by President Wilson. Sixty-six people had been killed and every claim of the union was refused.

In the decade before the First World War and earlier, there were many similar fierce industrial struggles. Occasionally the public conscience was alerted to the plight of exploited workers, for example by the Triangle Shirtwaist Company fire in New York City in 1911, when 146 workers, mainly immigrant women, were killed. The factory was badly overcrowded, fire exits were illegally locked, and most of the victims died jumping from upper floors beyond the reach of the firemen's ladders. In the 1900s some reforms were passed, such as state laws to provide compensation for industrial injuries. But the workers' right to humane conditions and a fair reward for their labour–and to organize trade unions to work for these improvements–was not yet generally recognized in America. Many people saw the activities of the IWW and the infant Socialist Party, founded in 1901, not as a justified corrective to the overwhelming power of employers, but as a dangerous 'rising tide of Socialism' which must be firmly resisted.

The 'rising tide' was effectively stemmed during the First World War, which was opposed by Socialists in America (and by some in Europe too) as an imperialist war which went against the interests of working people. Under the Espionage Act of 1917 most of the IWW and Socialist Party leaders were imprisoned for disloyalty, and this marked the end of radical trade unionism in the United States. For the time being only the conservative AFL with its small membership of 'the aristocrats of labour' was left in the field.

Thus in the 1920s the vast majority of workers had no one to plead their case. Even the AFL's membership declined during the decade, partly because in the boom years just enough prosperity trickled down into workers' pockets to soften their grievances, but also for deeper reasons: trade unions seemed almost 'un-American' in the political climate of that time. Once again, it was only the change of mood (and of government) in the 1930s which finally made membership of a trade union legal and 'respectable' in American society.

*GLOSSARY

anarchist, a person who believes that people should not be ruled by authority but should rule themselves.

culture, this word has several meanings; here it is used as the sociological term for the whole way of life, including beliefs and customs, of a society.

flappers, a slang word for 'liberated' young women in the 1920s.

ghetto, area of a city where blacks or other minority groups live.

libertine, a free-thinking or free-living person.

moonshiner, a maker of illegal spirits ('moonshine').

reactionary, very conservative or backward-looking.

KEYWORD

materialism, valuing the possession and display of things that you can touch, see and use above 'spiritual' qualities like freedom and beauty, or human virtues like kindness to other people. From a materialist point of view it is more important for a man to earn money and 'get on' than to paint beautiful pictures which don't sell, or to work for some ideal like 'a fair society'.

Many people think that the growth of materialist values comes from – and causes – a decline in religion. Most religions teach that 'doing good' is more important than 'doing well,' but Protestants also believe that hard work and economic success are part of man's duty to God. America's reputation for materialism increased in the 1920s, when economic progress made widely available for the first time so many material comforts – cars, fine clothes, heated houses, household gadgets.

Questions

Did you notice?

1. American women got the vote in (a) 1900 (b) 1925 (c) 1920
2. A monopoly is (a) a large business company (b) a card game (c) an electrical gadget
3. The 18th Amendment (a) banned the Ku Klux Klan (b) brought in national Prohibition (c) corrected Darwin's evolution theory
4. Speak-easies were (a) liberated girls (b) illegal bars (c) gangsters
5. Eugene Debs was (a) a Communist (b) a judge (c) a Presidential candidate
6. True or false?
   (i) In 1925 the American Ford factory produced 1 car every 10 seconds
   (ii) In 1920 most black Americans lived in city ghettos
   (iii) Sacco and Vanzetti were definitely guilty of robbery and murder
   (iv) American governments followed a policy of *laissez-faire* in the 1920s
   (v) American trade unions were strong in the 1920s
7. Which statement is *more* accurate?
   (i) Americans were frightened by the Russian Revolution because
      (a) they were sorry for the Russian people
      (b) Communism is an international doctrine
   (ii) Prosperity in America in the 1920s was enjoyed
      (a) only by people who were rich already
      (b) by some people more than others
   (iii) American farmers earned less in the 1920s because
      (a) they did not work hard enough
      (b) they produced too much

Can you explain?

8. Why was the American economy booming in the 1920s?
9. What does the term *laissez-faire* mean, and how far did it apply to the American economy in the 1920s?
10. Who gained most from prosperity, and why? Who did not benefit from prosperity, and why not?
11. Briefly summarize the ideas of the 'old' and the 'new' cultures which opposed each other in the 1920s.
12. On the whole liberal ideas won the 'social civil war' in the 1920s, but reactionary movements had some success. In what ways were they successful?

What's your view?

13. Many WASP Americans tend to look down on blacks and recent immigrants and for this reason treat them unfairly. In what other countries are minority groups unfairly treated? Do you think this is inevitable in a mixed society?
14. A British newspaper reported the death of the artist Picasso with the headline, 'Millionaire Painter Dies.' Does this headline tell us anything about the 'values' of our society? In what other ways does our society show its values? What do *you* think is most important in life?
15. There is no doubt that alcoholic drink and cigarettes are harmful to many people. What does our government do to discourage drinking and smoking? Do you think the government should do more or less in this field?

3

America in the Thirties

Although prosperity was not equally shared by all, in the 1920s the main feeling in America was one of success. In the 1930s, when America was hit by the worst depression in her history, the dominant feeling was one of failure. How did this hopeful atmosphere – and the lives of so many Americans – change so dramatically?

THE WALL STREET CRASH

Stock market speculation

In a Capitalist economy, the making and selling of goods is done by private companies. Most companies are owned by shareholders who buy and sell their shares or stocks on the stock market. There are two reasons why people buy shares: (1) for the income from the annual dividend (a share-out of the company's profits); (2) to increase their own capital by selling their shares at a higher price than they paid for them. Some investors (shareholders) speculate in shares or 'play the market' by trying to spot a company whose share values will increase quickly, so that they can make a quick capital gain. The amount of the company's dividend – and the value of its shares on the stock market – varies according to how well the company is doing. When its product is successful and selling well, it pays shareholders a higher dividend and the market price of its shares goes up.

The general prosperity of American industry in the early 1920s naturally brought a steady rise in share values. With so many 'winners' to choose from, people with cash to spare were tempted to gamble on the stock market. This was shown in the huge increase in stock market trading: in 1923, 236 million shares were sold and in 1928, 1,125 million. And we know that if lots of people want to buy something its price will go up, and the more people want to buy it, the more its price will go up. This is just what happened in the 1920s: share prices soon leapt ahead of their real value as measured against the success of the companies concerned. Prices were forced up just because so many people wanted to buy them. In three short months from June to August 1928, share values increased by 25 per cent!

Everyone joined in

The 'pickings' were irresistible. Speculation became a craze among ordinary people who did not *own* anything – a house or land, for example – which they could sell if the gamble didn't come off. Let's suppose that such a man had saved or borrowed $100 to 'play the market'. At that time a stockbroker (a dealer in shares) would accept a mere 10 per cent deposit, so $100 would buy $1,000 worth of shares. If the purchaser had to pay the full price, or increase his 'margin' (the deposit) to the stockbroker before pocketing his gains, his bank manager would gladly lend it to him at a low rate of interest. Confidence in the economic boom was so high that everyone was ready to lend or borrow freely. But note – our speculator is now considerably in debt, and his only safeguard against bankruptcy is a piece of paper which he thinks is worth $1,000 and which he hopes will be worth more in a few months' time.

In fact the bank manager was also busy

buying shares with his clients' deposits. He saw no serious risk in investing in a 'booming' stock market and like other speculators, he did not enquire too deeply into the company whose shares he was buying. Very likely he bought those of an 'investment trust' which did not manufacture anything at all. Investment trusts were companies set up to buy shares in manufacturing firms and sell shares *in themselves* to speculators. But they sold far more shares to the public than they held in producing companies! So the only 'prosperity' of the investment trust (remember, all this *began* with real prosperity) was the bubble of speculation itself. When the bubble burst, the shares in the investment trust would be worthless. Thus even the savings of thrifty people who thought their money was safely stowed away in the bank was put at risk by 'experts' in finance who should have known better, and by rogues who deliberately took advantage of the happy-go-lucky mood of the moment.

Panic on Wall Street

In the late 1920s cracks began to appear in the *real* prosperity on which this fantastic bubble of speculation rested. Producers began to have difficulty selling their goods, workers were laid off ... rumours spread in Wall Street (the financial district of New York) ... Suddenly, everyone wanted to *sell* – quick, get rid of them before they fall any further! In October 1929, panic broke out on the stock exchange. Now everyone wanted to sell, but nobody wanted to buy. Share prices fell dramatically, but regardless of the price, people who had borrowed money to buy *had* to sell, to save what they could from the wreckage. On 24 October 13 million shares were sold; on 29 October 16½ million. Between September and December 1929, share values fell by $40,000 million! From then on it was downhill all the way, to rock-bottom in mid-1932.

The banking crisis

The Crash had a serious effect on the economy. Many small speculators lost everything, of course, but bigger fish had been hooked too. Financiers and bank managers, whose business is lending money, were not in a mood to lend any more – if they had survived the Crash at all. Six hundred and fifty banks went bankrupt in 1929. Banks were unable to recover what they had lent (or lost in the Crash), and at the same time depositors hammered on the door to withdraw their savings. Bank after bank closed its doors: by 1933 over 4,000 had done so. By then the banking system had more or less collapsed.

In normal times a business can be helped over difficulties with a loan. But at this time there were no loans to be had, so factory owners had no choice but to close down. Between 1929 and 1932, 110,000 companies closed – and, of course, more and more men were thrown out of work. By 1933, industrial production was halved and about 15 million men – 25 per cent of the total labour force – were unemployed.

THE GREAT DEPRESSION

The 'downward spiral'

Economic depression tends to be self-perpetuating – that is to say, it makes itself worse all the time. As men become unemployed, they stop buying goods – so more men are thrown out of work. They in turn stop buying – and so the effect goes on. In America after 1929 the downward spiral quickly developed. It was made worse because there was no 'dole' (social security) of any kind. That would not have fitted the *laissez-faire* theory already described, in which both employer and workman had to sink or swim by their own efforts. So the unemployed man soon could not meet his rent – or his mortgage payments – and was put out on the streets with his family. They slept in parks, subways or 'shanty-towns' at the edge of cities, in shacks made of tin and sacking or any useful material from the rubbish tip. For food they rummaged through waste bins or joined the mile-long queue at the charity 'soup kitchen' (Figure 3.1).

But all too soon the soup ran out. Private charities had no funds to cope with a crisis like this – nor had state or city governments. Who could help now? The trouble was that it was nobody's job to help. The Republican President Hoover saw no reason to act, for according to *laissez-faire*, in which he strongly believed, the depression would soon cure itself. He knew that falling prices would increase the demand for goods, which would need more men to make them, which would mean more jobs . . . and so on. Although there was no sign of this happening, Hoover was certain that it would, and that there was noth-ing to do but wait. 'Prosperity is just around the corner,' he said in 1930.

Revolution in the air

But prosperity was not round the corner, and the mood of the country became uglier as the months went by. In July 1931, 300 un-employed men stormed food shops in Henry-etta, Oklahoma, and there were other similar incidents. The most famous protesters were the Bonus Marchers of 1932. They were a small 'army' of First World War veterans* who came to Washington, with their families in tow, to demand payment of a post-war bonus they had been promised by the govern-

Figure 3.1   Children queue for bread – a common sight during the depression.

ment. But they met no sympathy from the White House. Instead the army was called out to disperse them with tear gas, tanks and fixed boyonets; their scrappy tents and shacks were burned.

The Bonus Marchers and others who felt they had 'done their bit' for America were very bitter indeed. But even usually conservative people like farmers were angry. As the President of the Farmers' Union of Wisconsin said, 'I am as conservative as any man could be, but any economic system that has it in its power to set me and my wife on the street, at my age – what can I see but red!'

Who was to blame?

Hoover was blamed – then and afterwards – for doing little to help these men. Shantytowns were called Hoovervilles, and the newspapers people wrapped around themselves for sleeping on park benches became 'Hoover blankets'. But to blame Hoover for not acting was perhaps unfair: in the early years no one suggested the drastic steps that President Roosevelt later took. It was *the system* that had failed. The economy was not behaving according to the rules, and entirely new remedies had to be found for the sickness that had overtaken America.

Hoover did set up a federal agency, the Reconstruction Finance Corporation, to lend money to banks and other failing concerns, and the Home Loan Bank to help householders meet their mortgage payments. In 1931 he also excused foreign debtors for one year from paying their war debts (in the end, this act cancelled those debts forever). This was an attempt to increase American exports, but by now it was too late for that. No one overseas had a penny to spare. The economies of many countries – especially that of Germany – had been floated on American loans in the 1920s, and when these were withdrawn after the Crash, the Great Depression quickly spread round the world.

What had gone wrong?

The Wall Street Crash and the resulting banking crisis contributed to the slump but *it did not cause it*. The underlying difficulty was the lack of demand for goods which began to show itself in mid-1929. This earth-tremor shook to bits the ramshackle financial structure which had trapped so many people: banks with empty vaults, phoney investment trusts, and the colossal debts which speculators had built up by buying shares 'on margin'. With no 'shock-absorbers' – bank loans or temporary cut-backs in production – to take the strain of falling demand, what began as an economic decline turned into national disaster. Why was there a lack of demand for goods at a time of prosperity?

No American buyers

We saw in Chapter 2 that prosperity was not shared by all. In 1929 at least one-third of all personal income was going to the top 5 per cent of society while as many as 60 per cent of Americans were only making subsistence incomes – that is, they could afford food, clothes and rent, but had no spare cash to buy goods. So it was inevitable that when the 5 per cent of 'big spenders' had bought all they wanted – even if it was a radio for every room, and three cars in the garage – the home market would be glutted, and could absorb no more of the output of industry. Plenty of Americans still had no car, no radio – but they couldn't afford them.

The vital point about the new-style economy of the 1920s was the sheer number of goods being produced. In an economy of *mass production* there must be *mass consumption*: if one Ford car is made every ten seconds then someone – somewhere – must buy a Ford car every ten seconds. Since many American workers were not earning enough to buy the products they made, America must find enough rich people in other countries to buy her extra goods. But in 1929 there was no chance of selling more American goods abroad. Her foreign markets, too, were shrinking fast.

No foreign buyers

To buy foreign goods a country needs to earn the currency of its trading partners by selling its own products to them (all trade is in fact a process of exchanging the goods of one country for the goods of another). So in order to sell her own products abroad, America had to accept foreign goods in her market. In the 1920s this was even more necessary for her European trading partners who owed war debts to America. These debts had to be paid out of dollar earnings before Europeans could order tractors, radios and fridges from American producers.

So in the 1920s America should have been encouraging imports to increase her own exports. But instead, Republican governments gave way to the short-sighted demand of their own manufacturers for protection from foreign competition through high tariffs – that is, high customs duties on imports. In 1922 the Fordney–McCumber Tariff Act raised import duties higher than ever before. For a time the unhealthy situation was disguised because more and more loans were made overseas, and these could be used to buy American goods. But after the Crash American lenders called in their loans, and then even that buying-power was removed.

For a country that needs to export, a high tariff policy is always short-sighted because it provokes retaliation. In the 1930 Hawley–Smoot Tariff America raised her barriers still higher. So foreign governments raised their tariffs – 'If you won't buy our goods, we won't buy yours' – and the situation became even worse for American exporters. By 1933 foreign trade was down to one-third of the 1929 figure. It seemed that America's economy would gradually grind to a full stop.

A change of leadership

In the presidential election of 1932 Hoover

was swept aside by the Democratic Party and its leader Franklin Delano Roosevelt (FDR). What a contrast between the old President and the new! While Hoover was glum-faced and silent in public, having run out of empty promises by 1932, FDR was cheerful, energetic and full of plans. He spoke sympathetically of 'the forgotten man at the bottom of the economic pyramid', and championed that man's rights. FDR himself came from the 'top drawer' of American society but he was shocked to see millions of his countrymen 'living in conditions labelled indecent half a century ago'.

Above all, FDR brought boundless confidence to the task of pulling America out of deepening despair. He told Americans they had 'nothing to fear but fear itself' and promised 'a New Deal for the American people'. This name came to be used for a whole series of reforms passed during the first two terms of FDR's presidency, which lasted from 1933 to 1945. FDR was re-elected three times: in 1936, 1940 and 1944 – one sign of the New Deal's popularity with a majority of Americans.

THE NEW DEAL

The New Deal was certainly *new*. The changes it brought challenged two of those cherished ideals of America: *laissez-faire* Capitalism and individualism. But it must be said at once that FDR was a reformer, not a revolutionary. His long 'reign' in America altered but did not destroy those ideals and the society based on them.

The first important fact about the New Deal is the sheer number of laws that were passed. So many swept through Congress in the 'First 100 Days' of 1933 that it was difficult to set up fast enough the agencies to administer them. America had rejected a 'do-nothing' government and now had one which seemed to 'do everything'.

The second important fact is the experimental spirit of FDR's programme. He gathered around him a group of advisers and together they would try anything to help the situation. If a law did not work as intended, they would re-write it and try again. FDR was not working to a thought-out plan – but nevertheless, in the New Deal as a whole, three important themes can be seen: the three Rs of Relief, Recovery and Reform.

Relief, Recovery and Reform

Study Topic 4 (page 40) briefly explains some of the best-known New Deal laws. Look for the three Rs in studying this list. It is more important for you to recognize *themes* in the New Deal than to remember the many agencies and the dates they were set up.

The New Deal is also sometimes divided into two phases: the First New Deal of Relief and Recovery, lasting from 1933 to mid-1935 – and the Second New Deal, containing most of the Reform measures, from 1935 to 1940. But all these categories overlap: some laws were partly Relief, partly Recovery; and many of the long-term Reforms were already being planned in 1933.

This is what the three Rs were trying to do:

(a) Relief

The most urgent task was to bring immediate help to hungry, homeless people. The Federal Emergency Relief Administration is an example of this: it filled up the empty soup bowls and gave temporary housing to those with no home but the streets. Emergency loans were also arranged for failing banks and businesses.

(b) Recovery

Next, the government had to find ways to get the economy back on its feet so that once again a man could work, get paid, buy things that he needed and live in a home of his own. This was the aim of government help to farmers, for example: by buying up surplus farm production and then paying farmers to grow less wheat or cattle next year, prices were pushed up and farmers could make a liv-

ing from what they sold without glutting the market. Other steps to Recovery were the many government agencies that created jobs to give men wages to buy goods, and so to start the wheels of industry turning again.

(c) Reform

Thirdly, there must be changes in the economic system to prevent a depression on this scale from happening again. Examples of Reform are the Social Security Act of 1935, providing a dole for sickness, unemployment and old age, and the Wagner Act of 1935 which gave working men the legal right to form or join a trade union.

New Deal principles – the 'Keynesian revolution'

You can also see, in the list of New Deal activities (pages 40–41) some very important new economic principles at work. These were the new remedies for a situation that *laissez-faire* could not cure. FDR did not realize it at the time – he was not an economist, and arrived at these remedies by trial and error – but he was putting into practice the principles of a new economic era – what is sometimes called *the Keynesian revolution.*

In a book published in 1936 the British economist J. M. Keynes offered a formula to cure depression, the world-wide economic sickness of the 1930s. You can see how the New Deal expressed his three main recommendations, which we can summarize briefly like this:

1. Instead of sitting back and waiting for economic forces to cure a failing economy, the government must take positive action to help. This would cost money of course, but a government must be prepared to go into debt to take the necessary action.

2. Spending-power, i.e. money in the pocket, must be given to consumers through social security – or better still, by providing jobs for them to do. The government itself should prime the pump* by employing men on public works. Their wages could

then be used to buy the products of other workers, and this demand for goods would start the economy working naturally again.

3. Businesses should be supported through a crisis and encouraged to expand by making sure they could borrow money easily and cheaply – i.e. at low interest rates. If 'cheap money' was not available from private sources, the government must provide it.

The common thread in all this is *strong government action* to influence the economy. In America this was very significant for two reasons: first, it was a complete break from *laissez-faire*; and secondly, it led to a great increase in the power of the federal government over state governments.

Although FDR was not deliberately following Keynes' prescription, the actions of his government came close to what Keynes was asking for. Figures 3.2 and 3.3 show the increase in people working for the government, and in government spending, which he recommended.

Keynes' ideas were not generally accepted in the 1930s, as they were later. The Keynesian revolution and the New Deal in America eventually led to the mixed economy which

America and other Capitalist countries operate today – that is, a mixture of *laissez-faire* principles and firm government control. Look at the economic life around you and you will see both of these elements in our society today.

Opposition to the New Deal

FDR was naturally popular – almost the object of worship – among the 'forgotten men' who at last had a pay cheque to spend and could openly wear a union badge, as a direct result of New Deal laws. But as you might expect, the New Deal was not popular with all Americans. Opposition came from three main sources:

1. The political Right

Businessmen welcomed the financial support from government, but disliked being forced to operate the 'fair practices' that were now the law of the land: for example their workmen's right to belong to a trade union, and legal limits to hours of work and rates of pay. They saw in these controls – and they were right – an end to the historic freedom of the individual from which, until the New

Figure 3.2   The number of paid civilian employees of the federal government, 1920–65.

Figure 3.3   Federal government annual surplus or deficit, 1920–65.

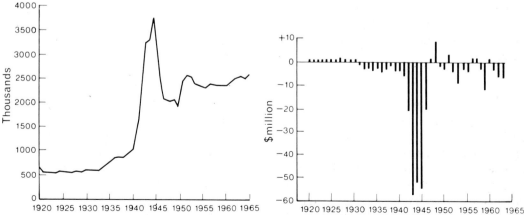

SOURCE: Daniel Snowman, *USA: The Twenties to Vietnam* (Batsford, 1968), revised edition *America Since 1920* (Heinemann Educational Books, 1978).

Deal, they were able to profit at the expense of other men's freedom.

Conservative supporters of traditional 'states rights' were also resentful of the greatly extended power of the federal government. Throughout American history there has been a tug of war between state governments and the federal government in Washington. It has often been a conflict between rural states with a fairly small, conservative population and a national government following more liberal policies approved of by the people who live in cities. After the New Deal, Washington won that battle all along the line, until in recent years distrust of the federal government has begun to reassert itself (see ahead, Chapter 7).

2. *The political Left*

There were others – Socialists or Communists – who thought that the New Deal did not go far enough. It checked the worst abuses of *laissez-faire* and forced some redistribution of wealth by higher taxes on the rich and social benefits for the poor, but it did not seriously interfere with a rich man's freedom to make money by exploiting other men's labour.

Among the people who campaigned on these lines were some who were not really Left but extreme Right in politics. One of these was Governor Huey Long of Louisiana. He became popular on the slogan 'Share Our Wealth', but when he achieved power he set up a kind of strong-arm government in which he was a one-man dictator. Perhaps fortunately, his career ended in assassination before he could challenge FDR for the Presidency, as he hoped to do.

3. *The Supreme Court*

FDR nearly met his match in the opposition to the New Deal that came from the Supreme Court. In several judgements, some by a 5 to 4 majority, they found some important New Deal laws 'unconstitutional' – i.e. they said that the federal government was going beyond the powers allowed to it by the Con-

stitution (see Study Topic 1, page 15). These laws were therefore cancelled and had to be rewritten in order to pass the Supreme Court's inspection, or abandoned.

FDR proposed to reform the Supreme Court itself by increasing the number of judges and then 'packing the Bench' with men more sympathetic to his policies (Supreme Court judges are appointed for life by the President). In the end this was not necessary – the Court began to take a broader view of what the Constitution allowed – but FDR's campaign against the Court damaged his reputation. He seemed to be getting too big for his boots, ready to attack the very structure of the American system of government – a judgement echoed by all his right-wing critics.

How successful was the New Deal?

The success of the New Deal is mostly to be seen in the confidence it restored to Americans, and in the long-term changes it introduced. Unemployment was reduced, but by no means ended. You can see from Figure 3.4 that the number of unemployed did not drop below 6 million until 1941. That was the year when America entered the Second World War.

FDR's greatest quality was boldness. It was this try-anything spirit that he communicated to other Americans in the darkest days of the depression. He was the first American President to project a personal image to the public through his press conferences, cinema newsreel interviews and above all his radio 'fireside chats', which often included domestic news about his family and his little dog Fala.

But in a sense FDR was not bold enough, at least according to the Keynesian 'rules' which governments adopted later. By 1937 the American Government's debts were very high, and many cautious advisers told FDR to *stop*! According to Keynes, a government should be ready to spend money almost without limit to cure unemployment – but that new idea was far from accepted in the 1930s,

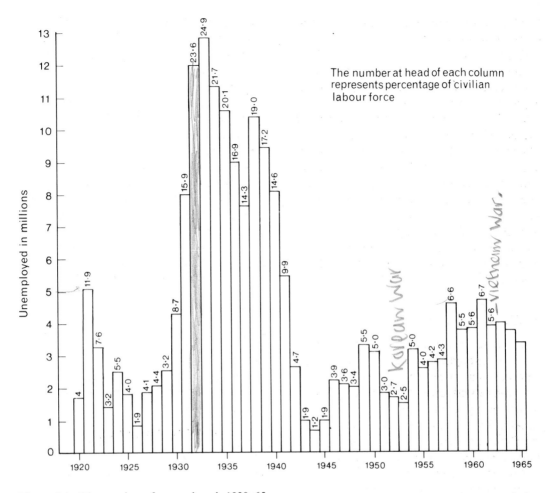

The number at head of each column
represents percentage of civilian
labour force

Figure 3.4   The number of unemployed, 1920–65.
SOURCE: Daniel Snowman, *USA: The Twenties to Vietnam* (Batsford, 1968), revised edition *America Since 1920* (Heinemann Educational Books, 1978).

and FDR did not dare to go further 'into the red'*. So he cut back government spending, and unemployment at once began to rise again.

There is only one situation in which a government does not worry at all about getting 'into the red' – and that is when it goes to war. In Keynesian terms, a rearmament programme funded by a government at war is the biggest public works project imaginable! Look back at Figures 3.2 and 3.3 (page

37), and notice the dramatic rise in the number of people employed by the government, and in the federal government's budget deficit, between 1941 and 1945.

It was in fact the preparations for war that FDR began in 1939, and greatly expanded after 1941, that finally cured the Great Depression in America. And in the period after 1945, as we shall see, high defence budgets have helped to keep her out of another one.

Study Topic 4

The New Deal Programme

1933

Immediately he took office FDR proclaimed a Bank Holiday or temporary closing of banks so that panic-stricken depositors could not withdraw their savings and force more banks into bankruptcy. Under a temporary Banking Act the government lent money to keep banks open and working, and later the 1935 *Banking Act* increased government control over banks.

FDR devalued the dollar by just over 40 per cent. This meant that foreigners could now get more dollars in exchange for their own currency, and therefore might buy more American exports.

The Federal Emergency Relief Administration (FERA) made $500 million available to state governments for emergency relief. It helped to finance soup kitchens, etc. It did not provide jobs like later agencies.

Aid for Mortgages – the Farm Credit Administration refinanced 20 per cent of farm mortgages and the Home Owners Loan Corporation did the same for 20 per cent of mortgaged private urban dwellings. Without these agencies people would have lost their farms or houses because of failure to keep up mortgage repayments.

Civil Works Administration (CWA). Set up to create jobs with minimum pay. Replaced in 1935 by WPA, the best-known 'public works' agency.

National Industrial Recovery Administration (NRA). Intended to regulate industry by allowing employers to fix prices in return for guaranteeing workers a minimum wage and the right to form trade unions. Companies which adopted NRA 'codes' could display its Blue Eagle symbol. The NIR Act also set up the Public Works Administration (PWA) with $3,300 million for major projects such as road-building and slum clearance. The Act was declared unconstitutional by the Supreme Court in 1935. Some NRA work was taken over by other agencies.

Agricultural Adjustment Act (AAA). Under this Act the government paid farmers to reduce their production. For example in 1933 it organized the ploughing up of 10 million acres of cotton and bought up and slaughtered 5 million pigs. This policy of artificial scarcity did increase gross farm income by 50 per cent between 1932 and 1936, but it mainly benefited large landowners and had the side-effect of evicting thousands of black farm workers in the South as their employer/landowners cut back production. Also cancelled by the Supreme Court in 1936, its work passing to other agencies.

The Reconstruction Finance Corporation (RFC) was inherited from Hoover but became very active under FDR. It was a government agency to invest government money in banks, so that they had more credit, and in industry to help maintain employment. By 1940 it had invested $15,000 million.

The Civilian Conservation Corps (CCC) offered 6 months' work to unemployed young men aged 18 to 25, mainly on conservation work. They were paid $30 a month and had to send $25 home to their families. In nine years it employed over 2 million; many rejoined the scheme after their first 6 months.

The Tennessee Valley Authority (TVA) was a bold experiment in the planned development of 41,000 square miles of the Tennessee Valley, including conservation (irrigation, planting forests, etc.) and government-controlled hydro-electric schemes. It was attacked as 'dangerously Socialistic' because the government was undertaking work which Capitalists believe should be done by private enterprise.

1934

The Securities and Exchange Commission (SEC) was established to regulate the conduct of the stock exchange and the way stocks were offered for sale. For example, it could require a down-payment of 50–60 per cent to be paid at the time of purchase.

1935

The Works Project Administration (WPA) took over and expanded the work of the CWA. Over the years the WPA hired 8½ million people for 1,410,000 projects. It built or improved 2,500 hospitals, 5,900 schools, 10,000 airports, 13,000 playgrounds, 124,000 bridges, 125,000 public buildings and 8,200 parks. Even artists, writers and musicians were hired to paint murals in public buildings, write tourist guides or put on plays and concerts.

The Farm Security Administration (FSA) was formed to help evicted sharecroppers and others to find homes and loans. It also employed a team of photographers– Dorothea Lange, Walker Evans and others–whose work became world-famous as a record of the suffering of the poorest Americans during the depression.

The National Labour Relations Board (NLRB) was set up by the *Wagner Act* to ensure workers' rights to form and join trade unions (previously often denied by so-called 'yellow dog' employment contracts in which workers pledged not to join one).

Unions needed a helping hand from government. In 1935 the Congress of Industrial Organizations (CIO) broke away from the American Federation of Labour (AFL) to organize the unskilled workers of the new mass industries. There were several big CIO strikes in the mid-1930s; in Chicago in 1937 ten strikers were shot by police in 'the Memorial Day massacre'. But employers now had to give way to the pressure of a militant union organization and the Wagner Act. Between 1933 and 1939 union membership rose from 3 million to 9 million, and expanded even faster during the Second World War.

The Social Security Act created the foundations of a welfare state in providing old age pensions, unemployment pay and sick pay. These schemes were jointly financed by federal and state governments.

1938

Fair Labor Standards Act. This law established maximum hours of work and minimum wages, and controlled the use of child labour.

Limited reform

The New Deal brought many overdue reforms, but it did not fully protect the most vulnerable workers. The Social Security Act offered no health insurance. Domestics, migrant workers, farmers and their labourers were excluded from its benefits and also did not qualify for minimum wages and limits on hours of work in industry. Many black workers slipped through the safety net in this way, and were also widely discriminated against in getting jobs. In 1941 FDR set up a

Fair Employment Practices Committee, a first step towards a 'new deal' for America's black citizens which was still 25 years ahead (see Chapter 6).

*GLOSSARY

into the red, getting into debt.

prime the pump, originally, to wet the mechanism of a pump to start it working; now the meaning has been extended, as here.

veteran, someone who has grown old in or had long experience of service (especially military service) or of an occupation. In America the word is applied to any ex-soldier.

Questions

Did you notice?

1. Investment trusts sold (a) cars (b) radios (c) shares
2. 'Hoover blankets' were (a) newspapers (b) car rugs (c) temporary housing
3. In 1933 the number of unemployed was approximately (a) 1 in 50 (b) 1 in 4 (c) 1 in 10 of the work force
4. The Social Security Act of 1935 was mainly an act of (a) Recovery (b) Relief (c) Reform
5. The CCC was (a) the Chrysler Car Corporation (b) the Civilian Conservation Corps (c) the Child Care Charity
6. True or false?
   (i) The main cause of the depression was the lack of demand for goods
   (ii) Huey Long was a Communist
   (iii) The New Deal made the federal government more powerful
   (iv) FDR's supporters were mostly right-wing
   (v) The main purpose of public works was to provide jobs
7. Which statement is *more* accurate?
   (i) There was no 'dole' in 1930 because
      (a) the *laissez-faire* theory said it was wrong
      (b) the government could not afford it
   (ii) In 1931 the Republican Government
      (a) did not want to increase exports
      (b) made it more difficult to sell American exports
   (iii) J. M. Keynes recommended that
      (a) a government should go into debt to cure a depression
      (b) a government should go to war to cure a depression

Can you explain?

8. Why was it so difficult to obtain a bank loan after the Wall Street Crash? What effect did this have on industry? *P32.*
9. Why did American exports decline after 1929?
10. Give two examples of New Deal laws which applied the economic principles of J. M. Keynes, explaining how they did so.
11. Which groups of Americans opposed the New Deal, and (in each case) why did they do so?
12. How successful was the New Deal in curing unemployment?

What's your view?

13. Many hard-working, thrifty Americans disapproved of people who were speculating on the stock market. Why do you think they disapproved? Do *you* think the speculators were doing anything wrong?
14. FDR was a very 'strong' President and it has been said that this is one reason why he was so popular. Do you think most people like a strong leader? If so, why? Can you see any danger in having a strong leader, even one (like FDR) who seems to be doing good for his country?
15. President Hoover's Government saw the Bonus March of 1932 as a sign of revolution, and therefore felt justified in using force against it. Was this a correct view of the Bonus Marchers' protest? In a democracy like ours or America's, what methods of protest or complaint are available to citizens? At what point, if any, do you think citizens are entitled to use *violent* methods of protest?

4

American Foreign Policy to 1945

The main concern of this book in regard to foreign policy is the World Powers' relations with each other after 1945 (see Part IV). That story is so highly coloured by the ideological war between Capitalism and Communism that you might think that is *all* it was about. But whatever political mission a government may undertake in the world, its foreign policy will also reflect its own national self-interest. It is easy to see this in the context of one nation's history, and America provides a good example.

Every government's foreign policy starts with three basic aims: to remain independent and defend the country from attack; to protect its citizens abroad; and to promote its own trading interests overseas. In the brief account that follows, notice the way American foreign policy changed to fit the needs of her own development. By the twentieth century she could not remain 'uninvolved' in world affairs, although many Americans still wanted her to do so.

No 'entangling alliances'

The thirteen colonies which formed themselves into the United States of America in 1787 had recently thrown off British rule in the American War of Independence. The new nation was at first small and weak, and naturally its first concern was to avoid being attacked or re-colonized. The main enemies at that time were the military giants Britain and France, who both had colonies and ambitions in the Americas.

The USA therefore took up a firm policy of neutrality, in which she would make no 'entangling alliances' with other nations and would not take sides in any dispute. Equally she wanted no interference in her own affairs. At that time she was busy colonizing the rest of her continent (or as much of it as she could) and developing its resources. In 1823 this attitude was made clear by President Monroe in what was later called the Monroe Doctrine. It said 'Keep off!' to any foreign power with greedy eyes on the territory that America regarded as her sphere of influence.

America acquires an empire

Towards the end of the nineteenth century the Monroe Doctrine was used to justify a kind of overlordship which the USA assumed over Central and South America and the Caribbean area. A symbol of her growing interest in the region was her acquisition, by less than fair means, of a ten-mile-wide strip of Panama in 1903. There American engineers constructed the Panama Canal, opened in 1914, which greatly facilitated American trade with the Far East and South America. Her trading interests developed accordingly, especially in her Latin American 'back yard'. She did not make outright colonies of Latin American countries, but did not hesitate to 'send in the marines' to protect the interests of American or other foreign investors. But as American investment increased, other foreign interests were pushed out: between 1914 and 1929 the American share of all investment in Latin America rose from 17 per cent to 40 per cent.

The seizure of the Panama Canal Zone was part of a sudden outburst of *imperialism* (k) at the turn of the century in which the United States did acquire a few actual colonies:

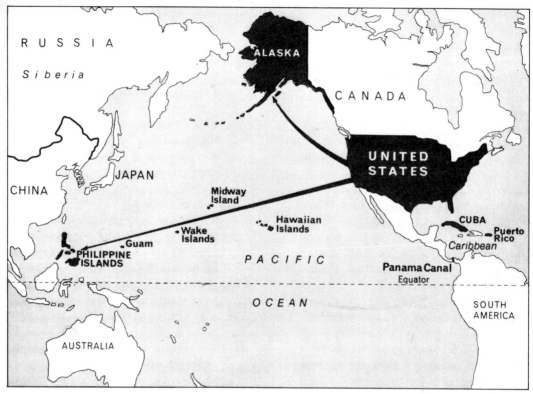

Figure 4.1   American imperialism around 1900.

Hawaii, the Philippines, Puerto Rico and Guam, and economic rule over Cuba (Figure 4.1). She had also bought Alaska from Russia in 1867, and purchased the Virgin Islands, in the Caribbean, from Denmark in 1917. Colonies are useful to the mother country as a source of raw materials and as a market for her own finished goods. By 1900 the American economy needed this kind of trade just as much as other colonial powers like Britain and France. Even so, many prominent Americans were against having colonies; they wanted their country to 'do right' in the world and not follow the bad example of other strong powers in suppressing weaker peoples for their own benefit. But this anti-imperialist feeling could not outweigh the temptations of great-power status which the United States had by now achieved.

Towards the rest of the world, however, the United States did hold to her policy of neutrality. This came to be regarded as her traditional or 'normal' policy, arising out of her own history. But you can see that the second and third aims of foreign policy – the protection of a nation's citizens and interests abroad – were already making it very difficult for America to remain neutral. In 1917, as we saw earlier ('Starting Point: the First World War', page 2), these interests led her to declare war on Germany and make an 'entangling alliance' with Germany's other enemies.

Foreign policy between the wars

After the First World War, President Wilson wanted to keep America involved in world affairs, but he was overruled by the strong desire of Congress and other Americans to return to her 'normal' policy of neutrality (or *isolationism*). You will remember that the 1919 peace settlement included the League of Nations and its plan for collective security

45

to keep the peace of the world. This was what worried Congress: the possibility that America might have to go to war unwillingly, to fulfil her pledge as a member of the League. So the Senate refused to ratify the Treaty of Versailles and the League of Nations Covenant, and America took no part in trying to enforce them. With sixty-four other nations, she did sign the Kellogg–Briand Pact of 1928 'to renounce war as an instrument of national policy', but this was really just a paper promise which was later disregarded by most of its signatories.

But American businessmen always had an eye on their overseas interests, especially in Latin America and the Far East.

1. America's 'back yard'

Latin America was still the exception to America's policy of non-interference in the affairs of other countries. But the *style* of American control there began to change. Under President Roosevelt's 'good neighbour policy' American troops were withdrawn from Haiti and Nicaragua in the 1930s and the United States waived its right, forced on 'independent' Cuba in 1903, to intervene in Cuba. 'Dollar diplomacy'† continued, but more subtly. America's new way of ensuring stability in any 'risky' country was to support a local strong-man or oligarchy* who could be trusted to maintain friendly relations with the 'good neighbour' to the north. Some of these American-backed régimes of the 1930s lasted for generations: Batista in Cuba, Trujillo in the Dominican Republic, Somoza in Nicaragua. At times their tyrannical methods were an embarrassment to the United States, but their usefulness was obvious. As FDR once said of Rafael Trujillo, the brutal dictator of the Dominican Republic, 'He may be a son-of-a-bitch, but he's *our* son-of-a-bitch'.

2. The Far East

The United States had a long-standing

†The meaning of this term is included in the explanation of imperialism on page 49.

interest in trade with China and was resentful when this was threatened by Japan, who sought exclusive rights to pursue her own interests there. In a bid for great-power status in the early twentieth century, the Japanese navy then began to rival the navies of Britain and the United States. At the Washington Conference of 1921, and again at the London Naval Conference of 1930, Japan accepted limits to the growth of her navy, but in 1934 she repudiated these treaties and began a naval arms race with the United States.

3. Threats to world peace

In the next few years Japan and other aggressive states became ever more defiant and bellicose. In 1931 Japan had occupied the Chinese province of Manchuria and was 'punished' only by the condemnation of the League of Nations and the United States. In 1933 Hitler came to power in Germany and began to rearm the country. In 1935 Italy, under the dictator Mussolini, easily conquered the small country of Ethiopia to make it an Italian colony, and once again the League did not intervene. In 1936 General Franco rebelled against the democratic government of Spain and it soon became obvious that the other European democracies would not intervene in the Spanish Civil War to prevent him from winning it (which he did in 1939).

These events were watched by the United States with concern, but she was no more ready to take action to prevent them than the states which had solemnly promised to do so through the League of Nations. In 1937 Japan launched a full-scale invasion of China, accidentally sinking an American gunboat in the process. America meekly accepted compensation for the loss, but despite increasing public hostility towards Japan, she would not be drawn into conflict. Isolationism was still supported by most Americans, whose main worry was the depression at home.

The Neutrality Acts

America's determination to 'stay out' was shown by her Neutrality Acts of the 1930s. When fighting broke out in Ethiopia, in Spain, and then in China, it seemed that America might be dragged into war 'accidentally'. One reason why she had felt bound to go to war in 1917 was to protect the investment of Americans who had sold arms to the Allies on credit, and because Germany had sunk American ships. If it were publicly known now that no American ships were carrying arms to a nation at war, there would be no excuse to sink them. So in 1935 and 1937, Neutrality Acts were passed to make it illegal to sell war materials to any belligerent state, and any other materials they might buy had to be paid for in cash and could not be carried in American ships. Of course America had a perfect right, as a neutral, to trade freely with anyone, but she was prepared to forgo this right to avoid getting involved.

Isolationism begins to weaken...

By 1939 military dictatorship had triumphed in Europe. Italy, Spain and Germany had Fascist governments. Britain and France had not resisted when Hitler ignored the Treaty of Versailles to rearm Germany, reoccupy the Rhineland and unite with Austria. In 1938 they had allowed him to take part of Czechoslovakia, and in 1939 he took the rest of it without asking. It looked as though the next target for German aggression would be Poland, Russia's neighbour (in Chapter 11 you will see how the Soviet government reacted to that threat, and what Fascism meant in the 1930s and in politics today).

American public opinion now began to change. Many Jewish refugees from Hitler's Germany arrived in America. If war came, American sympathies were bound to lie with the democracies–the Allies, as they again became when war did break out in September 1939. In November 1939 a new Neutrality Act allowed the sale of *any* material to a state at war, although still subject to the 'cash and carry' rule. Britain was already at war and at once bought vast amounts of war supplies from America. But by 1941 she was running out of money and could no longer buy on a cash-down basis.

FDR's sympathies were strongly towards Britain. After 1940 Britain stood alone against Hitler's forces which by then had overrun all of Western Europe. But Americans still did not want war and in the Presidential election campaign of 1940 FDR promised that 'No American boy will die in any European war'. Nevertheless he went as far as he could to help the Allied cause:

1. The *Lend-Lease Act* of March 1941 allowed America to 'transfer or lend' any article useful for the defence of any country whose survival was vital to American security. $7,000 million was made available immediately, and with this Britain bought arms and other vital supplies such as food. After June 1941, when Hitler attacked the USSR and thereby made her another Ally, Lend-Lease was also extended to Russia.

2. In August 1941 FDR met Winston Churchill aboard ship to sign the *Atlantic Charter* (Figure 4.2). Although the USA was not yet at war with Germany, this was a declaration of war aims rather like President Wilson's Fourteen Points in 1918. Again it contained high-minded plans for the post-war world: the right of all peoples to choose their own government; no territorial changes without their consent; and 'a wider and permanent system of general security'–in other words, a new version of the League of Nations.

Meanwhile, as Germany overran the countries of Western Europe, her ally Japan was occupying their Far Eastern colonies. America's relations with Japan worsened. While talks to resolve them were actually in process, on 7 December 1941 Japan attacked and devastated the American fleet at Pearl Harbor, Hawaii. America then declared war on Japan and a few days later Germany and Italy, Japan's allies, declared war on the

Figure 4.2   President Roosevelt greets Winston Churchill on board ship at the start of the Atlantic Conference, August 1941.

United States. And so America joined Britain, France, China and the USSR in the Alliance which, after many reverses, eventually won the Second World War. Since France and China (for reasons we shall see later) were unable to play much part in the war, it was the Big Three of Britain, the USA and the USSR who took all the important decisions.

America's part in the Second World War

At the beginning of Part IV we shall briefly look at the course of the Second World War, where the sources of post-war conflict between the World Powers can already be seen. But there are two important points which need to be mentioned here. They help to explain FDR's attitudes and policies at the end of the war, and also the readiness of the American people to abandon isolationism after 1945.

1. FDR's attitude to his allies

FDR strongly disliked colonialism – but one of the Big Three, Great Britain, was a major colonial power. FDR hoped to see the vast British Empire gradually dismantled after the war and the colonies given self-government in line with the declared aims of the Atlantic Charter. But he foresaw – rightly, as it turned out – that Britain (and France in her turn) would not do this willingly. Britain's leader, Winston Churchill, was a strong supporter of the Empire, and his first post-war wish would be to strengthen it and recover areas (such as Malaya) which had been occupied by Japan.

FDR's attitude to his other ally, the USSR, was open-minded. He was less scared of Stalin and Soviet Communism than earlier (or later) American Presidents. He had, after all, seen the need to amend American Capitalism in his own New Deal – although in spite of what his right-wing critics said, that was far from a Socialist programme. At the various

Big Three conferences, FDR got on well with Uncle Joe (Stalin's chummy wartime nickname in the West) and was inclined to trust him. He thought that if the West dealt fairly with the USSR after the war, and recognized her legitimate interests, the USSR would become a responsible and useful member of the international community.

But Churchill was not inclined to be 'soft on Stalin'. As Germany's defeat came closer, his main worry was the chance this would give to the USSR to increase her influence in Europe. Churchill thought that this must be firmly resisted, and after the war he was the first Western statesman openly to say so.

While the war continued, however, all these tensions between the Big Three were subordinated to the common aim of defeating Germany and Japan.

2. The USA's contribution to the war effort

The Pacific War against Japan was mainly fought and won by the United States, and her troops also helped to win the war in Europe. Throughout the war, America supplied the Allies with war materials of every kind. Americans became emotionally committed to the war effort in a way that had not happened in 1917–18. Like other people in the West, they were horrified to realize the extent of Nazi cruelty when concentration camps and other war crimes were uncovered. When the war ended, although America wanted to 'get the boys back home' as quickly as possible, there was no question of another retreat into isolationism. It was obvious now that the strongest nation in the world – and one with interests in every part of it – could not stand apart.

America's new foreign policy

FDR died in April 1945, two months before the founding of the United Nations. But his successor President Truman was just as committed an internationalist as FDR had been. From its beginning, the USA was a strong supporter of the United Nations and contributed a large proportion of its budget.

In every other sphere, too, America has been continuously involved in world affairs since 1945. She had been drawn into two world wars not only to defend Democracy but to protect American interests, and for both those reasons she would stay involved in the post-war world. In fact her foreign policy now became interventionist to the point where many people resented American interference in what they regarded as the concerns of other countries.

*GLOSSARY

oligarchy, literally this word means government by the few, but it is often used more loosely to denote a small 'ruling circle' of very powerful people.

KEYWORD

imperialism, rule of an empire, or the process whereby one (usually strong) nation imposes its rule over another (usually weak) nation or people. In history, the term 'imperialist' refers to countries like Britain and France which built up huge overseas empires of colonies in Africa, India, etc.

Nowadays we also speak of economic imperialism, where a powerful state does not actually rule another country but owns a lot of businesses there, or has lent a lot of money to its government. It can then put pressure on the small country's government and so undermine its independence. American 'dollar diplomacy' in Latin America is imperialism of this kind.

Often arising out of economic imperialism there can also be cultural imperialism – the spreading of one nation's ideas or way of life to other countries. Britain spread her way of life to her colonies in this way, but in the twentieth century America is the main example of this: Hollywood movies and the sales campaigns of big American companies have spread products like Coca-Cola and chewing gum to every corner of the world.

Questions

1. A policy of neutrality means (a) having no foreign policy (b) joining the League of Nations (c) not taking sides in disputes between other countries
2. America did not take action against Japan in the 1930s because (a) she did not mind what Japan was doing (b) she had signed the Kellogg–Briand Pact (c) she wanted to avoid war
3. In 1936 Ethiopia was conquered by (a) Italy (b) Germany (c) Spain
4. The Atlantic Charter was (a) a pact to outlaw war (b) a declaration of neutrality (c) a statement of war aims
5. FDR was re-elected in (a) 1939 (b) 1942 (c) 1940
6. True or false?
   (i) Malaya was part of the British Empire before 1939
   (ii) Hitler attacked the United States at Pearl Harbor
   (iii) President Truman was an isolationist
   (iv) The United States gave Lend-Lease aid to Soviet Russia
7. Which statement is *more* accurate?
   (i) Colonies were useful to the mother country mainly
      (a) to protect her from attack
      (b) as a source of raw materials and a market for goods
   (ii) One purpose of the 'cash and carry' rule was
      (a) to recover First World War debts
      (b) to prevent the sinking of American ships
   (iii) FDR hoped that after the Second World War
      (a) the British Empire would be dismantled
      (b) the Soviet Empire would be expanded

Can you explain?

8. In what way did American imperialism in Latin America differ from the imperialist policies of other strong powers in the nineteenth century?
9. What did 'back to normal' mean in 1920, so far as American foreign policy was concerned?
10. How did the Neutrality Acts of 1935 and 1937 show the strength of American isolationism?
11. Give an example to show isolationism weakening after September 1939. Why was American policy beginning to change?
12. At the end of the Second World War, how did FDR and Churchill differ in their attitude towards the Soviet Union?

What's your view?

13. Many times in her history the United States has intervened in Latin America to protect her interests there. Do you think a country has the 'right' to intervene in the affairs of another? If so, how far should it go to enforce its right?
14. In 1940, when Hitler had overrun Western Europe, most Americans thought that he should be stopped from defeating Britain. Why did the American Government not declare war on Germany in 1940? Do you think it was right not to do so?
15. In defence of past empires it is often said that colonial rule brought benefits to the colonies as well as to the mother country. Considering the case of any ex-colony you know about: what benefits to the colony, if any, did its former ruler bring? What disadvantages are there in being a colony? Do any difficulties arise *after* independence which come from having been a colony?

5

The Fifties: Affluence and Anxiety

It is difficult to arrange the next few topics of our history of the United States in neat chronological order. The 'affluent society' which developed in the 1950s is still largely the picture in America today, while the problems which erupted in the 1960s had their roots in earlier times and are still far from solved. Chapter 5 is chiefly about America's post-war economic success story, and alongside this, the rather disgraceful period of McCarthyism in politics. Chapter 6 takes up the social problems which mainly affect America's long-neglected minority groups – the blacks, the poor, and most of all those who are poor *and* black.

Many things in post-war America will remind you of our own society today. By studying America's history of the past forty years, we are seeing our own present. In the same way, many of America's problems today may be ours tomorrow.

America's war effort

American society was remarkably united during the war. Businessman or trade unionist, immigrant or native-born – all Americans felt they were on the right side in the world conflict, and wanted to win it. This feeling of national purpose was shown in the stupendous achievements of American industry between 1941 and 1945: it fed the Allied forces with 86,330 tanks, 296,400 aircraft, 2,681,000 machine guns, 64,500 landing craft, 6,500 naval ships and many other supplies of conventional warfare. And of course it was the American Manhattan Project – 'the best-kept secret of the war' – which produced the

Atom bomb to end the war against Japan in August 1945.

Many people feared that when orders for war equipment came to an end, America would fall back into depression. Some difficulties did occur as soldiers came home looking for jobs, but there was no serious rise in unemployment. The reasons why this did not happen are explained below.

The legacy of the New Deal

In 1945 President Truman announced a Fair Deal programme: a mini New Deal with plans for expanded social security, government housing and other public works projects. In 1946 an Employment Act was passed setting up a Council of Economic Advisers to keep up employment. It was clear that the precedent set by the New Deal would continue: the economy would not be allowed to 'run itself' by market forces alone. In fact all American governments since 1945 – Republican or Democrat – have been ready to intervene in the economy when it seemed to be necessary. Thus a Republican Congress under Eisenhower in 1956 passed the $100 billion Interstate Highway Act similar to FDR's public works projects, while Kennedy (a Democrat) in 1961 cut businessmen's taxes to encourage business expansion and therefore more jobs.

American governments have kept to another rule of Keynes in keeping up the numbers of their own employees, mainly in the defence and space industries, as we shall see. They have also, like our own government, repeatedly tried to control inflation, but with little success. Inflation, the steady upward climb of prices and wages, has become the chronic post-war sickness of all Western Capitalist economies, as unemployment had been before the war. So far no government has found a satisfactory way to check it (Chapter 7 explains this problem more fully, and the American government's efforts to deal with it).

A 'rebel' Congress

Truman had a rough ride in the Presidency. As soon as the war was over, organized groups in the community again began to fight for their own interests. The familiar struggle between employers and trade unions broke out: there were a number of serious strikes, but business interests retaliated sharply with the 'union-bashing' Taft–Hartley Act in 1947. This law restricted the unions' power and made them liable to be sued by an employer for 'damages' to his company's trading during a strike.

In the mid-term elections of 1946 a Republican majority had been returned to Congress which was able to pass this law over President Truman's veto. Here is an instance of the discord between President and Congress which can result from the system of 'checks and balances' written into the American Constitution (see Study Topic 1, p. 15). The intention was to prevent the President from becoming too powerful, but he is sometimes prevented from doing anything!

This is what happened to Truman in 1946. Congress was able to torpedo most of his Fair Deal plans, and there were signs that the long rule of the Democrats (since 1932) was coming to an end. It was widely expected that the Republicans would sweep the board in 1948, but although they did well in elections to Congress, Truman was returned as President.

THE AFFLUENT SOCIETY

Perhaps Truman owed his victory to post-war prosperity. Within a few years of the end of the war, things were going very well indeed in America. It was obvious to the world – and Americans proudly pointed it out to anyone who hadn't noticed – that they were the best-fed, best-dressed, best-educated, most comfortable people in the world. The American economy had reached another upward climb into what is called *the affluent society*. As in the 1920s, the most striking feature of this prosperity was the new life-style of Americans. The new boom had its own dangers, as we shall see, but there were significant differences which made it more secure than the boom which had ended in the 1929 Crash. One was the watchdog role of government described above. But there were other new factors too.

Better balance between producer and consumer

On the production side of the economy, the power of big corporations (the monopolies we looked at in Chapter 2) had continued to grow. The small-time producer found it impossible to compete. A big company can afford research to improve and develop its products and it can also benefit from economies of scale – Henry Ford's principle that the more you make of one standard product, the less your production cost per item. In the post-war years the expanding production of these big manufacturers was shown in the rise of national income from $213 billion in 1945 to $500 billion in 1961.

But on the consumers' side of the economy there was now big bargaining power too, which balanced the power of big producers.

1. Developments in marketing

Very large marketing organizations had developed: chains of department stores, supermarkets and mail-order businesses. Because they bought such vast quantities of goods, they could bargain for a very low price: a manufacturer with the chance to sell his product in millions will be ready to cut his profit per item to the minimum. So, for example, Sears Roebuck (a mail-order business) could buy tyres from the Goodyear Company as much as 40 per cent below the usual market price. Sears Roebuck could itself sell the tyres at a low price and still make a handsome profit.

2. *Trade union strength*

Since their New Deal 'charter of freedom', the Wagner Act of 1935, trade unions had grown enormously in strength and had won from their employers a much larger slice of industry's profits. This was resented (as the Taft–Hartley Act shows), but it was healthy for the economy as a whole: unlike the 1920s situation, there was an expanding market for goods among working people. They could now afford the things their parents had only looked at in shop windows: a car, TV set, an all-electric labour-saving kitchen.

The consumer economy

One feature of rising prosperity is that nobody wants it to stop. When you're on an escalator, you don't look back at where you've come from (or at the people who are still way behind you): you look ahead to where you hope you're going – the top! This is called a climate of 'rising expectations' and it describes very well the mood of America in the 1950s. Although most people were already richer than their parents' wildest dreams, there was always more ahead and no one felt like saying 'Stop! I've got enough!'

So not content with one car in the garage, every family wanted two. And not your sturdy workaday Model T which 'any hick up a dirt road' could mend and mend again with just a spanner and a can of oil. A Model T was made to last a lifetime – but who wants a car to last a lifetime when next year its tail-

Figure 5.1   The consumer economy: Las Vegas.

fin will be the wrong shape? Henry Ford's idea of a cheap, standard product for 'everyone' had worked very well for a time, but even in the 1920s more far-sighted manufacturers had realized that to absorb the vast output of a mass-production economy it would soon be necessary to stimulate a taste for variety and change among buyers.

You can see that the producer needs to sell you a new car much more than you need to buy it! The affluent society depends on an ever-expanding market, a 'growth economy' as it is called. When everybody has got one of everything, it is necessary to sell them another—and another. This is *the consumer economy* we live in today. Its main features are these:

1. *The advertising industry* has the most important job of creating needs. 'For the man who has everything' said a 1951 Christmas ad. in the *New Yorker* magazine, 'a mink-handled can-opener'. By 1956, $10,000 million a year was spent on advertising in the USA.

2. *Planned obsolescence* is also essential— no more 'last-you-a-lifetime' products. If you change the mechanism slightly so that last year's customer cannot buy spare parts, then you can sell him the latest model. The designer of shape and colour also has a part to play: this is where the changing tail-fin comes in.

3. *Hire purchase* is another necessary feature of a consumer economy. People who cannot afford the money to buy something this year must be lent the money to do so. Between 1956 and 1967, total consumer debt in the USA (the amount of money owed on goods already 'sold') rose from $42,500 billion to $99,100 billion, an increase of 133 per cent.

The producer in a consumer economy needs to keep selling, but indirectly the consumer needs to keep buying too. A man who makes cars and spends his wages on new clothes keeps the tailor next door in work, and vice versa.* Taken as a whole, the working population must keep buying to keep itself employed—*and* pay high taxes to provide basic public services.

Later it would be pointed out to prosperous Americans that a growth economy could not go on *for ever* (see ahead, Chapter 7), but in the 1950s there was the same carefree disregard for the future as in the 1920s. For the time being there was plenty of work making cars and food-mixers, and plenty of customers to buy them.

The move to suburbia

After the war several factors encouraged a dramatic shift of population from the major cities to vast new areas of 'suburbia' outside them. First was the increase of private cars (from 25 million in 1945 to 62 million in 1960) and 41,000 miles of new 'freeways' to drive them on; secondly, federal encouragement of long-term mortgages; and lastly, new 'pre-fabricated' building techniques. William Levitt was the Henry Ford of the building site: with a fair wind and no hold-ups, one house was completed every sixteen minutes in a Levittown. And as the people moved in, the shopping centre arrived with its huge car-park and supermarkets.

By 1960 a quarter of all Americans lived in suburbs. Sociologists found this new breed of American very conformist and materialistic– 'keeping up with the Joneses'* was almost an obsession in Levittown. One observer saw suburbia as a faintly sinister breeding-ground for the friendly and compliant 'organization man' employed by the big corporation, while another defended the right of suburbanites to be 'dull' and home-centred at a time when most of them were bringing up children.† Social surveys also noted that there was scarcely a black face to be seen in the new suburbs, and that poor non-whites were filling up the inner cities as richer whites

†The first study referred to is W. H. Whyte's *Organisation Man*, first published in 1956, and the second H. J. Gans' *The Levittowners*, published in 1967–two of many social analyses of post-war America.

moved out. The full significance of this development would only be realized later.

Faces at the window

In the 1920s you could measure prosperity in champagne suppers at the Stork Club in New York City. In the 1950s it was more like Saturday night in every local bar. But there were still seriously deprived groups, mainly non-whites in the inner cities, who could not afford to join in the party. In the 1960s they would rudely interrupt the general merriment with a brick through the window.

Spreading the American way of life

Again in contrast to the 1920s, in the post-war world America arranged for herself an expanding market overseas too. A walk down any British High Street will show you this. American companies like IBM, Ford, Safeway, etc., began to penetrate overseas markets to the point where countries in Western Europe which were political allies of the USA – France, for instance – began to resent the strong American influence in their economies.

If overseas customers could not afford to buy, they could be helped with gifts and loans. American aid programmes became a kind of international HP for overseas customers. Thus Marshall Aid in 1947, a $15,000 million programme to help West European recovery after the war, had the useful side effect of orders for American industry. In the same way the Alliance for Progress, launched by Kennedy in 1961 to encourage $400 million worth of private investment in Latin America, brought benefits to Americans as well as to Latin Americans. As with most other aid programmes from rich to poor countries, more money returned to the donor country in orders for goods and profits for shareholders than went into the receiving country in investment. This kind of aid also has the effect of encouraging an Americanized upper class at the top of society in the receiving country, while doing little to help

the majority of poor people. America has been loudly criticized for this.

The 'welfare-warfare state'

As we shall see in Part IV, by 1947 the West was already involved in a Cold War with its wartime ally the USSR. Both sides began a costly arms race: first more A-bombs, then H-bombs, then bigger ones, then nuclear missiles, then anti-missile missiles ...

This was another reason for high taxes and high employment in post-war America. States such as California became very prosperous on defence contracts. In 1958 the Cold War industry was further enlarged when President Eisenhower set up the National Aeronautics and Space Administration (NASA), and again in 1961 when President Kennedy promised an American on the moon within ten years. All this was set off by the Soviet triumph in 1957 in launching the first space satellite – 'Sputnik'.

One result of the huge national effort on the defence and space programmes was the growing power of what President Eisenhower called the *military-industrial complex* – the big industrialists and armed forces chiefs who worked closely together in the Cold War industry and who all had an interest in keeping it going. By its nature, what they were doing was Top Secret and therefore beyond the peering eyes of members of Congress who control the nation's budget. In post-war America the power of the 'barons of industry' like John D. Rockefeller and Andrew Carnegie had been cut back, but the influence of the military–industrial complex was perhaps even more sinister.

Here is a summary of America's economic life in the post-war years:

1. The affluent society spread downwards to far more Americans than 1920s prosperity, but still some groups were left out of it.
2. The consumer economy kept itself going by using and fostering the escalator of rising expectations, and by extending itself overseas. Again you can see the link between a nation's foreign policy and its

domestic needs: American overseas aid programmes also 'aided' Americans.

3. The economy was managed by government in many ways, and the government itself was a very large employer. If the Cold War industry ran down, a lot of workmen would lose their jobs – and many powerful corporations would lose government contracts. For that reason perhaps they used their influence in the government to keep the Cold War going.

ANOTHER RED SCARE

You have seen that Americans after the war had every reason to feel satisfied and confident. It was surprising that at a time of such prosperity and success they should suddenly develop another bout of 'Red fever', called McCarthyism, which lasted for about four years from 1950 to 1954. Once again America seemed to be suffering from a national persecution complex. The nation was being 'got at' by Reds under every bed! The very fabric of government had been eaten away by Communist agents! Even their own leaders were disloyal! So said Senator McCarthy, and millions of Americans believed him. But the real persecution was felt by thousands of her own citizens, who were accused of everything from 'a Pinko past' to outright treason. What set all this off? As with the Big Red Scare of 1919–20, the cause of the panic was outside America.

The Cold War – why are they winning?

Between 1946 and 1949 the Cold War between the West and Communism looked to Americans like a losing game. By 1948 the USSR had 'taken' Eastern Europe, including part of Germany. In 1949 the Russians exploded their first A-bomb – long before the West expected it. In the same year there was an even worse disaster for American prestige when a Communist government took power in China. For some years the American Government had given massive aid to the Nationalists who were now defeated, and the 'loss' of China was hard for many Americans to understand. They easily accepted the idea that the whole country had been forced against its will under the Red Hand of Moscow. As we shall see later, the triumph of Communism in China arose out of Chinese circumstances and had little to do with either Moscow or Washington. But it helps to understand America's reaction if we remember that in the long period of isolationism, few ordinary Americans knew or cared much about other countries.

It seemed to many Americans that 'our side' must have made terrible blunders to let all this happen. They saw evidence of mistakes in high places in several big spy trials after the war, in one of which a top British atomic scientist confessed that he had fed atomic secrets to the Russians. Even more sensational for Americans was the investigation of Alger Hiss, a former high official of the State Department (the American Foreign Office) who was accused of being a Communist agent by the Un-American Activities Committee of the US Congress, and subsequently convicted of perjury by a federal court. President Truman naturally denied the charges of mismanagement by his government, but he seemed to acknowledge the danger of infiltration by Communists when in 1947 he ordered an investigation into the loyalty of all federal government employees.

McCarthy seizes his chance

Into this nervous atmosphere stepped Senator Joe McCarthy, an unscrupulous right-wing Republican who saw a chance for personal fame and took it. In February 1950 he accused the State Department of sheltering 'known Communists' and was asked to prove these charges before a committee of the Senate. The committee dismissed them as 'a fraud and a hoax' – but the damage was done. A few months later the committee's chairman was defeated for re-election to the Senate when McCarthy spoke out against him.

McCarthy had suddenly become a power in the land, backed by many national newspapers and 'McCarthy clubs' of supporters. His campaign seemed further justified by the outbreak of the Korean War in June 1950, to which Truman responded with the military might that McCarthyite opinion demanded – though he stopped short of extending the war against China as some right-wingers wanted (see Chapter 23). At home McCarthy had everything his own way for a time. In public speeches, and later as chairman of a Senate sub-committee, he tore to shreds the reputation of many public servants. He called Dean Acheson, Truman's Secretary of State (Foreign Secretary), a 'friend of Moscow' and even attacked the popular Secretary of Defence, General Marshall, a wartime hero. In September 1950 the McCarran Internal Security Act was passed (over Truman's veto) requiring every 'Communist front' organization† to register a list of its members with the Attorney-General, and forbidding any subversive to enter the United States, even on a visit. This was a serious limitation on the liberties of thought and action that America claims to guarantee.

Level-headed politicians of both parties gave way to McCarthy and the tide of public opinion behind him – or used it for their own

†That is, organizations that were controlled by Communists or thought to be a cover for their activities.

purposes. Although Truman had tried to block the McCarran Act, his own government denied passports to people on the Attorney-General's list and unfairly investigated the loyalty of its own employees by giving suspects no chance to face their accusers. Some were dismissed or moved to 'safe' work. Similarly the 'respectable' end of the Republican party was glad to use McCarthy as a vote-catcher to end what he called the Democrats' 'twenty years of treason'. In 1952 they succeeded when Dwight Eisenhower, a popular Second World War general, became President (Figure 5.2). But McCarthy's crusade continued until, in 1954, he unwisely attacked the army. The committee hearings to examine his charges were televised, and now Americans saw – and were shamed by – McCarthy's brutal style of argument: shouting down witnesses and thumping the table with rage. Public opinion turned, the Senate passed a vote of censure on McCarthy and his career was finished. By this time, we should also note, the Korean War was over and East–West relations had thawed a little.

After 1954 American liberals could joke about 'McCarthy*wasm*', and in 1957 McCarthy's death passed almost unnoticed by the millions who had cheered or feared him four years earlier. But his campaign had left an ugly scar on America.

Figure 5.2   General Eisenhower sees victory ahead in the election campaign of 1952.

The effects of McCarthyism

Loyalty enquiries during the McCarthy period reached at least 9 million people working for the federal government or on government contracts, and millions more were required by state governments or private employers to sign a 'loyalty oath'. Teachers, trade union leaders and people in the entertainment business were particularly suspect: some lost their jobs on suspicion of Communist sympathies in their past, and once dismissed, found themselves on a black list – no one would give them a job. A new Lost Generation of artists and intellectuals left America to find work and a home in Europe, and some never went back. One of the best-known Hollywood refugees was Charlie Chaplin, who left in 1954 with a special kick in the pants from the Attorney-General notifying him that 'his re-entry would be challenged'. (When he returned on a visit in 1972 he was welcomed back with open arms and apologetic speeches. By that time most Americans were ashamed of this unsavoury episode in their history.)

A striking feature of the McCarthy 'witch-hunt' was the fearful and suspicious atmosphere it created. Most Americans did not believe his outrageous charges, but while he was at the peak of his power they were too scared to say so. One characteristic of American social life is conformism, and this was especially strong in the 1950s, as we have already noted. At all times it takes a brave spirit to be different in America, and in a period like McCarthyism it was downright dangerous.

The Radical Right smoulders on ...

McCarthyism was widespread but temporary – a brush-fire which did a lot of damage until it burnt itself out. But McCarthy's *ideas* were not extinguished. In the early 1960s there was a flutter of excitement about a new right-wing movement headed by the John Birch Society. 'Birchers' found Communism winning everywhere in American society – 'in the press, the pulpit, the radio and television media, the labour unions, the schools, the courts, and the legislative halls of America'. Even the Supreme Court was 'one of the most important agencies of Communism'!

As the tensions of the Cold War continued, some people feared that fanatical groups like the Birchers could provoke another wave of McCarthyism. But they remained little more than a lunatic fringe in American politics. In time Americans came to accept that Communism could not be wiped from the face of the earth with one swift blow (you will see later why it couldn't) and in this calmer mood they have weathered many international crises without looking for 'treason' at home to explain them.

In fact these two eruptions of the Radical Right may have had other origins than the Cold War. McCarthyism could be seen partly as a product of longstanding tensions in American society between status-seeking members of ethnic minority groups* (like the Irish Catholic McCarthy) and upper-class WASPs (like Alger Hiss). Birchism was more like the backwoods conservatism of the 1920s, a protest against *change* in a fast-moving era. In post-war life there were new things to hate – 'welfare', high taxes and the huge power of Washington – as well as the old enemies of Godlessness and liberalism; and one word could be stretched to cover all these 'un-American' things: Communism.† You will see further evidence later of the influence of strong right-wing feeling in the United States.

*GLOSSARY

ethnic minority group, a group of one race which shares a common culture, i.e. language, place of origin, history.

'keeping up with the Joneses', a slang term meaning trying to match everything your neighbours (the Joneses) have or do, to advance your own social status.

vice versa (Latin), the same the other way round.

†This was the analysis presented in Daniel Bell, ed., *The Radical Right* (Doubleday Anchor paperback, 1964).

Questions

Did you notice?

1. The Manhattan Project made (a) mink-handled can-openers (b) new highways (c) the A-bomb

2. The Taft–Hartley Act (a) restricted trade unions (b) kept subversives out of the USA (c) lowered tariffs

3. Sears Roebuck is (a) a tyre manufacturer (b) a McCarthy club (c) a mail-order business

4. In post-war America monopolies were (a) more powerful (b) less powerful (c) disbanded

5. An obsolescent product is (a) about to wear out (b) the latest thing (c) no use to anyone

6. True or false?
    (i) The Alliance for Progress helped Europe to recover from the war
    (ii) President Truman vetoed the McCarran Act
    (iii) Alger Hiss worked in the State Department
    (iv) McCarthy died a national hero
    (v) NASA is an advertising agency

7. Which statement is *more* accurate?
    (i) Continuous selling is needed in a consumer economy
      (a) to keep advertisers in business
      (b) to keep up employment
    (ii) 1950s prosperity differed from 1920s prosperity in that
      (a) more Americans benefited from it
      (b) no Americans were poor in the 1950s
    (iii) The military–industrial complex
      (a) started the Cold War
      (b) exerts a strong influence on the American Government
    (iv) 'Respectable' Republicans
      (a) found McCarthy politically useful
      (b) enthusiastically supported him

Can you explain?

8. In what way did post-war American governments carry on the principles established by the New Deal?

9. In the post-war economy of the United States, what was the part played by (a) advertising, (b) hire purchase, (c) overseas aid programmes?

10. What factors encouraged many Americans to move to suburbs in the 1950s? What were the new suburban communities like? What changes in the population of cities took place as a result of this exodus?

11. How did the defence and space industries benefit the American economy? What were the possibly harmful effects arising from the growth of these industries?

12. What was happening outside the United States in the late 1940s and early 1950s which worried many Americans? What was Senator McCarthy's explanation for these events?

What's your view?

13. American society (and British society) was more united during the Second World War than it has ever been since. Why is it so difficult to achieve a sense of 'national purpose' at other times? Is there any peace-time campaign or cause that in your opinion would be worth the national effort which won the war?

14. The consumer economy is part of the American way of life that many people in other countries try to copy. Why do they try to copy it? Are they right to do so, in your opinion? Will anything prevent a consumer economy from developing throughout the world?

15. Why do you think McCarthy's supporters were particularly suspicious of 'teachers, trade union leaders and people in the entertainment business'? Has society a right to expect especially high standards of conduct from any particular group of people? If so, which people?

6

The Sixties: Protest and Reform

This chapter of our American study concentrates on two social problems arising from American history and the way of life that earlier chapters have shown you: poverty and race discrimination. Both of these are worst in the cities, but the long history of racial inequality affects all blacks, wherever they live and at whatever level of society. The race issue needs separate treatment here, as it needed a special effort in America to try to solve it.

THE URBAN CRISIS

By the 1960s American cities were facing a crisis—we might call it a multi-crisis because it had so many interrelated causes. So far, all efforts to help the situation have been piecemeal—each tackling only one small area of the problem—and the results have been disappointing. The city crisis of the 1960s is still a major problem in the 1980s.

Some of America's city problems are common to other economically developed countries in the West, including Britain. We should briefly mention some of these before we look at particularly American features of her urban crisis:

Common city problems

In the 1950s most American cities—like some of ours a few years later—were sliced through to make way for increasing motor traffic. This was connected with the move to suburbia described in Chapter 5: suburban commuters were the main beneficiaries of the new roads, and once they were built, even more were encouraged to leave the city. But for those still living in the old, run-down tenement blocks it was no fun having the noise and dirt

of a freeway running past the window. The new roads also led to a decline in public transport which in some American cities has reached crisis point: if you don't have a car, you walk! And while it is true that most Americans have cars, many poor inner-city residents do not.†

The redevelopment of commercial areas of the cities, which most other people welcomed, also worsened living conditions for the poor who still lived there. As an economy becomes industrialized, more and more of the society's wealth comes from industry and commerce in cities. There is a big demand for city land, and the more crowded and concentrated a city becomes, the more the price of land will rise. A Capitalist economy allows private interests to profit from this situation: huge fortunes can be made by buying, developing, selling or just owning land.

After the Second World War it was profitable to bulldoze cheap down-town housing and offices and build new, high-rent commercial buildings. City governments often collaborated in these ventures, which would also provide amenities for their citizens and a higher tax revenue from the occupants of new buildings. Redevelopment took place in every American (and British) city, regardless of the social and environmental

†In 1970 only 20.5 per cent of all American households did not own a car. But among poor Americans the proportion of non-car owners was nearly 60 per cent, and among central city residents as a whole it was over 33 per cent. (SOURCE: US Department of Commerce Consumer Buying Indicators, July 1972.) *Note:* the official 'poor' are those below the poverty line, which was defined in 1964 as the lowest income on which a family of four could just about 'get by'. It would have to be frequently adjusted to take account of inflation and other factors. In 1964 the poverty line for an urban family was reckoned at just over $3,000 a year; in 1978 it was just over $6,000 a year.

consequences. The worst result, especially in America, was to drive the inner-city inhabitants into an ever-shrinking pool of run-down housing. In this example at least, there is some justice in the Socialist argument that Capitalism allows the already-rich to profit at the expense of the already-poor.

Violence Q. 8.

It was a series of city riots in the mid-1960s which first drew world attention to the extent of America's city crisis, and especially to the virtual state of war which exists between the police and the inhabitants of the ghettos – the area of the cities where most blacks and other minority groups live. There were riots in 1964 in Harlem (New York City), Philadelphia, and Rochester, NY; in 1965 in Watts (Los Angeles); in 1966 in Chicago and Cleveland; and in 1967 in Newark, New Jersey and Detroit. They were all suppressed with equal violence by the police. In the 1967 riots over eighty people were killed.

In 1967 President Johnson set up the National Advisory Commission on Civil Disorders to investigate the causes of this widespread city unrest. Its report in 1968 blamed ghetto conditions for the riots and condemned white America for the ghetto: 'White institutions created it, white institutions maintain it, and white society condones it.'

The significance of these riots is therefore not their violence but their *causes*, which we shall discuss presently. The fact is that violence has always been a common feature of American life. In recent years it is shown in the number of violent crimes at all levels of society; in political assassinations (President John Kennedy in 1963 and his brother Robert in 1968, black leaders Martin Luther King and Malcolm X); and in the brutal police methods applied to all protesters. It is not surprising that the bitter fury of the ghetto is expressed in this almost 'accepted' form of anger.

Day-to-day violence can be seen in any set of crime statistics for an American city. An example from the 1960s is given below (Table 6.1). These figures illustrate the general pattern: the poorer the district, the more crime occurs—no matter how heavily policed it may be. This is especially true, you will notice, of crimes against persons—and most of the victims of course are other residents of the ghetto. This leads to an atmosphere of fear which feeds on itself: when honest people are too afraid to walk in a city at night, there are fewer passers-by to help the victim of an attack.

Table 6.1   Incidence of index crimes† and number of policemen assigned per 100,000 residents in five Chicago Police Districts, 1965.

	High income white district	Low-to-middle income white district	Mixed high and low income white district	Very low income Negro district No. 1	Very low income Negro district No. 2
Number of Index Crimes against persons	80	440	338	1,615	2,820
Number of Index Crimes against property	1,038	1,750	2,080	2,508	2,630
Number of policemen assigned	93	133	115	243	291

SOURCE: Report of the National Advisory Commission on Civil Disorders (Bantam paperback, 1968), p. 267.
†'Index Crimes' are those involving violence or serious theft.

Poverty

Most ghetto areas included other poor people as well as blacks, especially Hispanics (Spanish-speaking groups like Puerto Ricans and Mexicans). But anyone who *could* leave the inner city did so: this was the 'white flight' to the suburbs already noted. And as affluent whites left, their places were taken by poor non-whites.† Once in the ghetto, blacks were kept there by the double barrier of *poverty* and *race*. In the suburbs the determination of wealthier white Americans to keep out black neighbours prevented any blacks who might overcome the poverty barrier from moving there.

The middle-class residents who fled to the suburbs took their taxes with them, leaving city governments with empty purses. This in itself is a serious problem, for the people who are left in the inner city pay least in taxes and need most in services. But far more serious is the poverty of the ghetto itself, which America began to recognize in the mid-1960s. In 1964 over 34 million Americans were living below the poverty line, and most of these were in city ghettos.

Poverty is always relative to better-off people in the same society. If everyone lives in shacks, no one feels poor. The inhabitants of American city ghettos feel poor because in every shop window and on every television screen they see evidence of the affluent society which they do not share. Their poverty is best understood as *deprivation* of things which other Americans take for granted.

Inhabitants of the ghetto are deprived in every way. The 'profile of poverty' in a typical ghetto community looks like this:

Low income level – from low-paid jobs and/or welfare payments.

High unemployment rate – especially among juveniles.

Poor housing – though not always cheap.

Poor schools – overcrowded; only the bravest teachers can bear to work there; high drop-out rate.

High crime rate – especially of juvenile delinquency.

Family problems – fatherless families, illegitimacy, crowding.

Poor general health – few, overworked medical facilities; insanitary housing.

High drug addiction rate – this is one escape from troubles, but it soon leads to others.

Depression and apathy – the mental condition of the poor that all social workers recognize.

It takes only a moment's thought to realize that all these problems are interconnected: family problems increase the school drop-out rate; low educational level means a poorly paid job – or none. The worst effect of this 'vicious circle' is on the young, who may grow up knowing nothing else.

The Poverty Programme

President Kennedy began the attack on poverty, but the main effort came with President Johnson's 'War on Poverty' and the Economic Opportunity Act of 1964. Under this law, federal funds were to be channelled into community groups within the ghetto. The idea behind this method was to stimulate self-help and also to provide administrative jobs in the ghetto itself. By 1967 the Office of Economic Opportunity had sponsored anti-poverty schemes affecting 9 million people, working through 1,100 community action agencies. These included educational 'head-start' programmes for ghetto children, training schemes for school drop-outs, launching funds for small businessmen and plans to help low-income students to earn while studying. The agencies also acted locally as 'a sort of supermarket of the social services'.

President Johnson claimed in 1968 that his campaign against poverty had raised 25 per cent of poor people out of it. Combined with his action on civil rights, there was certainly some progress for blacks, as we shall see later. But the War on Poverty was not a complete success. Many programmes were controversial: who was to judge which were 'worthy' projects among the many applications for funds? You can imagine the indignation

†In the 1950s the twelve largest cities lost about 3½ million whites but gained 4½ million non-whites, and the trend continued in the 1960s.

Figure 6.1   Blacks picketing a Washington bank.

when federal money was sometimes used to finance protests against city governments – or against respected institutions like banks (Figure 6.1). But in fact many projects were under-financed – and faced public opposition for a variety of reasons.

Obstacles to the Poverty Programme
1. 'They're all a lot of layabouts'

We have seen in earlier chapters the strong American belief in individual effort. There is a general feeling that if a man is poor, it is his own fault – he could get himself out of the mud if he tried. Welfare help will only encourage him to be lazy, so it is bad for him as well as for 'us' who pay for it with our taxes. The poor are all living on the dole because men who could work choose not to do so. The facts firmly disprove this: in 1967 the Secretary of the federal government's Department of Health, Education and Welfare pointed out that in the whole country only 50,000 families receiving welfare even included a man who could work – but the belief persists that 'welfare is wrong'.

2. 'Washington – keep out!'

Poverty Programme schemes were sponsored by the federal government, but had to be administered in co-operation with state governments and at their request. Yet only 22 out of the 50 states even took up the offer! This is another example of the old 'states rights' feeling we noted in Chapter 3. In spite of the obvious plight of ghetto citizens, a majority of state governments decided they either did not need or did not want federal help – perhaps because to accept it would look like an admission of failure.

3. The 'other war'

A third hindrance to the Poverty Programme was the war in Vietnam. In 1965 there was a massive escalation of American involvement in South-East Asia: by 1967 the Vietnam War was costing $30,000 million a year. Funds intended for the 'war' at home were diverted to the war abroad. As always, citizens at home – in this case the poorest – had to pay the price for their country's 'security' in the world.

4. *Private affluence – public squalor*

In spite of the example of the New Deal, there was still general distrust in America of public spending, while at the same time the spending of private money and effort – it scarcely mattered on *what* – was generally approved. As one American economist (J. K. Galbraith) put it, the scientist or research worker who devotes himself to developing a new hair-remover 'for which the public recognizes no need and will feel none until an advertising campaign arouses it, is one of the valued members of our society. A politician or public servant who dreams up a new public service is a wastrel.' The streets of the city might be full of pot-holes, the parks a playground for muggers, but behind his front door the private citizen was comfortable and secure with his two-inch-thick carpet – and a gun in the desk drawer. By the mid-twentieth century the American system had led to this striking contrast of what Galbraith called 'private affluence and public squalor'.

5. *'Does it do any good anyway?'*

Yet another source of public opposition to government spending on poverty was the marked lack of success of many projects which were undertaken. Perhaps because it was the most visible and shameful sign of poverty, slum housing was the first problem to be tackled. Many cities have built huge and costly housing estates – only to find, within a few years, that they were just as plagued with vandalism, destitution and squalor as the warren of scruffy streets and houses they replaced.

There are complicated reasons for this – including bad design of the housing itself – but the main lesson to be learned is that improving *one* part of the vicious circle does little to alter the profile of poverty. High-rise blocks and wire-cage playgrounds may look tidier (for a few years) – but the people who live in them are still unemployed, sick, little educated and *poor*. Moreover, the cost of these and other projects of LBJ's 'war on poverty' was astronomical. Could the American taxpayer afford it?

The Nixon administration which replaced Johnson's in 1969 savagely cut back on poverty programmes, including all federal aid for housing. This was not only the expression of a right-wing political view but a sign of widespread disillusion and perplexity about the problems of poverty and urban decay in American cities. How *can* they be solved? The harsh fact is that nobody knows. In the 1970s some new initiatives to revitalize down-town areas were partially successful, but the national poverty problem seemed to grow steadily worse.

In the 1960s, however, it was clear that a fundamental change of attitude towards blacks would help at least some of the ghetto inhabitants to escape. The *race problem* required urgent and special attention.

THE RACE ISSUE

There are 25 million blacks in the United States – about 12 per cent of the population. Throughout America's history they have been kept in a position of inferiority. In 1963, a hundred years after the end of slavery, President Kennedy could still say that a Negro born in America had 'about one-half as much chance of completing high school as a white ...; one-third as much chance of completing college; twice as much chance of becoming unemployed; about one-seventh as much chance of earning $10,000 a year; a life expectancy which is seven years less and the prospect of earning only half as much.'

To explain this situation, and to understand the black rage that broke out in the 1960s, we have to go back to the beginning of the story. Notice, first, three distinct forms of mistreatment by which blacks were kept down after the abolition of slavery in 1863:

intimidation – preventing blacks from taking advantage of their legal rights by terrorizing them. This was a method perfected by the notorious Ku Klux Klan, whose ultimate weapon was the lynch mob. The society was founded in the 1860s but was active in later periods too.

segregation – a rigid system of racial separation, similar to the policy of *apartheid* followed in South Africa today. It was finally made illegal in the United States by a Supreme Court decision in 1954, but still practised in the stubborn South after that date.

discrimination – the denial of equal chances to blacks by blocking their access to jobs, schooling, residential areas and other spheres of life 'reserved' for whites. Despite Civil Rights laws of the 1960s making these practices illegal, discrimination still persists in the United States today.

Slavery

From the sixteenth century on, Negroes were brought from West Africa to America and the West Indies to labour in the plantations where crops like sugar, tobacco and cotton were grown. A different kind of agriculture developed in the north of North America, and for this reason slavery did not spread there.

Slaves were the personal property of their masters and had no legal rights whatsoever. Apologists for this terrible crime in white history argued that most slaves were well looked after, as any piece of valuable property would be; but even if this is true it could not balance the appalling cruelty suffered by others. A good Christian slave-owner could only reconcile slavery with his Christian conscience by letting himself think that Negroes were not really human at all, so it was all right to treat them as animals. This defence of slavery was being put forward by some churchmen in America as late as 1900.

Runaway slaves

There were sporadic slave revolts and a constant trickle of runaways to the North, helped by anti-slavery Northern whites, the Abolitionists. This contributed to the tension between the so-called free North and the slave-owning South which led to the American Civil War of 1861–5. In 1862 President Lincoln's Emancipation Proclamation finally freed the slaves. In 1865 the American Constitution was duly amended to prohibit slavery

and to proclaim that 'The right to vote shall not be abridged by the United States or any state on account of race, colour, or previous condition of servitude.' So the Negro was now free – or was he?

'Jim Crow' and 'separate but equal'

Negroes in the South did not enjoy their freedom for long. Intimidation by the white population kept them in a state of constant fear, and a series of crafty laws systematically deprived them of their legal rights – *not* on grounds of race but by requiring that registered voters must be property-owners (which Negroes were not) or pass a literacy test (which Negroes could not). The literacy test was foolproof: a white examiner could ensure that, regardless of reading skill, whites would pass, and blacks would fail.

The all-white Southern state governments then passed a series of 'Jim Crow' laws which effectively segregated blacks from whites in every sphere of social life: schooling, residence, public transport, restaurants. The Supreme Court sanctioned the 'Jim Crow' system with its decision in the case of *Plessey v. Ferguson* in 1896 that separate facilities were constitutional, i.e. legal, so long as they were 'equal'. Of course they never *were* equal (in the 1930s, Southern governments spent $45 on a white child's education and $13 on a black child's) – but for fifty-eight years no one dared or cared to challenge this situation.

The North did not need to have an official system of segregation because there were few enough blacks in the North to be kept in their place by discrimination: white employers would not hire them, white trade unionists would not admit them to membership, white residents would not have them as neighbours. In this way they were kept out of all but the lowest-paid unskilled jobs and confined to slum housing.

Early black protest

Countless individual blacks resisted the system of segregation, which in practice was little better than slavery – but 'uppity niggers' were slapped down (or strung up) by almost un-animous white resistance to Negro progress. Negroes were a minority of the whole popula-tion – even in the South – and their leaders were perplexed to find a way out of their situa-tion. Three different approaches to the prob-lem were offered:

(i) Booker T. Washington, who founded the first Negro university, told his fellow blacks not to try to compete with the white man but to develop their skills within American society and so win white respect on their own merits.

(ii) W. E. B. Du Bois took the line that Negroes should patiently and deter-minedly work their way into white society by demanding their legal rights. In 1910 he founded the National Association for the Advancement of Coloured People (NAACP) which from that day forward has fought battle after battle through the courts.

(iii) Yet a third solution was suggested by Marcus Garvey who in the 1920s tried to launch a back-to-Africa migration. But it was too late for that; American Negroes were rooted in American society, for better or worse.

Their condition continued 'for worse' for many years yet. Blacks were worst hit in the depression, and often became scapegoats for America's troubles in those years. The Ku Klux Klan flared up again in the 1930s and dreadful crimes were committed against blacks. But still their fellow-citizens did not care to notice. The novels of James Baldwin or Ralph Ellison (see Further Reading, page 84) will tell you what it felt like to grow up a black American in those years. Perhaps the most damaging long-term effect of segrega-tion was psychological: it convinced many Negroes that 'whitey' must be right – they really *were* inferior. There was little evidence of black success anywhere to contradict this view.

The effect of the Second World War

The real breakthrough for black Americans came with the Second World War. The steady migration of blacks to Northern cities had begun between the wars. In 1910, 90 per cent of blacks lived in the South; by 1968, only 54 per cent remained there (look at Figure 6.2 (a) and (b)). Their social status in the North was little changed, but many found work in industry during the wartime boom. After the war, these now-skilled men (and their brothers returning from fighting for Demo-cracy) were not willing to put up with con-tinued suppression by white America – not without a struggle, anyway.

'Segregation is illegal'

Truman recognized the growing protest of black Americans and proposed various reforms which his conservative Congress would not pass – except for de-segregating the Armed Forces in 1948 (blacks and whites were no longer kept apart in separate units). But the big step forward came in Eisen-hower's time with the 1954 Supreme Court decision, *Brown v. Topeka Board of Educa-tion*. This reversed the 1896 'separate but equal' ruling by declaring that separate schools (and by implication all separate facili-ties) were illegal *even if* they were equal.

You might expect that in a generally law-abiding country, that decision would settle the matter! But 'whitey', especially in the South, had far from given up. In 1957 at Little Rock, Arkansas, federal troops had to force a way into the white high school for Negro children, against the loud protests of the state's Governor and a majority of the state's white citizens. In the following years, in place after place there had to be protest–demon-stration–riot before whites would put the law of the land into effect. The most famous vic-tory of the Civil Rights campaigns of these years (some of which were joined by white liberals, especially students, from the North) was the 1955 bus boycott in Montgomery, Alabama, organized by <u>Martin Luther King</u>. For a year, blacks refused to ride on buses in which certain seats were reserved for whites only. The bus company nearly went broke because blacks – the poorer end of the popu-

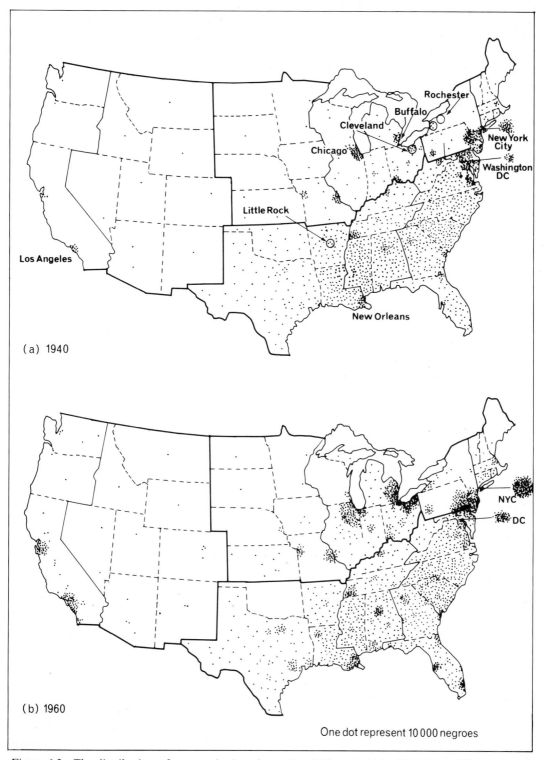

Figure 6.2 The distribution of negroes in America (a) in 1940, and (b) in 1960. The drift northwards accelerated during the Second World War.

lation – were their main customers. In the end, the company gave in.

The Civil Rights movement of the late 1950s and early 1960s is a dramatic story in itself – battles, victories, defeats, promises from on high which had little effect at the grass roots. In 1963 Martin Luther King led a march on Washington (a 'march of poor people', he called it) to which President Kennedy responded with the promise of laws to guarantee Negro voting rights and an end to social discrimination. But it was all so maddeningly *slow*!

Civil Rights – or black power?

By the mid-1960s a more militant 'black power' branch had broken away from the peaceful, non-violent protest movement of Martin Luther King. Stokely Carmichael and others argued that whites would never give way unless forced to do so by violent action. They could not see why Civil Rights protesters, sniped at and clubbed by white bystanders and white police, should just turn the other cheek and wait to be 'given' the rights that were theirs by law. Even more important was their call to fellow-blacks to turn their back on white society and build up *black power* – especially in the ghetto. Negro children should be taught their own history, and be proud of it! White businessmen who had long profited from black customers in the ghetto should be challenged – still better, replaced – by black-run businesses. Black youths were even armed and trained for battle with the 'pigs' – the white police.

Open war with white society was lost before it got started. Many black power leaders were imprisoned or killed in shoot-outs with the police, and the whole Negro protest movement was weakened by assassinations (Martin Luther King, Malcolm X) and by internal quarrels. But black power had built up *black pride* which the whites had stamped out in the blacks' long history from slavery onwards – perhaps the most useful weapon of all in the continuing struggle for equality.

Civil Rights – at last!

On the legal front, some whites at least were now ready to listen to their conscience. The Civil Rights Acts of 1964 and 1968 made race discrimination in jobs and housing illegal, and in 1965 the Voting Rights Act allowed the federal government to investigate areas (mainly in the South) where blacks still did not register to vote, or dare to stand for election, because of widespread intimidation by the local white population, who simply refused to operate a law they disagreed with.

But after 1965 scared blacks were coaxed and led to the voting booth, and at last there was real progress. The number of registered voters among eligible blacks increased from 35 per cent in 1964 to nearly 65 per cent in 1969, and the increase was most dramatic in the deep South: from 19 per cent to 61 per cent in Alabama, from 7 per cent to 67 per cent in Mississippi, from 27 per cent to 60 per cent in Georgia. In 1975 over 3,000 blacks held elected offices, including 18 seats in the federal Congress and 278 in state governments, while 120 large towns and cities had black mayors.

This trend continued: in 1983 there were 240 black mayors of American cities, including some with a *white* majority. President Carter appointed the first black ambassador to the UN, Andrew Young; in 1982 Mayor Tom Bradley of Los Angeles narrowly missed becoming the first black State Governor; and by 1984 there was a black contender, the Reverend Jesse Jackson, for the Democratic Presidential nomination. But blacks still took up a smaller share of elected offices than their proportion of the general population, partly because so many blacks were still *poor*.

One-third of blacks were still poor

After 1965 there was a surge of blacks into upper income levels, but this soon slowed down (see Figure 6.3). Discrimination in employment lessened, but did not disappear; blacks still needed more talent and effort than whites to overtake them on the pro-

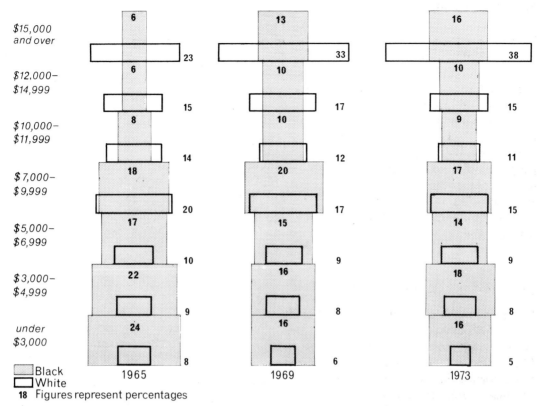

$15,000 and over

$12,000–$14,999

$10,000–$11,999

$7,000–$9,999

$5,000–$6,999

$3,000–$4,999

under $3,000

Black
White
18 Figures represent percentages

1965   1969   1973

Figure 6.3   The changing pyramid of black family income. Despite the improvement for middle-income blacks, there are still too many in the lowest income groups.
SOURCE: US Department of Commerce, Bureau of the Census.

motion ladder. Nevertheless the reforms of the 1960s did enable significantly more blacks to 'make it' to responsible jobs and a comfortable income. They were further helped in the 1970s by a federal policy of 'affirmative action', a kind of reverse discrimination in their favour. The expanding black middle class naturally had the same aspirations as whites, and were now able to improve their social status more easily. Between 1970 and 1976 the number of blacks in higher education doubled and in the same period the number living in suburbs increased by 36 per cent, despite continued discrimination in housing which was very hard to eradicate. But when the government tried to re-locate *poor* urban blacks in the suburbs, black residents were just as hostile as their white neighbours to the threatened invasion. 'Black solidarity' which had seemed so strong in the 1960s was weakening; blacks were now dividing along class lines into 'us' and 'them'.

And the number of 'them' was still alarmingly high. The most disappointing result of the 1960s reforms was the lack of change after 1969 at the bottom of black society. In 1969 32 per cent of blacks were in the lowest two income groups, the official 'poor' at a time when the poverty line was about $5,000 a year (Figure 6.3). In 1973 the figure was even higher, and since that date it has never been less than 30 per cent.

But the situation of the 7 to 8 million poor blacks was no worse than that of other poor Americans. In 1978 there were nearly 26 million below the poverty line and by 1983, as economic conditions worsened, the number had risen to 34.4 million–one in every seven Americans. Racial prejudice was only one element in a serious and widespread *poverty problem* which no one knew how to solve.

Questions

Did you notice? *Pop: 200m*

1. In the mid-1960s the estimated number of poor Americans was (a) 10 million (b) 25 million (c) 34 million *15%*
2. Among other things, the 'War on Poverty' provided (a) funds for small businesses (b) arms for Vietnam (c) weapons for the police
3. Abraham Lincoln (a) owned slaves (b) approved of slavery (c) freed the slaves
4. 'Jim Crow' was (a) a series of laws (b) an abolitionist (c) a Civil Rights leader
5. Roughly how many blacks living in America are still poor? (a) one-fifth (b) 90 per cent (c) one-third
6. True or false?
   (i) Most black Americans are living on welfare
   (ii) Stokely Carmichael believed in black power
   (iii) In 1975 black mayors ran many American towns and cities
   (iv) Southern agriculture needed more workers after the depression
   (v) Southern states pay less welfare than Northern states
7. Which statement is *more* accurate?
   (i) 'Private affluence and public squalor' suggests that
      (a) America cannot afford efficient public services
      (b) Americans prefer to spend their money privately
   (ii) 1960s city riots were mainly the result of
      (a) the widespread violence in America
      (b) conditions in the city ghettos
   (iii) Since 1964, discrimination in employment and housing
      (a) has been practised by all whites
      (b) has lessened but not disappeared

Can you explain?

8. What evidence from recent American history suggests that 'violence is a common feature of American life'?
9. Most ghetto families have a TV set, and some even have a car. Why are they described as poor?
10. Why was there opposition to the Poverty Programme from many American citizens?
11. How were the following methods used to keep blacks 'in their place' after the abolition of slavery?: (a) segregation, (b) intimidation, (c) discrimination.
12. What were the differences in tactics between the Civil Rights campaign of Martin Luther King and the 'black power' movement led by Stokely Carmichael and others? Did 'black power' achieve any results?

What's your view?

13. Both in Britain and America it sometimes happens that a man can get more in welfare benefits than in wages from the only kind of job available to him. Does this mean that welfare payments are too high? Is a man in this position justified in not working?
14. Like 'urban renewal' in the United States, 'slum clearance' schemes in Britain have come in for much criticism. Do you know what objections have been made? What are some common problems on large housing estates? Can you suggest how they might be solved?
15. Do you know of any laws in Britain similar to the American Civil Rights laws? Do you think they are necessary here? Can race prejudice ever be eliminated, in your view? If so, how?

7

Right Turn into the Eighties

The previous two chapters have examined a few important themes in detail. This one deals more sketchily with a series of events and Presidents from the late 1960s to the early 1980s, a period in which you will recognize some of the traditional strands in American history outlined in Chapter 1: the resentment of most Americans at 'too much government'; the influence of some puritanical religious sects; the abuse of power by some politicians–and the painstaking exposure of it by others. It was a period, like the 1920s, when social divisions were more evident than social cohesion. But whereas the 1920s ended with a 'Left turn' into the 1930s, the general trend in these years was the reverse.

It will be helpful first of all to set out the rather complicated Presidential framework of the period:

1968 Richard Nixon (Republican) was elected President by a small majority.

1972 Richard Nixon was re-elected President with an increased majority.

1973 Vice-President Spiro Agnew resigned after a corruption scandal. Nixon appointed Gerald Ford, Republican leader of the House of Representatives, to replace him.

1974 Richard Nixon resigned as a result of the Watergate scandal. Gerald Ford then became President.

1976 Jimmy Carter (Democrat) was elected President by a small majority.

1980 Ronald Reagan (Republican) was elected President by a substantial majority.

Conservative reaction to the liberal mood of the 1960s was under way before the decade was over. Many of the causes and campaigns of those years–or at least the extreme versions of them–deeply offended the 'silent majority' whom Nixon called on to elect him President in 1968.

OTHER ISSUES OF THE SIXTIES

Many Civil Rights campaigners saw an obvious connection between their cause and the Vietnam War (Figure 7.1). Bitterly they pointed out the high proportion of poor blacks who were drafted to fight and die there, while many middle-class whites could get deferment as students or evade the draft in other ways. The fusion of Vietnam with Civil Rights in protests and demonstrations made them doubly repugnant to patriotic white Americans, many of whom also wanted 'out' of Vietnam, not because America was 'wrong' to be there but for old-fashioned isolationist reasons. By 1968 Vietnam had overtaken Civil Rights as the most bitter controversy of the decade (Chapter 25 will fully explain why). But there were other divisive issues too.

1. 'Black consciousness' of the 1960s sparked off *ethnic consciousness* among other Americans (a marked departure from the traditional idea of America as a 'melting-pot') and led other minorities to claim their rights. If 'black power' had given blacks a new status in American society,

Figure 7.1 Anti-Vietnam demonstration, 1966. For many protesters Civil Rights and Vietnam were one issue.

could 'red power' do the same for the most deprived minority of all, the American Indians?† And what about the rights of prisoners in American gaols, of whom a high proportion were black or brown or red, and *poor*? There were violent outbursts from these social outcasts too in the sixties and early seventies, giving further cause for alarm to the 'silent majority'.

2. But it was the students – those unpatriotic draft-dodgers – who upset them most of all. The Vietnam War was a central issue

(though not the only one) in *the campus revolt* which came to a peak in 1968 and was paralleled by student protest in many countries of the world, most violently in France and Japan. In America the revolt was accompanied by an 'alternative life-style' which was truly revolting to many older Americans. Skirts went up to the thigh or down to the ankle; curly hair became an Afro mop while the straight hair of girls *or men* could hang to the waist unwashed for weeks (or so their parents thought). These were the years of hippies and drugs, of Beatle-mania and the cutting lyrics of Bob Dylan's protest songs. Serious political issues merged with pot-smoking and bra-burning at music festivals and rallies; it was hard for liberal parents to know where to stop if they followed their children down the protest road.

†There were less than a million American Indians in 1980, more than half living on reservations and most of the rest in cities. 'Wherever they lived, they were the poorest of the poor, at the end of the line in employment, income, education, health, and life expectancy. The suicide rate among Indians was twice that of the rest of the population.' John M. Blum *et al.*, *The National Experience*, Part 2, fifth edition (Harcourt Brace Jovanovich, 1981), p. 892.

3. Many suburban mothers, if not fathers, eagerly joined the 'serious' end of *the women's liberation movement* inspired by the publication of Betty Friedan's *The Feminine Mystique* in 1963. 'Consciousness-raising' women's groups sprang up across the country and began to demand not only equal rights before the law but an end to the overt or unwitting 'sexism' of men. Their efforts won the support of millions of women—more than half the population, after all!—and the justice of their case was recognized by Title VII of the Civil Rights Act of 1964, which outlawed discrimination on grounds of sex as well as race. But that was not the cure-all for women's grievances. Thereafter the National Organisation for Women (NOW), founded in 1966, and other more radical groups carried the cause of women's liberation into many other areas of life.

4. Another cause which attracted respectable support was the issue of *environmental protection*. Like many other problems newly 'discovered' in the 1960s, this one was not new. Measures had been taken in the United States before the First World War to protect areas of America from the greed of industrialists in their quest for raw materials. By now runaway technology and the ever-rising standard of living in the Western world had created, in the view of some scientists, an environmental crisis. Books and reports of the period identified the issues: Rachel Carson's *Silent Spring*, first published in 1962, pointed out the effect on birds and other wildlife of the profligate use of pesticides; in 1972 a group of American scientists† published *Limits to Growth* indicating that the depletion of natural resources in the world placed a ceiling on economic growth and increasing material comfort, which up to now governments and most of their citizens had assumed could go on indefinitely. By that time sensible Americans had made a start on this complicated problem, which will certainly preoccupy their government (and

†Donella and Dennis Meadows and Jay Forrester, at the Massachusetts Institute of Technology.

ours) for the rest of the century. Federal and state clean air and water Acts were on the books, and in 1970 a federal Environmental Protection Agency was set up. The urgency and importance of the 'save the environment' campaign was brought home to all Americans by the energy crisis of the 1970s (see below).

The New Left

In fact these campaigns of the 1960s were *all* legitimate causes with some degree of justice in them. But as often happens in politics, it was the extremist view which attracted media attention and alienated 'moderate' opinion. The radical New Left fiercely condemned America as 'a sick society', drunk with the power of its own technology, a society in which the interests of blacks and American Indians, of women and homosexuals and youth were all sacrificed to the values of masculine, middle-aged, middle-class 'middle America'. And since in their view nothing would be done by governments—no matter what political party was in power—the only path to reform was protest politics: sit-ins, street demonstrations, draft-card burning. In 1968 this gave Richard Nixon a campaign slogan—'Law and Order'—which was bound to appeal to Middle America. And so it did—but only *just* enough of them rallied behind Nixon to elect him; 13½ per cent of electors voted for an even more right-wing candidate, the populist Governor of Alabama, George Wallace.

Nixon in office

Once in office, Nixon was flexible in economic policy. His main problem was the increasing rate of inflation—that is, the *speed* at which prices were rising. Having tried to reduce it by 'conservative' methods, in 1971 he declared 'We are all Keynesians now' and imposed short-term wage and price controls which made some of his right-wing supporters wince (this point is fully discussed further on). He also devalued the dollar to increase the flow of American exports, which had fallen below imports for the first time since 1893.

Naturally he continued to denounce the protest movements, especially those against his policy in Vietnam. Nixon's main interest was in foreign affairs, where he made both useful and harmful contributions, as you will see in Part IV. At home, as the election of 1972 approached, he concentrated on building up an 'unbeatable' majority by winning over the Wallace vote. To attract Wallace's supporters, he soft-pedalled federal policies of the 1960s which assisted the advance of blacks, and took up an extreme-right position on other issues important to them.

The Watergate scandal

Nixon's election tactics were successful: in 1972 he greatly increased his 1968 majority. But his obsession to be unbeatable at the polls, by fair means or foul, led to his downfall two years later in the notorious Watergate scandal. This began with a burglary of the Democratic Party's headquarters by members of the Campaign to Re-Elect the President ('CREEP'), one of the many 'dirty tricks' of the campaign which were later exposed by the patient investigation of two reporters from the *Washington Post*, and a Congressional committee of enquiry. Worse than the 'dirty tricks' was the fact that Nixon himself had helped to cover up the crime. As the evidence of his guilt mounted, he tried to conceal incriminating tape-recordings, until forced by public indignation and a Supreme Court decision to reveal them. In August 1974, under threat of impeachment, he finally resigned—the first American President to do so—and was immediately 'pardoned' by the incoming President, Gerald Ford, for crimes which the general public could still only guess at.

That pardon was unwise: why should Nixon go scot-free when so many of his

underlings went to gaol?† Ford's refusal to 'let it all come out', coupled with his ineffectual personality—which everyone agreed was honest, but little more—made him an unimpressive candidate in the Presidential election of 1976. Jimmy Carter, as a Democrat who had spent his political life in his native state of Georgia, was untainted by Watergate and the other political intrigues of Washington. Although a professed liberal, he was also a 'born again' Baptist, a successful businessman, and a spokesman for 'states' rights' (always a popular cause in the South)—indeed his strident opposition to 'big government' was more in tune with his Republican successor President Reagan than with his Democratic predecessors Kennedy and Johnson. He was therefore an acceptable candidate to enough of Nixon's 'silent majority' for them to switch their votes to the Democrats and give Carter a narrow margin over Ford.

THE RIGHT GATHERS SUPPORT

By the mid-1970s most of the protest movements had turned away from militant direct action to seek redress for their grievances

†Some of them later made their names and fortunes with books and lectures 'revealing all' about Watergate. Nixon himself, although firmly retired from politics, retained the respect of many right-wing Americans who thought his achievements outweighed his crimes. More than 40 members of Nixon's administration, including his Vice-President and Attorney-General, were prosecuted for various crimes. Nixon's administration was not only the most corrupt in American history but had undermined the 'checks and balances' of the Constitution (see Study Topic 1) by abusing Presidential power. By laws of 1974, Congress reasserted its control over public funds, and also tried to limit the amount of private money used in election campaigns (but in 1976 the Supreme Court overruled Congress on this). Secondly, arising out of Johnson's and Nixon's conduct of the Vietnam War (see Chapter 25), the War Powers Act of 1973, while allowing the President to *declare* war in specified circumstances, required him to consult Congress at every stage of 'escalating' a conflict. Thirdly, the secrecy of the Nixon government led to a public demand for *more information* about what their rulers were getting up to. State 'sunshine laws' were passed, and full use made of the 1966 Freedom of Information Act, to give citizens the right to find out about the workings of government. Another result of public concern was Congressional investigation of the activities of the FBI and the CIA—see below, page 76.

Figure 7.2   An ERA rally, 1972. The new generation of radical feminists offended many Middle Americans.

through the courts. Disorderly violence had been replaced by peaceful reform, and Middle America sat back with a sigh of relief. But even peaceful reform was going too far for those a bit Right of the middle.

An excess of liberalism?

One of the unpopular spin-offs from the Civil Rights campaign was 'affirmative action'. In an attempt to help blacks to catch up with long-privileged whites, the federal government had encouraged employers and institutions of higher education to reserve special quotas for racial and ethnic minorities, even if this meant excluding better-qualified whites; while at a lower level of education black children were 'bussed' to schools in white neighbourhoods, and vice versa. Bussing led to near-riots in some cities: both white and black parents disliked sending their kids to schools miles from home. The quota system also came under attack, and not only from the political Right. It implied, after all, that the *quality* of a man or woman might depend on racial or ethnic origin rather than

personal characteristics, whereas the hope of many liberals was that a truly integrated society would in time become 'colour blind'. In 1978 a Supreme Court decision held that a white applicant to medical school, Allan Bakke, *had* been unfairly excluded in favour of less-qualified minority applicants; but that racial or ethnic origin might still be used as 'one element' in admissions policy, to ensure variety. After this supreme example of two-handed justice, support for affirmative action died away, leaving blacks, 'ethnics' and women (who had also benefited from the policy) to establish their credentials for jobs or education on merit alone.

But women were making great strides in other ways. In 1972 Congress had passed the Equal Rights Amendment to the Constitution (Figure 7.2), which would forbid any state or federal law denying or abridging equal rights on account of sex. As the ERA wound its way through state legislatures for the necessary thirty-eight to ratify it, in 1973 the women's movement scored another victory with a Supreme Court decision authorizing 'abortion by choice'.

75

The Court's decision on abortion especially offended traditionalist Catholics – but the advance of 'women's lib' in general upset many religious Americans, who saw it as a threat to family life. Even more subversive of their values was the increasing acceptance of 'gays' (homosexuals) as normal members of society, and a new habit among young Americans of living together, and even having children, without bothering to get married. Catholics now joined with fundamentalist Protestant sects like the Southern Baptists, Mormons and Seventh-Day Adventists to mount a counter-campaign against sexual permissiveness and the women's movement – and with a good chance of success. Unlike the moral crusaders of the New Left, the moral crusaders of the Right – the self-styled Moral Majority – could expect a sympathetic response from many upright, God-fearing Middle Americans.

The reaction of the 'religious Right' was provoked by liberal excesses which they saw as symptoms of moral decline within the United States. Equally disturbing to the 'political Right' were events in the outside world which signalled a decline of American influence abroad.

Wounded national pride

Every sordid detail of the Watergate affair had been beamed across the world by news coverage of that event, and patriotic Americans were further embarrassed by Congressional investigations in the mid-1970s which exposed the 'dirty tricks' of the Federal Bureau of Investigation (FBI) and the Central Intelligence Agency (CIA). But even more damaging to their national pride were a series of events which not only challenged American foreign policy but showed all too clearly the *limits* of Washington's power, even to protect the lives of American citizens abroad.

1. The oil crisis

In 1973 the Organisation of Petroleum Exporting Countries (OPEC) placed a temporary ban on the export of oil to the United States and its West European allies. This was a reprisal by Arab countries, who now dominated OPEC, against American arms supplies to Israel in the "Yom Kippur war' between Israel and surrounding Arab states. OPEC also quadrupled the price of Middle Eastern oil, contributing to the inflation which already bedevilled the Western world. This event forced America to modify its pro-Israel stand, and precipitated the energy crisis at home.

2. American withdrawal from Vietnam

The most dramatic evidence of America's diminishing power in the world was the failure of her policy in Vietnam (see Chapter 25). In 1973 American troops were withdrawn, with the brave pretence that they had *not* abandoned their ally South Vietnam to be swallowed up by the Communist North. But in April 1975 South Vietnam went down with a gulp. Once again America's humiliation was witnessed by the world as TV cameras recorded the chaotic evacuation of staff by helicopter from the roof of the American embassy in South Vietnam's capital.

3. The Mayaguez affair

Three weeks after the fall of South Vietnam, the next-door Communist state of Cambodia captured an American merchant ship, the *Mayaguez*. President Ford lashed out with a marine attack to rescue the crew – even while negotiations for their release were in process. Ford's action was applauded by most Americans as a demonstration that America could not be pushed around, but some were discomfited to notice that more marines were killed than sailors rescued.

4. The Iranian hostages

In 1979 American lives were again under threat when the new Islamic fundamentalist

Figure 7.3   The gates of the US embassy in Tehran, where Iranian students held fifty American hostages for over a year. President Carter's decision to admit the refugee Shah to the United States further inflamed anti-American feeling in Iran.

régime in Iran took fifty American embassy staff and held them as hostages for fifteen months (Figure 7.3). This was in retaliation for long-standing American support of the hated Shah of Iran, who had just been deposed. Right-wing American politicians fumed with rage and urged President Carter to 'do something'. In 1980 he sent a rescue mission, but this ended dismally with crashed helicopters and the loss of their crews.

The 'loss' of Iran, hitherto the guardian of American interests in the Middle East, was a foreign policy disaster on the scale of Vietnam (see Chapter 27). At home the plight of the hostages dominated President Carter's last year of office: their eventual release in January 1981 came too late to save him at the polls and neatly wiped the slate clean for the incoming President.

5. The Panama Canal treaties

The last in this series of wounding events was the Panama Canal treaties negotiated by President Carter in 1977 and pushed through the Senate, against stiff opposition, in the last months of his Presidency. Under the new agreement American military bases would be gradually withdrawn from the Canal Zone, and ownership of the Canal would revert to Panama by the year 2000. Moderate Americans saw this as a correction of past injustice (see page 44) and a way to improve America's reputation in Latin America. 'We stole it, and removed the incriminating evidence from our history books', said the New York Times. But 'We stole it fair and square', growled a right-wing Senator, one of many who saw the Panama treaties as the 'last straw' in all the indignities heaped upon the American eagle in the previous few years.

The energy crisis

Meanwhile, President Carter was not having much success in domestic affairs. To reduce 'America's dark and dangerous dependence on foreign oil' he made a bold attempt to rally Americans behind a comprehensive energy programme, but his proposals got bogged down in Congress. But federal encouragement of research into alternative energy

77

sources (such as wind and solar power) started a trend which continued into the 1980s, even after President Reagan's cutback of funds for this purpose. Americans strongly resisted being *controlled* in this area of economic life, as in others; but privately they showed an awareness of the energy problem by buying smaller, fuel-efficient cars, by moving to wood for heating (thus unfortunately contributing to smoke pollution!) and by reducing energy consumption in their homes by 20 per cent between 1973 and 1983. They also showed increasing suspicion of nuclear power, especially after a terrifying accident in 1979 at Three Mile Island in Harrisburg, Pennsylvania, which *almost* caused incalculable damage and loss of life in the area. In the early 1980s the nuclear power industry was in a slump. Unfortunately the same was true of other areas of the economy.

America's economic troubles

All American Presidents in recent years have had to grapple with complicated problems in the economy. In the 1930s, high unemployment had been cured by Keynesian methods which had the uncomfortable – but temporary – side-effect of high budget deficits (see Chapter 3). In theory, renewed prosperity would produce a budget surplus as the government's tax revenue increased – and in some years after 1945, it *did* (look back at Figure 3.3 on page 37). Prosperity might also have the uncomfortable side-effect of inflation, caused by increasing demand for goods and higher wages – but this could be kept under control so long as productivity (the average output per man-hour of work) was rising: the population could 'pay itself more' because it was producing more. And American productivity *did* increase at about 3 per cent per year until the mid-1960s. But in the 1970s the United States had all the economic diseases together – high unemployment *and* high inflation *and* budget deficits *and* a near-standstill in national productivity. A sick

patient indeed!

It was widely recognized that this was 'a new kind of depression', but economists could not agree about its causes and therefore could not suggest a simple remedy. In the absence of a magic cure, governments fell back on old-fashioned 'orthodox' or 'Keynesian' economic policies, the choice usually depending on their political philosophy. In general the Right saw *inflation* and *budget deficits* as the worst evils and thought that both were due to *high government spending*, which they therefore tried to cut back. They also favoured a 'tight money policy' – that is, high interest rates, which would discourage business expansion and 'slow down the economy'. For Keynesians, on the other hand, *high unemployment* was the worst problem; they argued that controls could be used to check inflation if necessary (as Nixon's wage and price freezes had done in the early 1970s), and that government spending must be kept up to alleviate poverty and prevent unemployment rising even higher. But both sides in this argument had to admit, under criticism, the bad effects of their policies: rising unemployment when orthodox rules were in force, and rising inflation when Keynesian methods were applied – *except* under wage and price controls which no one in a free society could tolerate (not yet, at any rate) as more than a temporary measure.

Despite this attempt to simplify the issues, they are not simple! Nor was there a clear split in Presidential policy between 'Keynesian Democrats' and 'orthodox Republicans': Nixon had resorted to Keynesian controls, while both Ford *and* Carter followed orthodox policies. But Carter got the blame – whether fairly or not – for everworsening conditions during his term of office: inflation rose from $4\frac{1}{2}$ per cent to nearly 15 per cent by 1980, while unemployment and budget deficits also remained high. In keeping with their general attitude, the Right still saw inflation and the national budget as the key to America's economic sickness, and in 1980 their new

President set out to cure it with 'Reaganomics'.

The Right victorious

By now you can see several currents in the rising tide of right-wing feeling in the United States. First there was general disillusion with ineffective poverty programmes of the 1960s which had bequeathed to the taxpayer a much-enlarged 'welfare budget';† and a feeling, even among liberals, that reform movements had gone far enough. Secondly, the religious Right were now aroused to the moral danger, as they saw it, of sexual permissiveness and women's liberation. Thirdly, some far-right politicians (now being called the New Right) were disturbed by the decline of American influence in the world and wanted an 'aggressive' foreign policy to counteract it. And lastly, *everyone* was worried about the economy.

In 1980 this combination of issues and voting strength ushered Ronald Reagan into office with a comfortable majority. He promised a self-assertive and strongly anti-Communist foreign policy to bring an American 'renaissance' in the world, and a domestic policy which would promote economic growth by cutting taxes, reduce inflation and budget deficits by cuts in public spending, and above all get the government 'off the people's backs'. In 1983 it is too early to assess the success or failure of these policies except by up-dating some of the themes of the last two chapters.

The 'social agenda'

Several of the social issues prominent in the 1970s were soon concluded to the satisfac-

tion of right-wing opinion. Affirmative action was now a dead duck, ceremonially buried by the criticism of some of those it was supposed to benefit—for example a young Mexican, Richard Rodriguez, who came to think he had been given unfair help to climb the educational ladder. What finally convinced him was the comment of a Jewish fellow-graduate on the number of top jobs offered to Rodriguez, while he had none: 'There isn't any way for me to compete with you. Once there were quotas to keep my parents out of schools like Yale. Now there are quotas to get you in. And the effect on me is the same as it was for them . . .'‡

In 1982 the ERA was finally defeated when it failed to get enough state governments to ratify it, despite a two-year extension of the seven years allowed for that purpose. Its defeat was partly due to campaigners like Phyllis Schlafly, 'sweetheart of the silent majority', with her reassurance to women that they were not domestic slaves but 'home executives'. She herself, as a Harvard graduate, author of nine books, mother of six children and a self-proclaimed 'super executive', seemed to prove her argument that the ERA was not needed. Supporters of the ERA fell back defensively on economic issues, pointing out that working women on average still earned only 59 cents for every dollar earned by men—but in vain.

But the more extreme campaigns of the Moral Majority were not so successful. The anti-abortion 'right to life' cause made little headway against the firm belief of most women that this *was* a matter of personal choice. And in 1981 the Senate ignored the furious lobbying of a fundamentalist radio preacher and confirmed unanimously the President's appointment of the first-ever woman judge to the Supreme Court. But in spite of this appointment, many women thought Reagan too dismissive of their grievances.

---

†Another example of the 'tax-payers' revolt' was Proposition 13, passed by referendum in 1978 in Ronald Reagan's home state of California, which prohibited local authorities from increasing property taxes (rates). Its purpose was to reduce government waste, but its effect was to force city authorities to raise money from private sources for projects such as renewing San Francisco's worn-out sewers and cable-car system.

‡Richard Rodriguez, *Hunger of Memory—The Education of Richard Rodriguez* (Bantam paperback, 1983), p. 171.

The economy

By 1982 Reaganomics was having the usual effect of 'orthodox' economic policies, only more so. Inflation was down from 14 per cent to 8 per cent, but the promised reduction in the budget deficit had not occurred, mainly because of high defence spending–the necessary back-up to Reagan's aggressive foreign policy. Nor did tax cuts stimulate business activity as had been hoped; in fact high interest rates were causing business failures and farm bankruptcies at a rate un-equalled since 1932. Industrial production continued to fall. Unemployment rose to 10 per cent–over 10 million people, and double the average for the pre-recession decade, 1963–72.

The social consequences of continued recession were also predictable. The squeeze on welfare–tightening up the rules for eligibility and cutting benefits wherever possible–left the poorest Americans in dire straits. The equivalent to 1930s soup kitchens appeared in the form of 'cheese lines' and other charitable hand-outs; in 1983 in Alabama, 250,000 people were regular recipients of such free food. The Census Bureau reported 34.4 million below the poverty line and pointed to the 'welfare squeeze' as a contributing factor.

As usual the worst conditions were to be found in inner-city ghettos. Unemployment was 18½ per cent among blacks–50 per cent among *young* blacks–and 14 per cent among Hispanics, who were now a larger group than blacks in some ghettos. In 1980 there had been race riots in Miami, Florida, causing fifteen deaths–an echo of the mid-1960s, but also a pointer to a new problem at the bottom of American society. One reason for the resentment which boiled over in Miami was the growing number of refugees from Haiti–estimated at between 10,000 and 20,000–in addition to many Cuban refugees already there.

The changing population balance

The number of Haitians in Miami was 'esti-mated' because no one knew how many there were, or indeed how many Hispanics there were in the United States as a whole. This too was an unforeseen consequence of a 1960s reform. In 1965 a new Immigration Act had abolished the old quota system, in force since 1924, which had favoured immigrants from Anglo-Saxon countries (see page 24). After 1965 the number of immigrants from Europe declined, while the number from other countries increased–especially from Latin America. The 1965 Act put a limit on the number from the Americas which seemed to meet the demand from those countries at that time. But for various reasons (usually political repression or economic difficulties at home) far more Latin Americans now wanted to emigrate to the United States than the law would allow, and those who could not enter legally did so illegally, especially across the long border with Mexico, which could not be effectively patrolled. The number of illegal immigrants in the country was esti-mated at about 7 million in the late 1970s, most of them Spanish-speaking Hispanics, in addition to 12 million 'legal' Hispanics. The Census Bureau predicted a continuing rate of immigration in the 1980s of about one million a year, of whom half would be illegal immigrants, mainly from Latin America.

This large group of poor illegal immigrants presented obvious social and economic problems: they formed an 'invisible subculture' beyond the normal institutions of society (schools, hospitals and so on) and were preyed upon by unscrupulous employers and landlords who could threaten to 'turn them in' at any time. Apart from the problem of controlling illegal immigration, the long-term effect of increased Hispanic influence in America was impossible to assess. It seemed that America's population was undergoing a subtle shift comparable to that in the nineteenth century caused by the influx of mainly poor Catholics from Europe, which challenged the dominance of the established Protestant majority (see page 12). With the decline of the national birth-rate, immigration accounted for 25 per cent of total population growth by the late 1970s.

A Republican ascendancy?

Despite the loss of Republican seats in Congress in the mid-term elections of 1982, President Reagan remained personally popular with most Americans. But the prospect of a long period of Republican rule, which some people thought was heralded by Reagan's 'landslide' of 1980, would depend on many other factors. Less than 54 per cent of electors bothered to vote in 1980 – in fact low turn-outs were a feature of all recent elections – and most of those who didn't vote were undoubtedly poor blacks and recent immigrants. But nine out of ten blacks who *did* vote supported the Democrats. Black activists were quick to notice that a fully-mobilized black vote could have defeated the Republicans in 1980, and began a campaign to register *all* eligible blacks and get them to the polls in 1984.

Our survey of American history concludes as it began, with a government in power whose main concern was to ensure the continued prosperity of richer Americans. Two periods of reform had smoothed out the most obvious inequalities in American society, but there was still a wide gulf between the 'comfortable' two-thirds and the 'deprived' one-third of Americans. If the aspirations of the poor cannot be satisfied by increasing economic growth (as the rich continued to hope), social stability in the future may only be assured by a more equal share-out of America's existing wealth. But that would mean 'socialistic' policies, a prospect that few Americans in 1983 were ready to face.

Questions

82

Did you notice?

1. American Indians in the United States today (a) are the most deprived minority (b) outnumber blacks (c) all live on reservations

   A

2. Rachel Carson (a) burnt her bra at a protest rally (b) wrote a book called *Silent Spring* (c) was 'the sweetheart of the silent majority'

   B

3. In political orientation the 'Wallace vote' was (a) New Left (b) Democratic (c) extreme Right

   C

4. The energy crisis of the 1970s was precipitated by (a) the Panama Canal treaties (b) the disaster at Three Mile Island (c) the OPEC oil embargo

   C

5. In economic policy the Right favoured (a) a tight money policy (b) wage and price controls (c) increased government spending

   A

6. True or false?
   (i) Americans ignored the question of environmental protection
   (ii) The New Left were admired by Middle Americans
   T (iii) Nixon followed Keynesian economic policies
   T (iv) 'CREEP' was successful in getting Nixon re-elected
   F (v) The Moral Majority supported 'abortion by choice'

7. Which statement is *more* accurate?
   (i) In 1978 the use of the 'quota system' for higher education
      (a) was condemned by the Supreme Court
      (b) was accepted as 'one element' in admissions policy
   (ii) The Equal Rights Amendment failed because
      (a) insufficient states ratified it
      (b) Title VII of the Civil Rights Act made it unnecessary

   (iii) One reason why Jimmy Carter was elected in 1976 was that
      (a) most Americans had 'turned Left' again
      ✳ (b) he campaigned against 'big government'
   (iv) One aim of 'Reaganomics' was
      (a) to reduce inflation
      ✳ (b) to increase unemployment

Can you explain?

8. Briefly describe *either* the campaign for environmental protection *or* the women's movement, adding any other information or arguments in support of it which you may know about.

9. What factors contributed to the success of Jimmy Carter in the Presidential campaign of 1976?

10. What objections were raised to the policy of affirmative action? Which people opposed it, and for what reasons?

11. Why were patriotic Americans upset by events in Vietnam in 1975, and in Iran in 1979?

12. All American governments of the 1970s were concerned about rising inflation and high unemployment. What were the essential differences between 'orthodox' and 'Keynesian' policies in tackling these problems?

What's your view?

13. Do you think blacks and other people who had suffered discrimination in the past deserved the extra help offered by affirmative action? Do you think a similar policy is necessary in Britain? What would be your attitude if you were *excluded* from a university place or a good job by the operation of such a policy?

14. It is estimated that traditional Catholics and fundamentalist sects together number about 75 million of America's population. Why did they call themselves the Moral *Majority* in their campaign against sexual freedom? How far do you think 'moral crusaders' should go in trying to put their views across—e.g. should they try to get laws changed, or strict censorship enforced, or just distribute propaganda?

15. Many suggestions have been made about controlling illegal immigration into the United States, but as yet no law has been passed by Congress. How would *you* tackle this problem?

Further Reading

SUPPLEMENTARY READING

James Baldwin, *Notes of a Native Son* and *Nobody Knows My Name* (both Corgi, 1969). Two volumes of essays on the problems of blacks in America.

J. R. Brooks, *The USA 1919–81* (Harrap, 1982). Also deals with foreign policy.

Denys Cook, *Presidents of the USA* (David and Charles, 1981). Briefly describes main features and events of each Presidency, with notes about Acts of Congress.

R. Currie, *The United States of America Today* (Blackie, 1980).

C. P. Hill, *The U.S.A. Since the First World War* (Allen and Unwin, 1967).

D. B. O'Callaghan, *Roosevelt and the United States* (Longman, 1971), and *The United States since 1945* (Longman, 1983).

W. P. Rae and N. C. Coutts, *Contemporary Files: Book 2 The World* (Heinemann Educational Books, 1980). A 'topic book' in which *The Washington File* examines several relevant problems: race, urban crisis, the economy, presidential power.

Studs Terkel, *Hard Times: Oral History of the Great Depression in America* (Allen Lane, 1970), *Division Street America* (Pantheon, 1966), similar oral history of Chicago in the mid-1960s.

Among the best-known of numerous novels and autobiographies which illustrate the history of the period are these:

James Baldwin, *Another Country* (Corgi, 1965) and many other novels.

T. Dreiser, *An American Tragedy* (Chivers, 1973).

Ralph Ellison, *Invisible Man* (Penguin, 1965).

F. Scott Fitzgerald, *The Great Gatsby* (Heinemann Educational, 1969). Modern Novels Series.

George Jackson, *Soledad Brothers: Prison Letters* (Penguin, 1970).

Harper Lee, *To Kill a Mockingbird* (Heinemann Educational Books, 1966).

Sinclair Lewis, *Main Street* (Cape, 1966), *Babbitt* (Cape, 1968).

W. Motley, *Knock on any Door* (Fontana, 1969).

John Dos Passos, *U.S.A.* (Penguin, 1966).

John Steinbeck, *The Grapes of Wrath* (Heinemann, 1965 and Penguin, 1970).

Richard Wright, *Native Son* (Cape, 1970).

The Autobiography of Malcolm X as told to Alex Haley (Penguin, 1968).

MORE ADVANCED

D. K. Adams, *America in the Twentieth Century* (OUP, 1967).

F. L. Allen, *Only Yesterday* (Harper Row, 1964). About the 1920s. *Since Yesterday* (Harper Row, 1972). About the 1930s.

John M. Blum *et al.*, *The National Experience: Book 2: A History of the United States since 1865* (Harcourt Brace Jovanovich, 5th ed., 1981).

Alan Conway, *The History of the Negro in the U.S.A.* (Historical Association pamphlet No. 67, 1968).

J. K. Galbraith, *The Great Crash* (Penguin, 1969), *The Affluent Society* (Deutsch, 3rd ed., 1977).

Paul Goodman, *Growing Up Absurd* (Vintage Books, 1973). A critique of American society and values which greatly influenced the New Left and student revolt of the late 1960s.

P. Goodman and F. O. Gateley, *America in the Twenties: The Beginnings of Contemporary America* (Holt, Rinehart and Winston, 1972).

M. Harrington, *The Other America: Poverty in the United States* (Penguin, 1963).

William E. Leuchtenburg, *The Perils of Prosperity, 1914–32* (University of Chicago Press, 1958). *Franklin D. Roosevelt and the New Deal, 1932–40* (Harper Row Torchbooks, 1963).

Isabel Leighton, *The Aspirin Age, 1919–41* (Penguin, 1964).

Peter J. Mooney and Colin Bown, *Truman to Carter* (Edward Arnold, 1979).

Vance Packard, *The Hidden Persuaders* (Penguin, 1960), *The Waste Makers* (Penguin, 1963).

Richard Polenberg, *One Nation Divisible: Class, Race and Ethnicity in the United States since 1938* (Penguin, 1980).

James Shenton, *History of the United States from 1865 to the Present Day* (Doubleday, 1964).

Harvard Sitkoff, *A New Deal for Blacks: The Emergence of Civil Rights as a National Issue* (OUP, 1979).

Daniel Snowman, *America Since 1920* (Heinemann Educational Books, 1978).

Howard Zinn, *A People's History of the United States* (Longman, 1980). An 'alternative view' of American history, emphasizing ordinary people's lives.

History of the Twentieth Century magazine series (see Notes on Resources, page xii for full information); the issues particularly relevant to this Part of the book are:

Chapter 2: No. 41.

Chapter 3: Nos. 47, 53, 55.

Chapter 5: Nos. 79, 82, 95, 96, 104.

Chapter 6: Nos. 90, 92, 104.

Feature Films Illustrating American History

Many topics of American twentieth-century history – or earlier – could be illustrated with feature films made or set in the period. Jack Babuscio, Lecturer in American History and Film studies at Kingsway–Princeton College, has drawn up the following short list of films which might be used in this way. Full particulars of the distributors are given at the end.

First World War

All Quiet on The Western Front – USA, 1930. Director: Lewis Milestone. 103 mins. Distributors: Columbia–Warner.

One of the strongest anti-war statements made on film, *All Quiet on the Western Front* points to the futility and inhumanity of all war and, in particular, the Great War.

Prohibition and gangsters

The St. Valentine's Day Massacre – USA, 1967. Director: Roger Corman. 99 mins. Distributors: BFI.

The lawlessness of the Prohibition era of the 1920s is shown in a film that concentrates on the short and violent career of Al Capone.

The Depression

Our Daily Bread – USA, 1934. Director: King Vidor. 62 mins. Distributors: BFI.

The most famous depression film of the 1930s, Vidor's story describes how a group of unemployed artisans come together to reclaim a derelict farm and lay the foundations of a self-supporting rural community.

American values

Ruggles of Red Gap – USA, 1934. Director: Leo McCarey. 90 mins. Hire charge approximately £10. Distributors: Columbia–Warner.

Charles Laughton is an English butler who shows his newly-rich employers that they have lost touch with their country's ideals, and teaches them all about the American Dream.

Technology

Modern Times – USA, 1935. Director: Charles Chaplin. 85 mins. Distributors: Peter Darvill Associates.

Chaplin's famous satire takes a highly irreverent attitude towards that 'sacred cow' – American technology.

Social reform

You Only Live Once – USA, 1937. Director: Fritz Lang. 93 mins. Distributors: BFI.

Lang's melodrama is a powerful indictment of the injustice, prejudice and brutality that is sometimes directed in the name of justice against an ex-criminal. With Henry Fonda and Sylvia Sidney.

Migrant workers

The Grapes of Wrath – USA, 1940. Director: John Ford. 129 mins. Distributors: Columbia–Warner.

Odyssey of the Joad family from the Oklahoma dust bowl to California, the 'Promised Land'. Faithfully follows the John Steinbeck novel. With Henry Fonda.

Power of the media

Citizen Kane – USA, 1941. Director: Orson Welles. 115 mins. Distributors: BFI.

Thinly fictionalized account of the rise and fall of William Randolph Hearst, America's great newspaper tycoon, with Orson Welles playing the central role as Charles Forster

Kane. Of special interest is the way Hearst/Kane manipulated public opinion to get America to declare war on Spain in 1898.

Corruption in politics

All the King's Men – USA, 1949. Director: Robert Rossen. 109 mins. Distributors: Columbia–Warner.

Thinly disguised portrayal of the rise and eventual assassination of Governor Huey P. Long, played here by Broderick Crawford as Willy Stark, who lifts himself out of the despair of the depression and promises the people of his state that they will 'share the wealth'. The point made is that power corrupts and absolute power corrupts absolutely.

Trade Unions

On the Waterfront – USA, 1954. Director: Elia Kazan. 107 mins. Distributors: Columbia–Warner.

Marlon Brando as Terry Molloy, ex-prize fighter who becomes the dupe of a mob which controls the longshoremen's union. Thought by some today to be basically reactionary in its message, it is one of several films dealing with labour and unionism made during the McCarthy period.

McCarthyism

McCarthyism spawned a number of anti-Communist feature films (*I Married a Communist*, *I was a Communist for the F.B.I.*, *My Son John*), but these are not readily available for hire. A useful film to illustrate this theme would be the following:
See It Now – USA, 1954. 38 mins. Distributors: BFI.

Edited recordings from the Edward R. Murrow TV programme of the same name which deals with the career of Senator Joe McCarthy. This was seen by an audience of 65 million and helped to turn public opinion against McCarthy. Sound quality is poor; teachers should preview.

City problems

Blackboard Jungle – USA, 1955. Director: Richard Brooke. 94 mins. Distributors: Ron Harris Cinema Services.

Based on the Evan Hunter novel dealing with some of the more gruesome facts of life in American big-city schools.

The military machine

Patton: Lust for Glory – USA, 1969. Director: Franklin Schaffner, 171 mins. Distributors: Film Distributors Associated.

A fascinating look at the military machine by close concentration on the Second World War general whose 'lust for glory' is the subtitle of Schaffner's film.

DISTRIBUTORS

Columbia–Warner Distributors Ltd., Film House, Wardour Street, London W1V 4AH.

British Film Institute Distribution Library, 9 Chapone Place, Dean Street, London. W1V 6AA.

Peter Darvill Associates, 280 Chartridge Lane, Chesham, Bucks., HP5 2SG.

Ron Harris Cinema Services Ltd., Glenbuck House, Glenbuck Road, Surbiton, Surrey.

Film Distributors Associated Ltd., Building No. 9, G.E.C. Estate, East Lane, Wembley, Middlesex, HA9 7QB.

Part II

The USSR since 1917

A poster honouring the Red sailors who helped to usher in the first Socialist state in 1917.

8

Russia: The First Socialist State

The land and peoples of the USSR

Many things in Russia have changed since 1917 – even her geography! In 1923 she officially became the Union of Soviet Socialist Republics, but the name of the largest republic is still often used for the whole country. In 1917 her territory included Finland and the Baltic states (Latvia, Lithuania and Estonia) and much of present-day Poland. These areas were lost, and later mostly recovered, within the period you will study. In area the USSR is the largest country in the world: it covers one-sixth of the world's land surface and straddles half the globe from Europe in the west to the Soviet Far East. But much of this is the nearly uninhabitable region of Siberia, which is only now being settled and developed. The USSR, like America, could be self-sufficient, although she has not yet achieved that economic balancing act.

Over half of the USSR's total population of about 265 million are Russians, but there are other small and large national groups, each with its own language and culture, which were gathered into one Russian Empire by the Tsars. Some, like the Georgians and Ukrainians, today have republics of their own. On paper the USSR is a federal system of fifteen republics, but in practice the Soviet Government allows little more self-government to national minorities than they had under the Tsar.

The local nationalism of Georgians and other non-Russian groups is one of the continuous threads in Russian history which can still be seen today. These people resented being 'Russified' under the Tsars and they still chafe against the tight control of Moscow.

Another recurrent theme is Russia's fear of attack from the west. This arises from her geography: from Poland to Moscow and beyond there is no natural barrier to hinder an invading army. In 1812 it took Napoleon three months to reach the gates of the capital, and in 1941 Hitler made it in six.

As we suggested in our survey of America, the last half-century of a nation's history can only be fully understood with some reference to earlier events and the cultural traditions of her people. Regrettably these aspects receive scant attention here, for any short history of twentieth-century Russia is bound to be dominated by one theme of overwhelming importance: the origins and principles of Socialism. It is one of the ironies of history that the version of Socialism practised in Russia today was not Russian but European in origin, and that it arrived there almost by accident.

'Slavophils' and 'Westerners'

Throughout the nineteenth century Russian thinkers divided into 'Slavophils' or 'Westerners'. The Slavophils thought that Russia would follow a path of its own into the twentieth century, arising from its own traditions and resting on three principles: the absolute power of the Tsar as the 'little father' of all the Slav peoples, the sanctity of the family as the basic productive unit of society, and the spiritual rule of the Orthodox Church. The Westerners on the other hand looked to the increasingly democratic countries of the West and compared their progress to backward Russia, where serfdom (slavery) existed until 1861, where the Church taught unthinking submission, and the Tsar ruled through his secret police and the threat of exile to Siberia. In 1825 a handful of idealistic army officers conspired to proclaim a constitution and the end of serfdom. They were executed. For the rest of the century, one revolutionary group after another sought by every means from education to terrorism to change Russia. They all failed.

One of these groups was the Russian Social Democratic Labour Party, strongly 'Western' in outlook, with ideas derived from a German thinker, Karl Marx. Like most other revolutionary opponents of Tsarism, in the early years of this century their leaders— including Lenin–were in exile in Siberia or Western Europe, where they continued to plot the overthrow of the Tsarist régime.

The Bolshevik Revolution

The sudden downfall of the Tsar in 1917 led to political confusion which gave Vladimir Ilyich Lenin the chance he had been waiting for. Within six years he had stamped on Russia an entirely new system of government based on the ideas of Karl Marx. This achievement against tremendous odds shows the power of a small band of dedicated men, inspired by one man's will, to alter the course of world history. It was all the more remarkable because Marx had based his theory on European conditions and had never intended it to be applied to a backward peasant country like Russia. It was not a seaworthy ship of state but a rusty old hulk that Lenin launched into the uncharted waters of a Socialist future.

Almost at once it nearly sank in the storms of civil war and foreign attack. Lenin was forced to recognize Russia's weakness in the face of Capitalist encirclement and in 1921 he was wise enough to berth his Socialist ship for urgent repairs. By the time she was stocked up and ready to continue her voyage, the wizard pilot was dead.

Economic development

Lenin's successor Josef Stalin tackled another superhuman task: to give agricultural Russia the industrial strength to withstand future attacks. Everything, including the lives of millions of Russians, was sacrificed to this aim, which was achieved only just in time. From 1941 to 1945 the economic fortress that Stalin had built was shaken to its foundations by the Second World War. But it did not fall. It is perhaps not surprising that after the war Stalin was still obsessed by foreign threats to Soviet security, a story we shall follow up in Part IV.

Post-War Russia

In the 1950s Russians were still waiting for the good life that Socialism promised, and were restless under political repression as cruel as the Tsar's. After Stalin's death Nikita Khrushchev inherited a Russia rather like that of 1917, in which pressures had built up ready to 'blow the lid' unless some of the steam could escape. Khrushchev lifted the lid–just a bit. He relaxed the political terror of Stalinism and began to raise the standard of living of ordinary Russians. In foreign policy his initiative for 'peaceful coexistence' with the Capitalist West eventually eased the dangerous tensions of the Cold War.

These new policies gave Soviet citizens a taste of material comfort and political freedom, and whetted their appetite for more. Already they have new housing, stylish clothes and TV. Now what about a car for every family? Free speech? And freedom to travel? Rising expectations at home have put today's leaders in an ideological fix. On the one hand, they have developed a Western-style consumer economy which underlines existing social inequalities (since the cheapest car costs more than an average family's yearly income, only a few privileged families have one). On the other hand, they wield a rod of iron in political and cultural life which seems little better than the old Tsarist system that ended in 1917. And yet they claim that the

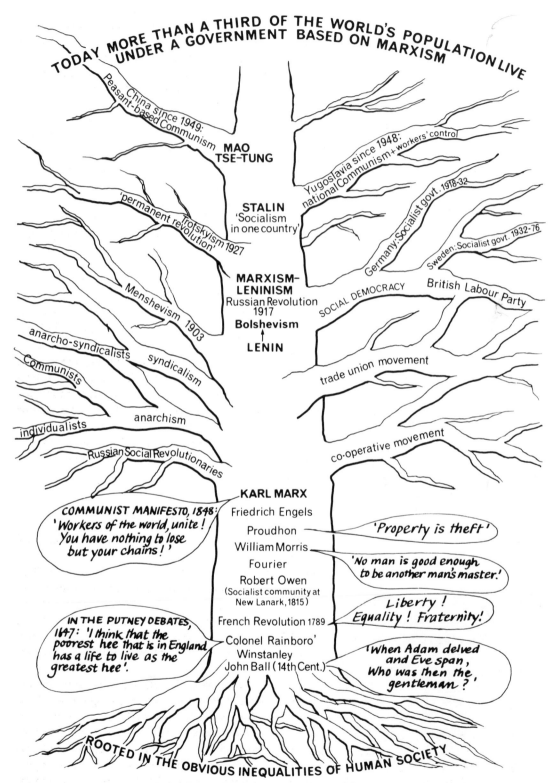

Figure 8.1   The 'tree of Socialism'.

Soviet Union is the foremost Socialist state, well on the way to a classless society which, according to Marx, will need no government at all!

Many other Socialists today would dispute that claim. Strict followers of Marx and Lenin in China, for example, alleged that after Stalin's death Soviet policies veered right away from the Socialist road. Others say that things began to go wrong much earlier than that: the Bolshevik version of Socialism was never what they understood by the term, and they soon came to dislike it just as much as Capitalism.

The history of Soviet Russia since 1917 will help you to judge this issue for yourselves. But first we must look at the original ideas on which the Soviet system was based. For the Bolsheviks were only one branch of a wide-spreading 'tree of Socialism' (Figure 8.1) which was well-rooted in history long before 1917.

SOCIALISM AND COMMUNISM

Throughout human history some people have thought (and many religions have taught) that it is wrong or unfair for some men to assume power over others and to think themselves better than others. This leads to the idea of *Socialism* or *Communism* (k) which says that society should be organized to prevent inequality, and that the collective interest of the whole community should come before the individual interests of its members. In such a society, men should be encouraged to co-operate rather than compete with one another. These ideas are obviously very different from the eighteenth-century philosophy of Capitalism which encouraged men to compete with each other for wealth and power and saw nothing wrong in the social inequality which resulted, since everyone had an equal chance to get rich.

By the mid-nineteenth century the 'success' of Capitalism had indeed made many people rich and powerful. But the dark side of their prosperity was the obvious misery of millions

of others who owned nothing, worked long hours for pitiful wages, lived in poor housing and unhealthy conditions, and had little or no chance to break out of these conditions. Even some Capitalists felt guilty about this situation, and many Socialist movements began actively to oppose it. This led to revolutions in Europe, which were all suppressed. But more successfully, Socialism was expressed in the growth of trade unions, co-operative movements and Socialist political parties. All these groups wanted to ameliorate the evil effects of Capitalism by curbing the power of unscrupulous Capitalists and providing some kind of welfare for the social casualties of the system.

Some Socialists came to their political beliefs through religion, some by sheer compassion for the underdog, some by their disgust at the growth of Capitalist industrialism, which spawned filth and ugliness for the increasing number of people engaged in it. Some wanted merely to help the poor; others wanted to create an entirely new, more just society. In 1890 a Socialist could be anyone from a Methodist minister organizing a miners' Sickness Benefit Fund to a terrorist anarchist planning to assassinate the head of a big business.

The ideas of Karl Marx

The most sweeping and powerful criticism of Capitalism came from Karl Marx (1818–83). Marx (Figure 8.2) was a giant thinker. The strength of his ideas can be seen in the single fact that today, more than a third of the world's people live under a government based on Marxism (see Figure 8.1). Why has this particular brand of Socialism been so successful?

Most other Socialists of that time merely *wished* that things would change. Even those who saw Capitalism as the main enemy were not sure how to bring about its downfall, or what to put in its place. Marx offered certainty about what to aim for, and a clear programme of action for those who accepted his vision. He believed that mankind was moving

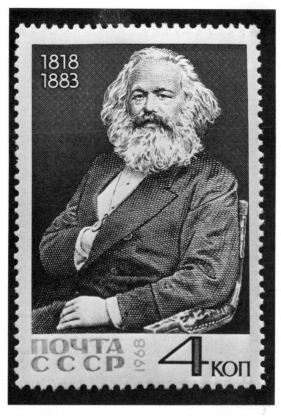

Figure 8.2   A Russian postage stamp commemorating Karl Marx.

inevitably towards Socialism and then to a new and final stage of Communism. The ruling minority of Capitalists would be swept away when the deprived majority rose up to claim its rightful share of society's wealth.

Marx thought this would happen at some time or other by a 'law of history' which could not be prevented, but nevertheless it was the duty of a Communist to help it along. This was the job of a Marxist political party: not merely, like other groups of reformers, to try to improve the condition of the oppressed, but to push and pull the whole cart-load of human society towards the next era of history.

Now the more militant Socialists knew *what* to do, but they could not all agree on how to do it. Marxists soon divided into those who believed that Socialism would be reached by *evolution* – that is, by peaceful and gradual development – and those who believed in *revolution*, violent if necessary, as the only means to overthrow the existing Capitalist system.

Marxism–Leninism

The most important of the revolutionary Marxists was Lenin. In 1903 the Russian Marxist party split into Mensheviks ('the minority') and Lenin's group of Bolsheviks ('the majority').† The Mensheviks were ready to link arms with other Socialist groups and advance with a broad front to overthrow Capitalism. Lenin on the other hand wanted a small, tightly disciplined party as the tool for revolution, and organized the Bolsheviks in this way. His formula for an efficient Communist Party, and other ideas he wrote about,

†These terms are rather misleading. At a Party congress in 1903 Lenin won majority support for his policy – hence the name of his group – but in the Party as a whole there were more Mensheviks than Bolsheviks.

expanded Marxism into Marxism-Leninism. It is this set of ideas which the Soviet Government and most other Communists believe in today (see Study Topic 5).

Hopes for a better world?

After 1917 the Soviet Union came to stand for the whole philosophy of Socialism in some people's eyes, and its unpleasant features gave useful ammunition to the many critics of Socialist ideas. But Marxists were only one kind of Socialist, and the Bolsheviks were only one kind of Marxist: the hard-line variety. They despised ineffectual 'do-gooders' collecting pennies for sick miners, and regarded non-revolutionary Marxists as 'idle dreamers'. For their part other Socialists found the Bolsheviks far too ruthless and arrogant. They preferred to approach Socialism step by step, and above all by *democratic* means. These differences were hotly argued at international Socialist meetings in the early years of this century.

In October 1917, nevertheless, Socialists all over the world eagerly picked up their binoculars to watch 'the great Socialist experiment' in Russia. Despite their misgivings about the Bolsheviks they at least hoped to see something better than the medieval cruelty of Tsarist Russia and the equally inhuman system of Western industrial Capitalism. In the following chapters you will see how far these hopes were justified.

KEYWORDS

Communism, Socialism, mean different things according to the context in which they are used.

1. In a *general* sense they both mean a political or moral philosophy based on two central beliefs:

(a) that the collective interest of the whole community should come before the individual interests of its members;

(b) that property (perhaps excepting personal possessions) should be owned communally and not by individuals.

Ideas of Fraternity (the brotherhood of man), Equality (the classless society) and Co-operation (rather than competition) are Socialist or Communist principles which follow from these two beliefs.

2. In present-day politics the words have different meanings:

(a) *Socialist* parties – in Western Europe they are often called Social Democratic parties – nowadays follow moderate Socialist policies which vary from one to another. They all at least support welfare programmes and some degree of public ownership of industry. The British Labour Party is a moderate Socialist party like this. Its own roots were in non-conformist Christianity and the trade union movement, which explains its strong trade union connection today.

(b) *Communist* parties follow the ideas of Marxism–Leninism. They were formed after the Russian Revolution, hoping to repeat that example in their own countries, and had strong ties with the Soviet Communist Party. Today their policies for achieving Communism vary according to local circumstances, and many no longer accept the leadership of the Soviet Party.

3. In the context of Marxist theory, Communism and Socialism have special meanings which are fully explained in Study Topic 5.

9

Putting Theory into Practice

PEACE AT ANY PRICE

The Bolsheviks come to power

In the introductory section, 'Starting Point: The First World War', pages 2–4, we followed the events of 1917 in Russia to the October Revolution when the Bolshevik Party took over the government. In the period of Dual Power after the fall of the Tsar in March, Russia had been governed jointly by the official (middle-class) Provisional Government and the more militant (working-class) Soviets, in which the Bolshevik voice became the loudest. When the ineffectual Provisional Government failed to meet the press-

Figure 9.1   Lenin urges on his followers. November 1917.

ing demands for 'Peace! Bread! Land!', many people looked to the Soviets for a lead. This gave the Bolsheviks their chance. In November they seized power on behalf of the Soviets, but in fact for themselves.

The Bolshevik Party, which soon adopted the name Communist Party of the Soviet Union (CPSU), has run the government of Russia ever since 1917. Yet at that time it represented only a handful of Russia's population of 153 million, most of whom had never heard of the Bolsheviks and the policies they stood for. Their seizure of power was an amazing feat of daring – but even more amazing was their success in holding on to it after 1917. Both these achievements were due to the exceptional skill and judgement of Lenin (Figure 9.1), a revolutionary leader of rare talent. Lenin knew exactly how to exploit the confused situation after the Tsar's abdication. And once the reins of power were in his hands, he rode the bucking bronco of opposition like a rodeo cowboy. Nothing could loosen his grip!

The Treaty of Brest-Litovsk

Peace was the first desire of the Russian people which the Bolsheviks had promised to fulfil, and they urgently needed it themselves to build their new Socialist society. They at once began negotiations for peace with Germany, but they were taken aback by the harsh terms Germany offered. Many leading Bolsheviks (including Lenin's right-hand man Trotsky) felt they could not accept such catastrophic losses for Russia. But Lenin argued that peace was their first priority and after much argument, his view prevailed.

In March 1918 the Treaty of Brest-Litovsk was signed. It was a cruel blow for Russia: she lost Finland, the Ukraine, the three Baltic states (Lithuania, Latvia and Estonia) and other areas. These included Russia's most fertile land, most of her industrial resources and 60 million of her people. Petrograd (later called Leningrad) was so close to the new

border that the capital was moved inland to Moscow.

To accept such humiliation for Russia was a bad start for the new leaders. But Lenin was ready to swallow the bitter pill for two reasons:

1. Without peace, the revolution at home would be lost.
2. The treaty would be temporary anyway. Lenin was sure that a revolution like Russia's was imminent in Germany, and a Socialist Germany would of course give back the lost lands to Socialist Russia. Even if the revolution did not happen, the Allies would defeat Germany in the end and Russia would recover her losses in the general peace settlement.

In fact a German Communist revolution did happen in 1919, but unlike Russia's it was crushed. And Germany did lose the war, but the Treaty of Versailles in 1919 recognized most of the former Russian areas as independent states (see page 4). Russia's revenge for Brest-Litovsk was delayed until 1939 when a new, strong Russia was able to grab back the lost areas, as we shall see later.

The question of the peace treaty reveals Lenin's special gifts as a leader and also the nature of the Bolshevik Party in his time. At the top there was room for argument about policy, but Lenin – whose judgement of a situation was usually correct – tended to win the arguments. Later, discussion within the Party gave way to one-man dictatorship by Stalin, a very different leader from Lenin.

Immediately after the October Revolution Lenin said, 'We shall now proceed to construct the Socialist order.' For years he had plotted the route to this moment in history, but he had not thought out in detail what to do when it arrived. But ready or not, he now had the chance to try out Marx's ideas in real life. As we go along you can measure the Soviet 'Socialist order' against the blueprint from which it was built (the ideas of Marx and Lenin are explained in Study Topic 5).

BOLSHEVIK RULE

Within six months of coming to power the Bolsheviks had established a very harsh one-party dictatorship. But *also* within six months they had to mobilize every ounce of strength to fight a civil war and foreign armies of intervention. It is true that the harshness of Bolshevik rule was partly due to the pressures of the war – which is how they justified it. But whatever the excuse for their ruthlessness, it had tragic results for the Russian people. In the economy the forced pace of socialization brought disaster. In political life the Red Terror of the early years set a precedent for the mass terror of Stalinism later. And both these policies followed logically from Bolshevik beliefs, as you will see.

This chapter deals with domestic matters – the 'home front' in the civil war years from 1918–21 – so that you can clearly see how the new state was organized. In Chapter 10 we shall briefly describe the military events: who was fighting whom, and why, and the devastating effect of the civil war on an already exhausted country and people.

One-party dictatorship

Once the Bolsheviks had taken power they did not intend to share it with anyone – not even with other Socialist parties like the Mensheviks and Social Revolutionaries. Trotsky put this point in a nutshell with his reply to the Mensheviks' call for a coalition* of revolutionary forces: 'Your part is over. Go to the place where you belong from now on – the dustbin of history!' This was the Bolshevik attitude to all allies once they had ceased to be useful to their cause. Another example was their treatment of the Ukrainian anarchist leader Makhno, who fought their own enemies in the civil war. While the war was going against the Reds, Makhno was a friend and ally. Once the Red Army's victory was assured, Makhno and his men were driven out of Russia.

Before the October Revolution, plans had been made to elect a Constituent Assembly whose job would be to form a permanent government to replace the Tsar. The Assembly met once, in January 1918. But when the Bolsheviks failed to get a majority, they simply dismissed it and continued to govern the new state by decrees from the Congress of Soviets, in which they had a majority, and the all-Bolshevik Council of People's Commissars. This was a sort of cabinet which made all the major decisions. Later they created a full structure of government and wrote a constitution for the re-named Union of Soviet Socialist Republics. The most important fact about this Soviet system was (and is) that the Communist Party controls every organ of government.

The Red Terror

A second early sign of the Bolshevik style of rule was the Cheka, whose job was the same as the former Tsar's secret police: to prevent the government from being overthrown. There were indeed many counter-revolutionaries who threatened it, but the Cheka soon began to imprison or execute *anyone* who criticized Bolshevik policy. The Cheka set the pattern of Soviet internal security which has been carried on ever since through a series of organs under different names: OGPU, NKVD, MVD and (today) the KGB.

The Red Terror alarmed some Socialist onlookers abroad, who protested that it put Bolshevism in the same category as Tsarism. Trotsky sharply replied that Bolshevik terror was entirely different!

> The gendarmerie of Tsarism throttled the workers who were fighting for the Socialist order. Our Extraordinary Commissions [the Cheka] shoot landlords, capitalists, and generals who are striving to restore the capitalist order. Do you grasp this distinction? Yes? For us Communists it is quite sufficient ...†

Other Socialists were ready to accept this principle that 'the end justifies the means'.

† From a pamphlet written in 1920, *Terrorism and Communism*, replying to criticism from the German Socialist Karl Kautsky.

Their view was summed up in the famous remark attributed to a visiting British Socialist in the 1920s: 'You can't make an omelette without breaking eggs.'

Few Western Social Democrats today would swallow that 'apology' for Soviet methods of the 1920s or later. It is clear now that the Bolshevik leaders were determined to hang on to power no matter what the cost in blood and the lost friendship of well-wishers – *not* for personal glory or profit, however, but because they were utterly convinced that their cause was right. Fools who could not recognize this truth must have it thrust upon them for their own good. By the same logic, unquestioning obedience was demanded from the lower ranks of the Communist Party.

'The Party is always right'

Imagine a Tory or Labour supporter ready to die for his party! – but in those early revolutionary days, at least, many a Soviet Communist *was*. 'The Party' was much more than 'a party' as we understand it. The Party was the source of all leadership, the fount of all wisdom, the focus of all personal loyalty. Sad and distasteful as this may seem to us, we should remember that the ordinary Russian had had precious little personal freedom in Tsarist days. In October 1917 he merely swapped one set of masters – the Tsar, the Church, the landlord – for another set: the Communist Party.

In 1920, however, this situation was not yet apparent. Lower-ranking party members expected to have a say in the new Socialist world – wasn't that what a 'workers' state' was all about? And for the millions of non-Communist Russians the new servitude looked a much better bargain than the old one, for many unheard-of benefits seemed to be coming their way.

State control of the economy

The land

Even before October 1917, exasperated peasants had begun to seize the land without waiting for the land reforms so often promised to them. The Bolsheviks in their rise to power had championed the peasants' right to do this, and now they 'legalized' the take-over by decree. The land was taken from its former owners and the peasants could occupy it but not *own* it, since private ownership was to be abolished in the new Socialist society. The peasants did not notice the subtle difference between occupying and owning: so far as they were concerned, the land was theirs at last. This misunderstanding was to lead to serious trouble later.

Nationalization*

Workers were immediately given a share in the management of their factories, but except for banks and a few key industries (arms factories, for example), the new régime did not at once take over all enterprises. Lenin's plan was a *gradual* transfer to state ownership and control. But during 1918 the government began hastily to take over all units of industry and trade, without compensation to former owners. There were two reasons for this: first, to mobilize every resource to fight the civil war which by then was raging; and secondly, to assert central government authority over local soviets which had begun to take over factories and run them themselves. This shows us another very important aspect of Bolshevik policy which continues in the Soviet Union today: all power is centralized in Moscow.

Social reform and experiment

Perhaps the most praiseworthy features of the Soviet Union as it later developed were the social reforms it pioneered: free state-run schools, welfare and medical services for all, and equal rights for women. By the 1930s Soviet welfare provision could put to shame far richer Capitalist societies. In the 1920s – understandably – social services were mostly paper promises, but an immediate start was made to provide elementary education for the

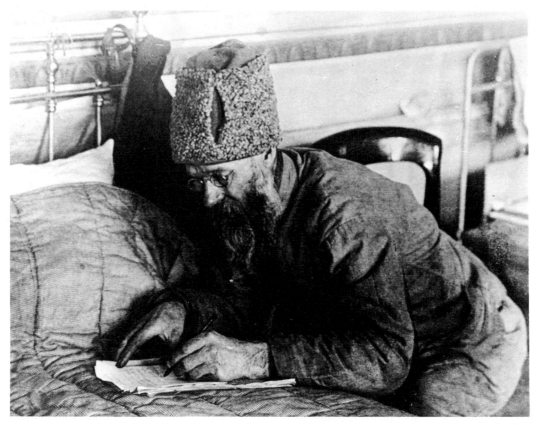

Figure 9.2 A student at a worker's university, Petrograd, 1919. He and many others had reason to be grateful to the new government.

millions of illiterates (Figure 9.2).

At this stage of Soviet development there was considerable freedom outside the sphere of politics. After the long repressive centuries of Tsarism, in Bolshevik Russia there was an outburst of creativity and experiment in the arts and in social life. The Soviet film-maker Sergei Eisenstein, for example, was a pioneer in the new art of cinema who attracted world-wide admiration. New ideas were tried out in marriage and divorce laws, education, and the treatment of criminals. Many social reformers in the West were excited and impressed by Soviet experiments of the 1920s which were revolutionary at that time. But this experimental spirit was totally crushed in the later period of Stalinism, when the Communist Party spread a blanket of conformism over every aspect of Soviet life.

WAR COMMUNISM

Lenin had intended to build his Socialist order slowly. He had to adapt Marxist theory to the actual conditions he found in Russia and he knew that Communism would not be achieved overnight. But his hand was forced by events. By the middle of 1918, sporadic resistance to the Bolsheviks had developed into full-scale civil war. A series of White Russian armies now organized themselves to overthrow the Reds and for the next three years the new régime was fighting for its life.

Trotsky hastily set up a Red Army to fight the war, and every Russian who had not joined the Whites was expected to help the Reds. No peep of protest was allowed. Workers who had just thrown off their Capitalist masters now had to work long hours under Bolshevik orders, for little or no pay. Peasants were asked to supply food for the cities and the army, but no goods were offered in exchange because there were none to spare. If they would not give up their grain voluntarily for the cause, it was seized from them by force.

Private traders and businessmen were pushed out of their jobs so that they could not sabotage the Reds' war effort. But the government did not have time to develop a state system of production and trade to replace private enterprise. The result was chaotic. The currency system broke down and simple barter took its place. By 1921 every town's market-place was full of pathetic, hungry people offering their household goods and clothes in exchange for food.

This harsh economic régime was known as 'War Communism'. It tested Russian loyalty to the revolution before most people knew what the revolution meant – and the Bolsheviks had not had time to tell them. Peasants began to hide or bury their grain rather than surrender it without payment. The bitterness of their feeling is shown in the story told by a supporter of the 1917 revolution who later left Russia, deeply disappointed with what the Bolsheviks had made of it. In a country lane in 1920 he came across the body of a member of a Bolshevik grain-collection squad. The man's belly was ripped open and stuffed to overflowing with grain, as if to say 'You want food? Right! Here it is!'

By 1921, resistance to War Communism was itself a serious threat to the Bolshevik Government. But by that time the Red Army had won the civil war – or perhaps it is truer to say the Whites had lost it. In the next chapter we shall see how this victory was accomplished.

*GLOSSARY

coalition, in politics, a temporary combination of distinct parties for a special purpose.

nationalization, making something into national or state property.

Study Topic 5

The Ideas of Marx and Lenin

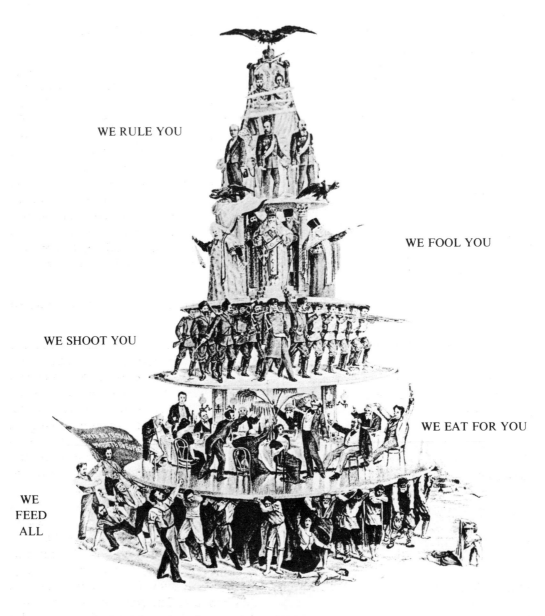

WE RULE YOU

WE FOOL YOU

WE SHOOT YOU

WE EAT FOR YOU

WE
FEED
ALL

Figure ST 5.1   A Marxist view of pre-revolutionary Russian society, from a propaganda poster of 1901.
Some of the oppressed bottom layer are beginning to protest—the proletarian revolution is on the way!

Defining Socialism and Communism

There have been – and still are – many small communist societies which are nothing to do with Karl Marx. Any group living or working together and sharing its possessions might be described as 'communist': a group of nuns or monks, for example, or people who band together to run a shared household. They all believe in communal living and ownership of property.

In the nineteenth century a political version of communism grew up in opposition to the inequality and exploitation of Capitalism. This political creed was more commonly called Socialism, and one of its spokesmen was Karl Marx. Marx used the two words in a special way: he described a Communist ideal society as the destiny of mankind, and Socialism as a stage on the way to it. His ideas are usually called Communism (with a capital letter), and we speak of Communist countries like Russia or China which are based on Marxism. But since no Communist country has yet got beyond Marx's transition stage of Socialism, they describe themselves as Socialist – for example, the Union of Soviet Socialist Republics.

Karl Marx, 1818–83

Marx was a German Jew who lived much of his life in England (he is buried in Highgate Cemetery, London). His ideas were put forward in the *Communist Manifesto* (1848), and in three successive volumes of a massive work, *Das Kapital* (in English, *Capital*), which were published in 1867, 1883 and 1890. The last two volumes were prepared for publication after his death by his collaborator, Friedrich Engels. Marx based his analysis of Capitalism on Engels' study of industrial conditions in the England of the 1840s – the most advanced Capitalist society at that time.

MARXISM

Some people regard Marxism as a religion, and Marx as its prophet. In some ways it is a faith, and some Marxists are as passionate in their belief as religious fanatics. But unlike most religions, Marxism is based on a mass of facts about human society, and it is concerned only with this world, believing that there is no other. We might call it an atheist's religion. It is a prescription for the way man should live – and *will* live in the future, Marx predicts.

1. History is a series of class struggles

Human society at any point in history is marked by *class struggle*. There is always one group on top and another underneath, and their interests are always opposed (Figure ST 5.1). In medieval England, for example, the king and aristocracy were on top of 'the rest'. The power of this upper class was based on land. If you owned some land and could hang on to it, you were all right, and if not you were some kind of slave to a landowner. Land produced food, the one essential commodity in this pre-industrial, self-sufficient economy. This kind of society is called *feudalism*.

2. Each stage of history gives way to the next

History is a process of change. As trade and industry developed, the power of landowners was taken by a new class of merchants and factory owners. In the new industrial society called *Capitalism*, these people were powerful because they owned the means of production (factories), distribution (railways, shops, etc.) and exchange (banks). Marx called this new upper class the *bourgeoisie*, and their rise to power was the bourgeois revolution.

Capitalism has also produced a new oppressed class – the *proletariat* of factory workers. Class conflict continues, but in a new form: the minority, the bourgeoisie, exploit the majority, the proletariat, by paying them only a fraction of the value of what they produce. The rest – the *surplus value* – they pocket for themselves. Capitalism also brings a new kind of suffering to the oppressed class. A peasant at least organized and understood his own work and breathed country air; but the proletarian is a mindless cog in a complicated industrial process and lives in abysmal city slums. He has become 'alienated' from his work and brutalized by the conditions of his life.

Nevertheless, in Marx's view, Capitalism was a step forward from feudalism because it could produce more goods and therefore a better life: the means of production had been improved.

3. Capitalism has produced its own 'grave-diggers'

As Capitalism developed, the greed of the bourgeoisie would drive them to ever more ruthless exploitation of the workers – the rich would get richer and the poor poorer. But the proletariat would not endure cruelty and injustice for ever. Eventually they would throw off their masters and demand a fair share of the goods they produced. To meet this demand, more goods must be made and a different kind of share-out arranged.

Of course the bourgeoisie would cling on to their privileged status and try to prevent change. But now they were a barrier to progress and no matter how hard they resisted, the proletarian revolution would sweep them aside. Capitalism must now give way to the new historical stage of *Socialism*, in which the production process would be expanded and distribution re-arranged to provide abundant food and goods for all.

4. The classless society

Socialism would soon lead to the ultimate utopia of *Communism*. When there was no shortage of food and goods, men would not need to compete for their share so they would not become unequal. In this society class struggle would disappear at last. Then there would be no need for authority to regulate social relations and, in time, the structure of government would 'wither away'. Under Communism, men would naturally co-oper-

ate in a classless society based on this simple economic principle: 'From each according to his ability, to each according to his needs'. Each man would freely give to society the work he was best able to do, and take from the common pool only what he needed and no more.

Marx was much clearer about the past and present than about the future. He did not describe in detail how a Communist society would be organized, nor exactly how to reach it. His followers therefore interpreted these points differently.

LENIN'S CONTRIBUTION

Lenin expanded some points of Marxism to include aspects of Capitalism which had developed since Marx's day. He said little more about the eventual Communist society: his main concern was how to get there.

1. Monopoly Capitalism and Imperialism

(a) Monopolies had grown in power to the point where the government might even take them into public ownership. But this kind of 'State Capitalism' should not be mistaken for Socialism. It would not benefit the masses because the government and all its agencies – the army, police, law courts and so on – always worked in the interests of the bourgeoisie.

(b) In the age of Imperialism, the bourgeoisie of Capitalist countries like Britain and America were now oppressing the proletariat of other countries as well as their own. So when the revolution came, it must be *world wide*.

2. The Revolutionary Party

The bourgeoisie would never be persuaded to give up their privileged status willingly, so *revolution* was the only means to overthrow them. 'Reformism' – improving the condition of the oppressed class bit by bit – was a betrayal of Marxism because it delayed the inevitable, necessary clash between the proletariat and the bourgeoisie. There must be *confrontation* rather than negotiation with the enemy.

The effective tool of revolution was a small but dedicated and disciplined Communist Party. When the moment for action came, every member must know exactly what to do, and do it. Once a general policy had been agreed by majority vote, there must be unquestioning obedience to orders from the top. This kind of decision-making was known as Democratic Centralism.

3. The Dictatorship of the Proletariat

The transitional period of Socialism after the revolution would be a 'Dictatorship of the Proletariat'. The workers would take over state power and use it to smash the bourgeoisie and prevent counter-revolution. They would 'Socialize' the economy and organize the new state in the interests of the workers.

The revolution and the period of workers' dictatorship might be harsh – but the workers were the majority of society, after all, and the bourgeoisie were only the minority. The proletariat and the Communist Party were the servants of history and should not flinch from necessary violence in carrying out their appointed task.

No one could tell how long the Dictatorship of the Proletariat would last. The bourgeoisie were cunning and powerful and would try hard to make a come-back. Only when all opposition had been crushed could society move on to the final stage of Communism that Marx had outlined.

MARXISM IN PRACTICE

Unlike theories of physics or mathematics, a theory of social science cannot be definitely proved true or false. It is more 'a way of looking at things' which makes sense to some people, but not to others. Marxism can be argued about for ever!

Much can be said to 'disprove' Marx. Russia in 1917 was not the advanced Capitalist society that Marx thought must come before Socialism, but a largely feudal one with about two million factory workers and a very backward economy. And in advanced Capitalist societies the condition of the proletariat has not worsened, as Marx expected, but steadily improved. In Britain today, for example, a proletarian revolution seems much less likely to happen than in Marx's time.

On the other hand, Lenin was able to establish his Dicatorship of the Proletariat even in 'unripe' feudal Russia. Socialism has brought spectacular economic progress to Russia, even if not yet abundant goods for all. And today the global class struggle seems to be developing as Marx and Lenin said it would: year by year, the few rich get richer while the many poor get poorer. The world bourgeoisie of Western Europe and America shows no willingness to share out its riches with Third World countries in Asia, Africa and Latin America. Up to now it is unmoved by any argument or even a feeling of guilt about the injustice of this situation. How long will the world proletariat put up with it?

So it is equally possible for Marxists to say 'It's all happening!' while non-Marxists say 'It's rubbish!' Millions of Socialists at least have found Marx's insight useful: they see many truths in his description of Capitalism, and a glimpse of refreshing sanity in his Communist utopia. But most people, Socialist or not, recoiled from Lenin's ruthless application of Marxism in Russia, and still more from the Stalinist terror which followed. Alexander Herzen, one of the many revolutionary exiles from Tsarist Russia, could see what might follow from Marxism long before Lenin and Stalin proved him right. In 1855 he commented on Marx: 'When people say we must kill millions in order that hundreds of millions might be happier, we can't ever be certain about the hundreds of millions; what is certain is that the millions are dead.'

Questions

Did you notice?

1. Lenin believed that the Treaty of Brest-Litovsk (a) would help to defeat Germany (b) was a fair settlement (c) would be temporary
2. Between 1919 and 1939, Latvia was (a) part of Germany (b) independent (c) part of the USSR
3. Makhno was (a) a Ukrainian anarchist (b) a Bolshevik leader (c) a Tsarist general
4. Eisenstein was (a) a film director (b) Marx's collaborator (c) a professor of physics
5. The Cheka was (a) the Tsar's secret police (b) the Bolsheviks' secret police (c) a group of White Russians
6. True or false?
   (i) Trotsky at first opposed the Treaty of Brest-Litovsk
   (ii) Mensheviks were Socialists
   (iii) In January 1918 the Constituent Assembly replaced the Congress of Soviets
   (iv) Karl Marx was a Russian revolutionary
   (v) All Socialists are Communists
7. Which statement is *more* accurate?
   (i) Nationalization means
      (a) workers' control of industry
      (b) public ownership of industry
   (ii) The Land Decree in 1917
      (a) gave the land to the peasants
      (b) took the land away from its previous owners
   (iii) According to Marx
      (a) Capitalism was better than feudalism
      (b) Capitalism was the worst system of all
   (iv) According to Lenin, the Dictatorship of the Proletariat
      (a) would be permanent
      (b) might last a long time

Can you explain?

8. Why did Lenin insist on 'peace at any price'? In what way was the Treaty of Brest-Litovsk 'a cruel blow for Russia'?
9. Bolshevik methods soon turned many other Socialists against them. But following *Bolshevik* logic:
   (a) why did Trotsky direct all other Socialists to 'the dustbin of history' in October 1917?
   (b) what was the justification for the Red Terror in the 1920s?
10. Despite the 'broken eggs' (see page 97), in the 1920s some Socialist onlookers were sympathetic towards the Soviet Union. What hopeful signs could they see at that time?
11. Lenin had intended gradual nationalization of the economy. Why did he speed it up in mid-1918?
12. What was the effect of War Communism on (a) industry and trade, (b) the peasantry?

What's your view?

13. Imagine yourself living in Manchester in 1850. Would you have been a Socialist? If so, what kind of Socialist, and why?
14. 'A proletarian revolution as Marx described it is unlikely to happen in Britain today.' Do you agree? If so, why isn't it likely?
15. In our study of America, or in the Capitalist world today, can you see any evidence to support Lenin's views about (a) monopolies, (b) imperialism?

10

Victory and Compromise

THE CIVIL WAR

Enemies at home

After the October Revolution most of the Russian aristocracy fled abroad, and in July 1918 the murder of the Tsar and his family destroyed the old ruling class for ever. The middle-class supporters of the Provisional Government (who had hoped for a parliamentary democracy after the Tsar's fall) were the hated bourgeoisie; they were dispossessed and branded as enemies. Other left-wing parties – Mensheviks, Social Revolutionaries and anarchists – all wanted revolution, but not the Bolshevik kind. When they objected to Bolshevik tyranny they became 'enemies' too, and were hunted down by the Cheka. By mid-1918 the only form of opposition for all these people was to join or support one of the White armies led by former Tsarist generals, or one of the so-called Green armies which fought both Reds and Whites.

Taken all together, the Bolsheviks' opponents were more numerous and better armed and trained than the Red Army. The Whites also had help, mainly in money and supplies, from foreign governments. In mid-1919 more than three-quarters of Russia was in White hands, and the Reds seemed close to defeat (Figure 10.1). But a year later the situation was reversed: the Reds had won (Figure 10.2), and two million White Russians fled their homeland to live in sad exile groups all over the world. How can we explain the Reds' success?

How the Reds won the war

The reasons for eventual Red victory can be briefly summarized.

1. Trotsky's command of the Red Army

Trotsky worked tirelessly to train and organize the Red forces, and directed their campaigns brilliantly. War Communism on the home front (see Chapter 9) made sure that Red soldiers were fed and armed, even if everyone else went cold and hungry.

2. The Whites lacked support

(a) Most of the peasants had no liking for the Reds, but a White victory might mean the loss of their precious land. When faced with a choice, they preferred the Reds and sabotaged White campaigns.

(b) Other political groups, like the Social Revolutionaries, also decided that the Reds were a lesser evil than corrupt White governments, and undermined their rule of White areas.

(c) Foreign backing of White campaigns sometimes failed. British or French troops felt no special sympathy for the White Russian cause.

(d) Foreign support for the Whites made them unpopular. Traditional Russian patriotism helped the Reds, who were 'defending the homeland against a foreign invader'.

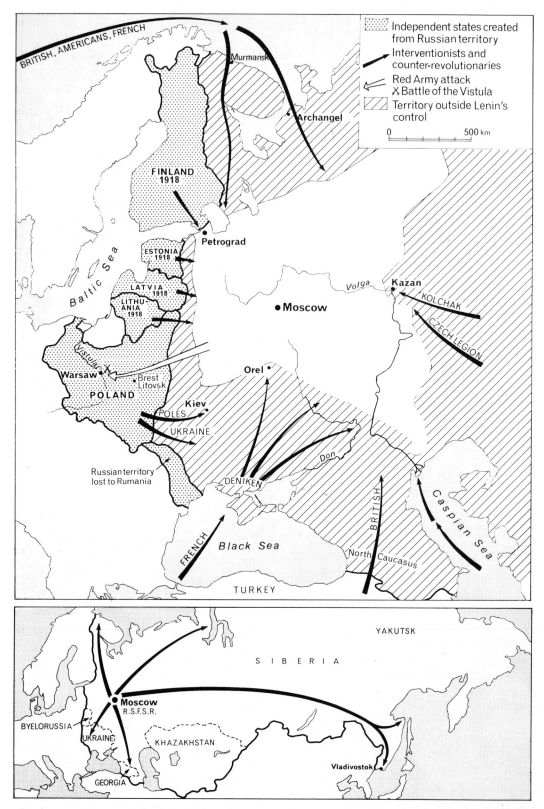

Figure 10.1 (*top*) Civil war and foreign intervention. Figure 10.2 The Communist triumph, 1919–22.

3. *Lack of White co-ordination*

The civil war was not really *one* war but a series of unco-ordinated campaigns which the Reds could deal with one by one: first Kolchak from the east, then Yudenich from the north-west, then Deniken from the south. In 1920 a last stand from General Wrangel was defeated. Then Poland launched a separate invasion, which ended with a peace treaty in 1921. Japanese troops were finally expelled from the Far East in 1922, and at last the whole of Russia was Red.

In war the will to win is often more important than superior numbers and weapons, and this was the Red Army's trump card. Red soldiers felt they had a stake in victory, whereas White soldiers were fighting to recover power and wealth for their generals! Moreover the Whites were a very mixed bag, with no common aim or unified leadership. The Reds would have beaten them more easily but for the help given to White armies by foreign governments, mainly Britain, France, America and Japan. Why did these countries interfere in a Russian civil war?

Foreign intervention

There were two reasons for foreign intervention – one military, the other political.

(a) *The military reason*

In the spring of 1918 the First World War was going badly for the Allies. The Bolsheviks' peace treaty with Germany in March was greeted with dismay. With Russia out of the war, German troops could be transferred from Russia to the Western front in France, and this might clinch a German victory. So one motive of the Allied governments was to restore the Provisional Government which, in its brief rule before the October Revolution, had continued to support the Allies in the world war.

(b) *The political reason*

From Marx onwards, Communism has been an international doctrine. 'Workers of the world, unite!' said the closing words of the *Communist Manifesto* in 1848, and as we have seen, Lenin thought his revolution would be only the first in a series which would liberate the world proletariat from Capitalism. To show they meant business, the Bolsheviks seized factories in Russia owned by foreign Capitalists and refused to accept responsibility for the foreign debts of the previous government.

Many people in the West saw the Bolshevik Government as a direct threat to their own way of life. Winston Churchill, then a Minister in the British wartime Cabinet, spoke for them when he described Lenin as 'a monster crawling down from his pyramid of skulls' and strongly urged a policy of intervention 'to strangle Bolshevism in its cradle'. Not everyone in the West felt like that, but it was a popular right-wing view.

The Soviet view of foreign intervention

Historians disagree about which of the above motives was the most important reason for foreign intervention. The defeat of Germany in November 1918 cancelled the military reason, yet help to the Whites continued until 1920. French reinforcement of the Polish army gained large areas of Russia for Poland in the last stages of the war. But on the other hand intervention was never a popular cause with war-weary Allied troops or people at home, and was carried out with little enthusiasm.

Whatever the real motives of Western governments, their actions had a harmful long-term effect. The Soviet Government was convinced that Western governments were determined to overthrow it, and would seize any future chance to do so. This belief strongly influenced Soviet attitudes to the West for years to come. It is often cited as the root cause of the East–West Cold War after 1945 which we shall be studying in Part IV.

COMPROMISE AT HOME AND ABROAD

1921 – year of crisis

So the Reds had won the war! But it was a hollow victory, for Russia was in ruins. In 1920 factories were producing only 15 per cent of 1913 output and food production was half the 1913 level. There was an acute shortage of metals, fuels and all imported goods. The railway system had more or less collapsed for lack of repairs and fuel.

The human statistics were even more tragic. At least 16 million had been killed in the two successive wars, and disease claimed many more (over 2 million died of typhus alone). And in 1921–2, despite international relief and the Soviet Government's efforts, 5 million more starved to death (Figure 10.3).

The famine was caused not only by the ravages of war but by the peasants' resistance to War Communism. Since their surplus production was requisitioned without payment, they planted only enough to feed themselves. Their attitude was 'We can do without boots – now see if you can do without food!' In 1921 a long drought made the harvest even worse, and millions began to die. Workers left the cities to scavenge in the countryside for food. Strikes and riots broke out and were harshly suppressed.

The Kronstadt Rising

On top of all this came a political crisis. In March 1921 sailors at the naval base of Kronstadt (near Petrograd) rebelled against the government. These men had taken a leading part in the October Revolution (see poster, p. 87) and were regarded as Red heroes – but three years of War Communism was more than they could stand. What kind

Figure 10.3   Starving, homeless victims of the Russian Civil War.

of workers' state was this, they asked, where every Bolshevik acted like a little tsar and every worker, peasant and soldier had only to *obey*? 'Soviets without Communists!!' was what they wanted now. But it was a vain cry. The Red heroes were ordered to surrender or be 'shot down like partridges'. And so they were.

The ground had been prepared for this betrayal well before 1921, but Kronstadt was a moment of truth in the history of Soviet Communism.

> The Kronstadt rising had a quality of nightmare not only for the slaughtered sailors but also for the Bolsheviks who so ruthlessly repressed them. It was as if the spirit of October 1917 had risen, after little more than three years, to reproach its leaders with having asserted the dictatorship of the Party over the proletariat ...†

In fact Lenin had already seen the warning signal of spreading discontent throughout the country. Now that the Red Army had driven its enemies out of Russia, the government must win back old friends (and make some new ones, especially among the peasants) or it would be overturned from within. So in 1921 Lenin made a sharp 'right turn' into the *New Economic Policy* (NEP).

THE NEW ECONOMIC POLICY

It is said that 'man does not live by bread alone', but without bread he doesn't live at all! This was Russia's basic problem in 1921. Somehow the peasants must be encouraged to produce more food. They had shown they would not do it 'for the cause', nor could they be forced by sheer brutality. Now NEP offered a Capitalist incentive – the chance of personal gain. This concession to the nation's bread-growers was the cornerstone of Lenin's new policy.

(a) *In agriculture* the surplus-requisition system was replaced by a state tax to be paid in foodstuffs. Above this amount, any

†Francis Wyndham and David King, *Trotsky* (Penguin, 1972), p. 87.

surplus could be sold for private profit. Peasants were also allowed to hire others to work for them.

(b) *In industry* factories employing less than twenty workers were returned to private ownership, or to local co-operatives set up to run them.

(c) Private enterprise in *retail trade* was allowed. Anyone could open a shop, set up a trading business or hire out a horse and cart for personal profit.

Some of the Party leaders strongly disliked the new policy. They were disappointed to give up the Socialist principles of War Communism, and saw NEP as a retreat back to Capitalism. But Lenin explained that it was only a temporary sacrifice, forced by the circumstances of the moment. He was careful to keep state control over what he called 'the commanding heights' of the economy: large factories, heavy industry, railways, banks and foreign trade. In due course the government would re-nationalize the rest of the economy and continue its task of building Socialism. These arguments convinced the doubters, as Lenin always did!

Like the Treaty of Brest-Litovsk in 1918, NEP was a desperate remedy for a desperate situation. Like Brest-Litovsk, it was only supposed to be a breathing-space before the next march forward. NEP has in fact been called 'a Brest-Litovsk on the economic front'.

NEP was a sacrifice of Socialist principles at home, and along with it came a parallel change in foreign policy. We know that the ultimate aim of a Marxist, and therefore of a Marxist state, is world revolution. But Lenin now had to ask himself, was this a realistic aim for the Soviet Government in the 1920s?

CAPITALIST ENCIRCLEMENT

In 1918 Lenin had confidently expected a Russian-style revolution in Germany and other Capitalist countries. In 1919 the Comintern (Communist International) had been set up to help foreign Communists, through national Communist Parties, to follow the Bolshevik example. The Comintern was *not* part of the Soviet Government, but its headquarters were in Moscow and in 1919, at any rate, its aims were the same. Foreign governments naturally saw it as an arm of Soviet foreign policy; to them it was further evidence of the Bolshevik threat.

For a time, Lenin's optimism about other revolutions seemed to be justified. In 1919 there were Communist risings in Germany, Hungary, Finland and the new Baltic states. But they were all put down. By 1921 the revolutionary tide in Europe seemed to have ebbed away, and the only role for a European Communist Party was to become a sort of 'Society for the Admiration of the USSR' – the only Communist beacon in sight!

Lenin was a long-term idealist, but a short-term realist. He saw that Russia was surrounded by a menacing circle of strong Capitalist nations who in the civil war had just demonstrated their hostility to the infant Soviet Government. But Russia needed trade and investment for the huge task of economic recovery and Socialist development, and only normal relations with Capitalist countries could provide this. The Soviet Government must recognize and adjust to 'Capitalist encirclement' as it had reacted to economic disaster at home – with compromise.

So in 1921 a new kind of 'Soviet agent' trooped off to Europe – very different from the popular image of the bearded and belted Bolshevik! These Russians arrived in pin-stripe suits and carrying brief-cases – the correct gear for their new task. They were looking for trade agreements and essential diplomatic recognition* for their government, and they were successful. In 1921 a trade agreement was signed with Britain, and in 1922 the Treaty of Rapallo with Germany provided for economic and military co-operation between the two countries. Britain recognized the new Soviet Government in 1924, France and others followed in 1925, though the United States held back until 1933. By 1925 the USSR had arrived in the diplomatic family of nations.

Which way from here?

These new policies at home and abroad were Lenin's last major contribution to Russian history. In 1918 he had been wounded by a bullet from Dora Kaplan, a Social Revolutionary; in 1922 and 1923 he had a series of strokes and in January 1924 he died, at the age of fifty-three. His death was a sad blow for the Bolsheviks and left several big questions to be discussed and answered. What do we do now? How do we do it? Who is to lead us?

The effects of NEP

Under NEP, food production and the output of industry gradually increased. The railways revived as the fuel crisis was overcome, and more than 1,000 new engines were imported from Sweden and Germany. By 1926–7, output of food and goods had regained the 1913 level and the two halves of the economy had achieved a fair balance – that is to say, agriculture was producing enough to feed everyone and factories made enough goods to go round.

But NEP also had some very undesirable effects from a Communist point of view. It licensed the very thing that Communism hoped to snuff out: every man's selfish desire to enrich himself. In no time at all thousands of small-time traders appeared – Nepmen, they were called. In the villages a new class of richer peasants called kulaks were soon enlarging their farms and hiring poorer peasants to work for them. In the climate of NEP these kulaks and 'petty bourgeoisie' (little Capitalists) were approved of because they produced more food and goods for the market. 'Enrich yourselves!' said Bukharin to the peasants, and so they did.

Bukharin's slogan was not echoed by all his fellow leaders, however. While ordinary Russians were getting back to normal life in the mid-1920s, the Communist Party leaders were arguing fiercely about the future policy of their government.

'Socialism in one country' or 'Permanent revolution'?

Bukharin and others supported NEP as part of a general Rightist policy which came to be called 'Socialism in one country'. The Rightists thought the government's first task should be to build up Soviet strength. Later, when the economy was strong, they could get back to Socialist principles at home, and the USSR would then be in a better position to pursue the long-term Marxist aim of promoting other Communist revolutions abroad. In other words the Rightists wanted to continue indefinitely the policies Lenin had started in 1921: a small amount of Capitalism at home, and uneasy coexistence with Capitalism abroad.

But there was an equally strong Leftist point of view whose supporters also claimed the authority of Lenin to back them up. Lenin had not meant NEP to be more than an emergency measure, had he? Lenin had not given up world revolution, had he? On the contrary, Comrade Lenin would turn in his grave to see these wretched little Nepmen and kulaks swarming all over the country! (Figure 10.4.) Comrade Lenin knew that our first priority is Communism, at home and abroad! So the Leftists argued for a policy of 'Permanent revolution' in foreign policy, and a return to full Socialism at home.

Unfortunately Comrade Lenin was not there to settle the argument. Two others both claimed to be his spokesman – Stalin for the Rightist point of view, and Trotsky for the Leftists.

The struggle for power – Stalin v. Trotsky

When Lenin died, Trotsky seemed the person most likely to succeed him (look ahead to Figure 11.3, page 120). A brilliant speaker and writer, commander of the Red Army, Lenin's

Figure 10.4   Honorary militiaman L. B. Kamenev bars the way to the NEP sledge – a Russian cartoon of 1924. Kamenev was a Leftist in the policy debate after Lenin's death.

right-hand man since 1917, Trotsky was the nearest to another Lenin that the Party had. Unlike Lenin, however, he was not personally popular with many other top Bolsheviks. He did not bother to curry favour with them; instead he tried to win their loyalty to his policies, which he declared and defended in fiery speeches at Party Congresses and meetings of the Politburo (the executive committee of the Party). But Trotsky's speeches at these meetings were not what counted in the end. Working behind the scenes, a much less likely candidate was slowly edging his way up to take Lenin's place.

Up to now Josef Stalin had not been outstanding among the Bolshevik leaders. His talent was in administration, and they were glad to let him get on with a dull administrative job as Secretary-General of the Party. In Trotsky's cutting phrase, Stalin was 'the Party's most eminent mediocrity' – in other words, a harmless nobody.

Lenin, as it happened, had seen more dangerous qualities in Stalin. In a political testament shortly before he died, he had made it clear that Stalin should not succeed him; he considered him 'rude' and said he should be sacked from his job as head of the Party. But after Lenin's death, in the interests of Party unity this advice was not discussed – in fact it was not openly published in the Soviet Union until after Stalin's death thirty years later.

So Stalin's future was ensured by Lenin's death. After it, he played a clever political game. As Secretary-General he could appoint his own followers to key posts in the Party – loyal yes-men whose votes could be relied upon at vital Party meetings. Unlike Trotsky he had no strong personal belief in a Right or Left policy, but he rightly sensed that in the blessed calm after the civil war no ordinary Russians, and few in the Party, wanted further upheaval. So he attached himself to the Rightist policy of 'Socialism in one country', and by 1925 this was the policy that the Party Congress approved.

Stalin then made short work of Trotsky. In 1926 he was expelled from the Politburo and in 1927 from the Party – along with seventy-five other leading Leftists. Trotsky was bundled off to a remote corner of the Soviet Union, and in 1929 pushed over the border into exile. After years of wandering from one country to another (no Western government wanted him as a permanent resident), he ended up in Mexico. During the 1930s his anti-Stalin writings and activities became a focus for Trotskyist opposition to Stalin's Soviet Union. In 1940 he was murdered by an agent of Stalin's secret police.

Stalin in control

By 1928 Stalin was the unquestioned leader of the USSR. He was to rule until his death in 1953. 'Socialism in one country' did become the theme of his régime, although not in the Rightist framework of NEP but a Leftist one much more like the previous period of War Communism. This was in fact the domestic policy advocated by Trotsky!

By opting for 'Socialism in one country' Stalin did not officially abandon world revolution – no Marxist could ever do that! – but he shelved it until some future unstated date. In foreign policy and at home, Stalin's overriding concern was *the strength and safety of the Soviet Union*, as the next two chapters will show.

*GLOSSARY

diplomatic recognition, a government's formal acknowledgement that a new group or party is effectively in charge of another country and is therefore its official government. This allows normal relations between the two governments to begin.

Questions

Did you notice?

1. Other left-wing parties were regarded as enemies by the Bolsheviks because (a) they tried to restore the Tsar (b) they wanted Russia to fight Germany (c) they opposed Bolshevik dictatorship
2. The system of War Communism (a) supported the Red Army (b) sabotaged White governments (c) earned the peasants' loyalty
3. Between 1921 and 1927, more than 1,000 railway engines were (a) imported into the USSR (b) exported from the USSR (c) made in the USSR
4. The Treaty of Rapallo was signed by (a) Britain and the USSR (b) France and Germany (c) Germany and the USSR
5. 'Nepmen' were (a) hard-working peasants (b) small traders (c) Bolshevik leaders who supported NEP
6. True or false?
   (i) Foreign intervention increased Soviet fears of the West
   (ii) Russia conquered Poland in 1921
   (iii) In 1921 Lenin abandoned all hope of world revolution
   (iv) Trotsky opposed NEP in 1925
   (v) In 1928 Stalin abandoned all hope of world revolution
   (vi) After 1928 Trotsky continued to oppose Stalin
7. Which statement is *more* accurate?
   (i) (a) Foreign intervention was only to keep Russia in the First World War
   (b) One reason for foreign intervention was 'to strangle Bolshevism in its cradle'
   (ii) Lenin did not want Stalin to succeed him because
   (a) he disliked Stalin's Rightist policy
   (b) he disliked Stalin's personality
   (iii) Leftist policies were not popular in 1925 because
   (a) they did not fit Marxist theory
   (b) they would mean further upheaval in the USSR

Can you explain?

8. What was the Soviet view of foreign intervention in the civil war? What evidence seemed to support this view?
9. Why is Kronstadt described as 'a moment of truth' in the history of Soviet Communism?
10. In what ways was NEP 'a Brest-Litovsk on the economic front'?
11. In 1921 Lenin recognized Russia's weakness in the face of 'Capitalist encirclement'. What changes did he therefore make in Soviet foreign policy?
12. In 1924–5, what were the main arguments put forward by opposing sides for (a) 'Socialism in one country', (b) 'Permanent revolution'?

What's your view?

13. Imagine yourself as a Bolshevik leader who firmly believed in the ideas of Marx and Lenin as outlined in Study Topic 5. Would you have supported NEP in 1921? Would you have supported it in 1925?
14. Many people in Britain shared Churchill's hope that Bolshevism would die in its cradle, yet there was little popular support for the British Government's policy of intervention in Russia in 1918–21. Why not, do you think?
15. Most Western governments disliked the new Soviet Government, but nevertheless they recognized it within a few years. The United States, however, withheld recognition until 1933. Why do you think her government delayed so long? What difficulties may arise when two states do not have diplomatic relations with each other?

11

Soviet Russia under Stalin

By 1928 the Soviet Communist Party had accepted Stalin as its leader and a new general policy of 'Socialism in one country'. The next big task was to make the USSR strong enough to resist attack from the Capitalist West. In 1928 there seemed no immediate danger of that, but after the experience of foreign intervention in the civil war, next time the Red Army must be ready!

The Party leaders were still disputing about the methods by which to build up Soviet strength. The Leftists wanted to get back to Socialist principles and were worried by the growing number of Nepmen and kulaks. The Rightists saw the contribution these 'little Capitalists' were making to national prosperity and thought the government should continue to encourage it. They were content to spread Socialism slowly through Russia's vast and mainly rural population.

As we saw in the previous chapter, Stalin was at first associated with the Rightist point of view. Historians are still not sure why he suddenly switched to Leftist policies so harsh that the scars are still visible in Soviet life today. Did he merely want to get rid of his rivals in the Party? Was he too impatient for the slower job of persuading the Russian people into Socialism? Perhaps he needed an atmosphere of continuous crisis to justify the ruthless one-man rule that 'Stalinism' came to mean.

For whatever reason, in 1928 Stalin embarked on a policy of forced industrialization at break-neck speed. In the course of this programme, not only Nepmen and kulaks but every opponent in the Party was trampled into the ground. Stalin's economic revolution transformed Russia far more radically than

the switch of control at the top that Lenin had accomplished: it *made* the Soviet Union of today.

Before we see how he did it, let's consider what this process of *industrialization* involves. We can understand it best by recalling the familiar pattern of Capitalist development in our own history.

What industrialization involves

Under Capitalism, industry was developed by private enterprise. Private individuals raised the money, or invested their own, to open a factory or sink a mine. If the business prospered, the owners made good profits and could invest some of this accumulated capital to expand the business or start a new one. The more capital they could accumulate, the faster their industries would grow. In late nineteenth-century America, for example, there was no brake on the power of industrial barons like Andrew Carnegie (US Steel) and John D. Rockefeller (Standard Oil) to exploit mercilessly both workers and consumers. They and others built up gigantic fortunes and gigantic industrial empires in one lifetime. Their enterprise, and the sufferings of the people they exploited, created America's advanced industrial economy.

Important economic and social changes followed from industrialization. As workers moved from farming into factories there were larger town populations to feed. The productivity of agriculture had to be raised (fewer men producing more) – or, as in Britain's case, extra food had to be imported. In fast-growing towns there was a shortage of housing and social amenities (roads, drains, transport, schools) which government or private enterprise was slow to meet. These social benefits, remember, *also* had to be paid for out of accumulated capital in the form of taxes paid to the government or by donations to charitable foundations. (If your local library was built around 1900, it may well have been paid for by the Carnegie Foundation. Many libraries in Britain were.)

Industrialization is a complicated and very costly process. It *must* involve saving and investment (which means that the work force must produce more than it consumes), and it is bound to bring social tension and hardship, at least in the early stages. This was certainly true of industrial development under Capitalism, where the social benefits were a long time coming. It was also true of industrialization under Socialism, or at least of the Stalinist version we shall now look at.

THE FIVE-YEAR PLANS

In 1928 Stalin abandoned the New Economic Policy and resumed state ownership of all industry and trade. A system of Five-Year Plans was introduced, in which the government would direct the economy in one vast national effort. This pattern of public ownership and planned production fitted the Marxist model of Socialism, but the aim of the Plans, on a national scale, was the same as any nineteenth-century Capitalist's: to accumulate as much capital as possible as quickly as possible, and spend these profits on expanding industry.

Stalin's government played the part of the hard-headed Capitalist and *managed* the whole economy of the Soviet Union like one huge firm. Workers were driven to produce as much as possible while consuming as little as possible. The farming sector must also serve the one national goal of developing industry: it was ruthlessly squeezed to give up workers for the new factories and to produce grain to feed them – and for export too. (This cruel story is told later, page 117.)

Throughout the 1930s the Five-Year Plans were pushed through like a steam-roller. Stalin's central theme was drummed into every Soviet citizen's ears: 'We are fifty or a hundred years behind the advanced countries. We must make good this lag in ten years. Either we do it, or they crush us.'

1. The development of industry

In the first Five-Year Plan from 1928 to 1932 (it was reckoned to be complete a year ahead of schedule), almost four-fifths of investment went into heavy industry. Before factories could turn out goods, they had first to be built, equipped with machines and supplied with power, i.e. the *means of production* had to be created before production could start. So the main emphasis was on energy supplies (coal, oil, electricity), construction materials (steel, cement, timber) and machine tools. By 1932, the output of machines had increased $4\frac{1}{2}$ times, and of electricity $2\frac{1}{2}$ times; 1,500 new industrial plants had been built (some of them massive, like the iron and steel complex at Magnitogorsk), and more than 100 new towns had appeared. By the end of the first Plan the balance of the economy had changed: industry now contributed 70 per cent of total national production.

Later Plans (the second from 1933–7, and a third begun in 1938 which was interrupted by preparations for war) gave some attention to consumer goods and to the quality of products (by one estimate, as much as 40 per cent of production in the first Plan had to be scrapped). But throughout the Plans, consumer goods were of secondary importance: low targets were set, and even these were often not met. A bitter little joke was passed around: 'Why are Soviet citizens like Adam and Eve? Because they live in Paradise and have nothing to wear!'

Another important feature of the Plans was the development of industry in safe areas east of the Ural mountains. (European Russia to the west of the Urals was vulnerable to attack: in 1941–2 it was almost all overrun by the Germans. As the Red Army retreated,

115

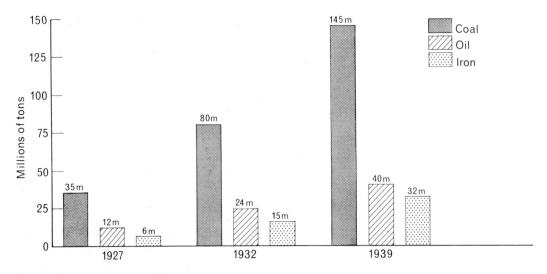

Figure 11.1 Russian production of coal, oil and iron, 1927–39. Under the Five-Year Plans Russia overtook Britain as an industrial nation and was surpassed only by the USA and Germany in 1939.

factories were dismantled and then re-built behind the mountain barrier.)

No one can check the accuracy of Soviet statistics in the 1930s, but today the official figures are generally accepted (Figure 11.1). In any case, the main achievement of the Plans was proved by the USSR's performance in the Second World War. In Churchill's words, it was the Red Army that 'tore the guts out of the German army', and most of their weaponry was Russian-made. In spite of the setbacks of the war, the Plans were a firm foundation for the Soviet Union's post-war industrial development. Today, her industrial power is second only to that of the United States.

How was this stupendous national effort of the 1930s achieved? The methods used were similar to those of War Communism – a mixture of brute force and unceasing propaganda.

Top-downwards planning

Plans for industry were drawn up and controlled by a State Planning Commission (Gosplan) whose job, in theory, was to arrange for the production of every single item from tractors to woollen socks. By gathering information from below, and by sideways co-ordination between different sectors of the economy, Gosplan was supposed to ensure a smooth supply of raw materials and paths of distribution for finished goods. On such a scale, this was an impossible task! Big mistakes were made – such as the decision to concentrate on coal production to the neglect of oil, and the huge resources spent on the Moscow underground when most of Moscow's inhabitants lived in hovels. Right down the line, targets were set and orders given which took no account of local circumstances or human exhaustion.

In the atmosphere of strict regimentation which developed, it became impossible to protest from below or to admit mistakes at the top. Often the only way to meet unrealistic targets was by fiddles or 'cooking the books'*, and this was certainly widely practised. When targets were not met, a worker or manager was branded as a 'wrecker' or an 'enemy of the state' and might end up in a forced labour camp run by the NKVD (secret police). The NKVD managed a convict labour force estimated at about 10 million; they did some of the heaviest construction work (building roads, dams, railways) in the harshest conditions. Untold numbers died in these camps.

Stakhanovites

On the factory floor the methods used to get maximum production were old Capitalist tricks like piece-work (paying for the number of items produced instead of hours worked) and bonus payments to workers who produced more than their fellows. There was a famous record-breaker called Stakhanov, a coalminer who one day in 1935 (working an easy seam and with the best tools and workmates) produced the astonishing output of 102 tons of coal. He and other 'Stakhanovites' became national heroes, rewarded with trips to Moscow, Party membership, medals, holidays and extra pay. Stakhanovite targets were then set as production 'norms' for other workers in the industry, who naturally failed to meet them and so could be paid less than the normal rate of pay.

An army of zealous Party workers (especially the members of Komsomol, the Party youth organization) had the special job of poking and prodding the workforce to ever greater efforts. One method was to organize competitions between one factory and another, but since competition is an un-Socialist word this was called 'social joint emulation'!

Life under the Plans

Ordinary life for Russian workers under the Plans was certainly grim and grey. All consumer goods were in short supply, housing was crude and insanitary, food was often rationed. But there was a positive side too. Many Russians, especially young people, could feel that their country was 'going places' at last. Of course Party propaganda repeated this message endlessly, but the evidence was there, in the new towns and industries springing up. And some of the benefits of planned Socialist development were already available in the 1930s: schooling and job-training for many, and basic medical facilities for people who had had none before. By 1940 there were more doctors per thousand people than in Britain or America. Before the idea of a worker's right to holidays

with pay was generally accepted in the Capitalist West, many Soviet workers had holidays organized and paid for by the state.

2. The collectivization of agriculture

Alongside the Plans in industry, in 1929 Stalin began the collectivization of agriculture. Individual farms and smallholdings were merged into large collective farms in which the land was jointly owned and worked by the peasants who lived on it.

Collectivization was most cruelly enforced. It left Russian agriculture bruised and bleeding. Even today the patient has not recovered, as is shown by the large imports of food needed by Russia – a country which in Tsarist times was an exporter of grain! The reasons for this harsh and short-sighted policy of collectivization are again to be found in the overall economic Plan and in Stalin's intolerance of *any* political opposition.

(a) The economic reasons

Under the Plans, industry had first priority and agriculture had to serve its needs. It was essential to increase the output of grain, not only to feed the growing town populations, but to trade for machinery and technical advice imported from the West. Production could be greatly increased, it was thought, in larger farming units run by the state. Tractors and scientific farming would gradually replace horses and hand tools, and everyone (when they were used to the idea) would cheerfully work for the success of this collective enterprise.

(b) The political reasons

The Land Decree of 1917 had never intended the land to become the personal property of the peasants. They were merely put in charge, as it were, until some form of common ownership and production could be organized. But very few peasants were followers of the Bolshevik Party, or even knew what their policies were. The only part of the revolution that mattered to them was the chance (as they interpreted it) to take what was rightfully theirs.

Since 1917 the land question had been shelved by force of events. In the famine of 1921 the nation's bread-growers had to be pacified by NEP, which had deliberately encouraged thrifty and hard-working peasants to enrich themselves even at the expense of poorer peasants in the village. Now the very success of NEP had become an embarrassment to the Party: a new class structure had begun to develop in the villages. Stalin saw the danger. These kulaks must be slapped down, and the Socialist plan for agriculture fulfilled at once!

The elimination of the kulaks

In 1929 Stalin announced that 'the kulaks must be eliminated as a class'. Squads of Party workers were despatched to the countryside to carry out his instruction. The historian J. N. Westwood describes what happened:

> ... 1929 and 1930 were the years of the collectivization drive. The richer peasants, who saw they had nothing to gain and then discovered they had nothing to lose either, expressed their despair by burning their crops, killing their cattle and destroying their machinery. In places there was armed resistance and in March 1930 Stalin ... realized that he had gone too far too fast. Accusing officials of being 'dizzy with success', he implied that collectivization had been rushed against his wishes. Many farms were de-collectivized but nevertheless by the end of 1934 87 per cent of farmland was collective, and 99 per cent by 1937.[†]

Some poorer peasants who owned little or no land were glad to move into the security of a collective farm. Many others disliked the new policy as much as the kulaks did. But however rich or poor they were, all who resisted were branded as kulaks. If they would not go into a collective farm they were deported to labour camps, transplanted to remote areas of Russia, or in the last resort they were killed. In this way the whole kulak class (about 5 million people) was destroyed by the mid-1930s.

The results of collectivization

The short-term result of all this was yet another terrible famine. To quote Westwood again:

> The chaos of collectivization – peasant resistance, lack of machinery, no clear idea of how the new farms were to be organized – led naturally to poor harvests. Nevertheless, all grain in the growing areas was collected by force and taken to the towns or exported. The peasants then began to die of starvation. About 10 to 15 million people died in the 1932–34 famine ... The government made every effort to conceal the famine from the outside world and this meant there could be no appeal for international aid. The U.S.S.R. continued to export grain in exchange for industrial plant. It has been alleged, probably with some truth, that the famine was not unwelcome to Stalin; it was an effective way to break peasant resistance.[‡]

The long-term results of forced collectivization were just as serious. The collectives were managed by Party officials who often had little knowledge of farming. There were not enough tractors in the regional Motor Tractor Stations (MTS) which were supposed to modernize farming techniques. The number of cattle, horses and pigs in the country was halved by the slaughter which accompanied collectivization. But most serious of all to Russian agriculture were the human losses: all the energetic and enterprising peasants had been swept away as 'kulaks' or to work in factories. Those who were left

[†]J. N. Westwood, *Russia 1917 to 1964* (Batsford, 1966) pp. 86–7.

[‡]Westwood, op. cit.

Figure 11.2   A cartoon in the Soviet magazine *Krokodil*, 1939, shows the peasant's 'selfish' pride in his private plot while the collective fields are neglected. This is still a problem for the Soviet Government today.

to run the collective farms were resentful and utterly dispirited.

The collective farms (*kolkhoz*), and a smaller number of state farms (*sovkhoz*) in which peasants are paid a wage like factory workers, are the basic units of Soviet agriculture today. As well as the land which is collectively farmed, each peasant family in a *kolkhoz* has a private plot – a large garden where they can keep pigs and poultry, grow vegetables, and produce dairy products. Until the 1960s the state bought the collective output of the *kolkhoz*, and an agreed quota from the private plots, at low prices; above this quota, peasants could sell their surplus for a higher price in private markets. Later they were allowed to sell *all* their private production in this way.

This concession to private enterprise was part of a determined effort by Stalin's successors to increase the nation's food supply (see Chapter 13). Official encouragement of private plot production nowadays shows that

the main weakness of the Soviet collectivized system still hasn't been solved. What is really missing from it is the 'TLC factor' (TLC =Tender Loving Care). In the collective fields the peasant does his duty and no more; his private plot gets his Tender Loving Care (Figure 11.2). The result is that although private plots occupy only a tiny percentage of cultivated land, they produce 25 per cent of total farm output. Not only peasant families but their customers in town markets have reason to be grateful for private plots.

THE PURGES

Up to this point the other Bolshevik leaders who helped Lenin to launch the first Socialist state have scarcely been mentioned. In this chapter their names appear, but only to have their epitaphs written in the horrific story of the purges. In a series of state trials after 1934 – or without even the formality of a

119

trial – all the 'old Bolsheviks' and countless thousands of lesser Party members were liquidated quite as ruthlessly as the kulaks. All the old gang save *one*, we should say – and no prizes for guessing the lone survivor!

First let's look at the bare facts of the story.

The victims

1. The Party

In December 1934 Kirov, a member of the Politburo and a possible rival to Stalin, was assassinated. His murder was probably arranged by Stalin to provide the excuse for the terror which followed. The crime was blamed on Leftists, including two of Stalin's other rivals, Zinoviev and Kamenev, who later confessed and were shot. In the next four years every anti-Stalinist was systematically combed out of the Party. They were accused of plotting against Stalin, spying, or spreading Trotskyist propaganda (Figure 11.3). Their sentence was death or a labour camp, which usually meant the same thing. Out of 139 members of the Party's Central Committee of 1934, 98 were later arrested and most were shot. Out of 1,966 delegates to the

Figure 11.3 Trotsky – the cause of all the trouble? Many of Stalin's purge victims were accused of conspiring with Trotsky in exile.

Party Congress of the same year, 1,108 suffered the same fate.

2. The Red Army

This was the next target. In 1937, starting with the Commander-in-Chief, Tukhachevsky (a hero of the civil war), a series of courts-martial removed two-thirds of the officers above the rank of colonel, including 13 out of 15 generals! They were all 'spies'.

3. The secret police

Even the purgers themselves were not safe. Stalin turned on the NKVD for all the world like a gangster rubbing out his own boys so they could not squeal on the boss! In 1936 the NKVD head Yagoda was tried, shot, and replaced by Yezhov. In 1938 it was Yezhov's turn: he and other officials were accused of 'excessive zeal' in carrying out the purges and were shot. Stalin's new man Beria took Yezhov's place.

The 'show trials' of 1936 and 1938 were the most dramatic feature of this blood-bath. Foreign observers, both enemies and friends of the Soviet Union, gaped in amazement to see well-known Bolshevik leaders paraded before the Chief State Prosecutor Vyshinsky, who accused them of every kind of treachery and treason. Even more amazing, they *confessed* to these crimes! A few committed suicide before the trial; a few withdrew their confessions in open court. Then the trial would be adjourned to refresh the victim's memory; when it resumed he admitted he was guilty after all, and was shot†.

Bukharin, Rykov, Radek, Tomsky – these names were as well known in the Soviet Union of the 1930s as Kinnock, Owen and Thatcher are known to us today. What did ordinary Russians think as one by one their respected leaders were denounced as traitors? Whatever their private thoughts, they had better say nothing. The NKVD's knock at the

†Arthur Koestler's novel, *Darkness at Noon*, gives a good idea of how these 'confessions' were obtained.

door in the night spread down to every local Party cell and even beyond Party membership. No one knows how many Soviet citizens disappeared in these years.

The results of the purges

After 1938 the worst of the terror died away. Perhaps Stalin realized the damage it was doing to the Soviet Union. By the end of the 1930s the Party – and therefore the government and administration of the USSR – had lost its most able and experienced workers. The Red Army had been 'be-headed': the disgraced senior officers were hurriedly replaced by raw young men with no combat experience. This almost led to disaster when Germany attacked the USSR in 1941.

The purges – along with the strong-arm tactics of the Plans and collectivization – made the Soviet people into a flock of trembling sheep. They were quiet, obedient and ready with exaggerated praise for 'the great leader'. Alongside Lenin, Stalin's face adorned every hoarding; heroic statues grew like mushrooms in every town square. Stalin himself rewrote the history of the Party to show himself as the right-hand man of Lenin, whom everyone worshipped. No bleat of protest was heard against Stalin until after his death in 1953.

Why?

Was the terror just an exhibition of Stalin's thirst for personal power? That was certainly an element in his character. But the great events of history are never solely the work of one man, though we are often tempted to think so. At least three other factors contributed to the purges:

1. The Five-Year Plans

The Plans set a pace of economic development which left no time to argue about this or that aspect of general policy. At the beginning other leaders did argue (it was said that Stalin's wife's suicide in 1932 was due to her distress at the cruelties of collectivization). But Stalin would not stop for debate. If others in the Party continued to criticize, they must be silenced altogether.

2. *The fear of foreign attack*

After 1933 the USSR had good reason to fear the growing power and aggressive policies of Hitler's Germany. (You will see in Chapter 12 that Stalin's foreign policy in this period turned this way and that to try to keep the Soviet Union safe.) When societies feel themselves threatened, they look for a strong leader. Criticism of 'Him' soon becomes unpatriotic: 'He' knows what to do, and we must obey! Stalin knew just how to exploit these fears.

3. *The ideology of Marxism–Leninism*

The ideas of Marxism–Leninism in a way 'justified' the purges. Loyalty to the State or the Party (in the Soviet Union it is the same thing) is more important than loyalty to the individual. Therefore to set yourself against the Party is the worst crime, for the Party *must* be right. In this way many Communists accepted the purges as a necessary 'purification' of the Party, and their acceptance of this principle helped Stalin to carry out his work. He used an army of other people and well-established practices to do it.

Above all, his policies rested on the nature of the Bolshevik Party. The top-downwards structure of the Party almost invited the top man to become a dictator. Usually Lenin did not exercise his power in that way – but Stalin did. It was also part of Bolshevik tradition to wipe out the opposition by force and Lenin must share responsibility for this. Lenin created the Cheka and in 1921 allowed the Red Army to shoot down 'like partridges' the sailors of Kronstadt. Stalin only carried to extremes what others had begun. And regrettably this thread of steel in Bolshevik thinking runs on from Lenin and Stalin into official Communist doctrine today. In 1977 a group of citizens in Communist Czechoslovakia were told by the Party newspaper to cease their campaign for civil liberties or they would get 'what they deserved'. 'Those who lie on the rails to stop the train of history must expect to have their legs chopped off.'†

WAS STALIN REALLY NECESSARY?

This heading for a final comment on Stalin's rule is borrowed from Alec Nove, a well-known writer on Soviet affairs. It is a question historians are still debating. Looking back on the 1930s after the Second World War, Western Europe had good reason to be grateful for Stalin's economic revolution: it gave the USSR the strength to beat the German army. This hard fact is often used to excuse the cruelties of Stalin's rule: 'Tough luck on the poor Russians, but thanks anyway, Uncle Joe!'

On the other hand many of Stalin's policies were not far-sighted 'good sense' but dangerous self-inflicted wounds. Although he recognized the threat from Hitler before Britain and France did, in the end Stalin badly misjudged Hitler's intentions and was taken by surprise when Germany attacked the USSR. The purges had so weakened the Red Army that it was almost defeated in the first year of the war. Collectivization had earned the Soviet Government such hatred that some peasants (in the Ukraine, for example) were ready to collaborate with the German invaders. It is sometimes said that the Soviet Union won the war in spite of, rather than because of, Stalin's pre-war policies. And it cost another 20 million Russian lives to do it.

Stalin, however, was not the only statesman to misjudge Hitler, as we shall see in the next chapter.

*GLOSSARY

'cooking the books', making false entries, e.g. in a company's accounts, to deceive an inspector.

†From an editorial in *Rudé Právo*, 12 January 1977, quoted in a BBC TV 'Panorama' programme, 13 June 1977.

Questions

Did you notice?

1. The Carnegie Foundation (a) developed Soviet industry (b) built libraries in Britain (c) exploited American oilfields
2. The first Five-Year Plan emphasized (a) heavy industry (b) consumer goods (c) the quality of goods produced
3. 'Stakhanovites' (a) were sent to labour camps (b) worked harder than their work-mates (c) built the Moscow underground
4. The kulaks were eliminated because (a) they were lazy (b) they used old-fashioned methods (c) they were becoming a political threat
5. A *sovkhoz* is (a) a state farm (b) a private plot (c) a tractor station
6. True or false?
   (i) Collectivization increased the number of pigs in Russia
   (ii) Vyshinsky was the head of the NKVD
   (iii) Peasants are allowed to sell surplus produce for private profit
   (iv) Electricity production more than doubled between 1928 and 1932
   (v) The USSR today is self-sufficient in food
7. Which statement is *more* accurate?
   (i) Many Communists believed the purges were justified because
      (a) this was the best way to ensure loyalty to Stalin
      (b) anyone who opposed the Party must be in the wrong
   (ii) The performance of Russian agriculture today suggests that
      (a) the peasants still dislike the collective system
      (b) the ideology of Communism is now accepted
   (iii) The Red Army's victory over the German army was due to

(a) Stalin's foresight
(b) the industrial achievements of the Plans

Can you explain?

8. Why was it necessary for Russian workers to produce more than they consumed in the 1930s?
9. In carrying out the Plans, what was the function of (a) Gosplan, (b) 'Stakhanovites'? a) P. 116   B) P. 117.
10. Why was it necessary to increase agricultural output under the Plans? How was collectivization supposed to achieve this? What were the 'human losses' which followed from this policy?
11. In what sense did the purges 'rest on the nature of the Bolshevik party'?
12. What were the overall results of the purges in the USSR?

What's your view?

13. One day in 1937 young Boris comes home to visit his parents. He now works in a lorry factory and is a keen member of the Komsomol. They reluctantly joined a *kolkhoz* five years ago, but they don't like it much. Think up a family discussion about what is happening in Russia.
14. Why are piece-work and bonus payments referred to as 'Capitalist tricks'? Why were they used in a Socialist country? Was there anything 'wrong' in doing so?
15. One historian writes: 'By 1941 the situation of the Soviet worker resembled Marx's description of the nineteenth-century European proletariat.' What does he mean? Was it entirely true? How might a loyal member of the CPSU answer this charge?

12

Soviet Foreign Policy, 1918–41

When the Bolsheviks took power in Russia they had two Marxist missions to carry out:

1. To create the first Socialist state.
2. To promote and encourage world revolution.

The first job was the task of the Soviet Government which they immediately formed. The second was assigned to the *Comintern*, set up in 1919. This was an association of national Communist parties, supposedly meeting on equal terms, but its headquarters were in Moscow and it was always, not surprisingly, dominated by the Soviet Party.

In the first flush of success after 1917, hopes were high for both of these aims. But as we have seen, the Party was soon blown off course by the struggle to stay in power. By 1921 Lenin was forced to recognize and come to terms with the opposition at home and abroad. It will be useful to recapitulate the events leading to this change of front before we see how Stalin developed Soviet foreign policy after Lenin's death.

FOREIGN RELATIONS IN THE 1920s

1918   The Treaty of Brest-Litovsk. To avoid being overrun by the Germans, the new government made peace with Germany. This was seen as a stab in the back by Russia's First World War allies, who therefore intervened in the Russian civil war.

1919   The Comintern was set up to help Communist revolutions abroad.

1918–21   Civil war. The Reds eventually won control from the Whites.

Foreign intervention was bitterly resented; it convinced the Soviet Government of undying Western hostility.

1921   The war had exhausted the Russian economy. Meanwhile, Communist risings abroad had been defeated. Lenin decided to soft-pedal world revolution and concentrate on building up Soviet strength. He introduced NEP and established diplomatic and trade relations with foreign governments – for example, the Treaty of Rapallo with Germany in 1922.

1928   Lenin's decision of 1921 was confirmed by Stalin's policy of 'Socialism in one country'. (Stalin's attitude to foreign affairs was a natural outgrowth of this policy, as we shall see.)

The activities of the Comintern

By 1921 the Soviet Government had come to terms with Capitalist governments abroad. But the Comintern was not disbanded, for to have done this would have looked like abandoning world revolution, which no Marxist party could do. For several years the Comintern continued to encourage Communist subversion abroad. Thus it would sometimes happen that Soviet diplomats were trying to negotiate an agreement with a government which the Comintern was working to overthrow! Foreign governments were annoyed at what seemed to them the 'two faces' of Soviet foreign policy, while the Soviet Government seemed to be genuinely surprised that its friendly approaches were so coolly received!

Under Stalin, however, the two faces did merge into one. He saw the Comintern as a useful instrument to promote Soviet interests abroad, and used it for that purpose. Thus if it did not suit the Soviet Union to agitate against the bourgeois government of another country, a new 'Party line' would be transmitted through the Comintern telling the Communist Party in that country to change its tactics. Moscow dictated the Party line and foreign Communists were just expected to follow it without question. When the line changed they often had to perform embarrassing somersaults which discredited the cause of Communism in their own countries. This did not bother Stalin, and we should not be too surprised at his attitude. Stalin was above all a national leader. He had inherited the Marxist duty to promote world Communism (and he continued to pay lip-service* to it) but he was always mainly concerned, as every national leader is, with his own country's interests.

STALIN'S FOREIGN POLICY IN THE 1930s

For some years after 1928 the Soviet Government was preoccupied with the economic development of the USSR and paid little attention to foreign affairs. Foreign Communist parties danced to Stalin's tune, and on his instructions they opposed all 'bourgeois' political parties in their own countries, whether of the Left or the Right. In Germany, for example, they regarded both the extreme right-wing Nazi Party and the moderate left-wing Social Democrats as equally reactionary 'class enemies'.

The menace of Fascism

But in 1934 Stalin had to sit up and take notice of what was happening in Europe. Hitler's Nazi Party, which he had mistaken for 'just another bourgeois party', was now in power in Germany and was showing itself to be something much more dangerous. Hitler was rapidly rearming Germany and announced his intention to recover German losses from the First World War and then to extend his new empire eastwards towards Russia.

Hitler's doctrine of Nazism was an extreme and vicious form of *Fascism*, a political creed which first appeared in Italy in the 1920s. There is no simple definition of Fascism: it can only be understood with reference to past and present Fascist régimes. Study Topic 6 (page 130) describes some of these and lists their common features. From this you will see that Fascism was anti-democratic but it was even more strongly *anti-Communist*. Each national version of Fascism had its own character, but they all gave more power to the existing ruling class, whether it was a traditional aristocracy or Capitalist 'barons of industry'. Fascism glorified The State almost to the status of a god which every citizen should serve and worship. International Communism, which called on 'workers of the *world*' to overthrow the ruling class, was therefore Enemy No. 1.

Nazism in Germany added a 'master race' theory: its own Aryan race was destined to rule, and had the *right* to rule, all 'inferior peoples' such as Jews, Slavs and non-whites of all kinds. Russians and East Europeans were Slavs, and their lands were marked out as *lebensraum* (living space) for the future masters of Europe – the Germans.

Steps towards the Second World War

Looking back at the 1930s it seems that the Second World War was inevitable from the moment that Hitler came to power in 1933. But at the time no one could bear to think of another war while the memory of 1914–18 was still so fresh and painful. Britain and France followed a policy of *appeasement* (k) by which they hoped to satisfy Hitler's appetite for territory, until in 1939 it became clear that nothing less than a German conquest of all Europe would do that. The Western democracies mistrusted Stalin as much as they dis-

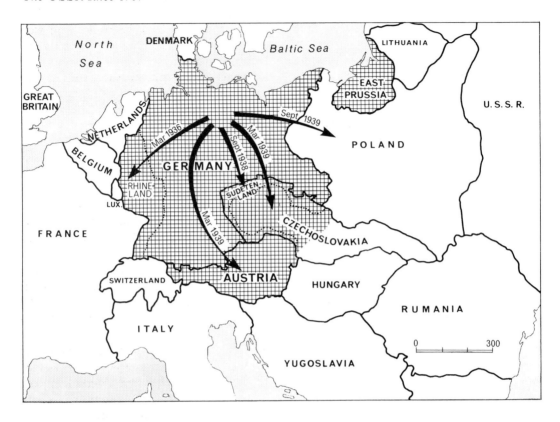

Figure 12.1   Steps to war, 1936–9.

liked Hitler and so they were unable to achieve a common front with the USSR against Germany until Hitler himself forged that partnership by waging war against all of them.

Here is a brief summary of the events leading to the outbreak of war between Germany and the USSR in June 1941. We follow them through Soviet eyes, and there is no space here to explain each event in detail. But it is not important to know all the details so long as you grasp the main theme of Stalin's policy: his desperate effort to avoid an attack on the Soviet Union. The map (Figure 12.1) will help you to see, as he did, the increasing danger of this with every passing year.

The starting point of Hitler's foreign policy was Germany's desire for revenge for the humiliating Treaty of Versailles (see page 4). Hitler promised to wipe out this shameful memory and make Germany great again.

1933	Hitler embarked on a huge re-armament programme. This was forbidden by the 1919 Treaty of Versailles, but no one could enforce it.
1934	Germany signed a pact with Poland (which had a common frontier with Russia and was a traditional enemy of hers). The USSR joined the League of Nations and began to look for friends.
1935	The USSR signed a mutual assistance pact with France and Czechoslovakia. The Comintern instructed European Communist parties to form a 'Popular Front against Fascism' (now recognized by Stalin as the main enemy) with all left-wing political parties.
1936	Germany sent troops into the

Rhineland (along her border with France). This also went against the 1919 Treaty: the Rhineland was supposed to remain a de-militarized buffer zone between the two countries.

Germany and Japan signed the Anti-Comintern Pact. Italy joined it in 1937.

1938   Hitler forced a union of Germany and Austria – also forbidden by the Versailles Treaty.

Sept.   *Munich Crisis.* Hitler demanded
1938   the Sudetenland, a German-speaking area of Czechoslovakia (see Figure 12.1). Stalin offered to help the Czechs, but under the pact of 1935 this action depended on France doing likewise. Instead, France followed Britain's lead: by the Munich Agreement Britain, France, Germany and Italy forced the Czechs to give up the Sudetenland. Despite their obvious interest in the matter, the Soviet and Czech governments were not represented at the talks which led to this Agreement.

March   Germany took most of what
1939   remained of Czechoslovakia.
1936–9   *Spanish Civil War.* Events in Spain reinforced Stalin's growing suspicion that France and Britain wanted Fascism to succeed, and might be glad to stand by while Fascism and Communism fought each other to death. In 1936 Franco launched a Fascist revolt against the legal Republican Government. Fascist Italy and Nazi Germany helped Franco, but Britain and France stuck to a policy of non-intervention. The USSR aided the Republicans but as usual Stalin's main concern was Soviet self-interest. Thus he tried to bend the Republicans' cause so that if they won, Spain would be a loyal Soviet pawn. But they

didn't: by 1939 Franco had won the war and established a Fascist régime in Spain.

Summer   Despite their basic distrust of each
1939   other, Britain and the USSR began talks to work out a common policy against the German threat. They failed to reach agreement.

Aug.   *Nazi–Soviet Non-Aggression Pact.*
1939   This sudden 'about-face' in Soviet policy astonished everyone. By secret clauses it gave Hitler a free hand in Western Europe, and Russia a free hand to recover territories she had lost by the Treaty of Brest-Litovsk in 1918. Soon after Hitler invaded Poland from the West, Russia moved into East Poland, Estonia, Latvia and Lithuania.

Sept.   Hitler invaded Poland. Britain and
1939   France then declared war, as they had guaranteed Polish frontiers. This was the beginning of the Second World War.

The Nazi–Soviet Pact

One British MP called the Nazi–Soviet Pact the 'double-dyed treachery of the Kremlin*' – and it certainly looked like a betrayal of everything that Communism (and Democracy) stood for (Figure 12.2). How can we explain Stalin's public somersault? Once again he had set aside all principle in sheer desperation to save the USSR from war. The Nazi–Soviet Pact was a policy of 'I'm all right, Jack' on an international scale. It was 'Socialism in *one* country – and the devil take the rest!'

Hitler's Blitzkrieg*

As German troops swarmed over Western Europe, Stalin continued to build up Soviet defences. In the winter of 1939–40 the USSR won a little war against Finland – not without difficulty – and took back part of that country

Figure 12.2   The 'double-dyed treachery of the Kremlin'–a British view of the Nazi–Soviet Pact, September 1939.

(also lost by the Treaty of Brest-Litovsk in 1918) as another 'cushion' to protect the Soviet Union. The USSR was 'punished' for this aggression by being expelled from the League of Nations.

During 1940 Stalin watched anxiously as Hitler conquered Western Europe with alarming speed. By June 1940 Britain stood alone against Germany ... But surely Hitler could not want a war on two fronts? He couldn't be planning to take on Russia as well, could he?

Operation Barbarossa

Stalin's behaviour in the next few months is hard to explain. Hitler was indeed planning an attack on Russia. Both British and Soviet intelligence services discovered details of this plan and told Stalin what was brewing. But he either refused to believe the reports, or he

still had faith – goodness knows why – in Hitler's promise of August 1939. Stalin was actually away on holiday when German troops launched their massive onslaught on Russia: Operation Barbarossa began on 22 June 1941 (see map, Figure 21.2, on page 226).

Like it or not, Britain and the USSR were now partners against a common enemy. Japan's attack on Pearl Harbor in December 1941 brought in the USA to make up the Big Three which eventually defeated Germany and her allies.

THE USSR AT WAR

The story of the Second World War will be briefly told later (pages 225–9). Here, as in our study of America, it is useful to make one or two points which will help to explain Soviet attitudes after the war.

1. The Big Three partnership

Despite their co-operation to win the war against Germany and Japan, it must be obvious by now that there was no other unity of purpose between the Big Three. Wartime propaganda in the West was full of (well-deserved) praise for 'our gallant Russian ally', and as a gesture of friendship the USSR dissolved the Comintern in 1943. But every Western politician knew that this did not cancel the international aims of Marxism!

The Russians were no less suspicious of the West. Since foreign intervention in 1918 the Soviet Government had always suspected the motives of Capitalist governments. The events of the 1930s had only confirmed in Stalin's mind this firm belief: no foreign government, except one under Soviet control, could ever be trusted. In 1945, whatever grandiose plans his wartime allies might have for 'a just and lasting peace', Stalin's foreign policy was still what it had always been: to preserve the security of the Soviet Union. He therefore insisted on a post-war settlement in Europe which would protect the USSR, regardless of other people's wishes.

2. Russian losses

The USSR suffered appalling destruction and loss of life during the war. The Germans at one time occupied an area of Russia which contained two-thirds of her heavy industry and four-fifths of her population. Much of the industry was moved eastwards and so were many minority peoples whose loyalty to the USSR was doubtful (many of them never returned to their homelands in Western Russia).† The human losses were terrible. Red Army victories were often won at the sacrifice of many thousands of men killed or captured. Millions died in prison camps. In German-occupied areas whole villages were destroyed and every inhabitant killed (Figure 12.3)–100,000 Jews in one massacre alone. Three million young Russians were deported to forced labour camps in Germany, and few returned. Over a million citizens of Leningrad starved in the two-year siege of the city, which never surrendered.

Twenty million Russian dead! Can we wonder that Stalin, even the cold-blooded man we have seen, was determined never to allow another foreign boot on Russian soil?

†See below, p. 141.

Figure 12.3   Russia at war: Russian partisans hanged by the Germans, 1941.

Study Topic 6

What is Fascism?

In the first place Fascism has a historical meaning as the system of government practised in Italy between 1922 and 1943 by the dictator Mussolini. Later the word was applied in a wider sense to other right-wing régimes with similar features. But we have to be careful here. In political argument the term 'Fascist' is sometimes used by left-wingers to describe any right-wing view they dislike, just as 'Communist' is used by right-wingers to label all ideas of the Left. To find a more exact meaning for Communism we can refer back to the ideas of Marx and Lenin. Fascism has no equivalent theory behind it – but it does mean something more than just right-wing.

Here is a brief explanation of Fascism in its historical context. From this we can arrive at a rough definition of what the word means in politics today.

FASCIST ITALY

After the First World War Italy had social and economic problems, as other countries of Europe did. There were strikes, riots and seizures of land by the peasants in the countryside. The middle classes – like those in other Capitalist countries – were frightened by the spectre of Bolshevism in Russia. All this was very unsettling in a country which, although it had a democratic form of government, had no strong political tradition to support Democracy – as Britain and America had, for example.

Against this background of confusion and anxiety Mussolini's Fascist Party grew in popularity. Fascism offered 'to save Italy from Bolshevism' and promised to restore to a demoralized country the power and glory of the ancient Roman Empire. The Fascist movement adopted as its emblem the *fasces*, a bundle of rods with an axe in the middle,

which was the symbol of state power in ancient Rome – hence the word Fascism.

Fascism attracted discontented people of all kinds: unemployed ex-soldiers, the depressed middle classes, patriotic youths, hungry peasants. The Fascists dressed in black shirts and boots and shouted about a great national cause which offered something to everyone: jobs, prosperity, national glory. Their 'political argument' was terrorism and street warfare which the government was too weak to control. When powerful industrial interests gave support to Fascism, Mussolini – *Il Duce* (the leader) – came to power with a march on Rome in 1922. He immediately set up a military dictatorship and organized the economy in what was called a Corporate State. The government undertook some public works similar to those of the New Deal in America. Mussolini built up the army and used it to extend the Italian empire in North Africa by conquering Abyssinia (the country now called Ethiopia) in 1935–6.

Fascism seemed successful because it imposed *order* on a disorderly country. Outside Italy Mussolini was regarded as a pompous clown, but people noted with approval that 'he made the trains run on time'. In recognition of that achievement his gangster methods were overlooked.

Mussolini tried to make his régime respectable by calling Fascism a philosophy, but there were no real ideas in what he said except the simple doctrine that The State (and therefore its Leader) must be worshipped and obeyed. He wrote down his 'theory' in grand-sounding but meaningless phrases like 'The State is the conscience and universal will of mankind.' His popular slogans were easy to understand, however: 'Mussolini is always right'; 'No discussion, only obedience'; 'Believe – Obey – Fight'.

Other right-wing dictators of the 1930s copied the political methods of Fascist Italy, adapting them to fit the circumstances and traditions of their own countries. In Spain, for example, General Franco allied the Army with the existing aristocracy and the Catholic Church. His Fascist régime lived on into the 1970s. Others like Nazi Germany and several régimes in Eastern Europe (and Fascist Italy itself) were defeated and disgraced in the Second World War.

NAZI GERMANY

By far the most 'successful' and sinister of all the Fascist states was Nazi Germany. After the First World War Germany had problems similar to Italy's, and she also had to bear the shame and punishment of losing the war. The shaky democracy set up in 1919 was never accepted by the upper class, who looked back with longing to the Kaiser's Germany. They and many other Germans welcomed Hitler's creed of Nazism, which was easily grafted onto well-established traditions in German history: obedience to authority, militarism, and a romantic worship of 'the Nation'. It also fitted in with widespread anti-Semitism* in Germany which Hitler did not invent, but exploited to the full†.

In Germany, the Fascist idea of national superiority appeared as a 'master race' theory which claimed historical roots in the ideas of nineteenth-century German philosophers. Since Germans were superior people, Germany's defeat in the First World War could not be the fault of the German Army, so scapegoats must be found. Hitler named them: Bolsheviks, Jews and Social Democrats had 'stabbed the army in the back' and now these people were the cause of all the post-war troubles. When the Great Depression made conditions even worse in the early 1930s, millions of Germans were happy to

accept Hitler's analysis of their situation. By 1933 the Nazis were the largest party and Hitler became Chancellor. Once in power, he dismantled the framework of democracy and established a one-party state.

Other features of Nazi Germany also followed the pattern in Italy. Hitler's methods of persuasion were the same as Mussolini's: the black-jack and a kick in the groin. The Nazis, like the Fascists, had the support of big business. Hitler too launched public works projects like road-building and, most important, a massive rearmament programme which provided jobs for the 6 million unemployed.

The efforts of Fascist governments to reduce unemployment suggest a link between Socialist ideas and Fascism (indeed the full name of the Nazi party was the National Socialist German Workers' Party). The common thread is *strong government action*, supposedly in the national interest. In their rise to power both Mussolini and Hitler vaguely promised a better deal for workers, perhaps to wean their votes away from left-wing parties. But the promise did not amount to much. Their régimes did not in any way alter the social structure: the same ruling class stayed on top. Except for a few individuals, both in Italy and Germany the upper class supported (and were supported by) the Fascist government.

Before long millions of Germans were ready to follow *Der Führer* (The Leader) to the ends of the earth. Anyone who doubted the new ideology either fled the country or fell into terrified silence. Those who spoke out against it were sent to join the Jews, gipsies and other 'human trash' in Nazi concentration camps. The Nazis had a flair for dramatic public display and soon had the whole nation (it seemed) chanting that mindless, fanatical slogan: 'One State, One People, One Führer'. Thus the whole nation backed Hitler's deadly philosophy: 'War is eternal. War is life.'

Hitler's so-called theories had no moral or scientific basis, but the policies he based on them were all too successful at first. His 'final solution' to the Jewish problem sent 6 million

†Similarly the British National Front party did not invent racialism in Britain today. As their national organizer told a reporter in 1976, 'It is not the Front who have "stirred up" racial intolerance. The feeling was there already. We are merely *organizing* it.' (Article by Tom Forester, 'The Front Line', in *New Society*, 15 July 1976.)

Jews to their deaths. His ambition for world conquest began the holocaust of the Second World War and ultimately brought disaster to his own country and people.

FASCISM AFTER THE WAR

After the Second World War Italy and the western part of Germany were both reorganized as liberal democracies. Fascism and Nazism were utterly discredited. But the fear of a Fascist revival persisted in the post-war world, especially in countries such as Soviet Russia which had suffered most from German aggression. This fear strongly influenced Soviet policy towards Germany, as we shall see in Part IV.

In a general sense Fascism lives on today in the practices of some extreme right-wing governments, for example the military dictatorship of 'the Colonels' in Greece from 1967–74, and in the attraction which Fascism holds for some people. Certain political groups in the West – the National Front in Britain, the John Birch Society in the United States – echo the ideas of pre-war Fascism. What *are* these ideas?

A summary of Fascist ideas

The writings of Mussolini and Hitler do not provide an intelligible ideology of Fascism – they are just confused scribblings. But we can make up a kind of 'identikit' of Fascist ideas – a list of common features which you can see in the historical examples described above, and in some right-wing régimes today: a strong leader; glorification of the state; denial of personal liberties; obedience to authority; aggressive nationalism; encouragement of violence and war.

To keep itself in power and to prevent the free circulation of ideas, an efficient Fascist government will try to control every aspect of national life: the economy, trade unions, the press, education, cultural activities, etc. Nazi Germany achieved a *totalitarian* system like this, but it was not so easily imposed on the more individualistic Italians.

Totalitarianism was also a feature of Stalin's rule in Russia. It was satirized in George Orwell's famous book *1984*, which summed up both Hitler and Stalin in one catch-phrase: *Big Brother is watching you.*

Why?

One big question remains. Why do people accept and support dictators, whether of the Left or the Right? Psychological reasons have been suggested. Social and economic difficulties often give some excuse for it. But until we have a fuller explanation of why ordinary people will allow one man, often acting in their name, to brutalize or kill millions of their fellow human beings, the world has no permanent safeguard against a future Hitler or Stalin.

*GLOSSARY

anti-Semitism, prejudice against Jews, or persecution of them.

Blitzkrieg (German), lightning war.

Kremlin, the main government building in Moscow, and the meaning is now often transferred, as here, to the Soviet Government itself.

to pay lip-service, to give formal approval to a rule or idea without intending to act upon it.

KEYWORD

appeasement, a policy of pacifying, or satisfying an appetite – for example, by throwing food to a hungry lion. The policy of Britain and France towards Hitler was called appeasement because they allowed him to take what he wanted (or even gave it to him), hoping he would not ask for more. The Munich Agreement of 1938 (see p. 127) is the main example of this. In the 1930s many people supported appeasement because they felt that Germany had justifiable grievances, particularly those arising from the 1919 peace settlement. Later it was thought that this weak-kneed policy encouraged Hitler's ambitions and therefore helped to bring about the Second World War. For this reason, in post-war politics appeasement was considered to be a dangerous and short-sighted policy.

Questions

Did you notice?

1. The Comintern was (a) a department of the Soviet Government (b) an association of Communist parties (c) a German political party
2. The failure to form a 'common front' against Hitler was due to (a) Stalin's opposition (b) Hitler's strength (c) distrust
3. The main aim of Stalin's foreign policy was (a) to protect the USSR (b) to come to an agreement with Hitler (c) to promote world revolution
4. Nowadays it is thought that 'appeasement' (a) helped to bring about the Second World War (b) was a sensible policy (c) prevented an invasion of Britain
5. 'Operation Barbarossa' (a) began the Second World War (b) was a Russian attack on Finland (c) ended the Nazi–Soviet Pact
6. True or false?
   (i) Britain warned Stalin of the German attack
   (ii) Russia invaded Poland in 1939
   (iii) Fascism was the system of government in ancient Rome
   (iv) In June 1941 Stalin was ready for the German attack
   (v) Nazi Germany was a totalitarian state
   (vi) Leningrad was occupied by the German army during the war
7. Which statement is *more* accurate?
   (i) One difference between Fascism and Communism was that
      (a) Communism appealed across national frontiers
      (b) Communism promised help to the working class
   (ii) Mussolini won international approval because
      (a) he made Italy a powerful country
      (b) he made the trains run on time
   (iii) A link between Fascism and Socialist ideas can be seen in
      (a) efforts to reduce unemployment
      (b) an emphasis on military strength

Can you explain?

8. What were the 'two faces' of Soviet foreign policy after 1921? In what way did Stalin 'merge them into one'?
9. Why were developments in Germany after 1933 so worrying to Stalin?
10. In what way did appeasement apparently encourage Hitler? Give *two* examples of events in the 1930s which seemed to do so.
11. Hitler's propaganda spoke of a 'Drive to the East' to claim living space for Germans. To Stalin it seemed that Britain and France tacitly agreed to this in the Munich Agreement of 1938. What made him think so?
12. By August 1939 Stalin had apparently decided that Germany would be a better friend for the Soviet Union than Britain or France. (a) List *all* the events since 1917 which had led him to that conclusion. (b) What advantages did the 1939 pact with Germany give to the USSR?

What's your view?

13. Many people considered Stalin treacherous for signing the Nazi–Soviet Pact. Do you share this view of his action? Which people in particular were betrayed by it? Did any other governments behave treacherously in this period?
14. Nowadays a policy of appeasement towards a leader like Hitler is condemned. But it is not always easy to recognize a Hitler in advance! How would you recognize another Hitler today? What difficulties and dangers may arise in a policy of 'standing firm'?
15. From the outline of Fascism given in Study Topic 6 and any other knowledge you have, what do you think is the special appeal of Fascist ideas?

13

Soviet Russia since Khrushchev

STALIN'S LAST YEARS

Post-war recovery

In 1945 the USSR faced a massive job of economic reconstruction. It was a situation similar to 1921, with the difference that there was now a firm industrial base on which to build. Recovery was also assisted by the spoils of war: large amounts of machinery were taken as reparations from Germany and from Manchuria, the area of China occupied by Japan since 1931. (The real victim of this confiscation was China, who regained her Japanese-occupied areas in 1945.) By 1953 pre-war levels of production had been surpassed, and the graphs of industrial production have gone steadily up ever since.

Foreign policy

The years 1945–9 were a period of great tension and danger as the Cold War developed between the USSR and the USA. As we shall see later, Stalin established a protective ring of Communist-run states in Eastern Europe (including East Germany) under tight Soviet control. An Iron Curtain clanged down to cut off all contact between East and West. The only exception was Yugoslavia: in 1948 Tito demanded the right to run his own kind of Communist system free of control by Moscow. To Stalin this 'treachery' was unforgivable: he broke off all relations and Yugoslavia (though still Communist) became an 'enemy' along with all the Capitalist states.

Stalinism at home

The 'cult of personality' (the worship of Stalin as the single-handed victor of the war and architect of Socialism) now reached absurd heights. It was shown in the numerous portraits and statues†, in the naming of cities and institutions (Stalingrad, Stalino, Stalinsk, etc.) and the new game of re-writing history 'to correct the distortions of the past' which Stalin had begun in the 1930s. The Nazi–Soviet Pact was explained as Stalin's clever trick to give the USSR time to prepare for war; military mistakes were caused by generals who ignored Stalin's advice, while victories were solely due to him. Hence the wry saying, 'Who can tell what is going to happen yesterday?'

There were also dark signs of new purges. In 1949 a group of top men in the Leningrad Party were executed. Late in 1952 nine eminent doctors were arrested, possibly suspected of trying to poison Stalin. Stalin told the Minister of State Security that if he did not obtain confessions from these men, 'We will shorten you by a head.'

Stalin's death

Fortunately for the Moscow doctors, Stalin died of a stroke on 5 March 1953. No sooner was he in his grave than the hard lines of Stalinist rule began to soften. The doctors were reinstated, a partial amnesty* was declared and various reforms were announced. Stalin's man, Beria, was removed from his job as head

†Some of these monuments did not last as long as Stalin intended–see Figure 13.1.

of the secret police (later he was tried in secret and shot). The Party leaders now proclaimed their loyalty to the principle of collective leadership instead of one-man rule. Nevertheless, there was some jockeying for the position of 'first among equals,' and by 1955 it was clear that Nikita Khrushchev had won that job. Khrushchev was never a dictator to compare with Stalin, but he dominated Soviet policy at home and abroad until 1964 when he was compulsorily retired by his colleagues. His influence turned out to be just as significant as Stalin's, both in the Soviet Union and in the world.

DE-STALINIZATION

The 'secret speech'

In 1956, at the Twentieth Congress of the CPSU, Khrushchev exploded a bombshell which echoed round the world. In a secret speech (which immediately became public knowledge) he made a sensational attack on Stalin. Overnight the cult of personality was turned upside down: now the list of Stalin's crimes was longer than the previous list of his virtues! Stalin, said Khrushchev, had ruled Russia as a tyrant. Under his rule 'Soviet citizens came to fear their own shadows'. They had been terrorized by 'mass repressions and brutal acts in violation of Soviet legality'. The Party delegates gasped as Khrushchev cited case after case of Stalin's injustice and cruelty.

So now the true history of all those years would be told! Or would it?

Was Stalin the only one?

'If we had known it was so easy to blame him, we could have committed many more crimes.' This was the caption of a German cartoon in 1956 showing 'Saint' Khrushchev heaping all the corpses of Stalin's rule onto a statue of Stalin. Here in a nutshell was the weakness of Khrushchev's speech. He said nothing about the role of other senior Party men – including himself – who had all risen to power

and served for many years under Stalin. It was obviously dishonest to blame one man for all the crimes of Stalin's rule. The public revelations of 1956 condemned the whole Party machinery and the traditions of Bolshevik rule since 1917 which had allowed one evil man to exercise such power. But no examination of the system of government which Stalin had used to his own advantage was ever made by the Soviet Party.

The effect of Khrushchev's speech

Khrushchev's 1956 speech began the official de-throning of Stalin in the Soviet Union. It had a shattering effect on the rest of the Communist world:

1. Rebellion broke out in the Soviet satellites of Eastern Europe: first Poland and then Hungary demanded freedom from the iron hand of Moscow (Figure 13.1).
2. Communist parties in the West now felt rather foolish for their previous slavish loyalty to the Soviet Party. In their eyes the CPSU had damaged the cause of Communism by supporting Stalinism, and they now made haste to dissociate themselves from it. After 1956 each national Party took up whatever line suited its own national circumstances.
3. On the other side of the world the Communist Government of China, already disenchanted with the Soviet Union in other ways, began to consider its own leader, Mao Tse-tung, to be the true 'heir' of Marxism–Leninism.

All these developments, together with Khrushchev's new foreign policy of 'Peaceful Co-existence' towards the West, we shall follow up in Part IV.

Khrushchev may not have foreseen the reaction to his 'secret speech' abroad. But it was necessary to de-throne Stalin in the Soviet Union in order to change Stalinist policies which were stifling human initiative and holding back economic progress. He therefore dismantled some of the machinery of repression and began new economic policies which would set Soviet citizens on the road towards a better standard of living.

Khrushchev breaks the mould

1. Political and cultural life

Stalin had set himself above the Party, which merely took orders from him. First on the agenda, therefore, was to reassert *collective leadership*. Now decisions would be taken by discussion and vote in the Central Committee and the 'inner circle' of the Politburo. The internal security police (KGB) was also brought firmly under Party control, and there would be no more 'violations of Socialist legality'–the automatic conviction of the government's enemies without due process of law. In 1958 a new Criminal Code insisted that prosecutions must go through correct legal channels, but Article 70 of the Code, forbidding 'anti-Soviet agitation and propaganda', could still be used to suppress any unwelcome protest.

For ordinary citizens the most dramatic relaxation of Stalin's terror was the release and rehabilitation of thousands of political prisoners (for those who were already dead, this took the form of a public announcement of their innocence). Imagine the relief and joy as the labour camps opened to let out all those 'wreckers', 'social parasites' and ex-prisoners of war in Germany, who had returned home after 1945 only to be locked up on Stalin's assumption that *any* contact with the West had made them potentially disloyal.

In public life, some criticism of the government was now allowed in the press, but censorship continued to ensure that it was kept within strict limits. Similarly some critical literature was allowed to appear, such as the poetry of Yevtushenko and Solzhenitsyn's *One Day in the Life of Ivan Denisovich*; but other works, such as Pasternak's *Dr Zhivago*, were not. The literary magazine *Novy Mir*, under its editor Tvardovsky, was the main vehicle for liberal opinion in a period of cultural relaxation which, as it turned out, would be all too brief. Even at this time cultural freedom was patchy–Khrushchev did not extend it to modern art,

for example, which he personally detested.

In any case freedom of expression for a few intellectuals was much less important, in Khrushchev's view, than a better standard of living for millions of ordinary people. By 1955 the USSR was an immensely powerful nation, but Soviet citizens lived very poorly compared with people in the West. Khrushchev now wanted to show that Socialism could provide as good a life as the mid-twentieth-century affluence that Capitalism had achieved. He therefore tried to make the Soviet economy more efficient and productive. It was not only a question of reforming the system, but of resisting the claims of other sectors of the economy (especially the 'metal-eaters' of heavy industry) to win a larger allocation of national investment for agriculture and consumer industries.

2. New economic policies

Stalin's direction of the economy was always rigidly controlled from Moscow. This was done through a vast bureaucracy which was wasteful and clumsy, and resented by people further down the line who felt themselves to be mere puppets. In 1957 Khrushchev set up 150 Regional Economic Councils (*sovnarkhozy*) to supervise the enterprises within their own areas. This was one attempt–later abandoned–to deal with problems of over-centralization which the Soviet government is still struggling to overcome.

Khrushchev's attempt to decentralize was accompanied by agricultural policies which he hoped would bring large increases in food production. In 1954 he launched the *virgin lands scheme* to reclaim and farm some 90 million acres of uncultivated land in Kazakhstan and Siberia. To encourage greater 'commitment' from collective farm managers he abolished the MTS (tractor stations)–a long-resented tool of control by Moscow–and allowed individual farms to buy up the machinery. In 1957 he boasted that the USSR would reach American *per capita* production of milk, butter and meat by 1962 (one of his many unfulfilled promises).

Figure 13.1 The head of a huge statue of Stalin toppled during the Hungarian Revolution.

Rural living standards were still far below those of town dwellers. Khrushchev began a determined effort, carried on by his successors, to improve the quality of rural life. After 1958 the peasants were able to keep (or sell in private markets) *all* the produce from their private plots, but alongside this concession to individualism Khrushchev continued the process, begun in Stalin's time, of gathering the collective farms into ever-larger units. One reason for this was to create large agro-industrial villages which could offer peasants some of the amenities of city life – an idea first put forward by Khrushchev in 1950, then dropped, and later carried through by Brezhnev. A further effort to hoist up rural living standards came in 1964, when old-age pensions and other social benefits long enjoyed by town workers were extended to peasants. In 1966 the annual 'share-out' of profits from the collective farm was replaced by a system of fixed wages plus an end-of-year bonus. There was now little difference between the 'truly Socialist' state farm (*sovkhoz*) and the collective farm (*kolkhoz*). But the problems of Soviet agriculture were far from resolved.

Along with his promise of more and better food, Khrushchev's most popular policies with ordinary citizens were his efforts to provide better housing and more consumer goods. In 1957 he began a twelve-year housing programme, but he did not succeed in diverting enough funds from the 'metal-eaters' to develop consumer industries as much as he wished; other leaders (and the armed services) did not share his view that defence spending could be reduced now that the USSR had nuclear weapons to match those of the United States.

Within a few years the reforms begun by Khrushchev did produce a remarkable improvement in Soviet living standards. Agricultural production increased by 50 per cent between 1953 and 1958 (Figure 13.2), and the leap in the output of consumer goods is shown in Table 13.1 (see page 138) – although in 1966 Soviet citizens still had far fewer of most items than Americans. But *they* did not make that comparison. Many Russians in the 1960s remembered the privations of the 1930s and the war years, and were well pleased with the progress they were now making. The big question was, could this progress be maintained? Soviet citizens now had their feet on the same 'escalator of rising expectations' as Americans in the 1950s, and their government would have to meet those expectations in the coming years.

Khrushchev's 'mistakes'

After Stalin's death Khrushchev had become 'top dog' against the opposition of some other Soviet leaders. In 1957 he survived one attempt to oust him, but by the early 1960s he had made a number of 'mistakes' in foreign and domestic policy, notably over the Cuba missile crisis (see ahead, Chapter 24), and in agriculture. His boastfulness and occasional outbursts of temper (or humour)–in sharp contrast to the tight-lipped public face of other Soviet leaders–apparently made him an unworthy representative of the USSR in their eyes. Finally he was unwise enough to propose a reorganization of both the armed forces and the Party, thus threatening two sets of powerful vested interests. In 1964 he was quietly voted out of office and spent the rest of his life as a private citizen.

THE BREZHNEV ERA

The new First Secretary† of the Party, Leonid Brezhnev, took care not to antagonize other powerful men in the government

†In 1966 the term General Secretary, used in Stalin's time, was resumed.

Figure 13.2 Khrushchev viewing the Russian grain crop during a farm tour. The poor performance of agriculture was one problem he tackled.

and the Party. His tactics were compromise, not confrontation. In the early years of his rule he shared the limelight with Premier Kosygin and the head-of-state President Podgorny, but he gradually took over Kosygin's role and in 1977 took the Presidency into his own hands. Unlike Khrushchev, whose death in 1971 went unmarked by his countrymen, Brezhnev went to his grave in 1982 weighed down by medals, awards and popular adulation. In spite of his personality cult, however, he did not become a one-man dictator like Stalin, nor did he even wield as much personal power as Khrushchev. If Khrushchev was a kind of trapeze artist–a daring show-off, apt to miss his catches–Brezhnev was surely a skilled tightrope-walker, able to balance and

Table 13.1 Distribution of consumer goods in the USSR and the USA

	Number of each item per thousand of the population		
	USSR, 1955	*USSR, 1966*	*USA, 1966*
Radios	66	171	1300
Cars	2	5	398
TV sets	4	82	376
Refrigerators	4	40	293
Washing machines	1	77	259
Sewing machines	31	151	136

SOURCE: J. N. Westwood, 'Khrushchev and After', *History of the Twentieth Century*, vol. 6, ch. 3.

appease the various interest groups in the Soviet hierarchy, and retain the confidence of all of them. This seems to be the secret of success in Soviet politics nowadays, and it gave the USSR eighteen years of stable and conservative government under Brezhnev.

It was a period of considerable achievement. Economic growth was sufficient to pay for increased arms spending *and* a substantial rise in living standards. In foreign policy Brezhnev developed 'Peaceful Coexistence' into a period of *détente** with the West in the mid-1970s, symbolized by Soviet–American arms control agreements, trade deals with many Western countries, and the European Security Conference held at Helsinki, Finland, in 1975 which agreed a mutual policy of non-interference in Soviet and Western spheres of influence. By the early 1980s the USSR was an acknowledged global superpower, with an apparently docile and contented population.

That docility was achieved at considerable cost, however, and the contentment of ordinary people rested on economic progress which could not be maintained indefinitely without more efficient production methods. Brezhnev did *not* find the secret of success here; his successors still face the problem.

Brezhnev mends the cracks

1. The dissident movement

Encouraged by the sweet air of freedom when Khrushchev lifted the lid of Stalinism, a number of Soviet writers and others among the professional élite began to demand 'human rights' for themselves and other victims of the Soviet system. Western literature was now available in the USSR, and a monthly journal, *Foreign Literature*, published translations of contemporary writing. Cultural and professional visits, radio broadcasts and tourism revealed glimpses of Western life and affluence, at least to the educated few. They now wanted the same freedoms as their Western counterparts, and were encouraged to press hard for reforms when the Soviet government promised at the Helsinki conference (see above) to increase personal freedoms for its citizens.

There were many voices in this community of dissidents–sometimes called the Democratic Movement, although it was never *one* organization–which in the 1970s became the nearest possible to a political opposition in the Soviet Union. Some wanted a return to the true ideals of Marx and Lenin which had been betrayed by Stalin and, to their disappointment, were not resurrected by his successors (one of their causes was Stalin's brutal treatment of national minorities–see below). A few, like the novelist Solzhenitsyn, wanted to go back even further to pre-revolutionary, Christian, 'Slavophil' Russia (see page 88), while others were social democrats in the Western mould. Jews, officially assimilated Soviet citizens but in practice still subject to discrimination, demanded the right to emigrate to Israel. Writers wanted to print what they liked, and when this was denied they resorted to *samizdat* ('self-publishing', i.e. privately circulated typescript) or *tamizdat* ('publishing out there', i.e. in the West).†

With one eye on Western opinion, which had to be kept sweet for foreign policy purposes, the Soviet government handled the dissident problem carefully. Some offenders were tried and sentenced to terms of imprisonment (usually three to five years) for spreading 'anti-Soviet propaganda', and were then re-admitted into Soviet society if they behaved themselves. Others were declared 'mad' and consigned to mental hospitals. Thousands of Jews and others were allowed to emigrate–what better way to get rid of discontented citizens?–while a few real trouble-makers were forcibly deported to the West (like Solzhenitsyn in 1974) or sent into internal exile (like the physicist Sakharov in

†The best-known example of *samizdat* was the *Chronicle of Current Events* documenting violations of human rights. Among many works of *tamizdat* was Andrei Amalrik's *Will the Soviet Union Survive until 1984?* –for which he served five years' imprisonment and was then exiled to the West.

1980). And *all* the dissidents were worn down by official disapproval and relentless KGB harassment. Expelled from their professional organizations, constantly watched and followed, their papers confiscated or ransacked, deserted by their emigrating or exiled comrades, the few remaining dissidents at last fell into exasperated silence. In 1982 the last remnants of the 'Helsinki Group' disbanded itself.

This steady and successful persecution was carried on against a barrage of protest in the West, which the Soviet government usually ignored but would occasionally respond to by releasing particular victims whose cases were publicized in the West. But the dissidents aroused *no* widespread support among ordinary Soviet citizens, who were easily convinced by the government that they were 'renegades' and 'traitors'–although how many of the new occupants of labour camps† shared that view, no one could know for sure.

2. Religious and national minorities

Soviet ideology had always claimed that there would be no need for religion in the ultimate Communist society,‡ and similarly that national boundaries within the Russian Tsarist empire would eventually disappear in the new Soviet state. After 1917 Soviet propaganda (and occasional outbursts of church-smashing) tried hard to eradicate persistent religious belief, while the Tsarist policy of 'Russification' was continued by ensuring that Party leaders in the national republics were either Russians or 'russified nationals'. Nevertheless the federal constitution of the USSR gave separate representation to the fifteen republics in the Council of the Nationalities, and also guaranteed freedom of religious belief. During the Second World War Stalin saw the need to reach an 'accommodation' with the Russian Orthodox Church in order to draw on the deep loyalty to Mother Russia of its 30 to 40 million members.

After the war religious sentiment and national loyalty were still tolerated, though frowned upon. But Khrushchev, impatient to reach the goal of true Communism (which he said would be achieved in the Soviet Union by 1980), barged recklessly into these sensitive areas of human feeling. His claim that national minorities would soon 'merge' into one Soviet people, and the sacking of Party officials in several republics for 'nationalist tendencies', alarmed Georgians and Uzbeks who thought of themselves as Georgians and Uzbeks *first*, and Soviet citizens *second*. His frontal attack on religion–closing churches and seminaries and even banning private religious meetings–provoked open protest from militant sects like the Baptists and sent religious observance 'underground', where it was far more dangerous than out in the open.

Brezhnev manoeuvred tactfully to repair the damage. Church closures stopped, new ones were allowed to open–but religious *propaganda* was harshly penalized. A new 'accommodation' was arranged with the Orthodox Church which brought a political pay-off in the Church's support for government policy–ironically, the same function it had performed for the Russian Tsars. In the 1960s, as a member of the World Council of Churches, the Russian Orthodox Church took a 'Soviet voice' into international religious debates.

The nationality issue was rather more complicated. There are about 130 distinct nationalities in the Soviet Union, some of which (like the 42 million Ukrainians and over 12 million Uzbeks) are much more than fragments. Many of them live in border areas of the USSR and have cultural and religious ties with people in neighbouring countries—see Figure 13.3. Some were once independent states and would like to be so again; some are united internally, or with their neighbours, by a strong religious faith which

---

†Variously estimated to be between two and five million in the late 1970s.

‡Marx called religion 'the opium of the people'. Belief in Heaven was an understandable 'escape' from the misery of life under Capitalism, but it would fade away when Communism provided true fulfilment in this world.

could be dangerous for a Communist government (as the example of Catholic Poland shows—see ahead, Chapter 27).

Presumably for compassionate reasons, some of the minorities cruelly uprooted by Stalin in 1944 (see page 129) were restored to their homelands in the 1960s—but others, notably the Meskhetians of Southern Georgia and the Crimean Tatars, were not. Similarly some were allowed to emigrate: Armenians to join other Armenians in the United States, 60,000 Germans to East and West Germany, along with 250,000 Jews who went to Israel and the United States. But when it came to the question of autonomy for the national republics, Moscow as usual wanted to tighten the reins. The debate over 'national' versus 'Soviet' control of the internal affairs of the republics delayed the

new Brezhnev Constitution,† originally promised for 1975, until 1977. When it came, the old structure of theoretical self-government for the republics was still there, and Brezhnev indicated that the time was not yet ripe to centralize the Soviet system further. In other words the nationalists had won the argument—for the time being.

National and religious divisions in Soviet society are only thinly papered over. What if Catholic Lithuania should follow Poland's example? What if the five Central Asian republics, united by their Moslem faith, should

†There had been three previous Soviet Constitutions: 1918, 1924 and 1936. *The Cambridge Encyclopedia of Russia and the Soviet Union* (Cambridge University Press, 1982, pp. 319–20) describes an apparently democratic system which includes the guarantee of many personal freedoms. The account concludes with the significant sentence, 'In practice this whole machinery is controlled by the CPSU.'

Figure 13.3   The fifteen republics of the USSR today. Note the large Moslem area bordering on other Islamic countries.

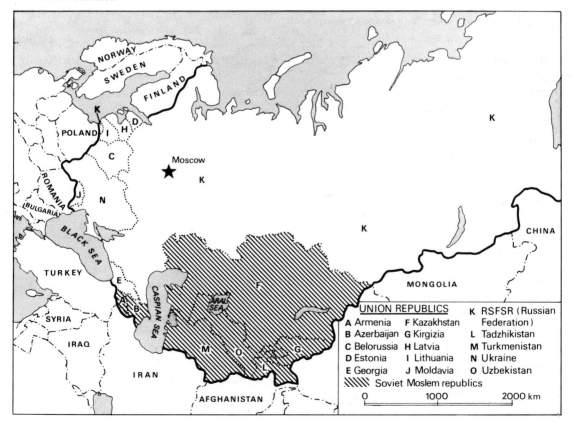

141

catch the infection of Moslem fundamental-ism over the border in Iran? Moslems at present form about 16 per cent of the Soviet population, and because of their high birth-rate are expected to reach 25 per cent by the year 2000. In the late twentieth century the Soviet Union may well be affected by ethnic, religious and nationalist passions which seem stronger than ever in other parts of the world.

Economic progress...

Sit tight, here come the statistics! Unfortu-nately they can't be avoided in any discussion of economic matters, but don't panic. Con-sider each point carefully and relate it to what you know of economic life in Britain and what you have learned about the American economy. You don't have to memorize the figures–they are there as *evidence* of the points raised.

The improvement in Soviet living stan-dards under Khrushchev and Brezhnev can be seen in the increased output of 'consumer durables' between 1955 and 1966 (Table 13.1, page 138) and in the continued growth of per capita consumption (Table 13.2). To update the consumer durable figures of 1966, by 1980 it was reported that 85 per cent of families owned radios, 83 per cent had TV sets, 86 per cent had refrigerators and 70 per cent had washing machines (cars were still the exception, however–only 9 per cent of

families owned one).† Diet was also healthier (more meat, milk and vegetables–less bread and potatoes), while most urban families now had their own flats, even if they had to share kitchens and bathrooms (about 30 per cent still did). In rural areas life was much more comfortable in the agro-industrial villages which had now been built, and average wages merged with those of town workers by the end of the 1970s. Education and other ser-vices were not so good as in towns, but it was significant that peasants no longer had to be kept on the land by force: in 1981 they were issued with the internal passport which enabled them to leave their jobs and move house if they wished, as town workers had been allowed to do since 1945.

The rise in living standards was achieved with a mixture of luck and good judgement. By 1971 Brezhnev had persuaded the 'metal-eaters' that more resources must be allocated to consumer industries and to agriculture, which received more than 25 per cent of investment after that date. In the 1970s some of it was used to improve rural housing, but the main aim was to raise agricultural output. Spectacular grain yields

†These figures were 'reported' in Gail Warshofsky Lapidus, 'Social Trends' in Robert F. Byrnes, *After Brezhnev: Sources of Soviet Conduct in the 1980s* (Indiana University Press, 1983), p. 193. But in some cases they may indicate *access to* these appliances rather than private ownership–e.g. a TV set in a rural community centre, or a washing machine shared by several families in a block of flats.

Table 13.2 Average annual rates of growth in consumption per capita in the USSR, 1965–81

	1966–70	*1971–5*	*1976–80*	*1981*
Total consumption	5.1	2.9	2.2	1.8
Goods	5.4	2.8	2.1	1.8
Food	4.3	1.6	1.0	1.4
Soft goods	7.1	3.0	3.1	2.1
Durables	9.1	10.0	5.4	2.7
Services	4.3	3.0	2.5	1.9
Personal	5.8	4.6	3.4	2.1
Education	2.9	1.5	1.6	1.3
Health	3.2	1.4	1.4	−0.2

SOURCE: Gertrude E. Schroeder, 'Soviet Living Standards: Achievements and Prospects', US Congress, Joint Economic Committee, *The Soviet Economy in the 1980s: Problems and Prospects* (US Government Printing Office, 1982), p. 5.

from Khrushchev's 'virgin lands' in the early years had fallen off by 1960 due to soil erosion, lack of fertilizer and the uncertain climate of those regions. Under Brezhnev a large input of fertilizer and new farming techniques brought better results, and the harvest from Kazakhstan was a godsend when the 'bread basket' of the Ukraine was half-empty, as happened in 1972. In the more friendly atmosphere of *détente* the USSR was fortunately able to make up grain deficiencies with imports from the West. As an exporter of oil and natural gas she benefited from rising energy prices in the 1970s, and with her profits from this trade she bought food and Western technology.

... and economic problems

Soviet economic achievements of the 1960s and 1970s brought great satisfaction to millions of her citizens, as Study Topic 7 illustrates. But long-term trends were not encouraging. From a high point of 6–7 per cent per year in the 1950s, economic growth slowed to an average of 5 per cent in the 1960s, 3 per cent in the late 1970s and 2 per cent in the early 1980s. Look again at Table 13.2 and you will see that although people were better-off each year, the *rate* of increased consumption fell steadily from 5.1 per cent in the late 1960s to 1.8 per cent in 1981. To put this in human terms, a family which in 1969 was saving up to buy a TV set in 1970, in 1981 could only look forward to a few extra pairs of shoes in 1982. This might not be so bad if they already had all they wanted, and of good, lasting quality–but this was far from the case.

Soviet industry is not a shining example of high productivity and efficiency. The main problem is chronic *shortages* and the notoriously *poor quality* of many products.† Every Soviet housewife faces the problem every day. 'Shopping' in the USSR is much more

†The notable exception was the quantity and quality of Soviet *weapons*, which began to alarm Western governments in the mid-1970s. *Détente* began to fade and was replaced by renewed East–West tension.

than just walking down the street to buy what you want. First you must find a shop which has it in stock, and then join the queue ... Or wait till your friend's friend tells you that the shop where she works has just received a new supply, and ask her to save you one. And what will your new toaster be like? In the West we have the 'Friday car' (the one made on Friday, that falls apart before you get it home)–but in the Soviet Union the problem is said to be so bad that the canny shopper will not buy a product date-stamped after the 15th of the month, when the workers are rushing to fulfil their month's quota after 'slacking' for the first fortnight.

Faulty goods piling up in the warehouses means frustrated shoppers with cash in their pockets but nothing to spend it on. One result of this is a thriving 'underground economy'. Almost any item or service can be had *na levo* ('on the left') if you have the right contact and can pay cash, or offer something in exchange. Another effect of having a hoard

Figure 13.4
'Where did you get that sheepskin coat?'
'My daughter brought it back from Paris.'

of spare money is the lack of incentive to earn any more: why bust a gut to earn a bonus, just to fill the bank vaults? In 1979 more than half of disposable money income (that is, what people have to spend after paying for necessities) was sitting in savings accounts.

The government is well aware of these problems. Departments of the bureaucracy which are users of products will often refuse to accept them from producers, and the state sets aside $1 billion a year to cover such losses. At citizen level, one Soviet economist estimated that a quarter of all fruit and vegetables spoiled on their way to the customer, while another lamented that 'a large part of the population is preoccupied with the search for scarce goods'. Moreover the younger generation compare their own life-style not with Russia of the 1930s but with Western Europe of the 1980s (Figure 13.4). No doubt Brezhnev was mindful of that when he warned the 26th Party Congress in 1981: 'The things we are speaking of–food, consumer goods, services–are issues in the daily lives of millions and millions of people ... The people will judge our work in large measure by how these questions are solved. They will judge strictly, exactly. And that, comrades, we must remember'.

The most serious weakness in the Soviet economy is lack of self-sufficiency in food. When Brezhnev died in 1982 his successors† faced a problem which had defeated *all* Soviet leaders before them: *the low productivity of collective agriculture.* Brezhnev had tried hard to raise output. Between 1965 and 1980 $500 billion was invested in agriculture–but grain imports in the same period cost $15 billion. In 1981–2 the grain gap was 44 million tonnes. Output did increase at about 2 per cent per year–but

†Brezhnev's immediate successor was Yuri Andropov, whose 15-month rule was chiefly notable for a bold attack on high-level bureaucratic corruption. After several months of serious illness, Andropov died in February 1984. His successor Konstantin Chernenko, a 72-year-old Brezhnev disciple, was regarded by Western Kremlin-watchers as a caretaker ruler who would inevitably be replaced before long by a younger man. Until that happened, the Brezhnev style of rule was expected to continue.

only by using 20 per cent of national investment against the pressing claims of other sectors of the economy. Compare this with the performance of American agriculture, where 7–8 per cent of national investment per year produced enormous grain *surpluses* (much of it exported to the USSR). Of course this comparison is not quite fair. Many regions of the Soviet Union have climatic problems: hard frosts and weak sunshine, or erratic rainfall. Newly-developed areas lacked the basic infrastructure of paved roads, grain silos, refrigerated transport and so on, which were paid for in the United States by earlier generations. But the inescapable fact is that Soviet peasants produce much less than they *could.*

Efforts to reform the system

Under Khrushchev and Brezhnev several different tacks were tried, but they all foundered on two rocks built into the Soviet system: the determination of the Party to retain control of every step in the production process, and the danger of allowing personal profit to creep into a Socialist way of life.

In industry Khrushchev began to reform the system in which managers were just robots carrying out orders from higher up. They were given more freedom to run their enterprises and were allowed to keep 40 per cent of their profits to spend on new machinery, or extra benefits and pay for the workers. For a while Brezhnev allowed these reforms to spread, while at the same time Khrushchev's Regional Economic Councils were abolished so that Moscow could resume its close surveillance of individual factories. The economist Liberman and other advocates of apparently 'Capitalist' incentives to managers and workers pointed out, as Lenin did when introducing NEP in 1921, that the state still *controlled* the economy at every vital point. But Party ideologists took fright: could a Socialist system enshrine the profit motive so blatantly? Evidently not. By 1970 the reforms had died away; Brezhnev called for 'discipline' and 'patriotism' to make everyone work harder–and raised the price of vodka.

In agriculture the problem was always to coax the peasants to give the same Tender Loving Care to the collective fields that they lavished on their private plots (see p. 119). In his drive to hurry on to full Communism, Khrushchev tried to squeeze private plots and organized large brigades of peasants to look after large acreages of collective land–but in 1962–3 there was a disastrous slump in output. Brezhnev recognized that private plots *had* to be allowed: using only 1 per cent of cultivated land, they produced 25 per cent of total farm output, and 30 per cent of all livestock products. In the mid-1960s the government even toyed with the idea of extending the 'TLC principle' to collective production: under the experimental 'link' system, five or six workers were linked to a small area, and allowed to make personal profits from it. This was remarkably successful, especially on the experimental farm run by one Ivan Khudenko. But it too threatened Party control and encouraged the profit motive. Khudenko was imprisoned for alleged theft, and the link system was abandoned.

Can it work?

The complexity of Soviet economic problems goes far beyond the scope of this book. But the problem of *incentives* is easy enough to understand. Every schoolboy knows that if 'Sir' gets a ten-page essay out of him this week, he won't be satisfied with two pages next week. And it's no use Sir just *telling* him to work harder 'for the good of the school' or even 'to get a good job'. Unless he can believe in those goals himself, and derive some interest and satisfaction from the work he's asked to do, the wily schoolboy (and the Soviet worker) will remain 'a slacker'.

What do Soviet workers think of a 'Socialist' system where there is such an obvious gap between *their* living conditions and those of the privileged élite? Party and government officials and the professional middle class all have access to private cars, special shops and foreign imports which are only available *na levo* to ordinary citizens (in the words of a Soviet comedian, 'We have everything–but not for everybody'). Eventually the demands of ordinary people may force changes in a system which doesn't deliver the goods they want, but they are unlikely to move towards Capitalist individualism. There is more to a happy life than an electric toaster, after all. Study Topic 7 reminds us that a Socialist ideology has allowed Russians to retain a traditional sense of community which is markedly absent in the competitive 'status race' of Western life. And while we rightly value the personal freedoms they lack, we have less cause to feel smug about our economic system, which also has social injustice and grave economic problems, not to mention 'Friday cars' and a busy unofficial economy out of sight of bosses and tax inspectors.

Perhaps outsiders expected too much of 'the great Socialist experiment' which began in Russia in 1917. 'I have seen the future–and it works!' said an American journalist who visited the Soviet Union soon afterwards. But does it work? Obviously not for the victims of Stalinism, and today's dissidents. And nearly seventy years after the revolution the Soviet Union still has to prove that it 'works' in providing the social equality and abundance for all that Socialism promised.

Study Topic 7

Life in Russia

The following short extracts from Jack Miller's *Life in Russia Today* (Batsford, 1969) describe some features of Soviet life which affect ordinary citizens. Jack Miller was until 1970 Senior Lecturer in the Institute of Soviet and East European affairs at the University of Glasgow. He is the editor of *Soviet Studies*, a quarterly journal published by the University of Glasgow Press.

Marxism–Leninism

The government of the USSR expects all citizens to know and to believe in a set of ideas called Marxism–Leninism, and does everything possible to make sure that they do so. Since the government is a powerful and determined one, and has many means of influencing people's minds, the consequences on the everyday life of the citizens are considerable. The system of ideas is more comprehensive and elaborate than any of the world's traditional religious or philosophical systems. It is not easy for the over 240 million inhabitants, with very different levels of education and belonging to many nations of very different background, traditions and religions to fulfil this expectation. Nevertheless, the Soviet Government acts on the assumption that this aim is perfectly reasonable and that it is, indeed, already largely achieved, except for the survival of religious ideas inside the country and the influence of foreign ideas. [*p. 1*]

The effect of all this on the life of the country is four-fold. Firstly, the newspapers, radio, television, films, theatre, literature, trade union meetings, entertainments and all other media of public communication are used for a didactic purpose. Thus, all domestic and foreign news is slanted in accordance with the system of ideas. Secondly, the educational services, from nursery schools to postgraduate studies, are used to inculcate the mental system, both by

presenting subjects of study in accordance with it and by making Marxism–Leninism one of the subjects taught. Thirdly, a special network of adult educational institutions exists, from workers' circles to the Higher Party Schools, for instruction in Marxism–Leninism which at its lower levels involves about a quarter of the working population at any one time. Fourthly, daily life is affected by the many ways in which the authorities seek to prevent any expression of ideas which conflict with the official ones, or any criticism of them. [*p. 4*]

Elections

There is, theoretically, always a possibility that the Supreme Soviet† may become a genuine parliament, but the entire political atmosphere of control by the party leaders would have to change first, as well as the mode of election to the Supreme Soviet. It has never been known, since the first elections under the 1936 Constitution, for more than one candidate to stand in any constituency, or for less than about 99 per cent of the electorate to vote for that candidate, or for any member of the Supreme Soviet to vote against a measure or even abstain, or for the membership of the Supreme Soviet not to conform to the plan issued from party headquarters – so many members from each occupation, a certain proportion of men to women ... and so on. [*p. 34*]

Rural progress

The rural population came, in Khrushchev's time, to regard its conditions as intolerable, though there had been much improvement since Stalin. Khrushchev's successors have had to meet this mood by further increases in the state's

---

†The top of the 'pyramid of soviets' which is the structure of government. Each soviet elects representatives to the next higher up, and that one to the next, and so on.

procurement prices, much bigger investments in agriculture, social insurance and something akin to wages for the collective farmers ... (*pp. 83–4*)

Housing

Since 1958 about 70 million square metres of new housing has been built in the towns each year. During this period the urban population has risen by about $3\frac{1}{2}$ million people a year. This means that the new housing is equal to 170 square feet, or one medium-sized room, per additional person. The net increase in dwelling space is less, since some old housing has been demolished to make way for the new. However, the overcrowding was so severe (for example in Moscow, 40 square feet per head) that this rate of new construction has eased it despite the rise in town population. Far more important than the gain in space is the gain in privacy. For millions of families the nightmare of sharing with four, six or ten other families the single kitchen and lavatory of a badly maintained pre-1914 flat has given way to the joy of a flat of their own. It is an emotional experience to be shown by Russian friends around their new flat; the tiny size of bathroom and kitchen, general gimcrack construction, thin walls which may be no barrier to neighbours' noise, are almost irrelevant. The new housing is mostly very small flats in very large blocks of six to eight stories, like huge boxes. This makes for a kind of overpowering monotony in the new suburbs, relieved since the early 1960s by the use of colour and different lines of balconies, and more recently by much taller blocks in some cities. [*pp. 89–90*]

Postscript

Many parts of the Soviet scene have been omitted from this book ... the most important aspect that has been left out is happiness. People make the best of their circumstances anywhere.
They get what satisfactions and enjoyments may be going. And they cope with their own governments and bureaucracies more readily than foreigners may find credible. They know the short cuts. Plenty of happiness is to be found in Russia. Watching the thousands of young people going out skiing on a Sunday morning, picking mushrooms with a family party in the woods ... one feels that a suspicious, strident and interfering government does not loom so large after all. In any case, there is deep satisfaction in the sense of community, the feel of a whole nation as a kind of large family, which remains fairly strong in Russia. The Soviet system itself is in some way an outcome of the Russians' reluctance to lose this sense of community as they came into the modern world during the past three or four generations.

But while one must bring in simple happiness to keep the record straight, the preceding paragraph is not true as it stands. The system cannot really be escaped. The young skiiers are old enough to have mastered something of the finesse of the Soviet double life. Not only the parents but the children in the family party may be considering as they picnic in the woods whether certain neighbours know that they are spending a day with a foreigner ... Finally, whatever success the Russians may have achieved in their great effort to avoid the loneliness and aimlessness of Western individualism, their Marxism–Leninism is at least as conventional as religion in the West, and their informer system makes for a special isolation of people from each other. [*p. 185*]

*GLOSSARY

amnesty, a general pardon (sometimes given to political prisoners when the government 'forgives' them).

détente (French), the ending of strained relations between states (later in the book we shall see what East–West *détente* meant in practice).

Questions

Did you notice?

1. The USSR had surpassed pre-war industrial production by (a) 1953 (b) 1960 (c) 1964
2. Beria was (a) a victim of Stalin (b) a follower of Stalin (c) a Soviet novelist
3. Khrushchev's 'secret speech' was addressed to (a) the world Communist movement (b) Western journalists (c) members of the CPSU
4. Compared to Khrushchev, Brezhnev was (a) more personally powerful (b) a more tactful leader (c) more tolerant towards dissidents
5. The word *samizdat* means (a) a kind of Russian soup (b) a Regional Economic Council (c) typescript literature
6. True or false?
   (i) Russian peasants can sell privately all the produce of their private plots
   (ii) The 'virgin lands' scheme was a complete flop
   (iii) Khrushchev was imprisoned in 1964
   (iv) Georgians and Uzbeks are Soviet citizens
   (v) Under Khrushchev the MTS (tractor stations) were abolished
7. Which statement is *more* accurate?
   (i) In the view of Jack Miller (see Study Topic 7), the Supreme Soviet
       (a) is much like any other parliament
       (b) is unlikely ever to become a real parliament
   (ii) Since 1958 political offenders in the Soviet Union
       (a) sometimes have a fair trial according to Soviet law
       (b) are always considered mad and sent to hospital
   (iii) The main aim of Khrushchev's reforms in industry was
       (a) to introduce Capitalist ideas
       (b) to improve efficiency

   (iv) Brezhnev put more money into agriculture
       (a) to raise output
       (b) to introduce the 'link' system

Can you explain?

8. What signs of Stalinism at home and in foreign policy could be seen in the last years of his rule?
9. What was the main weakness of Khrushchev's secret speech?
10. What changes were made under Khrushchev and Brezhnev to improve rural living conditions?
11. How did Brezhnev's government 'mend the cracks' in regard to (a) political dissidents, (b) the Russian Orthodox Church, (c) national minorities?
12. Describe the material situation of an average urban family in the USSR in 1981. What household equipment were they likely to have? What were their prospects for improving their standard of living?

What's your view?

13. In Study Topic 7 Jack Miller explains how Soviet citizens are encouraged to believe in Marxist–Leninist ideas. Is there any comparable effort in our society to encourage a belief in the ideas of Democracy and Capitalism? Do you think there should be?
14. It is suggested in this chapter that a free enterprise economy is more responsive to consumer needs than a centralized state-run economy. Nevertheless, is our economy entirely satisfactory from the consumer's point of view? Does the consumer have any protection against greedy or unscrupulous producers?
15. Western observers have suggested that ordinary Russians do not care too much about their lack of political freedoms. Why is this so? Will anything change their attitude, do you think?

Further Reading

SUPPLEMENTARY READING

Graham Bearman and Peter Lee, *Russia in Revolution* (Heinemann Educational Books, 1974). History Broadsheets.

David Fry, *Russia: Lenin and Stalin* (Hamish Hamilton, 1966).

I. Grey, *The First Fifty Years: Soviet Russia 1917–67* (Hodder, 1967).

Graham Lyons (ed.), *The Russian Version of the Second World War* (Leo Cooper, 1976). An edited translation of Soviet secondary school textbooks.

M. McCauley, *The Soviet Union since 1917* (Longman, 1981).

Jack Miller, *Life in Russia Today* (Batsford, 1969).

R. W. Pethybridge, *A History of Post-War Russia* (Allen and Unwin, 1966).

Sally Pickering, *Twentieth-Century Russia* (OUP, 1965).

W. P. Rae and N. C. Coutts, *Contemporary Files: Book 2, The World* (Heinemann Educational Books, 1980). A 'topic book' in which *The Kremlin File* examines several relevant subjects: Communist ideology, human rights in the USSR, economic planning, living standards.

John Reed, *Ten Days That Shook the World* (Penguin, 1970).

John Robertson, *Russia in Revolution* (OUP, 1983). From Tsarism to Stalin only.

John Robottom, *Modern Russia* (Longman, 1972).

Alexander Werth, *Russia at War, 1941–1945* (Barrie and Jenkins, 1964), *Russia: Hopes and Fears* (Barrie and Jenkins, 1969).

J. N. Westwood, *Russia 1917 to 1964* (Batsford, 1966).

There is much literature relevant to this period, especially the books by Russian authors published after Stalin's death but referring (in most cases) to the years of Stalinism. Alexander Werth discusses Soviet literature in its historical context in *Russia: Hopes and Fears* (Barrie and Jenkins, 1969), ch. 18.

Arthur Koestler, *Darkness at Noon* (Penguin, 1969).

George Orwell, *Animal Farm* (Heinemann Educational Books, 1972), New Windmill Series; *1984* (Heinemann Educational Books, 1965), Modern Novels Series.

N. Ostrovsky, *How the Steel was Tempered* (Central Books, 1973).

Victor Serge, *The Case of Comrade Tulayev* (Penguin, 1968), *Memoirs of a Revolutionary, 1901–1941* (Oxford paperbacks, 1967).

Mikhail Sholokhov, *And Quiet Flows the Don* (Penguin, 1967).

Published after Stalin's death:

Andrei Amalrik, *Involuntary Journey to Siberia* (Harvill Press, 1970). *Will the Soviet Union Survive Until 1984?* (Allen Lane, 1970). Not a novel but a speculation on the future.

A. Anatoli (Kuznetsov), *Babi Yar* (Sphere Books, 1969).

V. Dudintsev, *Not by Bread Alone* (Hutchinson, 1957).

Ilya Ehrenberg, *The Thaw* (Harvill Press, 1955).

Boris Pasternak, *Doctor Zhivago* (Fontana, 1969).

Alexander Solzhenitsyn, *One Day in the Life of Ivan Denisovich* (Heinemann Educational Books, 1974), *The First Circle* (Fontana, 1970), *The Gulag Archipelago, 1918 to 1956* (Fontana, 1974), and others.

Valeriy Tarsis, *Ward 7* (Collins, 1975).

Yevgeny Yevtushenko, *Selected Poems* (Penguin, 1969).

MORE ADVANCED

Svetlana Alliluyeva (Stalin's daughter), *Twenty Letters to a Friend* (Penguin, 1968).

Michael Binyon, *Life in Russia* (Hamish Hamilton, 1983).

Robert Conquest, *The Great Terror* (Penguin, 1971).

Edward Crankshaw, *Khrushchev's Russia* (Penguin, 1966).

Isaac Deutscher, *Stalin* (Penguin, 1970).

H. Montgomery Hyde, *Stalin: The History of a Dictator* (Hart-Davis, 1971).

R. G. Kaiser, *Russia – The People and the Power* (Secker and Warburg, 1976).

N. S. Khrushchev, *Khrushchev Remembers: The Last Testament* (Deutsch, 1974).

Lionel Kochan and Richard Abraham, *The Making of Modern Russia* (Penguin, 2nd ed., 1983).

David Lane, *Politics and Society in the USSR* (Martin Robertson, 2nd ed., 1978).

Peter J. Mooney, *The Soviet Superpower: The Soviet Union 1945–80* (Heinemann Educational Books, 1982).

J. P. Nettl, *The Soviet Achievement* (Thames and Hudson, 1967).

Alec Nove, *Economic History of the USSR* (Penguin, 1972), *Stalinism and After* (Allen and Unwin, 1975).

T. H. Rigby, *The Stalin Dictatorship: Khrushchev's 'Secret Speech' and Other Documents* (Spectrum Books, 1966).

Rius, *Marx for Beginners* (Writers and Readers Publishing Co-operative (Society Ltd.), 14 Talacre Road, London, NW5 3PE. Published

1976.) A cartoon treatment, but quite difficult even so.

History of the Twentieth Century magazine series (see Notes on Resources, page xii for full information); the issues particularly relevant to this Part of the book are:

Part III

China since 1911

Laying water pipes – a painting by a commune member from Shensi province.

14

China: Victim of Imperialism

Land, people and food

Like the other two World Powers, China is a huge country – larger than the United States but smaller than her gigantic northern neighbour the USSR. But her population of over one billion is more than theirs put together! There are also several million overseas Chinese living mainly in South-East Asia, who keep up cultural and other ties with their homeland.

Most of China's people are crowded into the eastern half of the country, while much of the west is thinly populated and undeveloped. More than 700 million are Han people, considered the true Chinese; the rest are national minorities such as Mongolians and Tibetans. China's structure of government, like the American, allows considerable self-government to the provinces, and many of the national groups live in autonomous (self-governing) areas. But China, like Russia, is wary of separatist movements which may undermine the authority of the central government in Peking.

China is still a mainly agricultural country. In fact she is only a few steps beyond a subsistence economy where flood or drought can cause millions of deaths. One triumph of the Communist Government is that this no longer happens in China, but keeping the balance between people and food supply is still a problem. The government is now trying hard to check population growth and to spread the existing population more evenly throughout the country. The government is also developing industry, but – for reasons we shall discuss later – China decided not to copy the Soviet industrial 'leap' of the 1930s to catch up with the West. So far China's industrialization is a gradual process, geared to the needs of agriculture – not, as in Russia, the other way round.

Imperialism – Nationalism – Communism

China was one of the main victims of Western imperialism, both by economic penetration and military conquest. The first phase of her struggle to escape from this situation was led by the Nationalist movement of Sun Yat-sen. His Kuomintang party eventually replaced the Manchu rulers who fell in 1911, but was itself unable to hold power against the double assault of Japan from the outside and Communism from the inside. Japan's aims in China were similar to Hitler's in Europe: to build up her own economy and find 'living space' for Japanese on the mainland. This ambition ended with Japan's defeat in the Second World War. Four years later, in 1949, the Chinese Communist Party took over the government of China.

Mao Tse-tung was China's Lenin, but the history of Communism in China is very different from the Russian example. The Bolsheviks seized power in the cities, and only then began to build their Socialist order throughout Russia. In China Communism began among the peasants and took twenty years to reach Peking. On the road to power the Communists had time to practise their policies before applying them to the whole of China. In the process Mao Tse-tung developed new ideas about Marxism which made his kind of Communism rather different from the Soviet system. As leader of the new state he tried to ensure that his Party did not forget its revolutionary past or the Marxist goal ahead. Mao Tse-tung's Communist revolution did not stop at Liberation in 1949; it was to be *a continuous process* of social transformation towards the promised class-less society.

China's influence in the world

Before 1949 China was the object of other states' foreign policies and scarcely had one of her own. For the next twenty years she was largely excluded from world affairs by un-relenting American hostility to the new Com-munist Government. At first China had the protective friendship of the Soviet Union to rely upon, but long-standing differences in outlook soon led to an open split between the two Communist giants. By the mid-1960s, feeling equally menaced by American 'Capi-talist aggressors' and Soviet 'Social imperial-ists', China had developed her own nuclear weapons to frighten them off.

China's military strength today does not match that of the other two World Powers except in millions of men. But in the ideologi-cal warfare of Capitalism *v.* Communism she may hold some trump cards. With her own experience of Western imperialism, and offer-ing a form of Communism tailor-made for peasant societies, China offers herself as an example to all 'oppressed' peoples with a similar history and similar problems to solve. She hopes that other countries in what is called the Third World will follow the escape route that China has marked out.

This is the starting point of China's twen-tieth-century history – the prison of imperial-ism and feudalism from which she had to break free.

IMPERIALISM

In the late nineteenth and early twentieth cen-turies the military and economic power of in-dustrial Western nations spread far around the globe. In their search for raw materials and markets for their own products they had acquired colonies or developed commercial enterprises in countries whose own govern-ments were too weak or unwary to resist. Officials and businessmen would be sent to the colonized country – and behind them, often a procession of missionaries to convert the 'poor heathens' to Christianity. Imperial-ist nations saw nothing wrong in this policy; indeed they felt they were bringing the benefits of trade and the light of 'true religion' to unfortunate, backward people. But the vic-tim's view of imperialism was rather dif-ferent!

China was one such victim (Figure 14.1), but many other countries suffered similar exploitation. When we see what imperialism meant at the receiving end, it becomes easier to understand the strong resistance move-ments which grew up in China and elsewhere.

China's humiliation

In the early nineteenth century the Manchu Empire stretched far beyond the China of today to include Mongolia and other areas to the north, Taiwan (Formosa) and other islands. Beyond there was an outer ring of countries under Chinese influence: Korea, parts of north India, Burma and Indo-China. The size and power of this huge Chinese sphere was gradually reduced during the period of Manchu rule. China was not carved up or completely taken over by her con-querors, but colonized through economic penetration by several competing powers.†

Phase 1: 'Forcing the door'

From the 1840s onwards, Britain led the com-mercial exploitation of China through Treaty Ports and other concessions such as the prin-ciple of 'extra-territoriality' by which foreigners in China were exempted from Chinese laws. The main Treaty Ports were opened to Western traders after the Opium

†The pattern of imperialism shown here is adapted from John Gittings, *A Chinese View of China* (BBC Publi-cation. 1973) pp. 186–8.

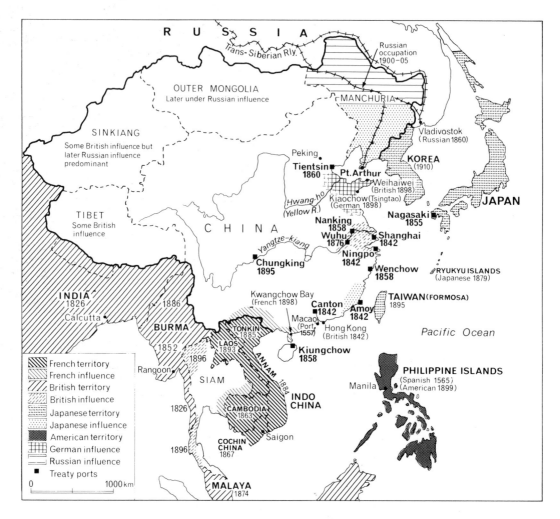

Figure 14.1   Imperialism in the Far East by 1911. (The Treaty Ports were open to European traders from the dates indicated.)

Wars of 1839–41 and 1858–60. Hong Kong became a British colony in 1841.

To understand what Treaty Ports meant to the Chinese, imagine that our own government had been forced to grant trading rights through our main ports (Liverpool, Bristol, Hull) to a strong, hostile nation – say the USSR. Certain districts in those cities would be out of bounds to British citizens. Russians living there could not be arrested by British police even for an offence committed outside their concession area. Russian trading companies could fix the import duty our government would receive on the goods they sold to

our citizens. Russian traders would be free to travel anywhere in Britain. Put like this, it is easy to see why the Chinese resented the Treaty Port system!

Phase 2: 'Peeling the onion'

In the late nineteenth century the outer ring of the Manchu Empire was stripped off by a series of 'unequal treaties' (so called by China because she was an unequal and unwilling party to them). Large areas in the north went to Russia; Korea, Taiwan and some other islands to Japan; Burma and north Indian areas to Britain; Indo-China to France. Further concession areas on mainland China went to Japan, Germany, Russia, France and Britain.

Phase 3: 'Dollar diplomacy'

The United States arrived late on the scene in the Far East and disliked the 'selfish' way in which the European nations had marked out exclusive little patches of China for themselves (Figure 14.2). In 1900 she got the other powers to agree to an 'Open Door' policy: all nations would be able to trade with China on equal terms. The 'Open Door' let everyone into China, and especially the United States.

China in 1900

At the turn of the century Japan was the only industrialized country in Asia. The tiny giant proved its strength by winning wars against China (in 1894–5) and the Tsarist Russian Empire (in 1904–5). In Russia the humiliating defeat of 1905 led to an unsuccessful revolution against the incompetent Tsar – a prelude to his overthrow in 1917. Chinese reformers also noted the significance of Japan's military success against these huge old empires – but their Manchu rulers did not.

The lesson was repeated by the Boxer Rebellion in 1900. An outburst of rioting against Western 'foreign devils' in China brought another thrashing for the proud Manchu Government, this time at the hands of a combined force of Western powers led by the Kaiser's Germany. The once-great Manchu Empire was no match for the industrial nations of the twentieth century, and its system of government was hopelessly out of date. But still the old Empress T'zu-hsi and the corrupt court officials who served her continued to regard Westerners as 'barbarians', beneath the contempt of 'superior' Chinese people. Despite the efforts of a few officials to reform it, the antiquated and inefficient system of government did not change.

The need for change was most desperate in China's vast countryside, where millions of

[From *Puck*, New York.]

JOHN BULL: "Remember, I am to have the Lion's share."

Figure 14.2 An American view of European imperialism in China. Russia and Germany carve large slices, France waits like a vulture, while Britain demands 'the lion's share'.

peasants were stuck in feudal conditions more like the fourteenth century than the twentieth.

FEUDALISM

About 80 per cent of China's population were peasants who scratched a bare living from the land. They lived a hand-to-mouth existence: what they grew in the summer was eaten in the winter. Hard work and lucky weather might produce a surplus which the peasant could sell or exchange for the things he did not make himself – but equally, a poor crop could mean going into debt to pay his rent and taxes.

A peasant woman's situation was even worse. She was the property of her father or husband and could be sold in hard times like any other article of value. A daughter was a liability because a dowry would have to be found for her eventual marriage; a son, on the other hand, would bring his wife's dowry to

155

his father's house. For this reason girl babies were sometimes left in the fields to die.

The downtrodden peasants had no control over their own lives. Local government officials were in league with the local gentry – indeed they were often the same people. It was almost impossible for the peasant to build up a reserve of grain: if it was not eaten by pests it would be snatched by the 'human vultures': the landlord, the tax-collector, the money-lender. When drought or flood occurred (and these were frequent in China) millions of peasants starved. No one in authority did anything to prevent a famine, or cared what happened to its victims.

NATIONALISM

Young, educated Chinese of the middle class were ashamed and resentful of China's weakness and humiliation at the hands of foreigners and heartsick at the condition of their fellow countrymen. Many of them had travelled in Japan and the West and enviously compared the economic progress of those countries with China's backwardness. They were also attracted to Western ideas of Democracy and self-determination – the right of nations to govern themselves. But in China they had little chance to use their skills or develop their political ideas. Government jobs were in the hands of corrupt Manchu officials, and business was monopolized by foreigners. Many left China to join the communities of overseas Chinese all over the world.

These young reformers in China and abroad were Westernized in outlook but they were also strongly *nationalist* (*k*): they wanted to get rid of foreign influence in China and begin a programme of democratic reforms and economic development. Knowing that nothing would change under the fossilized Manchu Government, they worked busily to overthrow it. The leader of these campaigns was Dr. Sun Yat-sen.

Suddenly the fortress of Manchu rule crumbled away. The old Empress had died in 1908 and various incompetent officials tried to hang on to the throne for its heir, the three-year-old Pu-yi. But in 1911 a series of uprisings in the cities sent them scurrying for cover. When news of the Nationalist Revolution reached Sun Yat-sen, who was lecturing in the United States, he hurried home to become the first President of the Republic of China.

KEYWORD

nationalism This word was discussed briefly under the keyword 'nationality' (see page 5). Nationalism means a desire or a policy to help one's country or nation, usually by uniting all its people into a strong, self-governing state. The form it takes will depend on the circumstances:

1. It may involve gathering under one government several neighbouring parts of a country, for example as the city states of Italy were united into one nation in the nineteenth century.

2. On the other hand, nationalists may want to separate their nation from a strong neighbour which imposed its rule on them at some point in history. Welsh and Scottish nationalist movements are examples of this kind.

3. It will often be necessary to get rid of a foreign ruler so that the people of the nation can govern themselves. This form of nationalism became very common in the twentieth century when the peoples of India, Africa and China, for example, wanted to free themselves from Western imperialism.

4. A nationalist is always a patriot who loves his country. Perhaps he even thinks it is the best country, and that the peoples of other nations are inferior to his own. From this kind of nationalism it is only a short step to wanting all foreigners to keep out of 'our' nation (they may 'pollute' it) – or to the idea that one nation has a 'right' to dominate others. Aggressive nationalism like this can easily become imperialism, as it did in Nazi Germany and Fascist Italy.

Figure 15.1   Sun Yat-sen.

Figure 15.2   Chiang Kai-shek.

Figure 15.3   Mao Tse-tung.

15

Nationalist China

The Nationalist Revolution of 1911 was like the demolition hammer on a fine old palace. When the comic opera façade of the Manchu court fell to the ground, everyone could see the neglected and worm-eaten structure behind it: China's cities half owned and run by foreigners, most of her industry and commerce in their hands, above all the wretched poverty of the Chinese peasants. This was the demoralized ruin that Sun Yat-sen hoped to reconstruct into a new, modern state! But however little protection it had given, the Manchu palace had at least spanned all China. Now that it was gone there was nothing to hold the millions together. Any strong man could come and build his own house in the rubble, and that is just what happened.

The Nationalists had first to win power before they could use it, and that task was not achieved until 1928. Before we look at the problems of China, here are the three main leaders who tried to deal with them.

Sun Yat-sen (Figure 15.1) is rightly remembered as a revolutionary leader, a thinker, statesman and politician. But he was not a soldier, and for many years after 1911 military strength was what counted in China.

Sun's successor, Chiang Kai-shek (Figure 15.2), was both soldier and politician. By 1928 he had established a national government which ruled China for twenty-one years. But Chiang used his military and political skills not so much in the service of the Chinese people as of his own party. Eventually he had to surrender the mainland to the Communists led by Mao Tse-tung.

Mao Tse-tung (Figure 15.3) also recognized that 'political power grows out of the barrel of a gun' – a remark that earned him the undying suspicion of Western democrats. But at least when he had won political power, he used it to bring in beneficial reforms.

157

This chapter sketches the rise and fall of the Nationalists between 1911 and 1949, and shows why they eventually lost popular support. Chapter 16 follows the footsteps of the Communists through the same disorderly period, and indicates the reasons for their success.

1916–28: THE PERIOD OF WARLORD RULE

For some years after 1911 Sun Yat-sen was overshadowed by Yuan Shih-kai, a former Manchu general who had pledged his support to the Republic but was actually planning to make himself the new emperor. The shaky Republic was saved from his scheme by Yuan's sudden death in 1916. Sun Yat-sen's party, now calling itself the Kuomintang (KMT), set up a government in the southern city of Canton, but northern China fell into the hands of local 'warlords'. Sometimes co-operating, sometimes warring among themselves, these robber barons carved out their own little empires, ruthlessly suppressing and exploiting their peasant subjects. For those poor people it seemed that things had only changed for the worse since the end of Manchu rule in 1911.

Life under the warlords

Even for better-off Chinese daily life was chaotic at this time. Think of something quite ordinary like sending a letter to your sister in Swatow, or a parcel to an export agent in Canton, and then read the annual report of the Chinese Post Office for the year 1917. Here is an extract, recounting the year's activities in the southern province of Kwangtung:

> KWANGTUNG – Until June the province had peace, but the events since then are now a matter of history. The establishment of the so-called Military Government; the opening of the extraordinary parliament; the differences of opinion between local officials and the Military Government; the revolt of troops at Waichow, which affected also Poklo and Sheklung; the declaration of independence against the Kwangtung Government by Defence Commissioner Mo Ch'ing-yu, of Swatow, with consequent fighting at Laolung, Chonglok, Hingninghsien, and a dozen other places; the assumption by General Lung Chi-kuang of the Inspector-Generalship of the Laing-Kuang, with the operations, naval and military, which that step entailed – all these have kept the province in a state of ferment. Courier services had occasionally to be suspended, coast and river steam-services were interrupted, commerce was at a standstill, and the whole Swatow section remained till the close of the year in a chaotic condition. In April and August there were severe floods; courier lines in the East, West and North River sections were interrupted, and postmen had to deliver mails by boats. There were sixty-five cases of brigandage and piracy, which resulted in loss of mails and postal property. In twenty other cases couriers were robbed of their own belongings. In twenty-five cases offices or the shops of agents and box-holders were pillaged, and in five cases similar establishments were destroyed by fire. In three instances couriers were so badly wounded as to be quite unfit for further duty. Thus the natural progress of the Post Office was impeded, and the results of the year's working, while satisfactory, are by no means what they would have been had the year been a peaceful one.[†]

Pity the Director-General of Posts, Monsieur Picard-Destelan, who must have felt close to despair as he gathered in twenty-odd similar reports from other provinces of China! You may notice, by the way, that he was not Chinese but a Frenchman. Right down to Transport Officer Signor A. Rosario in Shanghai, most important jobs in the so-called 'Chinese' Post Office were held by foreigners.

[†]This extract and other information about the Chinese Post Office is taken from the *China Year Book, 1919–20* (George Routledge and Sons Ltd.). This was a little encyclopedia of information about China's economy, politics and laws, invaluable for foreign visitors and traders in China at that time.

Foreign influence

The origins of this 'Chinese' Post Office provides a useful example of foreign influence in Chinese life at this time. In 1896, after many years of pressure from foreign governments, the Manchu rulers had permitted the British to organize a national postal system on Western lines. The new Post Office competed directly with two existing services, which explains the Peking government's reluctance to admit another one. By 1904, however, the British Inspector-General of Customs and Posts could report favourable progress: 'The native postal agencies linger on, but the competition is telling upon them, and in process of time the Post Office will be in fact, as in name, the National Post Office.'

This was the typical pattern of Western imperialism in China by the early twentieth century. Tentacles of foreign influence reached out in all directions until there was scarcely any sphere of life the Chinese could call their own. But at least Signor Rosario and his colleagues were providing a useful service and had not come to China to make profits for shareholders at home. This of course *was* the aim of foreign businessmen, and many were quite unscrupulous in pursuit of it. Their activities are further discussed in Study Topic 8 (page 163). In the early years of the Republic foreign powers paid no more respect to China's interests or the authority of her new government than they had to the old one. Indeed the Nationalists had yet to establish their authority!

The menace of Japan

Although Britain and other Western nations had powerful economic interests in China, by this date Japan was her most dangerous enemy. Japan was a small, crowded country bursting with military and industrial energy. In 1895 she had won the island of Taiwan (Formosa) from China, and in 1910 had taken control of the mainland country of Korea. After 1911, while the Nationalists and warlords struggled for control of China's govern-

ment, Japan watched lynx-eyed for every chance to extend her influence further. In 1915 she pressed Twenty-One Demands on the acting President Yuan Shih-kai which, if accepted, would have placed China under Japanese control. Yuan wriggled out of some of these Demands but was forced to grant others – for example, a half-share in China's most important iron and steel company, and extended leases on railways and ports in the Chinese province of Manchuria, which Japan had seized from Russian ownership in 1905.

1919: the May 4th Movement

Japan gained further advantage in China from the First World War. In 1917 the Allies had coaxed China to declare war on Germany so that they could attack German shipping and possessions in China. Unknown to China, these possessions had been secretly promised to Japan (one of the Allies) in the event of Germany's defeat. When this deal was revealed at the 1919 Peace Conference, China's indignant protest was expressed in a wave of strikes and demonstrations in China. This was known as the May 4th Movement. There were student riots in several cities, and a widespread boycott of Japanese goods.

The Kuomintang Nationalists were in the forefront of this protest. So also was a group of even more radical reformers in China – a handful of revolutionaries, impressed by the success of the Bolshevik revolution in Russia and the few Marxist writings they had read. In 1921 these people organized the first National Congress of the Chinese Communist Party (CCP) in Shanghai. One of the twelve delegates was Mao Tse-tung.

1923–7: the united front of the KMT and CCP

Sun Yat-sen's vision of China's future was a liberal-democratic one, mildly Socialist but not Marxist. In 1921 he declared the Kuomintang's policy – the Three People's Principles of Nationalism, Democracy and People's Livelihood.

1. Nationalism

The first aim of Sun's party was to unite China under a strong national government and expel foreign influence.

2. Democracy

Sun wanted eventual democracy for China on the Western parliamentary model. But since most Chinese were illiterate, and unused to democratic ideas, he envisaged a period of tutelage, under Kuomintang leadership, to guide and educate the people for self-government.

3. People's livelihood

Land would be redistributed on the principle of 'land to the tiller' (the person who worked it). The new government would undertake a programme of economic development. Like every developing country (then and now) it would need foreign loans and advice to begin with.

Sun Yat-sen appealed hopefully to the Western democracies for help with this programme, but got no response. In 1923, however, the Soviet Union – itself looking for friends in a hostile world – offered help to the Chinese Nationalist revolution. This began the first period of a 'united front' between Nationalists and Communists in China. The USSR sent advisers to China and Chinese Communists became members of the KMT. A young KMT soldier called Chiang Kai-shek was trained in Russia to head the KMT's military college, and the KMT itself was reorganized on the model of the Soviet Communist Party.

1926: the Northern March

In 1926 the 'united front' of KMT and CCP began a successful campaign against the northern warlords and rapidly gained popular support. But the activities of its Communist members soon began to worry some people in the KMT. The Communists were provoking a real social revolution as they advanced: peasants attacked landlords, workers sacked the premises of Chinese and foreign Capitalists. Foreign governments became alarmed and considered a military intervention to protect their own interests in China.

Now came a moment of decision for the KMT – they had to decide how far Left their revolution was going to be. Sun Yat-sen had belonged to the Left wing of the party, but he had died of cancer in 1925. His successor, Chiang Kai-shek, belonged to the Right – which in fact was more representative of the mainly middle-class membership of the party. For Chiang and like-minded members of the KMT, the next step was clear.

1927: the 'White Terror'

In 1927 Chiang decided to get rid of the KMT's embarrassing left-wing 'tail'. He turned on the Communists and massacred many thousands of them. Having 'purified' its own ranks, the KMT then went on to defeat the warlords and in 1928 established a government at Nanking which in due course was internationally recognized as the new government of China. Foreign governments with interests in China were now satisfied that Chiang would be a 'reasonable' man to deal with.

1928–37: THE KUOMINTANG MISSES ITS CHANCE

The Communist survivors of the 1927 White Terror had fled to the countryside of central China, and we shall follow up their story later. In the rest of this chapter they appear only as the Red 'bandits' whom Chiang tried again and again to stamp out.

Encirclement campaigns

From 1930–34 the KMT launched one campaign after another against the Communists centred in the hills of Kiangsi province. In 1934 the CCP broke out of the noose which threatened to strangle them and embarked on their epic Long March to the north-west province of Shensi. The KMT armies pursued them relentlessly, but could not defeat them.

Figure 15.4 Japanese expansion in China, 1931–9.

After 1935 the Communists had an impregnable base in their mountain stronghold, but still Chiang spent every ounce of Kuomintang strength on trying to dislodge them.

Japan on the warpath

Chiang was so obsessed with his internal enemies that he scarcely noticed the growing threat from Japan. In 1931, against very little resistance from the KMT, Japan had occupied the important Chinese province of Manchuria and set up a puppet state there. By 1936 it was obvious that Japan was planning further aggression, but Chiang Kai-shek still did not prepare for it. In the 'Sian incident' of December 1936 Chiang's own troops kidnapped him and then brought a Communist leader to bargain with their captive. Chiang was forced to agree to another 'united front' with the hated Communists, this time against Japan. And only just in time! In July 1937 Japan launched a general invasion and the Sino*-Japanese war began (Figure 15.4).

Chiang Kai-shek did not know it yet, but by 1937 the KMT had missed its chance to prove itself a worthy government for China. By the time Japan was defeated in 1945 – a story which is told in the next chapter – the Communists had taken the KMT's place as the hopeful reformers of China. In 1949 the KMT fled in disgrace to the island of Taiwan, where they still are today.

Limited reforms under the Kuomintang

Here, in conclusion, it is fair to record the limited progress which the KMT did bring about, and suggest some reasons why they did not do more. If we measure their reforms against the needs which Sun Yat-sen had recognized, we can see how inadequate they were.

1. Nationalism

The KMT did achieve a united government at Nanking, but further away from the capital their control over local warlords was often weak. And of course there were always 'Red' areas of China which the 'White' armies of the KMT never conquered.

The rights of foreigners were pushed back a little, but as Study Topic 8 shows, Western imperialism in China was not finally defeated until the Communists came to power in 1949. Worse than that, Japanese imperialism nearly strangled China during the KMT period, and Chiang could claim little credit for its eventual defeat. Nevertheless the KMT was a more patriotic and effective government than the Manchu rulers or the warlords.

2. Democracy

Chiang never seriously intended to create a democratic system in China. The KMT was the only legal political party, and even within itself it was hardly democratic: a small inner clique of wealthy men, with Chiang at the centre, took all important decisions. As time went on the KMT's government became more terroristic and corrupt until it lost the support even of many middle-class Chinese.

3. People's livelihood

Some industrialization took place in the KMT period, together with improvements in transport and communications. There were also some social reforms, notably in education. More schools were opened and universities expanded. The KMT even attempted a kind of cultural uplift in the New Life Movement which taught the value of honesty and devotion to the public welfare.

The status of women was raised in Nationalist China, especially by the example of Chiang's wife. Madame Chiang Kai-shek, an elegant, cultured graduate of an American university, was an international glamour-girl – the Jackie Kennedy of the 1930s! She represented the important American connection of one group of KMT leaders – the more liberal end of the party – which is further explained in Study Topic 9. Gradually their influence was pushed aside by other leaders, including Chiang himself, who were more traditionally Chinese. Significantly, Chiang admired the militaristic governments of Germany, Italy and Japan, and his own rule become increasingly like theirs. But he came to rely on America for his own survival.

Why did the Kuomintang fail?

The fundamental weakness of KMT rule in China was its failure to do anything for the peasants. Social improvements mainly benefited the minority of Chinese people who lived in the cities. No land reform took place. Some laws to reduce rents and taxes were passed, but they were never enforced. When famines occurred, no relief was organized and millions of peasants died. The peasant could well ask: was Chiang any better than a Manchu emperor or a warlord?

Looking back – especially if we look through Marxist spectacles, as the Chinese do today – the reason for the KMT's failure is plain. It was a middle-class party and served the interests of its own middle-class supporters: landlords, businessmen, financiers. Their wealth and privilege would have been threatened by any far-reaching reforms to benefit the masses of peasants and workers.

> Despite their fine words and outward reverence for the Three People's Principles, the Nationalists preserved many of the worst features of the old Chinese society. The familiar pattern remained: misery for the many and luxury for the few. The longer he remained in power, the more Chiang lost sight of the aims that had inspired Sun Yat-sen. Power corrupted the Kuomintang party. Its ideals were scrapped and it was left with one aim – to stay in power.[†]

Nevertheless the KMT lost that power to the Communists. In the next chapter we will see what they were doing in these stormy years of civil war and foreign invasion.

[†]H. Higgins, *From Warlords to Red Star* (Faber, 1968), p. 50.

Foreign Influence in China

Sun Yat-sen's Nationalist movement wanted first and foremost to liberate China from the bonds of foreign imperialism and re-make the old Manchu domain into a strong, independent state. But in the turmoil of the warlord period, the opposite happened. Two large chunks of mainland China broke away: Tibet declared itself independent in 1912, and Mongolia became 'independent' under Soviet domination in 1921. The Nationalist Government continued to claim these areas, but was never strong enough to try to recover them.

In the Chinese economy, too, the bonds of foreign control tightened. In 1911 two-thirds of the businesses in the Treaty Ports were foreign owned, as were 41 per cent of Chinese railways. The warlords were out for themselves and not concerned with protecting China; they sold more 'concessions' and accepted foreign loans at high interest rates which had to be paid back by later governments. In the 1920s nearly a quarter of China's national income was spent on repaying foreign loans.

It is often said that imperialism brought economic and cultural benefits to backward countries like China. Is there any truth in this claim?

THE EFFECTS OF WESTERN IMPERIALISM

It is true that Western influence usually (though not always) began to develop a feudal, agricultural system into a Capitalist, industrial one which can eventually provide a higher standard of living. This in turn brings the benefits of education, leisure and recreation which most people in the West value highly. The Nationalists in China in fact wanted development of this kind – as most poor countries do today – but under their own control.

Under imperialist Capitalist development the profits from foreign-owned businesses of course went to shareholders back home and did not benefit the colony as native Capitalism could have done. Foreign companies were much larger than local competitors, if any, and could prevent their growth by undercutting them. On the other hand some native people were employed by the foreign companies and they of course acquired a personal stake in perpetuating imperialism. In China the native agents of foreign companies were called *compradors* and they were even more hated by patriotic Chinese than the white officials of the company.

Moreover Western influence usually had a harmful cultural influence on the colonized country. It distorted the traditional way of life by driving out local products and deliberately cultivating a taste for more expensive imported ones. The following account of one large company's activities in China – British-American Tobacco (BAT) – will serve as an example of the way foreign companies operated once they had a foot in the 'open door' which the Manchu Government had been forced to grant. Incidentally, the methods used by foreign companies to develop new markets in Third World countries today are not much different from those employed by BAT in China all those years ago.

A case study of imperialism†

Chinese native tobacco was smoked in pipes or taken as snuff but was not suitable for making into cigarettes. Like any modern Capitalist marketing a new product, British-American Tobacco and other companies had to create a taste for Western cigarettes when they were first imported into China in the late nineteenth century. One company, it was reported, dropped free samples in the streets of Shanghai! In 1902 BAT established the first cigarette factory in China, using imported American leaf. In 1913 they began to import American tobacco *seed* and encouraged peasants in areas with a favourable climate to grow it. The company offered free seed and fertilizer and the loan of special tools needed at harvest time in return for a guarantee to buy the whole crop.

During the 1920s and '30s the cheaper native leaf was replaced by the better, but dearer, imported variety. (This pattern, repeated for other products, caused a sharp rise in the cost of living – one of the most harmful general effects of imperialism.) By 1933 1,800,000 peasants in China were producing an annual crop of 170 million lbs. of tobacco, and many thousands of Chinese worked in BAT factories. The peasant was now dependent on BAT agents and compradors for supplies of seed (no longer issued free!) and for loans. To get the fair price the company offered he had to take his crop to its own collecting station, sometimes many miles away, or risk being cheated by a local collector.

BAT factory workers were paid somewhat higher wages than those in Chinese factories. The usual pattern was to pay a few trusted Chinese very well to tyrannize the rest. These foremen and gang-masters had to be bribed for jobs and privileges and also acted as 'company spies'. BAT was one of the targets in a series of strikes and boycotts, especially the Shanghai Incident of 30 May 1925

†This account of BAT's activities is adapted from John Gittings, *The World and China, 1922–1972* (Eyre Methuen, 1974) ch. 1.

when British police killed and wounded some Chinese students, and another incident in 1926 when the British fleet shelled the city of Wanhsien, killing a number of Chinese roughly estimated as 'from 50 to 2,000'. Eventually BAT agreed to recognize its trade union, but it continued to resist every demand for better wages and conditions.

BAT, like other foreign companies, also strongly resisted paying taxes to the Chinese authorities. When the KMT Government was firmly established at Nanking its right to levy taxes was finally acknowledged, but BAT continued to lobby for tax rates which favoured their products over Chinese competitors. They also tried hard to stamp out a new cottage industry – hand-rolled cigarettes made with smuggled Japanese cigarette paper – and reduced the price of their cheaper cigarettes to undercut those from Chinese factories.

Only a few large Chinese companies – such as the Nanyang Brothers company in Hong Kong – were serious rivals to BAT. Foreign companies were not allowed to own land outside the Treaty Ports, but they could evade this law by buying land in the name of a Chinese comprador. When BAT's comprador was caught out and sued by a group of Chinese rivals led by Nanyang Brothers, the judge was successfully bribed to give a ruling in favour of BAT. This was typical of BAT's operations: they worked hand-in-glove with government officials at all levels.

But why did the Kuomintang Government allow this? Didn't they come to power with a policy of anti-imperialism?

The Kuomintang's record against imperialism

Anti-imperialism was indeed the main driving-force behind Sun Yat-sen's nationalist movement. And after 1928 the KMT Government did win back some rights from the Western powers – for example, the right to fix its own tariff rates. But Britain and the United States clung on to their privilege of extra-territoriality until 1943, when they gave it back as a friendly gesture to China, who by then was their ally in the war against Japan.

The KMT Government did not 'get tough' with strong foreign governments for fear of offending them. In fact there were many ties between China and the United States (Figure ST 8.1) which Chiang Kai-shek soon wanted to strengthen to help him against Japan, and later against the Communists. Eventually the KMT was being kept in power only by American support, and thus it became even further discredited in the eyes of patriotic Chinese.

In 1949 China 'stood up' (in Mao Tse-tung's words) after a century on her knees. It happened to be Communists who helped her to her feet, but millions of Chinese welcomed the new government regardless of its politics, just because it gave back to China her lost national pride.

Figure ST 8.1   Girl Guides in Nationalist China. Western influence spread into every sphere of life.

Study Topic 9

The Kuomintang's American Connection

Throughout her history America has prided herself on being anti-imperialist. In 1919 when the First World War Allies presented Japan with former German possessions in China (a promise made to Japan before America entered the war) there was an outburst of indignation in America in sympathy with the May 4th protest in China. You may also remember that President Roosevelt hoped to see the British and French colonial empires dismantled after the Second World War: he held the traditional American view that it was wrong for strong nations to impose their rule on weak ones.

Yet the United States joined in the exploitation of China through the activities of private companies like BAT, and insisted on their right to do so! This kind of 'double-think' now seems very hypocritical, but Americans saw no inconsistency in opposing the *open* imperialism of European powers, who had colonies and spheres of influence all over the world, while still encouraging their own businessmen and missionaries *privately* to spread Capitalism and Christianity to the poor 'backward' Chinese. At that time most Americans were confident, as many still are today, that their way of life and religious belief were 'obviously' the best. And what was good for America was 'obviously' good for China too.

In the 1920s and '30s many Americans were sympathetic to China's desire to rid herself of foreign influence, and wanted to help her economic development. American businessmen – even some tourists – travelled widely in China. American missionaries ran schools there and helped their pupils, sometimes from humble families, to get Western-style higher education in China or the United States. They brought home tales of their work, even to small-town church halls in the heart of 'isolationist' America, where a film show might be held after Sunday evening service to show what the Minister and his kindly wife were doing for the poor downtrodden Chinese. All this helped to build up in America a popular image of China as a kind of lumbering, backward child whom Uncle Sam could help to grow up Free and Democratic in the family of nations (Figure ST 9.1).

Most American observers in China saw Chiang Kai-shek and his charming American-educated wife as the saviours of China. A few recognized the increasing corruption and tyranny of the Nanking Government and were worried by it. They had heard about some energetic 'agrarian reformers' up in the hills and wondered if they might offer more hope to China than the KMT ...? But official American policy was to support the KMT – a 'reforming' party, it was thought, but not too extreme.

Japanese aggression in the 1930s was a serious threat to American interests in the Far East and a far worse threat to China. Some American diplomats in China (in particular 'Vinegar Joe' Stilwell, US Military Attaché in the 1930s) were ashamed of their own government's timidity in not resisting Japan, especially when she launched a full-scale war against China in 1937. But American isolationism in this period allowed Japan to stamp on American toes as well as trample all over China (as we noted in Chapter 4).

Japan's attack on Pearl Harbor in 1941 changed all that. The Sino–Japanese war then

得心應手

校長蔣中正贈

Figure ST 9.1   A Chinese flagmaker, 1944.

merged into the Second World War and the USA and China became allies fighting a common enemy. After 1941 America gave the KMT large amounts of money and military supplies to fight the war against Japan. Thus Uncle Sam's informal helping hand became a firm government commitment – and a financial investment – in the KMT's cause.

Japan was defeated in 1945, though not by any efforts of the KMT. In fact it was their lack of resistance to the invaders, on top of the other failures noted in Chapter 15, which finally lost the KMT all support in China. To the surprise of many Americans, Chiang Kai-shek's rule was immediately challenged by an internal force far stronger than Japanese aggression. Hastily they pumped more money and arms into the KMT, but in vain. In 1949 the KMT was roundly beaten and forced to flee to Taiwan.

Ordinary Americans were dismayed – and then furiously angry – to see their generous goodwill of many years past (not to mention the money!) wasted by the defeat of the KMT. Who were these guys who had crept down from the hills to snatch the soul of China from Democracy and Freedom? None other than the old familiar enemy – Commies! But these Reds could not be the intelligent, sensible Chinese the missionaries had known – they would not be taken in by such wicked ideas! No, this new breed of Chinese must be puppets manipulated by the deadly hand of Moscow!

Does this explanation sound familiar? (see page 56). This was the way Senator McCarthy explained the 'loss' of China to bewildered Americans. It was *his* analysis of the Communist victory which most of them accepted: that it was a plot directed from Moscow, helped by 'traitors' in the American Government. But this was a very mistaken view of what had happened, as the next chapter will show.

*GLOSSARY

Sino-, Chinese or to do with China; hence Sino–Soviet, Sino–American, etc.

Questions

Did you notice?

1. The May 4th Movement was a protest against (a) working conditions in China (b) Japanese imperialism (c) the Chinese Communist Party
2. Sun Yat-sen intended to introduce (a) immediate democracy (b) 'land to the tiller' (c) Marxism
3. In 1930 the official government of China was in (a) Nanking (b) Canton (c) Peking
4. In 1931 Japan occupied (a) Mongolia (b) Peking (c) Manchuria
5. A Chinese comprador was employed by (a) the Manchu Government (b) a foreign company (c) a Chinese Capitalist
6. True or false?
   - (i) In 1927 the Kuomintang's policy turned 'right'
   - (ii) The Long March of 1934 was against warlords
   - (iii) The Kuomintang was mainly a middle-class party
   - (iv) Many Americans sympathized with the May 4th Movement
   - (v) BAT paid its factory workers less than workers in Chinese factories
   - (vi) BAT introduced a higher grade of tobacco into China
7. Which statement is *more* accurate?
   - (i) In 1921 Sun Yat-sen
     - (a) did not want Soviet support for his Revolution
     - (b) would have preferred to get help from the Western powers
   - (ii) In 1936 Chiang Kai-shek's troops kidnapped him
     - (a) to force him to resist the Japanese
     - (b) because they disliked KMT rule
   - (iii) The KMT lost power in China mainly because
     - (a) it did not develop China industrially
     - (b) it did nothing to help the peasants

Can you explain?

8. In what way was the power of the Chinese Government (both before and after the 1911 revolution) reduced by (a) Treaty Ports, (b) 'unequal treaties', (c) the 'open door'?
9. Why did Chinese businessmen resent foreign imperialism so strongly?
10. What happened in the following years to increase Japanese pressure on the Chinese mainland?: 1910 1915 1919 1931 1937
11. What were the Three People's Principles of Sun Yat-sen? How far did the Kuomintang party carry them out?
12. What were the main weaknesses of the KMT as a suitable government for China?

What's your view?

13. What is your opinion about the activities of Christian missionaries in China, as described here?
14. Look at the definition of the keyword 'nationalism' on page 156. Do you know of any historical or present-day nationalist movement other than those mentioned here? Can you fit it into one or more of the four categories described? Is it or was it a justified cause, in your view?
15. In a study of Russia or China it is useful to understand the Marxist view of history which their leaders accept (even if *you* don't!). Before considering these questions you may like to remind yourself of the main ideas of Marx and Lenin (see Study Topic 5, page 100. In Marxist terms, what *kind* of revolution was the one that began in 1911? Who were the bourgeoisie in China in the 1930s? In what ways did they oppress the proletariat of workers and peasants? What evidence of Marx's class struggle can you see in China in the period 1900–1949?

The Rise of Communism

In the last chapter we followed events after 1911 from the Nationalists' point of view. We looked at China 'from the top down', as the Kuomintang always did. With his bird's-eye view Sun Yat-sen had surveyed China's problems accurately, but his successor Chiang Kai-shek did little to solve them. After 1928 the Nationalist Revolution became little more than a subject for tea-table discussion in Nanking.

The Communists' approach was quite different. They moved among the peasants of China – 80 per cent of her population – where backwardness and oppression were a daily misery. Under Mao Tse-tung they set out to change these conditions by a *real* revolution – from the bottom up.

1919: the May 4th Movement

The Chinese Communist Party dates its own history from the May 4th Movement, the series of riots and strikes in May 1919 protesting against the transfer of the German sphere of influence in Shantung to Japan. The future leaders of Communism in China – only just reading and learning the ideas of Karl Marx – were quick to realize that among Chinese students and workers there was a volcano of boiling rage against foreign imperialism which could be used as the spearhead of the revolution which had begun in 1911.

The Kuomintang was supposed to be leading that revolution, but at this stage it was making little headway. The warlords had seized power in most parts of China and Sun Yat-sen had neither the strength nor the money to carry out the fine-sounding Three People's Principles he announced in 1921. Meanwhile, in that year the Chinese Communist Party (CCP) was formed in Shanghai and began to spread Marxism among the

workers. They organized a number of successful strikes, notably the seamen's strike of 1922 which won substantial pay increases from the British shipowners. With these successes to its credit, the CCP's membership rapidly grew.

1923–7: united front of the KMT and CCP

Then in 1923 the Soviet Union gave Sun Yat-sen the backing he needed, and the energy of the Communists in China was harnessed to the KMT. Sun Yat-sen welcomed their support, and for their part the Communists were willing to co-operate (for the time being) with the middle-class Nationalist Revolution, which from their point of view had some good 'first-step' aims. In the Northern March against the warlords which began in 1926, their courage and propaganda helped to win popular support for the KMT's Revolution.

Nevertheless, the Communists always kept their eye on the ultimate Marxist goal of a working-class revolution. Their activities soon became an embarrassment to the KMT and in the White Terror of April 1927, many thousands of Communists were killed by the KMT. By this time Sun Yat-sen had died and the right-wing military leader Chiang Kai-shek was at the head of the KMT.

1927: turning point of the Revolution

The year 1927 was very important for the Chinese Revolution. The Kuomintang marched off 'rightwards' under Chiang Kai-shek and after that, it scarcely gave a backward glance at the fine Principles of Sun Yat-sen (see page 160). In fact after 1927 the Communists took over those Principles and moulded them into a Marxist shape. The same year was equally crucial for the Communists because it drove them into the countryside of China. By 1928 the main group of the CCP under Mao Tse-tung and the Red Army leader, Chu Teh, were strategically well placed in the Chingkang Mountains on the border of two provinces, Kiangsi and Hunan (Mao's home province).

1927–37: CIVIL WAR

The Red base areas

The KMT was strong in the cities, so for the time being the CCP had no choice but to work among the peasants. Mao already had considerable experience of this and had come to think that it was the most important part of the Revolution. He was a vigorous and inspiring leader in the Red base areas which the CCP formed in the provinces of central China. Land was seized from the landlords and redistributed to the peasants. Their debts were cancelled and Peasant Associations were set up to run the areas with the help of CCP and Red Army *cadres* (k).

The Communists worked mainly with the poor peasants, who made up 70 per cent of the rural population. But at this stage they trod gently so as to enlist also the support of the 'middle peasants' (those who owned their own land and were not so desperately poor) and even the small industrialists. This careful, soft-footed approach was typical of the Chinese style of revolution which the CCP began to develop in this period. No mercy was spared, however, for the landlords and 'evil gentry' who had ruled the countryside in their own interests for so long.

The Red Army

At the same time the Communists had to learn and apply revolutionary warfare. They were under constant attack from the KMT, and the Red base areas were drawn in and expanded, broken up or re-formed as the Red and White forces battled to and fro. Mao later wrote down the successful guerilla* tactics

practised by the Red Army and they have since been copied by leaders of other national liberation armies. Study Topic 10 illustrates this and other aspects of the Communists' success in the countryside.

The Red Army was a new kind of army in China. The soldiers did not live off the peasants, eating their grain and raping their women, but helped them in their work whenever they could. The famous 'eight-point code' for soldiers' behaviour shows their careful attention to public relations! There was more than one version of the code during the Red Army's history, but the spirit was always the same:

1. Speak politely
2. Pay fairly for what you buy
3. Return everything you borrow
4. Pay for anything you damage
5. Don't hit or swear at people
6. Don't damage crops
7. Don't take liberties with women
8. Don't ill-treat prisoners

The poor Chinese peasants, beaten down for centuries by every kind of exploiter, were bound to be impressed by this kind of treatment even if they hardly understood the Red Army's politics. In return they helped the soldiers by acting as scouts and bringing supplies, and many new recruits joined the Red forces. The Red Army also won recruits from the KMT armies with the same clever tactics used to enlist the peasants' support.

The CCP's Soviet connection

Within the CCP an argument now developed over future policy: should they attack the cities and rouse the industrial workers, or continue to work among the peasants and build up the Red Army? Marx had said that the proletariat of factory workers would be the vanguard of a Communist revolution, and some of the CCP's leaders, especially one called Li Li-san, wanted China's revolution to follow the pattern laid down by Marx. But there were only some 2 million factory workers in China's population of over 400 million. Mao Tse-tung, although trying his best to be a good Marxist, was becoming convinced that in China the peasants must be the driving force of the revolution. He had already argued this case in an important Report of 1927 which is explained in Study Topic 10. But so far his point of view had not been accepted by the other CCP leaders.

The Soviet Communist Party supported the Li Li-san line – in fact they were the authors of it. Stalin was trying to direct the Chinese Communist Revolution through the Comintern, whose job it was (remember?) to bring about world revolution after the Bolsheviks' victory in Russia. Stalin was ignorant of Chinese conditions and had already given the CCP some bad advice by telling them to stick to the united front with the KMT even when it was plain that Chiang Kai-shek was not going to keep his side of the bargain. The CCP naturally looked up to the Soviet Party and wanted to obey 'the experts', so they were loyal to the KMT until the White Terror of 1927 nearly wiped them out altogether.

Now Stalin insisted that the CCP must follow the Marxist rule-book and attack the cities. That's what the Bolsheviks had done, and it worked in Russia, didn't it? So the Li Li-san line – that is, Stalin's line – was adopted, and in 1930 the Communists attacked several important cities.

It was a tragic mistake. In every attack they were beaten back and lost many men. Li Li-san was called to Moscow to be reprimanded by Stalin, who was clever at blaming other people for his own mistakes. It was now obvious that whatever Marx had prescribed for nineteenth-century Capitalist Europe, and whatever tactics had brought Lenin success in Russia, Mao Tse-tung had seen the right way to Communist revolution in China. It must be a *peasant revolution*.

But victory was still a long way off. The Red bases in central China could be encircled by the White armies, and this was the KMT's strategy against them. In 1934 the CCP decided to make a strategic retreat to the remote north-west province of Shensi where they could defend themselves more easily. Thus began the epic Long March.

The Long March

The Long March is the most famous event in the history of Communism in China.† Some of China's leaders today are survivors of it. The heroic story deserves a chapter to itself, but you will have to find one in another book! Here (and in the map, Figure 16.1, on the next page) we can only suggest what a fantastic undertaking it was.

The marchers travelled 6,000 miles across some of the worst territory in the world. They crossed 18 mountain ranges and 24 rivers, poorly equipped and clothed for the extremes of climate they met along the way. They were constantly harassed by KMT armies. Of the 100,000 who set out, only 20,000 arrived at their destination. But all along the route they held political meetings to explain their policies; they gathered recruits and made themselves known in the remotest areas of China. The Long March was an incredible ordeal for those who took part, but it was also a 6,000-mile advertising campaign for Communism.

During the Long March, in January 1935, Mao Tse-tung was elected leader of the CCP, and from that time onwards the Chinese Communist Revolution was under his personal direction. The year 1935 also marks the end of Soviet influence on the CCP's struggle for power – and just as well, perhaps, for Stalin's advice so far had not been much help.

The cave university in Yenan

In October 1935 the survivors of the Long March arrived in the mountainous area of Yenan in Shensi province (Figure 16.2). For several years Mao had been writing and speaking to his followers about Marxism–Leninism and his own special views on how to apply these theories in the conditions of China. Now he developed this 'gospel' of Marxism–Leninism – Mao Tse-tungism into a kind of handbook for a peasant-based

†When President Nixon visited China in February 1972 he said in his first speech, 'And so let us in these next five days start a long march together …'

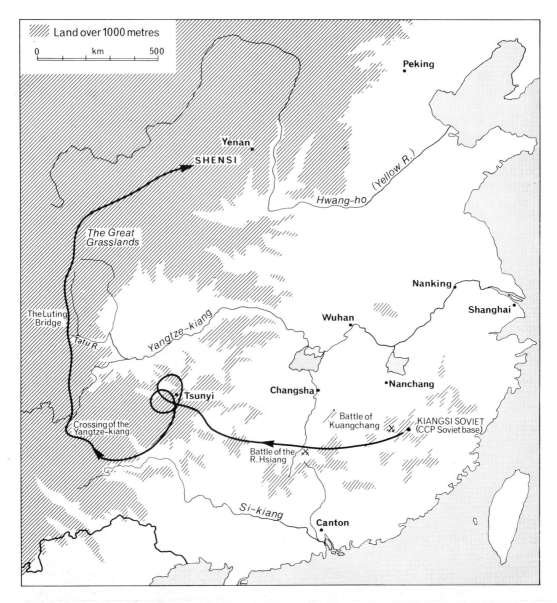

Figure 16.1   The Long March, 1934–5.

Marxist revolution. Together with other CCP leaders, Mao taught it to thousands of Red Army recruits at the famous 'cave university' in Yenan. His lectures and essays from the Yenan period became the philosophy of China's Communist Revolution and are frequently referred to – together with his later writings – in China today. These collected views are called Mao Tse-tung's *Thought*.

Many other patriotic Chinese who had

become disillusioned with the Kuomintang made their way to Yenan to see for themselves what this new group of revolutionaries were doing. The new arrivals were impressed because the Communists did not just *talk* revolution but practised what they preached. They carried out land reform, set up schools and workshops and helped people to run their own affairs through Peasant Associations. Yenan was a kind of shop window of China's future – and these window-shoppers liked what they saw!

Another united front

In 1936, as we saw in Chapter 15, the most urgent problem for China was the threat from Japan. For a year the Communists had been loudly calling for firm resistance, but Chiang Kai-shek did nothing until the famous Sian incident of December 1936 when he was kidnapped and forced to agree to another united front with the CCP. The Red Army became the 8th Route Army under Chiang's command and China now made ready for the Japanese invasion which began in July 1937.

The agreement with the KMT brought a double advantage to the Communists. It made them national heroes overnight, for all the Chinese people could now see who their real friends were. Secondly, it saved them from further attacks by the KMT which for years had been sapping their strength. But both Mao and Chiang knew that their truce was only temporary; when the common enemy (Japan) had been defeated they would return to their life-and-death struggle for the right to rule China.

1937–45 : THE SINO-JAPANESE WAR

The KMT'S war record

The war with Japan brought further misery to China. At first the KMT armies resisted the invaders, but by 1939 Japan occupied huge areas of northern, coastal and central China (see Figure 15.4). Chiang moved his capital to the inland city of Chungking and there he sat out the war in his mountain stronghold, out of reach of Japanese attacks except by air raids. After 1938 the only significant actions of KMT troops were occasional attacks on their 'allies' the Communists.

From 1937 onwards the KMT received substantial help from the Soviet Union. This may seem surprising, but it is explained by Russia's traditional fear of Japanese power in the Far East. Russia had historical interests in China – especially in Manchuria – which she hoped one day to recover from Japan. Once the KMT took up arms against Japan, and had (officially) stopped fighting the Communists in China, Stalin was ready to help even a 'reactionary' like Chiang Kai-shek.

When Japan attacked the United States in December 1941, the Chinese war became part

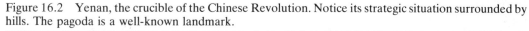

Figure 16.2   Yenan, the crucible of the Chinese Revolution. Notice its strategic situation surrounded by hills. The pagoda is a well-known landmark.

of the Second World War and China found herself one of the Big Five alliance against the Axis powers (Germany and Japan). For Chiang Kai-shek the USA's Lend-Lease Act of March 1941 opened the tap of American aid for which he had been waiting. But he wasn't going to waste it on fighting the Japanese when others could do that for him! Chiang was saving his strength for his internal enemies. The Americans became increasingly irritated when the money and supplies they sent to help the Chinese war effort produced so little result. In 1944 an American military mission visited the Communist base in Yenan and reported that American aid might be better used if it was sent there, but Chiang and his wife played up their personal American connection for all it was worth, and managed to keep the US Government's confidence. American aid continued to flow into Chungking; if Chiang Kai-shek would not fight the invaders, at least his refusal to surrender tied up Japanese troops on the mainland.

The Communists' war record

In contrast to the KMT, the Communists were brave and effective fighters against the Japanese. They put to good use the guerilla warfare they had practised earlier against the KMT by making persistent attacks behind the Japanese lines. In northern China the Japanese-held cities became 'islands' in the Communist-controlled 'sea' of the countryside. If Japanese troops ventured out, their trains were blown up and their soldiers mown down by guerilla bands of Communists and local peasants.

Note! – Communist soldiers *and peasants*. Wherever they fought, the Communists continued to preach and practise their own cause among the Chinese people. These were the years when the soul of China was finally 'lost' to Communism, and it should be very clear by now (whatever Senator McCarthy thought) that it was neither Russia's 'victory' nor America's 'fault' that this happened. From its beginning, the Chinese Communist Revolution was a *Chinese* affair. But we are

jumping ahead! The story is not quite finished.

1945–6: the post-war situation

On 6 and 9 August 1945, two Atom bombs were dropped on Japan. On 14 August Japan surrendered and the Second World War was over.

At the end of the war the Communists were in a very strong position in China. They had liberated 100 million people from Japanese occupation, and added further areas during 1945. Their reputation with the people was very high. The KMT's reputation, on the other hand, was at rock bottom. By 1945 the Party was little more than a corrupt military clique. The leadership had lost nearly all support even among the middle class, and it had never won any from the peasants and workers, except during the brief united front with the Communists from 1923–7.

But in 1945, very few outsiders recognized the true position: the wide support for the Communists and the lack of any for the Kuomintang. In any case, both the major powers on the scene regarded Chiang Kai-shek as the ruler of China now that Japan was defeated, and each for its own reasons wanted him to stay in power.

(i) *The Americans* had begun to have doubts about Chiang Kai-shek's fitness to rule China; the tyranny and corruption of his government was by now very well known. But they had a long-standing emotional and financial commitment to the KMT, and a strong dislike of Communism. Moreover, with the eclipse of Japan's power in the Far East they wanted a friendly government in China as a bulwark against Russian expansion into the area. So the Americans air-lifted KMT troops to take over northern cities of China as the Japanese withdrew, to prevent the Communists sweeping in from the surrounding countryside.

(ii) *The Russians* were mainly concerned about their own interests in China. The Allies had promised to support the Soviet claim, when Japan was defeated, that

Mongolia should remain 'independent' (in reality a Soviet satellite) and that historic Russian 'rights' to use two ports and railways in Manchuria should return to her. Six days before Japan surrendered, Russian troops occupied Manchuria and immediately the war ended they signed a treaty with the KMT confirming this post-war settlement of Russian claims.

Did Stalin (like others) simply not realize Communist strength in China? Or did he prefer a weak KMT government to a strong Communist one? We saw in our study of Russia that his foreign policy was always in the interests of the Soviet Union rather than foreign Communists. At any rate the Soviet Government took advantage of their last-minute occupation of Manchuria to strip its factories of $2 billion worth of machinery. They took this home as 'booty' when they handed Manchuria over to the KMT as the legal government of China.

You can imagine the CCP's reaction when their part in China's war against Japan went unrecognized and unrewarded. In fact the Americans at first rather naively hoped to harness the Communists' reforming energy to the 'acceptable' KMT party in a coalition government. In 1945 they sent General Marshall to China to arrange this, but the venture

was doomed from the start. The CCP protested that even while Marshall attempted to mediate their long-standing differences with the KMT, millions of tons of American war surplus material was being sold to the KMT.

For his part Chiang Kai-shek had no intention of sharing power with the CCP; he was itching for the chance to finish off the 'Red bandits' by the only method he understood. During 1946 civil war broke out again. The last phase of the long struggle for power in China had begun.

1946–9: CIVIL WAR AGAIN

In 1946 the KMT's armies greatly outnumbered the Communists and their American equipment was vastly superior. In 1948 another treaty with the United States brought further massive supplies. But instead of winning the war, Chiang Kai-shek dug his own grave with military mistakes in the field and gross incompetence at home. Chinese manufacturers were enraged by a flood of American goods into China under a commercial treaty of 1946. The Americans were irritated when, as usual, much of their aid was diverted to the black market by corrupt KMT officials. Soaring inflation and food shortages made daily life impossible for everyone. The few remaining supporters of the KMT backed away in disgust at this typical display of corruption and mismanagement.

The final triumph of the Communist forces can be quickly told. In their twenty-year struggle they had won the masses, and now even the middle class were ready to give them a try. In the later stages of the civil war whole KMT armies went over to 'the liberators', taking their American supplies with them. In January 1949 Peking surrendered; in April the KMT capital at Nanking did the same. By September the remaining KMT forces had retreated to the island of Taiwan, where they have been ever since.

On 1 October 1949 in Peking Mao Tse-tung proclaimed the People's Republic of China (Figure 16.3).

Figure 16.3   Mao leads the Communist victory parade, Peking, 1949.

Study Topic 10

Communist Success in the Countryside

Mao Tse-tung came from a peasant family, but by acquiring an education he moved first to the provincial town of Changsha and later to Peking. In 1921 he helped to found the Communist Party and in 1925 he began to work among the peasants, becoming head of the Party's Peasant Department in 1926, when the CCP was allied with the Kuomintang. In 1927 Mao wrote a controversial Report in which he argued that the peasants would be the driving-force of China's revolution. At that time his views were not shared by orthodox Marxists in his own Party, but by 1935 events had proved that for a country like China, Mao's was the best strategy.

Having defined the objective – a peasant revolution – Mao also developed the techniques to achieve it: revolutionary warfare coupled with continuous political education and practical work among the soldiers and peasants. His ideas on these matters are illustrated here with extracts from his own writings. How successful they were you can see from the last extract, an outsider's view of young peasant soldiers in Yenan.

THE PEASANT REVOLUTION

During my recent visit to Hunan I made a first-hand investigation of conditions in the five counties of Hsangtan, Hsianghsiang, Hengshan, Liling and Changsha ... All talk directed against the peasant movement must be speedily set right. ... For the present upsurge of the peasant movement is a colossal event. In a very short time, in China's central, southern and northern provinces, several hundred million peasants will rise like a mighty storm, like a hurricane, a force so swift and violent that no power, however great, will be able to hold it back ...
Almost half the peasants in Hunan are

now organized ... In force and momentum the attack is tempestuous; those who bow before it survive and those who resist perish. As a result, the privileges which the feudal landlords enjoyed for thousands of years are being shattered to pieces. Every bit of the dignity and prestige built up by the landlords is being swept into the dust. ... and the popular slogan, 'All power to the peasant associations' has become a reality ... The patriarchal-feudal class of local tyrants, evil gentry and lawless landlords has formed the basis of autocratic government for thousands of years and is the cornerstone of imperialism, warlordism and corrupt officialdom. To overthrow these feudal forces is the real objective of the national revolution. In a few months the peasants have accomplished what Dr Sun Yat-sen wanted, but failed to accomplish in the forty years he devoted to the national revolution. This is a marvellous feat never before achieved, not just in forty, but in thousands of years ...
The Revolution of 1911 did not bring about this change, hence its failure. This change is now taking place, and it is an important factor for the completion of the revolution. Every revolutionary comrade must support it, or he will be taking the stand of counter-revolution ...
(From *Report on an Investigation of the Peasant Movement in Hunan*, 1927)

Mao was a little over-optimistic about the strength of peasant revolt in 1927 – it was not yet a hurricane of 'several hundred million'. But the tone of his argument was designed to persuade his comrades to his point of view, and this is typical of all his writings.

REVOLUTIONARY WARFARE

Mao Tse-tung wrote at length on the strategy and tactics of guerilla warfare and the kind of military organization it requires. These extracts show what the Red Army was like in its early days of 'hit and run' warfare with the KMT, and some of the tactics it used.

The Red Army

The majority of the Red Army soldiers come from the mercenary [i.e. KMT] armies, but their character changes once they are in the Red Army. First of all, the Red Army has abolished the mercenary system, making the men feel they are fighting for themselves and for the people and not for somebody else. So far the Red Army has no system of regular pay, but issues grain, money for cooking oil, salt, firewood and vegetables, and a little pocket money. Land has been allotted to all Red Army officers and men who are natives of the border area ...

After receiving political education, the Red Army soldiers have become class-conscious, learned the essentials of distributing land, setting up political power, arming the workers and peasants, etc., and they know they are fighting for themselves, for the working class and for the peasantry. Hence they can endure the hardships of the bitter struggle without complaint ...

Ordinarily a soldier needs six months' or a year's training before he can fight, but our soldiers, recruited only yesterday, have to fight today with practically no training. Poor in military technique, they fight on courage alone ...

The reason why the Red Army has been able to carry on in such poor material conditions and such frequent engagements is its practice of democracy. The officers do not beat the men; officers and men receive equal treatment; soldiers are free to hold meetings and to speak out; trivial formalities have been done away with; and the accounts are open for all to inspect. The soldiers handle the mess arrangements and, out of a daily five cents for cooking oil, salt, firewood and vegetables, they can even save a little for pocket money ... [which] gives great satisfaction to the soldiers. The newly captured soldiers in particular feel that our army and the Kuomintang army are worlds apart. They feel spiritually liberated, even though material conditions in the Red Army are not equal to those in the White Army. The very

soldiers who had no courage in the White Army yesterday are very brave in the Red Army today; such is the effect of democracy. The Red Army is like a furnace in which all captured soldiers are transmuted the moment they come over....

The most effective method in propaganda directed at the enemy forces is to release captured soldiers and give the wounded medical treatment. Whenever soldiers, platoon leaders, or company or battalion commanders of the enemy forces are captured, we immediately conduct propaganda among them; they are divided into those wishing to stay and those wishing to leave, and the latter are given travelling expenses and set free. This immediately knocks the bottom out of the enemy's slander that 'the Communist bandits kill everyone on sight' ...

(From *The Struggle in the Chingkang Mountains*, 1928)

Guerilla tactics

Ours are guerilla tactics. They consist mainly of the following points:

Divide our forces to arouse the masses, concentrate our forces to deal with the enemy.

The enemy advances, we retreat; the enemy camps, we harass; the enemy tires, we attack; the enemy retreats, we pursue.†

To extend stable base areas, employ the policy of advancing in waves; when pursued by a powerful enemy, employ the policy of circling round ...

These tactics are just like casting a net; at any moment we should be able to cast it or draw it in. We cast it wide to win over the masses and draw it in to deal with the enemy. Such are the tactics we have used for the past three years.

(From *A Single Spark Can Start a Prairie Fire*, 1930)

Strategic retreat

What constitutes a defeat for the Red Army? Strategically speaking, there is a defeat only when a counter-campaign ... fails completely, but even then the defeat is only partial and temporary. For only the total destruction of the Red Army would constitute complete defeat in the

---

† This was the famous 'sixteen character slogan' which all Red Army officers knew by heart.

civil war; but this has never happened. The loss of extensive base areas and the shift of the Red Army constituted a temporary and partial defeat, not a final and complete one ...

We all know that when two boxers fight, the clever boxer usually gives a little ground at first, while the foolish one rushes in furiously and uses up all his resources at the very start, and in the end he is often beaten by the man who has given ground ...

It is extremely difficult to convince the cadres and the people of the necessity of strategic retreat ... It often happens that only by loss can loss be avoided; this is the principle of 'Give in order to take.' If what we lose is territory and what we gain is victory over the enemy, plus recovery and also expansion of our territory, then it is a paying proposition. In a business transaction, if a buyer does not 'lose' some money, he cannot obtain goods; if a seller does not 'lose' some goods, he cannot obtain money ... Sleep and rest involve loss of time, but energy is gained for tomorrow's work. If any fool does not understand this and refuses to sleep, he will have no energy the next day, and that is a losing proposition ...

After the October Revolution, if the Russian Bolsheviks had acted on the opinions of the 'left Communists' and refused to sign the peace treaty with Germany, the new-born Soviets would have been in danger of early death ...

'Fight when you can win, move away when you can't win' – that is the popular way of describing our mobile warfare today.

(From *Problems of Strategy in China's Revolutionary War*, 1936)

'Encircling the cities from the countryside'

The question is as follows: the enemy has occupied China's principal cities and lines of communication, and bases himself on the cities to oppose us; we base ourselves on the countryside to oppose the enemy. Can the countryside defeat the cities? The answer is that it is difficult ... For the cities as a whole are concentrated, whereas the countryside is scattered ... Nevertheless we must state that the countryside *can* defeat the cities ...

(From *On the New Stage*, 1938)

The truth of the last-quoted prediction was shown by what actually happened in the last stages of the struggle for power in China.

'RED DEVILS'

Very few people in the outside world knew anything about Communism in China in the 1930s. But one American, Edgar Snow, journeyed up to Yenan to see for himself what was happening there. His book *Red Star Over China*, first published in the West in 1937 (Gollancz), gave the world a glimpse of China's future.

Here is an extract from a chapter called 'Little Red Devils' in Edgar Snow's book:

Half-way round the crenellated* battlement I came upon a squad of buglers – at rest for once, I was glad to observe, for their plangent calls had been ringing incessantly for days. They were all Young Vanguards, mere children, and I assumed a somewhat fatherly air toward one to whom I stopped and talked. He wore tennis shoes, grey shorts, and a faded grey cap with a dim red star on it. But there was nothing faded about the bugler under the cap: he was rosy-faced and had bright shining eyes, a lad toward whom your heart naturally warmed as toward a plucky waif in need of care and affection and a friend. How homesick he must be! I thought. But I was soon disillusioned. He was no mama's boy, but already a veteran Red. He told me was fifteen, and that he joined the Reds in the South four years ago.

'Four years!' I exclaimed incredulously. 'Then you must have been only eleven when you became a Red? And you made the Long March?'

'Right,' he responded with comical swagger. 'I have been a *hung-chun* for four years.'

'Why did you join?' I asked.

'My family lived near Changchow, in Fukien. I used to cut wood in the mountains, and in the winter I went there to collect bark. I often heard the villagers talk about the Red Army. They said it helped the poor people, and I liked that. Our house was very poor. We were six people, my parents and three brothers, older than I. We owned no land. Rent ate more than half our crop, so we never had enough. In the winter we cooked bark for soup and saved our grain for planting in the spring. I was always hungry.

'One year the Reds came very close to Changchow. I climbed over the mountains and went to ask them to help our house because we were very poor. They were good to me. They sent me to school for a while, and I had plenty to eat. After a few months the Red Army captured Changchow, and went to my village. All the landlords and moneylenders and officials were driven out. My family was given land and did not have to pay the tax-collectors and landlords any more. They were happy and they were proud of me. Two of my brothers joined the Red Army.'

'Where are they now?'

'Now? I don't know. When we left Kiangsi they were with the Red Army in Fukien; they were with Fang Chih-min. Now, I don't know.'

'Did the peasants like the Red Army?'

'Like the Red Army, eh? Of course they liked it. The Red Army gave them land and drove away the landlords, the tax-collectors, and the exploiters.' (These 'little devils' all had their Marxist vocabulary!)

'But, really, how do you *know* they liked the Reds?'

'They made us a thousand, ten thousands, of shoes, with their own hands. The women made uniforms for us, and the men spied on the enemy. Every home sent sons to our Red Army. That is how the *lao-pai-hsing* treated us!'

No need to ask him whether *he* liked his comrades: no lad of thirteen would tramp 6,000 miles with an army he hated.

By 1945 these lads, and hundreds of thousands more, were fully trained and experienced Red soldiers. Four years later they had swept the Kuomintang armies into the sea and were ready to spread their Yenan-style Socialism throughout China.

*GLOSSARY

crenellated, built with battlements to give shooting-spaces, like the top of a castle wall.

guerilla, irregular warfare (or a person engaged in it), i.e. not between conventional armies with set battles.

KEYWORD

cadre, a nucleus of regular soldiers in a regiment, who are therefore the best-trained and most reliable. Communists often refer to those Party members as 'cadres', whose job is to organize and politically educate the masses. At the time of the Red base areas, when Communist ideas were new in China, the cadres would have been Party members or Red Army men. But in China today the term includes anyone in a position of leadership or management – for example, the members of a committee running a school or factory. Not all the cadres are members of the Party, but they are all helping to lead and organize society according to its policy.

Questions

Did you notice?

1. The Chingkang mountain area was (a) the KMT's wartime capital (b) a Red base (c) where the Long March ended
2. In the Red base areas the Communists had no mercy for (a) landlords (b) middle peasants (c) small industrialists
3. In 1930 Li Li-san wanted the CCP (a) to stay united with the KMT (b) to attack cities (c) to work mainly with the peasants
4. The cave university was in (a) Nanking (b) Chungking (c) Yenan
5. Mao became leader of the CCP in (a) 1935 (b) 1927 (c) 1949
6. True or false?
   (i) The CCP were never interested in organizing city workers
   (ii) The US Government was satisfied with the KMT's war effort against Japan
   (iii) Soviet troops invaded Manchuria in 1945
   (iv) In 1927 Mao believed Sun Yat-sen's revolution had failed
   (v) The Soviet Union aided the KMT's war effort against Japan
7. Which statement is *more* accurate?
   (i) In 1945 Stalin's main concern in China was
      (a) to assist the Communists to gain power
      (b) to recover Russian interests there
   (ii) General Marshall went to China in 1945
      (a) to arrange a coalition government
      (b) to help the KMT to take power
   (iii) Mao departed from Marxist theory in his belief
      (a) that the peasants should lead China's revolution
      (b) that the CCP should form a united front with the KMT

Can you explain?

8. Why was 1927 such a decisive date (a) for the KMT, and (b) for the CCP?
9. What were the special features of the Communists' work in the Red base areas and in Yenan after 1935?
10. What was the effect of Soviet influence on the CCP in the early 1930s?
11. In what ways was the Red Army different from most other armies?
12. Briefly, why did the United States want the KMT to stay in power after 1945? How did they try to ensure that it did so?

What's your view?

13. Consider again the *Three People's Principles* explained in Chapter 15 (pages 159–60). In what ways did the Communists 'take them over' after 1927?
14. In the extract from Edgar Snow's book (pages 178–9), what reasons does the boy give for the Red Army's popularity? Can you suggest any other reasons why boys like him might have joined it?
15. There are several examples in history of successful guerilla warfare against conventional armies. Do you know of any? Why is it so hard for conventional forces to win against guerillas?

17

Figure 17.1   A Russian poster of 1949 welcomes China into the Communist family.

CHINA'S FOREIGN RELATIONS AFTER 1950

'Leaning to one side'

The Soviet Union had continued to regard the KMT as the legal government of China until the eve of its departure to Taiwan. But when the new government was proclaimed, Stalin naturally welcomed it as 'a victory for world Communism' (Figure 17.1). Mao Tse-tung went to Moscow for two months of discussions, and in February 1950 the Sino–Soviet Treaty of Friendship was announced, from which China was to receive substantial military and economic help. The two states also struck a bargain over territory: China confirmed that Mongolia was no longer part of China, while Russia agreed to surrender her rights in Manchuria 'not later than 1952'. Arrangements were made for the joint de-

Constructing the Socialist State, 1949–56

velopment of Sinkiang, a border area of China where Russian influence had always been strong.

China now had a powerful friend in the outside world, and for several years she followed a policy which Mao called 'leaning to one side'. We shall see later that this friendship did not last for long, but in the early 1950s both Communist states felt reassured by their alliance. This was the iciest phase of the East–West Cold War.

Cold War with the West

Coming on top of Communist advances in Europe between 1945 and 1949, Mao's victory in China was not welcomed by the West. The Chinese Communists caused further disapproval by occupying Tibet in 1950 to restore former Chinese rule there. The West saw this as 'the conquest of a free country', for Tibet – although internally not a free society – had been ruling itself since 1912. The Sino–Soviet Treaty yet further increased Western fears of the vast Communist bloc which now confronted 'the free world'. Many people found it easy to accept the view that Mao's triumph was part of a global conspiracy for world conquest, master-minded in Moscow: Stalin was pulling the strings, and Mao was merely a puppet.

To cap all this, late in 1950 Chinese and American troops came face to face on opposite sides in the Korean War. As you will see in Part IV, this confrontation led to a twenty-year freeze between China and the United States. Their hostility also greatly restricted China's relations with other Western nations, and blocked the new government's admission to the United Nations.

So Communist China, like Communist Russia, started life in the international community as a 'black sheep'*. But her government had more than enough to keep it busy at home.

THE NEW GOVERNMENT

The Communist Government had the help of a loyal army and Party which had served a useful apprenticeship in the liberated areas before 1949. It also had two sources of strength among the people it was going to rule: first, the support of millions of peasants who had already tasted the benefits of Communist rule and, secondly, the goodwill of many non-Communist Chinese. We can understand the peasants' support, but why did others welcome the Communists? In one word – *patriotism*. The new rulers were a strong national government which had come to power without outside help. They had a record of patriotic resistance to foreign imperialists, and had defeated the American-backed KMT. They offered the hope of a strong and independent China in years to come.

The Kuomintang had been a disappointment to many who had originally supported it. Those who still did so went to Taiwan or elsewhere, but many of the middle class stayed in China in a mood of 'wait and see'. Others returned from abroad in the same spirit: at last there seemed to be an opportunity to use their education and talents in the service of their country.

These people were part of the 'bourgeoisie' and therefore in theory were enemies of a working-class revolution. But the Communists knew that their skills and experience would be needed to rebuild China. So they did not drive them out but encouraged them to stay, hoping to re-educate them to accept Socialism as China moved towards that goal in the coming years.

The aims of Mao Tse-tung

Mao Tse-tung's ideas and leadership had led the CCP to victory in 1949, and he was the dominant influence in the People's Republic until his death in 1976. To study the period 1949–76, which we might call the 'Mao dynasty' in China's history, it is important to understand the long-term aims of his policies.

Like Marx himself, Mao took a long view of human history. Socialism is only a stage on the road to the Communist 'classless society' which he believed involved nothing less than the transformation of man – the creation of new, unselfish human beings whose first loyalty is not to themselves or even to the family, but to 'the people'. He did not expect this to be achieved easily or quickly, for the ideas of hundreds of millions of people are not changed overnight. At times a special push would be needed, and we shall deal later with examples of this in the Hundred Flowers Movement, the Great Leap Forward and above all the Cultural Revolution.

How far a truly classless society can be achieved, in China or elsewhere, is a matter for the future. But this is what Mao was aiming for in his leadership of China's Communist Revolution. For Mao, 'Liberation' in 1949 was only a step on the road: the revolution itself is a continuous process stretching back to the 1920s and ahead for years to come.

The first job of the new government, however, was to construct a Socialist state by nationalizing the means of production and reorganizing other spheres of life on a Socialist basis. The rest of this chapter deals with this stage of the Chinese Revolution under three headings: the economy, social reforms and ideology.

THE ECONOMY

To begin with, the new régime had a basic task of recovery. China had been devastated by decades of civil war, Japanese occupation and natural disaster. Such industry as she had, in Manchuria, had been largely dismantled and looted by the USSR. Her people were hungry, disorganized, exhausted. Soaring inflation in the last years of the KMT régime had ruined confidence in the money system.

But for the strong and united new government, rehabilitation of the economy was a relatively easy task. To quote a US Congress Report of 1967:

> ... in a remarkable short time the new government had:
> suppressed banditry
> restored the battered railroad system to operation
> repaired and extended the badly neglected system of dikes
> replaced the graft-ridden bureaucratic system of local government with apparently incorruptible Communist 'cadres'
> introduced a stable currency and enforced a nationwide tax system
> begun an extensive programme of public health and sanitation
> provided a tolerably even distribution of available food and clothing ...†

Agriculture

In Socialist China, as in Russia, the system of land-holding and agricultural production was completely changed from small-scale privately owned farms to large-scale communally owned farms. In China there were distinct stages in this process: first, redistribution of land so that every peasant had his own patch; secondly, gradual collectivization into co-operative farms similar to the Soviet *kolkhoz*; thirdly, the formation of communes. The third stage was begun in 1958 and is described in the next chapter. Here we look at the first two stages.

Stage 1 – Land reform

Under the Land Reform Law of 1950, between 1950 and 1952 land was seized from the large landowners and redistributed among individual peasant families. This

†Joint Economic Committee of Congress, *An Economic Profile of Mainland China* (US Government Printing Office, 1967).

extended to the whole of China what had been done in Communist areas from the 1920s onwards. It finally fulfilled over the whole country Sun Yat-sen's original principle of 'the land to the tiller'.

There were both *political* and *economic* reasons for Stage 2, which began in 1952. To fit Socialist ideology, the reorganization of agriculture could not stop at redistribution: that would merely replace one group of individual owners with a larger group of individual owners. Before long there would be a 'kulak problem' like Soviet Russia's in 1928. In any case, as we know, Socialism means the *collective* ownership of the means of production. The Chinese Communists also had the same economic reasons as the Soviet Government for collectivizing agriculture: they wanted to increase production in larger farming units where mechanization and new techniques could be introduced.

Although the motives of the two Communist governments were the same, there were marked differences in *the methods* by which collectivization was carried out in each country. Mao was keenly aware of the need to tread softly, to coax and persuade the peasants into co-operative farming rather than forcibly dispossess them of their land and livestock as Stalin had done. In China, collectivization was carried out at a pace the peasants could accept.

Stage 2 – Collectivization

Between 1952 and 1956, the land was gradually collectivized in a step-by-step process:

(i) 'mutual aid teams' of 7–10 families were formed. They shared their animals, tools and labour, but each family continued to own its land and the crops it produced.

(ii) 'lower-stage co-operatives' were set up to farm the land co-operatively. But the families still owned their land and received a share of the profits according to how much of the co-operative farm was theirs.

(iii) 'higher-stage co-operatives' of 100–300 families were the next step. At first pri-

183

vate ownership continued, but after 1955 this was discouraged. Gradually the co-operatives bought the land, tools and animals from individual families who then became part-owners, along with all the others, of the whole co-operative farm.

By 1956, 95 per cent of the peasants were in higher-stage co-operatives. Collectivization had been achieved in Mao's way: steadily and firmly, but not cruelly. The lessons of 'Stalin's way' in Russia had been learned, and so far, at any rate, communal farming in China seemed to be successful.

Industry

China in 1949 was even more backward industrially than Russia in 1917. There was some light industry, mostly foreign controlled, and the Japanese had set up some heavy industry in Manchuria during their rule of that area since 1931. China's 'own' industry was mainly small handicraft workshops.

The years 1949–53 were a period of recovery and of taking over businesses owned by foreigners and former supporters of the KMT. Small Chinese-owned businesses were allowed to continue in private hands until 1956 – a few even until 1966. Small capitalists were allowed 5 per cent interest on investments until the mid-1960s. This is another example of the Communists treading softly so as not to make enemies of useful people.

In 1950–51 (while China was engaged in the Korean War) over 40 per cent of the state budget went to national defence. Nevertheless, in 1953 China began large-scale industrial development with her first Five-Year Plan.

Soviet-style planning at first

In the Sino–Soviet Treaty of Friendship the USSR had promised extensive economic aid: she would provide, over fifteen years, 300 modern industrial plants, and train Chinese workers to operate them, at a total cost of $3 billion in loans.

For the first few years, China's industrial development was a faithful copy of the Soviet model: 70 per cent of investment went to heavy goods industries, 13 per cent to consumer industries, and rather little (only 6·2 per cent of the state budget) to agriculture. Another Soviet feature that China adopted at first was centralized planning. By 1957, 68 Soviet projects had been completed and by 1960 (when Soviet aid was withdrawn), 154 were finished.

China's industrial progress in these years (shown in an economic growth rate of 12 per cent per annum) certainly owed much to Soviet help. But by 1956 Mao had begun to think that the Soviet model was not well suited to China. After that the emphasis of China's economic development changed, as we shall see in the next chapter.

SOCIAL REFORMS

From 1949 onwards, social life in China was overhauled in the same radical way as the economy.

Public health campaigns

Vast public health campaigns were carried out, which greatly reduced or eliminated chronic health problems such as the high infant mortality rate* and the widespread endemic diseases of pre-Communist China. An important long-term result of this was the creation of a hygiene-conscious people whose attention to public (as well as private) cleanliness is remarked upon by every foreign visitor.

Working conditions and welfare

Working conditions and welfare for the growing industrial work force were regulated and extended by a trade union federation set up in 1950. As in other Socialist countries, its function is to administer the laws of labour protection and social welfare rather than, as in the West, to bargain for higher wages. Retirement was fixed at between the ages of 45–55 for women and 55–65 for men. By 1960, an eight-hour day and a six-day week were fairly general.

Education

Education was radically 'reformed' after 1966, and we shall consider this topic in more detail later (Chapter 19). In the early years the main emphasis was on primary education and literacy campaigns (in 1949 at least 80 per cent of the population was illiterate). Simplification of the complicated Chinese language was begun. During the 1950s the existing patchwork of Christian-mission, state and private schools were merged into a national system.

The position of women

The most radical social change in the new China was in the position of women (Figure 17.2). As in many peasant societies today, women in feudal China were considered as possessions of men. They were subjected to cruel humiliations (like the practice of binding girls' feet from birth), they were married off in childhood and sold in hard times by their husbands or fathers. Under the KMT their status had improved a little, but they were still regarded mainly as domestic servants. In 1950 the Marriage Law abolished child marriage, infanticide (the practice of killing unwanted girl babies), bigamy and other marital inequalities. Other laws gave maternity benefits and equal pay to many working women and, in accordance with Mao's saying 'Women hold up half the sky', they are now legally on an equal footing with men. But to some extent traditional attitudes to women still persist, especially in remote rural areas. Women's Liberation is not yet nationwide in China!

IDEOLOGY

The aspect of Communist China which the West finds most distasteful – today as in the 1950s – is the determined process of re-making men's *minds* as well as their environment. Mao's writings make clear this basic policy, and the Cultural Revolution in the late 1960s was a startling demonstration of it. But that was only the biggest in a series of nationwide ideological campaigns since 1949 and, moreover, all these campaigns are only peaks in a continuous process of political education, of 'ideological struggle' between different groups and within each individual.

In the West we too have our evangelists*, both political and religious, who try to make converts. But in the West we can shut the door in the face of the political canvasser or the missionary – or the advertising man. We can simply refuse to submit to the conversion process. In China there is no escape! Since 1949 every person in China has been under pressure (at times very strong indeed) to accept the Party 'line' – or leave. And in 1949 there were still many unconverted peasants, not to mention the professional and intellectual middle classes, many of them Western educated. So there was a lot of Thought Reform to be done.

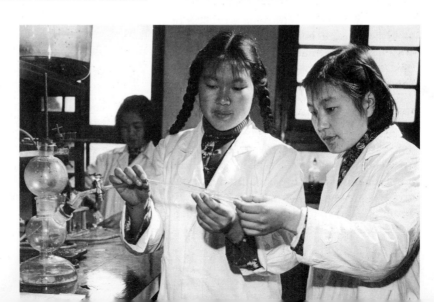

Figure 17.2 Communist China opened up a new life for girls like these two at the East China Institute of Textile Engineering in Shanghai.

Thought Reform

The cadres are sometimes the organizers of campaigns, sometimes the target of them. At all times they have the main responsibility for political education: in the 1950s it was their job to persuade the peasants into co-operatives, just as later they ran discussion groups to study Mao's *Thought*. In the early years there were three major campaigns:

> The Thought Reform campaign among intellectuals in 1950.
>
> The Three-Anti campaign (against corruption, waste and bureaucracy) among cadres in 1951.
>
> The Five-Anti campaign (against bribery, tax evasion, fraud, theft of government property and theft of state economic secrets) among merchants and industrialists.

The process of Thought Reform or 'ideological remoulding' provoked a horrified reaction in the West, where it was called brainwashing. It seemed to be a kind of magic spell which the demon Chinese were using on their 'victims'! In the 1950s some perfectly 'sane' Westerners arrived in Hong Kong from China parroting Mao's Thought as though they really believed it; soldiers taken prisoner in the Korean War returned from captivity in China confessing to 'crimes against the Chinese people' committed during the war.

In calmer mood, Thought Reform has been examined and described as a kind of group psychotherapy in which the individual is helped by his comrades through a process of self-criticism and confession, first to strip away his 'old' mental attitudes and then to construct a 'new' view of himself and his relationship to society. Once 're-made' in this way, he can be re-integrated into society.

Thought Reform may seem to us a kind of psychological torture. It is perhaps easier to understand if we think of it as an extreme expression of *social pressure*. This is the real ruling force in China today. China is a conformist society in which everyone is encouraged – even bullied – to accept a generally agreed set of ideas. We all know that it is much more comfortable to be in tune with other members of the society we live in than to be thought different, wrong or anti-social by everyone else. Imagine yourself as the object of a Thought Reform session: could *you* cling on to unpopular ideas through hours and hours of discussion in which it would be patiently explained, over and over again, that you were the one out of step, a leftover from 'old China' whose resistance to the new ideas was holding up her progress towards the new Socialist future? You would probably be glad to pin on your Mao badge and join the others under the red banner, as millions did in China after 1949.

Were millions massacred?

As a weapon of social control, Thought Reform is rather more humane than the usual ones of totalitarian states: imprisonment and death. Imprisonment is used in China too (they call it 'reform through labour'), and at times there has also been indiscriminate killing. It is hard to know exactly how much. One author suggests that about 500,000 people were killed in the Three and Five-Anti campaigns; other estimates reach 2 million or higher. In the West in the 1950s it was widely stated that 'millions' were being slaughtered, but there seems to be no firm evidence of massacres.† Mao's techniques of winning over the opposition without mass terror before 1949 were so well established, and so successful, that any killing that did take place was probably due to excessive zeal in the lower ranks rather than official policy.

*GLOSSARY

'black sheep', a despised and rejected outcast.

evangelist, a person preaching the Gospel; loosely used for anyone trying to spread a faith or belief.

infant mortality rate, the number of babies per 1000 born which die in the first year of life.

†See the discussion on this point in Study Topic 12.

Questions

Did you notice?

1. In the Korean War, Chinese soldiers fought (a) Americans (b) North Koreans (c) Russians
2. Collectivization was begun in 1952 because (a) the peasants disliked working alone (b) the USSR ordered it (c) private ownership conflicts with Socialist ideas
3. One feature of China's industrial development in the early 1950s was (a) centralized planning (b) an emphasis on consumer goods (c) huge investments in agriculture
4. China's main educational problem in the early 1950s was (a) existing missionary schools (b) illiteracy (c) too few universities
5. Mutual aid teams were (a) Thought Reform squads (b) adult education teachers (c) groups of peasant families
6. True or false?
   (i) Tibet was self-governing until China occupied it in 1950
   (ii) China's Communist Government was admitted to the UN in 1950
   (iii) All privately-owned businesses were nationalized by 1955
   (iv) The Marriage Law of 1950 brought complete Women's Lib. to China
   (v) By the Sino–Soviet Treaty of 1950 China lost Manchuria
7. Which statement is *more* accurate?
   (i) In 1949 many middle-class Chinese welcomed the Communists because
      (a) they wanted to see China strong and independent
      (b) they were attracted to Marxist ideas
   (ii) The Land Reform Law of 1950
      (a) began the collectivization of agriculture
      (b) gave 'the land to the tiller'
   (iii) Millions of Chinese were converted by Thought Reform campaigns because
      (a) there was strong social pressure to 'follow the crowd'
      (b) they would certainly be killed if they didn't
   (iv) In the period up to 1956 China copied Soviet methods
      (a) in the development of industry
      (b) in the collectivization of agriculture

Can you explain?

8. What were China's relations (a) with the USSR and (b) with the West, in the early 1950s?
9. In what sense is Mao Tse-tung's Communist revolution a continuous process?
10. What changes in the organization of Chinese agriculture were made between 1950 and 1956? What were the *political* and *economic* reasons for collectivization, and why was it carried out gently?
11. Which sector of the economy received most money and attention under the first Five-Year Plan? Why?
12. What is meant by the description of Thought Reform as 'an expression of social pressure'?

What's your view?

13. Why do you think people in the West were especially horrified by reports of brainwashing in China?
14. Do you think the ideas of people in Western societies are influenced by social pressure? If so, in what ways?
15. Western visitors to China notice that despite official policy, women are still under-represented in positions of authority and tend to hide behind their menfolk. Do you think this timidity is born into women, or merely the result of age-old customs and belief?

187

18

The Great Leap Forward: A Maoist Experiment

The first stage of China's Communist revolution – the construction of a Socialist economy – was mainly achieved by 1956. By then most businessmen had merged their concerns with state enterprises and had themselves become state employees. The government had begun many large industrial projects with Soviet help. By that date also, 95 per cent of China's agriculture was organized in completely Socialist higher-stage co-operatives in which land, tools and animals were collectively owned and used.

After 1956 China moved into a stormy period. In the next decade the Communist Government sometimes looked like a car with a drunken driver at the wheel, lurching first Left, then Right, then Left again in 1966 into the dramatic upheaval of the Cultural Revolution. It would be more accurate, however, to say that different drivers were steering at different times, and the sharp Left turns occurred when Mao Tse-tung was in control.

The image of a car on the road is deliberate, for when the debate over policy came to a climax in the Cultural Revolution of 1966 it was presented in China as a choice between the 'Capitalist road' of the Rightists and the 'Socialist road' of Mao Tse-tung. In fact Mao had begun to map out his Socialist road in policy debates within the Party ten years earlier.

The Socialist road

For Mao Tse-tung 1949 was only the beginning of a new phase in the struggle to achieve Communism in China. He believed that Marx's class struggle continues during the stage of Socialism in the sense that Capitalist *ideas* are still around and have to be recog-

nized and snuffed out whenever they reappear. These ideas are naturally attractive to middle-class people who had some special status in the old society, but even Communist cadres of humble origins may start 'putting on airs' when they get into positions of authority. So China's leaders must be ever-watchful to prevent any 'back-sliding' into old Capitalist habits, and the emergence of a new privileged class.

More than that, the government must constantly push China *on* towards the goal of a completely Communist society. Mao himself was ready to take great 'leaps' towards the Communist future, on the principle that if you drive very fast down a jungle track, sheer speed will get you quite a long way before the tangle of undergrowth forces the car to a stop. Then you may have to pause and repair the damage – but you are much further along the road than if you had cautiously stopped to cut down every bramble along the way.

Mao's techniques of conversion

Mao's bold style of leadership was often opposed by more conservative leaders in the Party's Central Committee. He did not simply purge the opposition and establish a one-man tyranny, but nevertheless he was quite determined that *his* vision of China's future should be accepted. In the period after 1956 he used two special techniques to accomplish this:

1. A public discussion was opened to let 'the broad masses' express their views. In the general debate which then followed, Mao used his own great prestige and a barrage of propaganda to help the masses to make up their minds.

2. A scapegoat was set up to take the blame for 'wrong' ideas and policies which were set against the 'correct' ideas and policies of Mao Tse-tung. In the late 1960s two prominent Party leaders, Liu Shao-chi and Lin Piao – both with a long record of loyalty and both at one time tipped as successors to Mao – were publicly disgraced in this way.

These techniques were largely successful in keeping China on Mao's 'Socialist road' until his death. But other Party leaders considered his drive towards ultimate Communism much too reckless and fast. In the twenty years after 1956 China got into grave difficulties and Mao's leadership was challenged more than once. This chapter and the next show how he overcame the opposition and how far he achieved his aims.

In the mid-1950s – to continue the motor car image – Mao was in the driver's seat, and he could see several big bumps in the road ahead. First there was the continuing struggle against Capitalist ideas, and secondly there were serious problems in the economy. We will take the question of ideology first.

THE HUNDRED FLOWERS CAMPAIGN

What the government needed most for its task of building Socialism was a group of skilled experts – educators, scientists, engineers, managers – who were dedicated to its own Communist programme. Few of the Party cadres – although their ideology was satisfactorily Red – had sufficient education and experience for important administrative jobs. But many of the intellectuals and professional people, who did have the required skills, had not been converted to Socialism by the Thought Reform campaigns of the early 1950s. These educated city-bred people despised the upstart cadres with mud on their boots, chanting their Communist slogans and bossing people about.

How could middle-class people with such un-Socialist attitudes be trusted in positions of authority? Somehow they must be persuaded into a Socialist way of thinking, and

it was clear that a more subtle approach than crude Thought Reform was needed to win them over. This was tried in the Hundred Flowers Campaign of 1956–7. Everyone was invited to 'let a hundred flowers bloom and a hundred schools of thought contend': in other words, to criticize and comment on the régime and its work so far. At the same time a Party rectification campaign was conducted against bureaucratic behaviour among the cadres.

At first the critics were slow to respond – perhaps they could not believe that their opinions were really being asked! – and in February 1957 Mao reissued the invitation in a speech which was published all over China. Then came a flood of criticism in speeches and in print. It was strongly anti-Party and even anti-Socialist; in some places there were student riots against Party officials. Suddenly the Party leadership took fright: they had hoped for constructive criticism, but they could not allow the basic Socialist framework of new China to be questioned. That was counter-revolution! So the Hundred Flowers Movement was abruptly halted and replaced by an anti-Rightist campaign which returned to the blunt methods of Thought Reform to *force* a transformation in people's thinking.

Meanwhile the Party leaders' attention was taken up by economic questions. Mao was marshalling support for a daring new policy which would help to solve these problems and would also continue to build up a truly Red ideology in China.

THE GREAT LEAP FORWARD

The large investment in heavy industry during the first Five-Year Plan, 1953–7, had achieved its goal of doubling overall industrial production in that period. But China's leaders were worried because China's economy was unbalanced in several ways:

1. The increased output from heavy industry was not much use while there were too few producer industries to use its products (bars of steel are only useful when they are made into something!). In particular, not enough tools and machinery for agriculture were being produced.

2. Industrial development was also geographically lop-sided. Most of China's industries were in a few coastal towns simply because that was the most convenient place for the foreign companies which had first developed them. Already there was a disturbing drift of even more people to these cities: between 1949 and 1956 the urban population had grown from 58 million to 89 million.

3. With most investment and effort going into industry, agriculture was lagging behind. China, like Russia in the 1930s, needed an agricultural surplus for export as well as to feed her own growing population. Until she could build up grain reserves and some defences against natural disasters, the old enemy – famine – could strike again at any time.

4. Lastly, it was clear that Soviet-style centralized planning was unsuitable for China. She did not have sufficient transport and trained workers to manage her economy in this way.

So far China's economic development had been under Soviet guidance and had mainly followed the Soviet pattern of the 1930s. But was this the right kind of development for China? Did she want to become a heavily industrialized country like the USSR? Mao Tse-tung was beginning to think out some entirely different principles for China's economic development in the future. He hoped they would lead to the kind of classless society he was aiming for in China.

When you come to think of it, what are class distinctions based upon? Mainly on differences of wealth of course, but there is also the extra prestige of education, of working with your brain and not with your hands, or operating a shiny machine in a modern factory instead of toiling away in muddy fields. There is even some social status (and this is especially true in poor countries) in being part of the 'up-to-date' life of a city instead of plodding along in the 'backward' countryside.

These differences already existed in China and – so it seemed to Mao Tse-tung – they

would become stronger, not weaker, unless her economic development changed direction. After much discussion in the Party's Central Committee, Mao gained support for a bold new policy. Early in 1958, China was launched into the Great Leap Foward.

The aims of the Great Leap Forward

In the first place, the Great Leap Forward was a spectacular attempt to increase production in both industry and agriculture. The propaganda slogans said it would accomplish the work of 'twenty years in a day'! China would 'outstrip Great Britain in fifteen years'! It would be 'hard work for a few years, happiness for a thousand'!

Secondly, the new policy was designed to correct the lop-sided features of China's economy and begin to iron out the differences between industry and agriculture, town and country. This was done in two ways:

(a) By developing small and medium-sized factories throughout the countryside, beginning with 600,000 'back-yard steel furnaces' to boost iron and steel production. These were to be set up and manned by peasants with the help of local cadres. They were mainly to produce tools and other requirements for local use, but enterprising workers might also discover new techniques or supplies of raw materials which could be used in other parts of China.

(b) Huge 'earth-works' were undertaken: reservoirs and irrigation channels, land-reclamation and flood-control schemes, tree-planting, bridge-building and road construction. These projects were mainly a long-term investment in agriculture: they would lay the foundations for increased production in the future and defend the fields against flood and drought.

But how on earth would all this be done? China had very few cranes, bulldozers and earth-moving machines. She also had very few technical experts – and those she had would not lend their skills to a mad-cap Communist adventure like this, which broke all the rules of Western and Soviet industrial development.

But what China did have was thousands of willing Party cadres and millions and millions of peasants. If the cadres and the peasant workers had no technical know-how, never mind! They would learn by doing! If China had no bulldozers, never mind! Use hands and feet and wheel-barrows and pick-axes!

Thirdly, then, the Great Leap Forward was also a huge propaganda exercise. Armies of peasants marched to the fields and construction sites with banners flying and drums beating. Slogans were everywhere. One of them, 'Politics in command!' thumbed its nose at all those superior people who would not roll up their sleeves and join in the great crusade. Reds were in control now, and experts who hung back or criticized were pushed aside. If they would not become Red, then the Reds must become expert, the quicker the better!

The 'blue ants'

It is difficult in a few words to describe the feverish atmosphere and activities of the Great Leap Forward. Thirty or 40 million peasants dug canals (Figure 18.1); 50 to 70 million planted new forests; other millions built roads, dikes and reservoirs. Six million

city-dwellers were sent to the countryside to help. Even Chairman Mao turned out to do a bit of digging! A Western journalist described the hordes of workers in their blue cotton working clothes as 'blue ants' – and the name has stuck, for this is still the way that huge construction projects are carried out in China: by the hard physical slog of hundreds of thousands of people, with scarcely a machine in sight.

To organize the setting up of new factories, and to marshal the armies of labour needed for big construction projects, a new kind of agricultural unit came into being: *the commune*.

People's Communes

During 1958 the higher-stage co-operatives were gathered into even larger units called People's Communes. A directive from the Central Committee recommended communes as 'the best form of organization for the attainment of Socialism and the gradual transition to Communism. They will develop into the basic social units in Communist society.'

Some enthusiastic cadres organizing the communes at once abolished all private property, set up communal kitchens and canteens and decreed that the peasant should be paid a fixed wage like a factory worker. But these

Figure 18.1   The 'blue ants': building a new canal near Peking.

'excesses' were resisted by the peasants. Within a few months they were corrected, and the too-large communes reduced in size.

The setting up of communes during the Great Leap Forward radically altered the pattern of collective farming and the Party's administration of China. For the next twenty-five years the commune was the basic unit of China's rural economy and government. Study Topic 11 (page 196) describes how they were organized.

Consequences of the Great Leap

'Back-yard steel furnaces' and other features of the Great Leap were watched with a smile of amusement and scepticism in the West and with strong disapproval by China's 'big brother' the Soviet Union. Would 'back-yard steel' really 'outstrip Great Britain in fifteen years'? Come now, be sensible!

In economic terms the Great Leap was a serious blunder. 'Back-yard steel' was of such poor quality that it was of little use for any industrial purpose. Dikes leaked and home-made clay drainage pipes cracked. Worse still, grain was left to rot in the fields while peasants were away digging reservoirs.

From 1959–61 China suffered three 'hard years' (as that period was later called) which almost took her back to the bad old days earlier in the century. Food was rationed and famine occurred in some areas. It is hard to assess the full extent of this: even after 1980, when the post-Mao leaders described the Great Leap as one of Mao's worst 'mistakes', the government did not issue a full account of its effects. But one Western journalist recently reported that 'about 16.5 million more people than normal died in the three years of food shortages caused by the Great Leap, probably from malnutrition and its effects', while another was told in 1982 that in one county, 60,000 people out of a total population of 380,000 starved during that time.†

This economic calamity was not entirely due to the Great Leap, however. It was made worse by two other factors:

(i) Disastrous weather caused poor harvests for three years in a row.

(ii) In 1960 the USSR suddenly withdrew all her aid and personnel, leaving factories half-built and Chinese workers half-trained. The effect of this was shown in 1961 when there was a 75 per cent drop in industrial output from the 1959–60 figure. It took China several years to recover from the blow.

The Soviet withdrawal of aid was part of a Sino-Soviet quarrel which had been developing behind the scenes for some years. It soon became a major split which profoundly affected relations between East and West, as we shall see in Part IV. The dispute concerned several issues, but we can already see a hint of these differences: China under Mao was becoming an entirely different *kind* of Socialist state from the USSR.

Clearly the Great Leap Forward went badly wrong. But it is fair to record some good results of it, and some sensible aims underlying this Maoist 'adventure'. Small local workshops did increase the supply of scarce products like cement and fertilizer, and continued to do so. They also began to develop simple industrial skills among the peasants, and provided alternative work during the slack season in farming. In agriculture, 30 billion trees were planted in 1958, and over 100 million acres irrigated between 1958 and 1960, which greatly increased yields in later years.

Visiting economists concerned with Third World development were impressed by several features of the Great Leap and the Chinese commune. These were often cited as useful lessons for other poor countries:

1. *Labour-intensive industry*. The Great Leap turned China away from large, high-

---

†The first quotation comes from Fox Butterfield, *China: Alive in the Bitter Sea* (Bantam paperback, 1983), p. 242. The second report was made by John Gittings in

'The Long March from Famine', *The Guardian*, 12 March 1982. See the discussion about the results of the Great Leap in Study Topic 12, p. 198.

technology industrial projects towards small, labour-intensive factories in which more people than machines were used. This is sensible for a country such as China which has millions of people but very little capital to spend on costly machinery.

2. *Rural development*. Mao believed that China should remain basically an agricultural country. One purpose of the commune was to develop a complete rural–industrial–cultural life to counteract the lure of cities, which in China and elsewhere cannot provide enough work and amenities for all the new arrivals. Many cities in the rest of the Third World are ringed by pathetic shanty-towns of envious onlookers, while the rural societies they have left behind disintegrate. Through the Great Leap and later policies, Mao tried to prevent this happening in China.

3. *Self-reliance*. The Great Leap emphasized local independence in the self-governing communes, and with its theme of 'walking on two legs' (meaning to combine old Chinese practices with new, modern technology). This encouraged a habit of self-reliance which was essential at national level: after 1960 China had to do without any foreign aid, on which most developing nations rely. It also gave the Chinese peasants confidence in their *own* ingenuity and customs. Too often in developing countries, 'progress' means only Western technology which has to be learned from scratch, and in the process traditional ways are abandoned as inferior.

These general points remain valid for China and other developing countries. But in 1959 the immediate problem was a dislocated economy and widespread hunger.

REPAIRING THE DAMAGE

The Great Leap Forward was mainly Mao's idea, so other leaders blamed him for its failures. In December 1958 he resigned as Chairman of the Republic, though he remained Chairman of the Party and its Central Committee. For a few years he gave his attention mainly to foreign affairs and the growing split with the USSR.

In mid-1959 a policy of back-pedalling in the economy began. China now shifted gear into conservative policies so similar to Lenin's New Economic Policy in Russia that the period 1961–3 has been called 'China's NEP' (although that term was not officially used in China).

In agriculture the principles of the communes were entirely reversed by the NEP. The commune structure remained, but the practice developed of taking the household as the accounting unit, thus encouraging family rather than collective enterprise. Private plots were extended and peasants encouraged to engage in side-line occupations on a family basis, with a free market for their products. A black market was tolerated in the cities, where prices were sometimes fifty times the official price. Private trade and speculation in foodstuffs rapidly developed and in the communes a 'kulak' class began to emerge. By 1962, for example, the private grain harvest in Yunnan province was larger than the collective harvest.

In industry there was a return to bonuses and prizes for good workers, and to bureaucratic control from above. There was a reinstatement of experts as managers, for technical skill was now considered more important than a Red ideology. In the Great Leap period workers had been offered political incentives: 'Work for China!' 'Serve the people!' 'Politics in command!'† Now they were offered material incentives: 'Work for more money! For personal glory!'

The new economic policies in China *did* help recovery from the hard years after the Great Leap Forward, just as Lenin's NEP had rescued Russia from the economic chaos

---

†They should really be called moral incentives. Maoist Communism was more like a religion than a political programme, so that arguments over policy became a choice between right and wrong. To 'serve the people' was right whereas to work for self-interest was wrong.

of 1921. Again as in Russia, these policies also provoked a spontaneous return to Capitalism which soon began to worry the Maoists. In 1962 Mao began a Socialist Education Movement against corruption and Capitalist practices, and from 1960 on, the Maoist Defence Minister, Lin Piao, conducted a re-education campaign in the People's Liberation Army (as the Red Army is now called). It was for this campaign that the *Little Red Book*, a digest of Mao's Thoughts, was first produced.

WHICH ROAD FOR CHINA?

As soon as the immediate economic crisis was overcome, a full-scale argument developed between Right and Left (i.e. Maoist) leaders in the Party. The argument centred on two important questions:

What kind of economic incentives should be used in Socialist China?

How much power and status and freedom should be allowed to the educated élite, especially to those experts in positions of authority whose ideology was not wholeheartedly Red?

The debate in China often referred to what had happened in the Soviet Union, the other main example of a Socialist country, and you may remember that the USSR had become rather like a Capitalist country in two important ways at least:

1. Stalin had used material incentives in the Five-Year Plans (bonuses and piecework payments, fame for Stakhanovites and disgrace for shirkers) and these practices have continued in Soviet industry. In the early 1960s, when Khrushchev was trying to boost production, material incentives were extended on the Capitalist principle that a man will work harder for more money.

2. In the USSR the élite of Party and government officials have great power and status. Indeed all educated people – writers, artists, scientists – live more comfortably than other Russians. So it could be said that a new bourgeoisie has arisen whose right to a privileged position is not questioned by the Soviet Party. In fact Party members benefit most from it.

To the Maoists, these developments in the USSR showed that the Soviet Union (especially under Khrushchev) had 'taken the Capitalist road'.[†]

On the other hand, many Rightist Chinese leaders admired Soviet achievements and thought that China could copy them without making the mistakes of Stalin and Khrushchev. They wanted an efficient economy, which meant experts not Reds as managers, and if material incentives increased production, then use them! Since the CCP, unlike the Soviet Party, knew that it was important to stay in touch with the masses, they would prevent the middle class from 'getting above themselves'.

There was also an important reason why these leaders wanted to make up China's quarrel with the USSR (Figure 18.2). In the mid-1960s American escalation of the war in Vietnam (on China's border) looked very dangerous. Suppose it should escalate further and involve China? China could not hope to go it alone against the military might of the USA, and where else could she get help and modern weapons but from the USSR? (By 1964 China had developed her own A-bomb, but she was still far behind in the nuclear arms race.)

But these arguments did not satisfy the Maoists. First, they considered that many Party leaders themselves were 'putting on airs', claiming status and privilege above the masses, so not only the un-Socialist middle class but Rightists in the Party must be brought down a peg or two. Secondly, it would be disastrous to sacrifice the Chinese Socialist road to the Soviet Capitalist road merely for self-protection. On the question of defence against the West, they offered Mao's view that 'people are more important than weapons'. Remembering the CCP's long struggle against the Kuomintang and Japan, the Maoists argued that China could win any

[†]Mao was also very critical of Khrushchev's foreign policies, as we shall see in Part IV.

war provided that her soldiers and people were armed with the invincible Red ideology that had enabled them to defeat better equipped enemies in the past.

This was the ferment of discussion that led up to the Cultural Revolution of 1966–9. To the Maoists it was a much more serious ideological split than at the time of the Hundred Flowers campaign in 1956. Then the Party was more or less united and the only problem was the left-over bourgeoisie who had not yet accepted Socialism. Now there was an even more dangerous enemy: 'Party persons in authority taking the Capitalist road' – that is, those Rightists who wanted to follow the Soviet example.

It should be very clear by now that one important quality of Mao's leadership from the 1930s onwards was his daring (his critics called it rashness). In the early 1960s it seemed to him that the whole future of the Chinese Revolution and of Communism was at stake. So he began a counter-attack – at first quite gentle – in the Socialist Education Movement begun in 1962, but when this did not correct the Rightist tendencies, he was ready to throw the whole of China into the turmoil of the 'Great Proletarian Cultural Revolution'. And all this at a moment when China's chief enemy, the United States, was getting deeply involved in an anti-Communist war on China's doorstep! No wonder that the reaction of outsiders to the Cultural Revolution – both in the West and in the Soviet Union – was one of amazement: 'Whatever are those crazy Chinese up to now?'

Figure 18.2　In July 1963 a Chinese Government delegation went to Moscow to try (unsuccessfully) to heal the breach with the Soviet Union. They were seen off at Peking airport by other top officials – an indication of the importance attached to their mission at a time when the Party leadership was predominantly Rightist.
Foreground, left to right: President Liu Shao-chi; Premier Chou En-lai; Secretary-General of the Party Deng Xiaoping (leading the delegation) and his fellow-traveller, Peking's mayor Peng Chen; and lastly, the President's deputy Chu Teh (in dark glasses).

Study Topic 11

The Chinese Commune

Communes were set up from 1958 onwards as part of the Great Leap Forward and were the final stage of the gradual process of collectivizing agriculture during the 1950s. But they differed in many respects from collective farms (the *kolkhoz*) in the USSR.

They were formed by gathering higher-stage co-operatives into larger units. These were soon found to be too large for efficient management and were reduced to a size of 5,000–20,000 people. Below commune level there were 5–10 Production Brigades, and below that, Production Teams of 20–100 families. In most cases the Production Team was the accounting unit, all its members planning the work and finance. The Team was usually an existing village, and therefore the natural focus of group loyalty. Attempts to raise financial responsibility to Brigade or commune level were always resisted by the peasants; they preferred to keep the purse strings within reach of every village.

Figure ST 11.1   Basket workshop in a commune.

The main function of the commune was collective farming, the particular crops varying according to the area. Workers received a ration of basic food crops and a share-out of group earnings at the end of the year, after state taxes and contributions to commune funds for schools, welfare clinics, etc. had been paid. Each family's share was based on work points earned by its members during the year. Each household also had a private plot from which its own food and income could be supplemented.

But there was much more to the commune than communal farming. It was also the basic unit of government and of the Party. Each controlled its own health and welfare facilities, education and cultural affairs, as well as production. By combining farming with small-scale industry it could use peasant labour previously wasted in the slack season. Communal childcare freed women to work in the fields and workshops (Figure ST 11.1), and the welfare amenities fulfilled the Socialist ideal of community care 'from the womb to the tomb'.

The Great Leap theme of self-reliance and 'walking on two legs' was a continuing principle of the commune. By joining with others, it could organize a large workforce for regional projects which could not be undertaken by smaller units, or the remote national government. Small commune workshops, mainly servicing agriculture, complemented larger, modern plants at regional or national level. Local clinics were staffed by 'barefoot doctors' (quickly-trained first-aid workers) and commune hospitals offered traditional herbal remedies and acupuncture alongside Western-style treatment and medicine.

The commune also organized the people's militia, numbering 10–12 million throughout the nation. Discounting nuclear warfare, Mao's idea was that a country organized into thousands of self-sufficient 'cells' would be almost unconquerable.

Study Topic 12

What Can We Believe About China?

One of the problems when studying very recent history is to find accurate and reliable information. History books are usually the result of research into contemporary records and documents of the period concerned, and these are often not available until many years after the date to which they refer–if ever. For this reason we shall probably never have a full record of Stalin's purges, for example.

The history of Communist China presents many political problems. During the 1950s most reports published in the West (especially in the USA) were very hostile. For example American newspapers often reported famine in China. Yet in 1967 the Joint Economic Committee of the US Congress made a detailed study (see extract on page 183) which produced no evidence of famine at any time since 1950. In 1972 it published a follow-up report, which revised some of the information given only five years earlier: 'In general, the assessment of the present volume is less pessimistic than the assessment of the 1967 J.E.C. study ... It is now clear that fairly impressive industrial growth occurred in the midst of the Leap Forward confusion ...'† But to judge from information gathered in the 1980s, famine *did* result from the Great Leap, while industrial growth in that period was negligible.

Another important example concerns the number of people executed or massacred by the Communists. The *Guinness Book of Records* states that 'the greatest massacre in human history' occurred in China during the period 1949–65, when '26,300,000 Chinese'

were killed. The entry continues: 'This accusation was made by an agency of the USSR Government in a radio broadcast on 7 April 1969.' It then gives an even higher estimate from the 'implacably hostile' Kuomintang Government in Taiwan: 'at least 39,940,000' killed between 1949 and 1969.‡

By describing the Taiwan Government as 'implacably hostile', the editors of the *Guinness Book of Records* suggest that its figure is perhaps not to be trusted. Since they do not suggest that the Soviet Government is 'hostile' to China, the reader might well assume that the lower figure of 26,300,000 is reliable. But can the Soviet broadcast of April 1969 be trusted? For several years before that, China and the USSR had been conducting a propaganda war against each other and in March 1969 their soldiers actually came to blows in a border incident.

Teachers of political history must try to be as fair and unbiased as possible. But when faced with conflicting accounts, and drawing on limited information, in the end we have only our own non-expert judgement to fall back upon. Perhaps 26,300,000 Chinese *were* massacred by the Communists between 1949 and 1965, but this high figure is not borne out by other reports. As for the Great Leap Forward, the present Peking government is so 'implacably hostile' to that Maoist policy that we may have to wait some years for a full and fair account of it.

In the next Part of the book, when we study the Cold War, we shall return to the question of political bias in history teaching.

†Joint Economic Committee of Congress, *People's Republic of China: An Economic Assessment* (US Government Printing Office, 1972) introductory summary by John P. Hardt, p. ix.

‡Norris and Ross McWhirter, eds., *The Guinness Book of Records* (Guinness Superlatives Ltd., 1972 edition) p. 201.

Questions

Did you notice?

1. From the CCP's point of view, the Hundred Flowers Campaign provoked (a) too much criticism (b) too little criticism (c) the wrong kind of criticism

2. One important economic problem in the mid-1950s was that (a) Soviet industrial projects in China were not successful (b) China did not need more industry (c) agriculture was falling behind

3. Which one of the following was *not* an aim of the Great Leap Forward? (a) to dig reservoirs (b) to increase production (c) to develop nuclear weapons

4. The term 'blue ants' refers to (a) Chinese construction workers (b) a plague of locusts (c) Soviet technicians in China

5. During 'China's NEP' (a) relations with the USSR were resumed (b) Maoists were in control (c) material incentives were used

6. True or false?
   (i) At first the communes were too large
   (ii) During the Great Leap Forward the grain harvest was neglected
   (iii) After 1960 China got loans from the West
   (iv) The *Little Red Book* was first used in the People's Liberation Army
   (v) Peasants are given everything free by the commune
   (vi) One principle of the commune is self-reliance

7. Which statement is *more* accurate?
   (i) 'Back-yard steel furnaces'
      (a) were a resounding success
      (b) produced poor quality steel
   (ii) In China 'walking on two legs' means
      (a) combining old and new
      (b) getting help from the Soviet Union
   (iii) The Maoists in China thought the USSR had 'taken the Capitalist road' because
      (a) private ownership of houses is allowed there
      (b) a new bourgeoisie has arisen in Soviet society

   (iv) Mao's phrase 'people are more important than weapons' suggests that
      (a) a country's best defence is the ideology of its army and people
      (b) China cannot be seriously damaged by nuclear weapons

Can you explain?

8. Why was the Hundred Flowers Campaign (a) started, and (b) stopped?

9. What was the purpose behind these features of the Great Leap Forward?: (a) 'back-yard steel', (b) reservoirs and other 'earthworks', (c) 'politics in command'.

10. What is the difference between political incentives and material incentives? Which did the Maoists favour?

11. Imagine the discussions of the CCP's Central Committee at different times in the period covered by Chapter 18. Indicate in note form: (a) the arguments Mao might have used when he proposed the Great Leap Forward in 1957; (b) the point of view of other members who argued for 'back-pedalling' policies in 1960.

What's your view?

12. Quite apart from her politics, China's economic policy of rural development is often held up as a good model for other developing countries. In what ways is China's example useful for them? Do you think a commune or anything like it could be achieved without the ideology of Communism behind it?

13. Do any people in our society work hard and devotedly without the rewards of good pay and/or public recognition? What is their motivation for doing so? Is there any job in which you would be prepared to work hard for little money?

14. Do you think that history is taught objectively in Russia and China? From your recollections of any British history you have learned, do you think it was taught objectively? Does it matter if history is not taught objectively?

19

The Cultural Revolution

China's Great Proletarian Cultural Revolution was a two-and-a-half-year debate all over China between the two lines of policy which by the mid-1960s had split the CCP into Rightist and Maoist factions. The Rightists thought that China should strike out for rapid Soviet-style economic development, relying on experts in the government and Party to lead the obedient masses. To them economic efficiency was more important than political purity – or as one of their leaders put it: 'What difference does it make if the cat is black or white, so long as it catches mice?' All the difference in the world! replied the Maoists. This was their view: Socialism must guide our progress, or it isn't progress at all. That means we must take the masses along with us step by step, and if that means slowing down to their pace, then slow down! In fact we must pause right now to involve them in our discussions about which road to take. The Party leads the masses – but it must also be directed by the masses. And they will certainly choose the Socialist road!

After months of wrangling within the Party, Mao therefore appealed over the heads of Party members to let 'the masses' decide the issue. To guide them towards the Socialist road he gave out directions from time to time. He hoped that through ideological struggle around these ideas everyone in China, and especially the youth of China, would be 'revolutionized': the Capitalist cobwebs would be swept away and replaced by firm Socialist principles.

This chapter starts by identifying the targets of the Maoists' attack, then follows the course of the conflict, and ends with a summary of changes in China after the Cultural Revolution.

THE TARGETS

The Maoists believed that theirs was the true Socialist road, the correct interpretation of Marxism–Leninism. Their propaganda accused the Rightists or 'revisionists' of revising Marxism–Leninism for their own purposes, just as the Soviet Union (especially under Khrushchev) had revised the true doctrine to suit its own national policy. The main culprits were a group of 'Party persons in authority taking the Capitalist road', and chief among these was China's President, Liu Shao-chi, 'China's Khrushchev' (Figure 19.1).

Figure 19.1   Khrushchev and Liu Shao-chi symbolize the 'supreme twosome of revisionism' on this Cultural Revolution poster.

These people were the primary target in the Cultural Revolution.

Secondly, education was singled out for 'complete transformation'. The existing system was said to be still dominated by the pre-1949 bourgeois élite who had never given their full allegiance to the new Socialist China, despite the attempt in the Hundred Flowers Movement to win them over (see page 189). Now, said the Maoists, they were 'training their successors for a Capitalist comeback' through the ideas which they transmitted to the young, and by discriminating against proletarian children through the examination system. This system of education, said a newspaper editorial in June 1966, 'is a great obstacle to the revolutionizing of young people's minds and encourages them to become bourgeois specialists by the bourgeois method of "making one's own way" and achieving individual fame, wealth, and position...' As early as 1964 Mao had described the education system as one which 'strangles talents' and had recommended that 'Students should be permitted to doze off when a lecturer is teaching. Instead of listening to nonsense, they do much better taking a nap to freshen themselves up. Why listen to gibberish anyway?'

So as well as 'Party persons in authority', teachers talking gibberish were approved targets for attack! In practice, as the struggle spread into all spheres of life, *anyone* in a position of authority was called upon to explain his past actions and pledge himself to the Socialist road.

'Bombard the Headquarters!'

The administrators of Peking University were the first victims when in June 1966 radical students put up a *dazibao* ('big character poster') criticizing them. *Dazibao* is a Chinese method of public argument: any person or group can put up a statement, then others add their views. Imagine poster-size 'letters to the editor' on every bare wall (Figure 19.2)–that

Figure 19.2 The Red Guards have run out of wall space for *dazibao* in a village commune on the outskirts of Canton.

was *dazibao* during the Cultural Revolution. (Arguments over policy at every level – within a factory, for instance – are still conducted in this way.)

After the students, Mao entered the fray. In July (aged seventy-two) he made an epic nine-mile swim down the Yangtse River before a cheering crowd of supporters and photographers. On 5 August he put up his own *dazibao*, 'Bombard the Headquarters!' – an invitation to attack the Party leadership. On 8 August the CCP's Central Committee issued the Sixteen Points Resolution (drafted by Mao) which laid down the 'ground rules' of

the coming struggle. From this comes the catch-phrase which represents a three-stage programme that everyone was supposed to carry out:

'Struggle!' (against 'Party persons in authority', etc.).

'Criticize!' (revisionist and reactionary ideas).

'Transform!' (education, literature, art, all over China).

It is hard for twentieth-century Westerners to appreciate the underlying *passion* of political debate during the Cultural Revolution, which was rather like a schism between

Figure 19.3 'Mao worship' during the Cultural Revolution: a gigantic parade in Kweichow province.

'true believers' and 'heretics' within a formerly united Church (the Communist Party). There was a comparable period in seventeenth-century England, when Nonconformists seeking to reform the established Church went around vandalizing churches and attacking respected priests and bishops for their 'wrong' religious ideas, just as Party officials in China were harassed for their alleged Rightist ideology.

But the political argument sometimes got lost in the excitement of the campaign. 'Struggle and Criticism' often degenerated into sheer power rivalry between different groups, each claiming to be the true followers of Mao, in whose name the revolution was being carried out.

'STRUGGLE AND CRITICISM': THE BATTLES OF THE CULTURAL REVOLUTION

The Red Guards of university and school students were Mao's shock troops in the revolution. Schools and colleges closed and they flocked to Peking on free travel passes. Mao received millions of them in gigantic parades (Figure 19.3); at the first of these on 18 August he symbolically appointed himself their leader by donning their red arm-band. These were occasions for mass 'Mao worship'. Perhaps the nearest parallel in the West would be the hysteria of young fans mobbing their favourite pop group; many of the Red Guards were just about 'teeny-bopper' age – twelve or thirteen years old.

The Red Guards camped in thousands all over the capital, causing shortages of food and other essentials. They tore down street names reminiscent of old China and replaced them with new ones. Shops were ordered not to sell 'decadent' Western items like cosmetics; city girls with Western hair-styles were forced to adopt modest pig-tails. The campaign against the 'four olds' (ideas, culture, customs, habits) led to rummaging through homes for 'bourgeois' personal belongings dating from old China, and to

some vandalizing of historic buildings and museums. Everywhere Party leaders and others in authority were forced to write self-criticisms or to confess their revisionist ideas before jeering crowds of Red Guards.

The *Little Red Book* was waved by chanting crowds, its quotations shouted and written up everywhere, along with the 'latest instructions' from Chairman Mao. The cult of Mao reached the height of absurdity in these years. For example: 'We must resolutely carry out the instructions of Chairman Mao whether we understand them or whether for the time being we do not yet understand them'!

In December 1966 the workers were called upon to join in the struggle and this led to widespread economic chaos during 1967. The most famous conflict involving urban workers was in Shanghai. The triumph of the Maoist forces there in January 1967 is regarded as the first major victory of the 'Socialist roaders' over the 'Capitalist roaders'. But there were still many battles to come.

As factories and transport came to a standstill, and serious fighting sometimes broke out, the People's Liberation Army (PLA) were used as mediators and to keep essential services going. At times the conflict certainly got completely out of hand. In the Wuhan incident in July 1967, military units in central China kidnapped a high-up Party leader who had been sent to mediate between local factions. This event shows the deep cracks in national unity at this time. This and other 'excesses' during 1967 brought an official 'cooling down' policy. Workers were sent back to their jobs and millions of Red Guards were sent to work in the countryside with the peasants.

Three-in-One committees

In 1968 the political situation was still far from clear. The Maoist groups seemed to be dominant throughout the nation, but the Party was in disarray. Who would now take control of schools, factories, local government? Gradually a process of rebuilding the Party began. A new formula for leadership evolved: Three-in-One Revolutionary Committees, consisting of:

1. PLA representatives.
2. Loyal Party cadres.
3. Representatives of the 'revolutionary masses', i.e. the workers or members of the institution concerned.

From late 1968 these Three-in-One Committees were set up all over China, and gradually the tumult of 'Struggle and Criticism' died down.

This system of leadership continued into the 1970s. At first the PLA was the dominant influence, but gradually the Party reasserted its authority. Special May 7th Cadre Schools were set up in 1968 to provide refresher courses for cadres: a programme of manual labour to keep them in touch with the masses, and political study to keep their ideology correct. After the great shake-up, only 1 per cent of Party members were expelled, though a larger proportion at high level. Liu Shao-chi, chief scapegoat of all the propaganda, was expelled in October 1968.

What was it all about?

The West watched the events of 1966–8 in China with astonishment. The revolution was variously assessed as a struggle for power, Mao's megalomania, or an army take-over. In fact it *was* a nationwide argument over which 'road' China should follow, initiated by Mao and supported by some Leftists in the Party, but bitterly opposed by others. By 1969 the Maoists had won the arguments of the 'Struggle and Criticism' phase, and the next stage of the revolution was the 'Transformation' of China. The following brief account of changes after 1969 is based on the reports of Westerners who visited China in the early 1970s. This was the general pattern of life until after Mao's death in 1976.

'TRANSFORMATION': CHANGES AFTER THE CULTURAL REVOLUTION

Visitors were often told that China was in a stage of transition and experimentation, and that many of the experiments might be modified or abandoned as time went on (in fact some very quickly were). The general aim of all social and economic policy was the elimination of the 'three great differences': between agriculture and industry, between town and countryside, and between mental and manual labour. The roots of these ideas can be seen in the earlier Maoist phase, the Great Leap Forward.

The economy

Eliminating the differences

The official economic slogan, 'agriculture the foundation, industry the leading sector', stressed that China is basically an agricultural country and not aiming primarily at rapid industrialization. The first duty of industry was to make the tools for farming, and consumer goods for all the people rather than for a privileged group of town-dwellers. But both sectors of the economy should try to be as self-supporting as possible–that is, farmers should also manufacture things they need, and factory workers should grow their own food. To encourage a collective spirit among the peasants there was a stronger emphasis on *the commune* as the basic production unit of agriculture, rather than the smaller Production Brigade or Team.

There was a renewed push against the growth of cities in what was called the 'back to the countryside' movement. Millions of city-dwellers, especially educated young people, were encouraged to live and work in the countryside: under this policy, for example, 1 million people left Shanghai. As we noted in Chapter 18, China's cities were already growing too large and it was hoped by this means to reverse the accelerating 'natural' drift of peasants seeking the higher standard of living, better social services and wider cultural life of the cities.

Differences of income continued. Except in a few politically advanced Production Brigades, which abolished private plots and practised a form of group assessment to decide each worker's share of the annual profit, a peasant family's income was based on work points earned during the year, and could be supplemented by a private plot (Figure 19.4). In other work, visitors found differences between the highest-paid and the lowest-paid usually in the range of 3 or 4 to 1 (compared with 20 to 1 in Britain). But the most determined effort to equalize the status of mental and manual workers was through education, which is discussed below.

'Politics in command' again

The Cultural Revolution did not, luckily for China, produce an economic crisis like that which followed the Great Leap. Economic growth continued steadily, but very slowly. There is still a shortfall in agricultural production, and shortages of farm machinery and fertilizers. China's leaders are aware of this, but in the afterglow of the Cultural Revolution the *style* of growth was considered more important than the *rate* of

Figure 19.4   Lunch in the courtyard for a peasant family in Tachai. They work early and late but take a three-hour lunch break at home.

growth. Once again it was 'politics in command' of the economy. What did this mean in practice?

In fields and factories alike, bonuses and prizes to individuals were out, but team competition was rewarded and encouraged. What made the best team? Not so much the amount produced as the workers' attention to quality, safety and helping other workers. Everyone in China was supposed to live and work in a spirit of 'Serve the People' (the slogan was cut into hill-sides, painted on walls and hung in the front room)—so *that* was the first principle of 'good work'. Individuals were admired and written up in the press—not (like Russian heroes of the Five-Year Plans) for the amount they added to the nation's wealth, but for the spirit in which they 'served the people' in whatever work they did.

At every level of the production process there was discussion. Workers, experts, cadres—all had their say. Western visitors often commented on the inefficiency of such clumsy decision-making and of making complex products in small factories with old-fashioned machinery when China could now build large, automated plants. In the West we are used to measuring everything by results—whatever produces more goods quicker and cheaper is best. But in Maoist China, as a British visitor put it, 'Socialism is a way of life rather than a way of growth.' In other words, the most important thing was to keep the social relations right as the economy developed, even at the sacrifice of greater efficiency and faster growth.

Could this system work?

Some economists thought that China's effort to spread economic progress evenly, and to involve everyone in economic development, might bring her long-term benefits by creating an efficient, committed work force who *feel* involved in the production process because they *are*. It might also avoid the split between advanced cities and backward countryside, and between highly skilled managers and workers trained only to be robots on an assembly line.

Others, however, saw China's clumsy Socialist style as a waste of time and energy when so many Chinese still live in extremely poor conditions. They argued that Western know-how and example could be used to raise China's standard of living much faster.

Living standards were still low. The official 'line' was that every household would soon have the few basic consumer goods – watches, bicycles, etc. – that many already had, and in the meantime the Chinese people were content with the simple essentials of life. (Or were they? One foreign student in Peking at this time noted that 'people talked a lot about the rising level of "Socialist consciousness" but they really measured China's progress in terms of their own bicycles, watches and sewing-machines.'†)

EDUCATION

Most secondary schools, colleges and universities were closed for several years after 1966 to 'reorganize'. When they reopened, every institution incorporated two important principles of the Cultural Revolution.

Theory and practice

The need 'to combine theory and practice' was a favourite theme of Mao's. He saw it not only as the best way to learn, but as a tool to undermine the reverence for Learning – and therefore for Learned People – which was characteristic of old China. So everywhere in China there was now great stress on mixing book-learning with social practice. Courses were shortened and all students, from the primary school up, must spend part of their time in productive work. Even high-level professors (*especially* high-level professors!) must mix their teaching of theory with field-work in their subject, while experienced workers, no matter how 'uneducated' themselves, came into the class-room to teach

†Beverley Hooper, *Inside Peking* (Macdonald and Jane, 1979), p. 20.

their skills. Everyone must 'learn from the masses' – and in doing so they would learn to respect manual workers.

Education for the masses

Exams came under careful scrutiny. Were they merely a hurdle to separate sheep from goats? Those that assist learning could stay, but fences which kept out the proletarian 'goats' must be discarded. Open-book exams and other methods of assessment were tried out in some institutions.

Most important in spreading education to the masses was the new system of enrolment to higher education. The following extract from the report of a Student Christian Movement visit in 1972 explains this:

> Before 1966, the majority of university students were the sons and daughters of intellectuals and leading Party members. Now there is discrimination in favour of workers, peasants and soldiers, and all young people must work for a minimum of two years before entering college. One typical example ... was a 21-year-old girl at Nanking University, who was studying English. She was a worker until May this year, and came to the university through the procedure now common. She heard from factory cadres that it was possible for workers to apply to study, and she expressed a wish to learn English. This idea was discussed by her work-group.... They discussed it with the factory Revolutionary Committee, who gave their approval, and so her application was sent to the university. There it was approved ... after she had taken a simple exam to ensure that she had sufficient literacy to take the course ...

All Middle School (that is, secondary school) graduates had to spend two years in manual labour before they were eligible to apply for higher education. Once they had completed their education, at school or university, they would probably be assigned to work in a village, perhaps thousands of miles from home, as part of the 'back to the countryside' policy. Thus their education would benefit rural areas where primary-school teachers and 'experts' of all kinds were needed.

Finally, what about the educational effect of just *living* in a society officially dedicated to serving the people?

The Maoist vision of a 'new man'

Western visitors were impressed by the seemingly genuine Socialist spirit of Maoist China. They reported with admiration the absence of many shameful problems of Western society: the old and disabled well cared for, streets and parks free of litter, social and family relations apparently harmonious. There were also none of the 'usual' features of poor countries–no beggars on the streets or bothersome hustlers trying to buy the Van Heusen shirts off their backs. The crime rate was astonishingly low and the level of courtesy and honesty very high.

Was this a sign of Mao Tse-tung's Socialist 'new man' in the making? Is it even possible to create a new, unselfish kind of human being, as he set out to do? On this point Western observers differed. Winston Churchill (grandson of the more famous one) gave one opinion: 'Mao is trying to change human nature, but I'm afraid even *he* can't do that.'[†] Barbara Wootton, a well-known sociologist, tentatively offered another view: 'On the whole, people do what is expected of them by the society they live in. If they are taught from the age of three to 'serve the people', then who knows? – it may become a habit.'[‡]

The Anti-Confucius campaign

To a considerable extent China *was* transformed by the Cultural Revolution, at least superficially. But although officially dead, the Rightist dragon would not lie down! Soon there were reports of material incentives reappearing in the economy; of city-dwellers creeping back from their mission in the countryside to become 'hooligans' in the cities; of resentful Party officials and intellec-

[†] In a public lecture at the Institute of Contemporary Arts, London, 7 June 1972.
[‡] In a public lecture at the Architectural Association, London, 17 January 1973.

tuals pulling strings to get their children into university along with the 'privileged' working-class candidates. So back came the Leftist crusaders to deal with the twitching corpse! Through wall-posters and newspapers, the Anti-Confucius campaign of 1973–4 tried to reassert the victories of the Cultural Revolution. Confucius, the ancient Chinese scholar and philosopher, symbolized Authority, Scholarship and Expertness.

In response to this new onslaught of propaganda, Party officials and cadres obediently renewed their pledges to the 'Socialist road'–but with a certain weariness. Yes, Chairman Mao had said there must be repeated Cultural Revolutions, but was it time for the next one *already*? By now many Rightist and 'moderate' leaders had been reinstated in the Party, with popular approval, and everyone was tired of 'struggling and criticizing'. In fact the new blast of ideological exhortation came from a small and unpopular group of Leftists led by Mao's wife, Chiang Ching. While Mao still lived, the Leftist line could not be openly challenged.

After Mao–who?

But the Great Helmsman was failing at last: by 1975 everyone knew that Chairman Mao was mortally ill. Who would succeed him? Two earlier candidates were now out of the picture: President Liu Shao-chi, chief Rightist target of the Cultural Revolution, had died in 1974, and Defence Minister Lin Piao, also disgraced during the course of it, had been killed in a plane crash in 1971 'while trying to escape after an attempt on Mao's life'. With Mao enfeebled by illness and no obvious successor in sight, his lifelong comrade-in-arms Premier Chou En-lai was the effective leader of China in the early 1970s. Chou had been a rock of calm moderation during the Cultural Revolution, and was an immensely popular figure. But he was seriously ill with cancer, and in January 1976 he died. This sad event cleared the stage for an undignified power struggle in the last months of Mao's life.

Questions

Did you notice?

1. Liu Shao-chi was said to be (a) an ultra-Leftist (b) 'China's Khrushchev' (c) a Maoist
2. A *dazibao* is (a) a wall poster (b) a Red Guard (c) a soldier
3. During the Cultural Revolution, which of the following did Mao *not* do? (a) ask people to criticize him (b) swim in the Yangtse (c) wear a red arm-band
4. To 'cool down' the Red Guards, they were (a) sent to work in the countryside (b) sent back to school (c) thrown in the Yangtse
5. After the Cultural Revolution, a university entrant must (a) have worked for at least two years (b) agree to study science (c) come from a working-class home
6. True or false?
   (i) Workers in Maoist China had a say in running their factories
   (ii) Defence Minister Lin Piao was accused of trying to kill Mao
   (iii) Only intellectuals in China can afford bicycles
   (iv) Confucius was a 'Capitalist roader'
   (v) Maoist China had a low crime rate
7. Which statement is *more* accurate?
   (i) The Sixteen Points were
      (a) policy differences between China and the USSR
      (b) directions for carrying out the Cultural Revolution
   (ii) The policy of 'eliminating the differences' was an attempt
      (a) to create a more equal society
      (b) to make all Chinese people think alike
   (iii) Workers were asked to teach school and college students because
      (a) students were supposed to learn from the masses
      (b) there were not enough qualified teachers in China

Can you explain?

8. The Maoists told their followers to 'struggle against' certain groups of people in particular. Who were their main targets?
9. Why was education singled out for complete transformation in the Cultural Revolution?
10. During the Cultural Revolution, what was the part played by: (a) the Red Guards, (b) the People's Liberation Army?
11. After the Cultural Revolution, what was the purpose of: (a) May 7th cadre schools, (b) the 'back to the countryside movement'?
12. Which new policies attempted to eliminate the difference between mental and manual labour in China?

What's your view?

13. Do any of the 'three great differences' exist in our society? If so, should we be trying to eliminate them?
14. Both in Russia and China, when Socialist propaganda and controls were lifted there seemed to be a 'spontaneous return to Capitalism' among the people. Does this mean that people are naturally self-interested? If so, is it possible and desirable to 'educate' them into co-operative ways of thinking and acting where the motive is not personal gain?
15. One purpose of the Cultural Revolution was to give workers and students a say in their daily work or education. How far are workers and students in our society encouraged to participate in this way? Should they be given more say, or less?

20

China After Mao

China-watching is rather easier than Kremlin-watching, through the numerous connections between the mainland and Hong Kong. From this observation post, outsiders were probably more aware than most ordinary Chinese of factional struggles behind the scenes in the last years of Mao's rule. But even the most watchful were surprised by the dramatic events of 1976 and the extent to which China would be changed after the death of Mao Tse-tung.

The struggle for power

After Chou En-lai's death in January, everyone expected his deputy Deng Xiaoping† to become the new Premier. Deng had been purged as a Rightist in the 1960s, but he had always retained Mao's respect and was regarded as the natural and welcome successor to the politically 'moderate' Chou En-lai. Instead, Mao appointed the almost unknown Hua Kuo-feng as Acting Premier, apparently as a gesture towards the small but noisy group of Leftists clustered around Mao's wife Chiang Ching. They had recently promoted a campaign against an 'unrepentant Capitalist roader'–unnamed, but known to be Deng–and in April they were able to get him blamed for an outburst of fighting in Peking between Leftists and thousands of mourners who had come to pay respect to Chou En-lai on the 'festival of the dead'. Deng was dismissed from his post as Vice-Chairman of the Party and Hua Kuo-feng was confirmed as Premier. Well-organized

†This is the new English spelling of Teng Hsiao-ping. See Note on p. vi.

but unconvincing demonstrations were held in support of Hua and the Party, while China waited quietly for Chairman Mao to die.

On 9 September Mao at last 'went to meet Marx'. Three weeks later his wife and her group of radical Leftists were arrested and a huge campaign was launched to 'smash the Gang of Four' (Madame Mao and three others). This began a process of de-Maoization in China which would be even more far-reaching in its ultimate effects than de-Stalinization in the Soviet Union. But instead of blaming Mao himself, the new leadership cleverly directed public wrath against his policies onto the already-hated Gang of Four. In the next few months the Gang were 'smashed' in a vicious campaign of personal abuse and almost laughable claims of their wicked influence in every sphere of life (Figure 20.1).

Figure 20.1 October 1976: demonstrators in Canton answer the call to 'smash the Gang of Four'.

As in Russia after Stalin's death, official propaganda turned upside down. The recent campaign against 'the Right deviationist wind' was forgotten now that the Gang of Four had been discovered as the real trouble-makers. But how could that be? They were 'Socialist roaders', weren't they, with the backing of Chairman Mao? Ah, but the Gang were Rightists *posing as* Leftists and *misrepresenting* Mao's real views. That 'nagging, scheming woman' and her three 'merry men' had misled *everyone* for their own sinister, selfish ends.

Meanwhile Hua Kuo-feng had slid into Mao's job as Party Chairman waving Mao's last hand-written instruction, 'With you in charge, I am at ease'. But Hua was scarcely known outside Party circles. So alongside the vilification of those 'cunning and treacherous sham Marxist political swindlers' went a counter-campaign in praise of the 'selfless, frank, open, above-board, honest, etc., etc.' Chairman Hua. Well perhaps he was all those things, but the twice-purged Deng Xiaoping was apparently more popular with the Party and the people. With the Gang out of the way, he now came bobbing back. In 1977 he was restored as Vice-Chairman of the Party and Vice-Premier of the state, and thereafter was acknowledged to be the power behind the throne, whoever might be occupying the front seats.† By 1981 Hua had surrendered both his offices, as Premier and Chairman, to Deng protégés.* His second demotion in 1981 was accompanied by the first thorough and official condemnation of Mao Tse-tung. Mao's contribution to the Chinese revolution was acknowledged, but after 1949 his 'mistakes', 'arrogance' and 'confused thinking' had led to catastrophic policies for the People's Republic–especially the Great Leap Forward and the Cultural Revolution.

† In 1983, while Deng held several second-tier offices, the front seats were occupied by President Li Xiannian, Premier Zhao Ziyang, and Secretary-General of the Party Hu Yaobang. In 1982 the office of Party Chairman was abolished, perhaps to guard against a personality cult of some future occupant (this was one of the accusations against Hua Kuo-feng).

CHANGES AFTER MAO

The indictment of Mao in 1981 came as no surprise. By that time his policies in every sphere of life had been dismantled and China was once again 'transformed' as thoroughly as she had been by the Cultural Revolution. But transformed into what? 'When the snow thaws, the road is very muddy', said a Chinese in 1979 to a foreigner in Peking.‡ This is an apt description of China in the first few years after Mao's death. Some observers saw a return to the Stalinist mould of the 1950s in the new concern to catch up with the West at all costs, while others took the many signs of 'Capitalism' as an indication that China might be on the verge of abandoning Marxism altogether. In the West Deng Xiaoping's policies were usually called 'pragmatic'–in other words, 'try anything that *works*'.

Here we can only follow a few tracks along the muddy road so far. Bear in mind that in a country of China's size and population, conditions and policies may vary widely from one area to another. This was true even when there was one firm 'line' issuing from Peking, and it is much more true in the 1980s when provincial and local authorities are being allowed some freedom to 'experiment'.

Political relaxation

However far they believed or followed the campaign to 'smash the Gang', there is no doubt that millions of Chinese were thankful to see the Cultural Revolution slip away into history. The 'Eleven Years' became a catchphrase for the 'lost years' of 1966 through 1976, when Maoist policies were in force, and in the new Deng Xiaoping era few would openly admit to supporting those policies. The perplexing question for outsiders is, how far were Leftist views genuinely supported at the time?

It is clear that millions were converted to a

‡ Beverley Hooper, *Inside Peking* (Macdonald and Jane, 1979), p. 178.

Maoist ideology in the late 1960s–especially the hordes of teenage Red Guards, the 'revolutionary successors' Mao was trying to train. Millions of others perhaps just kept their heads down, waiting for the storm to pass. But there was no escape for thousands of branded 'Rightists' who were cruelly humiliated and even beaten to death at 'struggle meetings', or driven to suicide by unfeeling harassment. In December 1980 the trial of the Gang of Four (and six others) for a long catalogue of counter-revolutionary crimes, including 'frame-ups' of their enemies during the Cultural Revolution, was an occasion to set the record straight. It was now stated that 34,800 innocent people had died and over 729,000 more had suffered 'unwarranted persecution' during that colossal 'mistake' of Chairman Mao's.

Foreigners in China in the late 1970s were regaled with innumerable tragic stories to illustrate these bare statistics. Many of the 'criticized' officials and teachers had been reinstated after a period of 're-education' in the countryside or cleaning out latrines, but only now were they free to tell the tale of their suffering. But they were still wary: who knew when the official line might change again? Unofficial fraternization with foreigners, expressly forbidden during the Eleven Years, is never encouraged by the Chinese authorities. One place where it did take place for a while was in front of Democracy Wall, a stretch of wall in central Peking set aside for posters. In 1978–9 this was a sort of 'Speaker's Corner' where people stood for hours reading and debating the day's crop of *dazibao* and home-printed journals which were handed around. The content of these was similar to *samizdat* in the Soviet Union: calls for personal freedom and constitutional government, and accounts of mistreatment at the hands of officialdom.

Some of the regular *dazibao* authors attracted great interest: were they the tip of an iceberg of political dissent in China? Maybe–but we shall never know. China's 'dissident movement' was silenced in 1979 with the closing down of Democracy Wall and the trial of the best-known dissenter, Wei Jingshen, who received a fifteen-year sentence for 'passing military intelligence to a foreigner' and publishing a dissident journal. Ironically, outspoken *dazibao* and other signs of free political debate in the late 1970s had been initiated by Rightist leaders to support their manoeuvres against remaining Leftists, the so-called 'whateverist faction' ('whatever Mao said and did was correct'), but by 1979 that narrow political objective had been achieved and the public debate was now closed.

'Open door' to the West

At the official level, however, certain kinds of foreigners were now very welcome in China. One of Mao's ideas that *did* live on was his conviction that the United States was a less dangerous enemy of China than the USSR. In 1971 China had finally been admitted to the United Nations and this began a slow process of *détente* with America which continued in the 1970s through all the changes of leadership in both countries, culminating in the resumption of full diplomatic relations in 1979 (the effect of this development in the triangle of East–West relations is described in Part IV).

It was therefore to the Capitalist West rather than her Communist partner of the 1950s that China looked for help with her spanking new economic policy, the Four Modernizations–of agriculture, industry, science and technology, and defence—through which she hoped to become a 'powerful modern Socialist state by the year 2000'. Contracts were signed with Western and Japanese firms for large amounts of advanced technology, mainly for heavy industry. But it soon became clear that China could neither pay for nor swallow such huge bites of sophisticated machinery at her present stage of development. By 1980 she was facing inflation and budget deficits, while new foreign-built plants like the vast Baoshan steelworks near Shanghai lacked the local infrastructure (transport, sufficient electricity, etc.) to make them operational. To the dismay of her foreign partners, in 1981 China cancelled $2 billion worth of foreign contracts as part of a sharp 're-adjustment' of economic policy.

But the door was kept open to foreign investment in four Special Economic Zones set up in areas near Hong Kong and the tiny Portuguese colony of Macao,† where foreign firms were invited to develop 'joint ventures' with Chinese authorities. Low taxation, low rents and above all low wages (an average of $50 per month on the mainland, compared to $250 in Hong Kong) made this an attractive proposition to foreign entrepreneurs, while China would benefit from the provision of jobs and industrial training, and the products of the new factories. Between 1979 and 1982 the Zones attracted nearly $5 billion in foreign investment, most of it from 'overseas Chinese' businessmen. To some ideologists in the Party these Zones looked uncomfortably like the foreign concession areas of pre-Communist China, but they were quieted with the assurance that Peking makes the rules there, and that what has been given can always be taken away.

After 1980 less was heard of the over-ambitious heavy industry projects of the Four Modernizations, while Deng gave more attention to agriculture and consumer industries. Feeding all the hungry mouths in China is still the first priority of her government, and it requires a two-pronged solution: first, to check the rate of population increase, and secondly to raise agricultural output.

Population policy

Most peasant societies, including China, traditionally favour large families, and this is understandable when the infant mortality rate is high and there is no state care for parents in their old age. When better health care is provided, and other 'natural' checks like famine and war are eliminated, these

†The present status of these two left-over Western colonies is explained in Chapter 26, pages 298–9.

developing nations all face a population explosion until parents feel secure enough to limit their families, and know how to do so. By the 1950s China had reached this stage, but at that time Mao foolishly dismissed advice to encourage birth control and even set off a 'baby boom' with his pronouncement that 'people are the most valuable resource'.

China now has a population problem of staggering proportions, fully recognized by the leaders in the late 1970s and confirmed by a United Nations-assisted census in 1982 which showed her population to be already over 1 billion, with an average age of 26 – the youngest in the world. Having set itself a ceiling of 1.2 billion by the end of the century, in 1980 the government brought in a set of arm-twisting disincentives far more strict than the previous promotion of a model two-child family. First there is an official marriage age of 25 for women and 27 for men, which can only be defied with intense social disapproval. Once married, a couple will find its family life regulated to a degree inconceivable in the West. To encourage a one-child norm, the first-born brings a 5 per cent pay rise for its parents, free medical care and priority for new housing and its own schooling. If a second child arrives these benefits are withdrawn, while a third shifts the scheme into reverse: both parents will have their wages docked by 5 per cent and the child goes to the bottom of the list for all scarce resources. 'Glory certificates' are issued for voluntary 'one child' pledges or sterilization after the first is born, and contraceptives and abortions are freely available.

The consequences of these measures have yet to be seen. It is especially difficult to enforce the rules in rural areas, where cultural traditions – including a preference for boy children – remain strong. At once there was a recurrence of female infanticide: in one district of Hubei province it was noted in 1983 that boys outnumbered girls by five to one among the under-fives (the population as a whole is already $52\frac{1}{2}$ per cent male). Apart from this unbalancing trend, which the government was trying to counter with propaganda, it had set itself a daunting task: in the 18 years from 1964 to 1982 the population grew by 310 million, while the target for the *next* 18 years was 190 million. To achieve the goal of a comfortable living standard for all, the one-child policy is designed to halve the present population and is supposed to continue for 100 years!

The food problem

The increase in food production since 1949 has only *just* kept pace with population growth. There has been no nationwide famine, but many lean years; as in the Soviet Union, the size of the grain harvest each year is crucial. But what about other nutritious foods? Only 15 per cent of China's land is arable, and it has been suggested that the protein content of the Chinese diet could be improved by producing more meat and dairy products on the grasslands. But the Chinese do not care much for these foods, so the food problem remains chiefly a grain problem.

The new leaders were less worried than Mao was about self-sufficiency in grain, however, and encouraged the growing of other crops while allowing grain imports to rise (from 9.4 million tonnes in 1978 to 16 million tonnes in 1982). In a country where 80 per cent of the population are peasants, agriculture must not only feed the whole nation but provide surplus funds for the government to develop industry, and crops to be traded for necessary imports. And of course the peasants themselves must earn enough cash to buy what they don't grow; they are the main domestic market for industry. All these factors boil down to a problem familiar from our study of Russia – how to increase China's farm output, with the added handicap of far less mechanization than in the USSR.

The commune never worked well as an organizer of agricultural production. Despite all Mao's propaganda, the peasants would not think of themselves as part of a Socialist

army of thousands, all beavering away without thought of personal profit. Even at village level it was hard to generate a truly communal spirit. A family which worked harder than others and expected recognition at the work-point assessment meetings of the Production Team would only poison social relations in the community, so few bothered to exert themselves. The new leaders therefore had to try other methods to increase production.

The end of the commune?

By the early 1980s important changes could be seen in rural organization. In a gradual process, so as not to jolt the existing system too sharply, the governmental functions of the commune were being restored to the township (the system which prevailed before 1958), while the commune acted only as a marketing and management agency for the various production units within its area. The abolition of the middle-tier Production Brigade left the organization of farming, and land ownership, to the Production Team – a village of a few hundred people. Some Teams still organized farm-work collectively (as described in Study Topic 11), but most had gone over to the family-based 'responsibility system' introduced in 1979. Each family was given 'responsibility' (not *ownership*, but there may be little difference in practice) for an area of land, and a contract with the Team to produce a certain output for the state; above that quota they could sell the crop and any side-line products for their own profit, at any price they could get. Since 1977 the government has allowed private markets in the towns and provides stalls and weighing-machines for them. As in the Soviet Union, these markets enrich the diet of town-dwellers as well as the pockets of the peasants.

Like the methods used to recover from the Great Leap Forward (see page 193), the responsibility system rested on the principles of Lenin's NEP in 1921, when peasants were urged to 'enrich themselves' and in so doing, swell the national output of foodstuffs. The new practices soon had the same desired effect in China–greatly increased output, and a marked rise in the prosperity of hard-working families (dare we call them *kulaks*?). It remains to be seen whether China's government will continue to tolerate the 'un-Socialist' results which were also appearing (as Stalin and Mao could not). In one province, by 1982 there was already a disparity of five to one between the incomes of the richest and poorest families, and the gap will widen as richer families buy machinery and livestock which their poorer neighbours cannot afford. The present government hopes that new, voluntary co-operation will spring up 'naturally' to replace the collectivism that Mao tried unsuccessfully to impose from above. But will it happen?

Some leaders have objected to encouraging 'petty Capitalism' in the countryside (see–the arguments are starting already!). And there are other consequences of the new policy which may cause the government to think again. Since a family's income now depends on its own efforts, and it is still forbidden to hire labour, there is an obvious incentive to have more children–and to keep them out of school to herd ducks or weed the onion patch. Absenteeism from rural schools has always been high, and in a country which now admits to an illiteracy rate of over 23 per cent, this is a serious matter.

The Chinese commune may have disappeared as 'the basic unit of the future Communist society', but it is too early yet to write its epitaph. There are impressive reminders of its work, and the now denigrated Great Leap Forward, in the vast irrigation schemes undertaken at that time. The commune structure may well be useful for similar large-scale projects in the future, or to revive that other Great Leap theme, the development of rural industries. In the next twenty years, by the government's own estimate, employment will have to be found for nearly 300 million surplus farm labourers, and the most constructive suggestion is that country towns and small industries should be

expanded to absorb them. Certainly they cannot be accommodated in the larger cities, which are already overfull and have unemployment problems of their own.

Back to the cities again

A most unpopular policy of the Cultural Revolution, once its effects were felt, was the 'back to the countryside' movement. In 1968 it was quite exciting for a city-bred Red Guard to go off for a few months to 'make revolution' among the peasants; it was even tolerable to work in a commune for two years before going on to higher education (many of the so-called worker-peasant students of the 1970s were in fact middle-class children who had to qualify for entrance by 'doing time' in this way). But to settle down for life in a remote village, to fulfil Mao's intention by trying to *become peasants*, was a disillusioning experience for the 16 million or so 'educated youths' who were sent off during the Eleven Years to do so. Even the most ardent followers of Chairman Mao began to weaken in their revolutionary resolve and many trickled back to the cities, where they hung around without jobs or ration cards, often resorting to petty crime.

In the late 1970s the trickle of returning exiles became a flood, making worse the existing shortage of housing and jobs and creating a small crime wave. In 1980 unemployment in the cities was admitted to be about 20 million, while 60 per cent of crimes were committed by juveniles. Officially the jobless were only 'waiting for work' (there is no 'unemployment' in a Socialist society), but in the meantime the government encouraged thousands of small, self-governing collectives to provide low-cost consumer products for the local community. Similarly, individuals and families were allowed to start up restaurants, shoe-repair services and so on, and by 1983 there were 2½ million of these small family businesses (Figure 20.2) competing with state-run shops and services. Both individual and collective enterprises pay a state tax of 30–40 per cent on their

Figure 20.2   A fast-food restaurant in Kwangchow set up by a Cantonese entrepreneur.

profits, and the rest can be spent as they like. Those who need a market-place to meet their customers can use the free enterprise markets which now exist everywhere.

Cash incentives in industry

To complete this picture of 'Capitalist restoration' in agriculture and petty trade there was a return to cash incentives for factory workers too. China's industry shows similar weaknesses to Russia's: many consumer products are more readily available than in the USSR, but there are shortages of some prized items like bicycles, and many complaints of poor quality. To improve efficiency the new leaders began experimental reforms like those tried in Russia in the 1960s (see page 144)–making managers 'market conscious', and their own rewards dependent on the profits of their enterprises–while shop-floor wages were also directly linked to output. In 1983 these ventures were being extended and the magic

label 'responsibility system' applied to them, but it is too early to assess the results. One practice which is *not* working, in the view of Western economists at least, is the use of bonuses in a negative rather than a positive way: instead of selecting the few best workers for extra rewards, *everyone* gets a bonus except the few worst.

The iron rice bowl

The 'automatic bonus' is part of an inbuilt inflexibility in China's Socialist economy which is called the 'iron rice bowl'. It is an article of Socialist faith that everyone should have the lifelong security of a job, and the support of social services outside the workplace. In China most of these services–and many other things, including housing, the timing of women workers' babies, and even the issue of cinema tickets!–are arranged by a person's *danwei*, or workplace, so that one's *danwei* is a kind of social identity card. For a government to deprive citizens of their *danwei* is to cast them into the wilderness! But the obligation to provide 'employment', even when there isn't any, leads to widespread overmanning, frustration for managers, and a couldn't-care-less attitude among workers who know they can't be fired.

This is a real crunch-point in the Socialism *v.* Capitalism debate. Outside critics say the iron rice bowl must be broken if China's industry is ever to approach Western standards of efficiency, and the first cracks are appearing in the Special Economic Zones, where businessmen used to the cut-and-thrust of Capitalist Hong Kong are demanding the same freedom in their 'joint ventures' on the mainland: the right to hire and fire their workers, and pay them unevenly. But the Socialist view still has its defenders, such as the economist Liu Zizhen, who offered a counter-argument to the Deng leadership: isn't it better to have three men doing one job slowly than one working like a demon and two on the dole? Or why not a four-hour working day?† If Hong Kong practices spread far on the mainland there will be similar arguments at a lower level too. Some workers will welcome the chance to become as rich as their Hong Kong cousins (they haven't seen the *other* side of Hong Kong's cut-and-thrust, of course), while others may prefer a system which allows them plenty of time to raise song-birds or practise the ancient Chinese art of calligraphy.

Dangerous foreign influences

Predictably, the new government was soon having difficulty resisting other insidious influences through the open door to Hong Kong, Japan and the West. In the late 1970s about 250,000 Chinese were leaving the

Figure 20.3   Japanese watches are readily available in this Peking store to those who can afford them.

mainland each year to try their luck outside the Socialist womb, most of them arriving as illegal immigrants in Hong Kong (in 1981 the British authorities there started sending back the ones they caught). Like Russia, China won't miss these discontented citizens – but the 'pollution' of cultural life on the mainland, especially youth culture, worried the government. It could be seen in the idolization of Western fashions and popular music, and in the hunger for consumer goods (Figure 20.3) which swept the country as soon as it was no longer 'un-Socialist' to admit to it. Millions of mainland Chinese have family connections in Hong Kong and with other overseas Chinese, and as visits from their cousins became easier many humble homes on the mainland were decked out with colour TVs, tape recorders and cassettes, luxuriant curtains and kitchen gadgets. The glitter of these shiny objects to peering eyes through the window was another factor contributing to juvenile crime and the discontent of millions of young people in China today.

The disillusion of young people is easy to understand. Young adults in the 1980s – and 65 per cent of the population is under thirty! – never knew the 'hard times' before 1949, and are sick of hearing about it from their elders. Those who became 'born again

---

†You may recognize a counterpart of this debate in the discussions about work-sharing and the 'right to work' in the West. Here it arises from high unemployment, which some economists think may be permanent: new technology and structural economic changes may mean that there will never again be enough jobs for everyone. Shall we have a few button-pushers working full time and an army of unemployed growing roses – or a three-day working week for all?

Marxists' during the Cultural Revolution were either stranded in a puddle of ideological purity by the U-turn afterwards, or became utterly cynical watching the revolving door of the leadership struggle in the 1970s. Many lost vital years of schooling when schools and colleges were closed during the Cultural Revolution, or spent so much time in political study and 'productive labour' that they are outshone by a younger generation now being trained in the traditional academic way. What is there to be idealistic about these days? Even their parents, who still keep a portrait of Chairman Mao in the parlour in gratitude for the Chinese revolution, seem to accept that *guan-xi* ('connections') and 'going through the back door' are once again 'the Chinese way' to a comfortable life, and that *comfort* is what life is mainly about.

The Party is doing its best to counteract apathy and cynicism through stern editorials in the press and 'uplifting' TV programmes, but these have little more effect than the sermons of our own moral guardians in the West; a rendering of 'The Nightsoil Collectors are Coming Down the Mountain'† by the massed bands of the PLA cannot compete with the dulcet tones of Teresa Teng crooning love songs over the air waves from Taiwan. In any case the Party's reputation for moral rectitude is not high. For the third time since he came to power, in 1982 Deng launched a 'rectification campaign' against corruption and 'bureaucratic tendencies' among its 39 million members, and to weed out Leftists recruited during the Eleven Years who might be soft-pedalling his new policies. But the devious bureaucrats may frustrate his intentions, as they have done before.

What we have left out

This chapter has emphasized areas of political and economic life where the switch from Maoist policies is most evident, and where comparisons can be made with similar problems in the Soviet Union. Many important topics have been omitted, such as the modernization of the Army (another object of Deng's attention in the early 1980s), and the introduction of new legal codes in 1980, a step towards the first comprehensive legal system in Communist China. Nor is there any mention here or in earlier chapters of the rich artistic heritage of China, which is so important to her people that it is always chosen by the Communist government as the first vehicle to transmit a new political 'line', or a full assessment of progress towards true equality for women under socialism.‡

One neglected topic deserves at least a postscript in a book intended for students. Many outside critics see China's deficient education system as one of the factors holding back her economic progress. The new government now sends a few high-level students abroad–there were 10,000 in the United States in 1983–but it has scarcely begun the necessary overhaul and expansion of the structure within China. Of the children who enter primary school, only 60 per cent complete the five-year course, and only half of *those* receive the full five years of secondary schooling. At the top of the pyramid, only 3 per cent of the eligible age-group can find a place at university (compared to 35 per cent in the USA and 27 per cent in the USSR), which leads to frantic cramming for the $12\frac{1}{2}$ hours of entrance examinations, or 'going through the back door' to get in. But the weakest area of the

---

†'Nightsoil' is the term for human excrement, which is collected from public latrines and houses all over China to spread on the fields as manure. This is one example of the way a frugal society recycles a useful commodity which is wasted in the West.

  To be fair to the Party, by 1982 they had dropped this particular song and were promoting another catchy number, 'The Three Main Rules of Discipline and Eight Points for Attention'.

‡In a word, it is patchy. Both in Russia and in China there are many more women in certain professions, such as medicine, than in the West; but observers have noticed that housework is still considered 'women's work' in the USSR, while in China it is *mothers* who are sometimes blamed and harassed for producing girl babies, despite government propaganda pointing out that a baby's sex is determined by the father's contribution. You can draw your own conclusions from this information.

whole system is the one which should be turning out millions of skilled engineers and technicians to carry through the Four Modernizations–vocational and technical education.

The Cultural Revolution emphasis on 'more practice and less theory' seemed to recognize this deficiency, but in fact it was the upper secondary schools and colleges, where vocational education should take place, that were most disrupted during the Eleven Years. And in their drive to eradicate every Maoist feature from China, in 1976 the new leaders reverted wholesale to the highly academic pre-1966 system. They do not yet seem to have realized the importance of practical education for the modern society they are trying to develop.

China's future

You can see that China does not rank alongside our other two World Powers, the United States and the Soviet Union, except in terms of her *potential*. She has considerable untapped resources in areas such as the Western province of Sinkiang, bordering the USSR, which could also accommodate millions more people if conditions were made attractive enough for them to settle there. Above all she has the energy and enterprise of the Chinese people, which have been amply demonstrated by the achievements of Communist China since 1949 and by the hard-working communities of overseas Chinese all over the world. Chairman Mao may have been guilty of confused thinking about numbers, but he was surely right that 'people are the most valuable resource'.

*GLOSSARY

protégé (French), a person protected by a powerful or important sponsor.

Questions

Did you notice?

1. Mao wanted his successor to be (a) his wife (b) Hua Kuo-feng (c) Deng Xiaoping
2. The Eleven Years refers to (a) the Great Leap Forward (b) 'China's NEP' (c) the Cultural Revolution and its aftermath
3. The 'whateverist faction' believed that (a) Mao was always right (b) the Gang of Four was always wrong (c) 'anything that works' should be tried
4. The 'iron rice bowl' means that (a) food is rationed in China (b) everyone is guaranteed a job (c) foreign employers can pay high wages
5. In the 1980s former Red Guards were likely to be (a) sent back to the countryside (b) Deng's strongest supporters (c) disillusioned
6. True or false?
   (i) The responsibility system transferred land ownership to the peasants
   (ii) Female infanticide reappeared in China in the 1980s
   (iii) In 1980 Communist China was not a member of the United Nations
   (iv) In 1983 some Chinese students were studying in the United States
7. Which statement is *more* accurate?
   (i) Democracy Wall
      (a) began a new era of free public debate in China
      (b) showed the existence of political dissent in China
   (ii) The Special Economic Zones attracted foreign investment because
      (a) foreign businessmen were given complete freedom there
      (b) wages in China were lower than elsewhere
   (iii) Under the new population policy, Glory Certificates were issued for
      (a) enforced sterilization
      (b) a promise to have only one child

Can you explain?

8. Describe the transition from the period of Leftist influence just before Mao's death to the condemnation of his policies in 1981.
9. Briefly describe the methods, and the reasons, for restoring 'Capitalist incentives' in: (a) farming, (b) small businesses and petty trade, (c) industry.
10. Even in the Rightist climate of opinion after Mao's death, some leaders had doubts about the new policies. What unwelcome consequences might result from: (a) foreign investment in the Special Economic Zones, (b) the family responsibility system in farming, (c) breaking the iron rice bowl?
11. What was the new population policy introduced in 1980, and why was it considered necessary?
12. What reasons are suggested in this chapter for the discontent and cynicism of many young people in China in the 1980s?

What's your view?

13. Why was the Chinese government worried about the 'pollution' of cultural values on the mainland through new contacts with the outside world? Were they right to be? Is there any way they could successfully counteract these influences?
14. One tactic used to 'smash the Gang of Four' in China was to accuse them of drunkenness, immorality and extravagant living. Are these methods ever used in our society to discredit public figures? Is it 'fair' to attack people in this way?
15. If you were a 25-year-old Chinese with no family connections outside China, would you try to emigrate, or escape to Hong Kong?

Further Reading

Every public library has a selection of the stream of books on 'China today' published in the last fifteen years. The view presented may depend on the author's political outlook and, even more crucially, bearing in mind the political zig-zags in China since 1965, on the date of publication. The same note of caution applies to any account of 'modern China' in a history book: does it include the switch of policies after Mao Tse-tung's death?

The following bookshops have a good stock of books on China:

Guanghwa Company, 9 Newport Place, London WC2.

East Asia Books, 277 Eversholt Street, London NW1.

Collets, 40 Great Russell Street, London WC1.

The Society for Anglo–Chinese Understanding (SACU) at 152 Camden High Street, London NW1, is similarly well stocked and will supply a book list on request. Publications of the Anglo–Chinese Educational Institute and those of the Foreign Language Press, Peking, can be obtained there.

SUPPLEMENTARY READING

Jack Belden, *China Shakes the World* (Penguin, 1973).

Colin Bown, *The People's Republic of China* (Heinemann, 1975). History Broadsheets.

Colin Bown and Tony Edwards, *Revolution in China, 1911–1949* (Heinemann Educational Books, 1974). History Broadsheets.

H. Fullard (ed.), *China in Maps* (Philips, 1968). With useful short text.

John Gittings (ed.), *A Chinese View of China* (BBC Publications, 1973). A collection of documents, with commentary.

Felix Greene, *The Wall Has Two Sides: A Portrait of China Today* (Cape, 1963) and several other books.

Hugh Higgins, *From Warlords to Red Star* (Faber, 1968).

Hilda Hookham, *A Short History of China* (Longman, 1969).

G. Long, *China Today* (Blackie, 1980).

G. Long and V. Oates, *China: Portrait of a Superpower* (Blackie, 1981).

P. Meigham and B. McWilliams, *China for a Change* (Harrap, 1983). Almost a cartoon treatment, but with substantial information, on the period up to 1949.

L. Mitchison, *China in the Twentieth Century* (OUP, 1970).

G. Moseley, *China: Empire to People's Republic* (Batsford, 1968).

R. C. North, *Chinese Communism* (Weidenfeld and Nicolson, 1966).

John Robottom, *Modern China* (Longman, 1970).

J. and G. Stokes, *The People's Republic of China* (Ernest Benn, 1975).

Edgar Snow, *Red Star Over China* (Penguin, 1972). Classic account of the Communists in the 1930s, first published by Gollancz in 1937. *Red China Today: The Other Side of the River* (Penguin, 1970).

Han Suyin, *China in the Year 2001* (Penguin, 1970).

Dick Wilson, *A Quarter of Mankind: Anatomy of China Today* (Penguin, 1968) and *Mao: The People's Emperor* (Hutchinson, 1979). A very readable biography by an 'old China hand'.

There is not much literature from or about China which is well known (and therefore available) in the West. One exception is an outsider's view of China in the 1930s. *The Good Earth*, by an American, Pearl Buck (Longman 1973); another is an insider's view by a Chinese novelist very popular among forward-looking Chinese in the 1930s and 1940s: Pa Chin's *Family* (Anchor, 1972). The three volumes of Han Suyin's autobiography, *The Crippled Tree*, *A Mortal Flower* and *Birdless Summer* (all Panther Books, 1972) are probably the most appealing to the modern reader. Han Suyin was born in China of Belgian and Chinese parents; her personal account of China before the Communists came to power makes it easy to understand her enthusiasm for post-1949 China.

A volume of *Poems* by Mao Tse-tung (translated by William Barnstone) is available from Barrie and Jenkins (1972) and the Quotations from Mao in *The Little Red Book* (Foreign Language Press, Peking, from SACU or other suppliers) are quite comprehensible to young readers. Many of his sayings are 'timeless' but it is also interesting to discuss them in their historical context (the source and date of each quotation is given). Many of his poems also have a political message of course.

MORE ADVANCED

Colin Bown, *China 1949–76* (Heinemann Educational Books, 1977).

David Bonavia, *The Chinese* (Penguin, 1982). The best of several recent journalistic accounts; very informative on the immediate post-Mao period.

Jerome Ch'en, *Mao* (Prentice-Hall, 1969). Great Lives Observed Series.

Philippe Devillers, *Mao: What They Really Said* (Macdonald, 1969).

C. P. Fitzgerald, *The Birth of Communist China* (Penguin, 1970).

Jack Gray, *Mao Tse-tung* (Lutterworth Press, 1973). A short biography showing the influence of Mao's ideas on the course of events.

Louis Heren and others. *China's Three Thousand Years: the Story of a Great Civilisation* (Times Newspapers, 1973).

William Hinton, *Fanshen: A Documentary of Revolution in a Chinese Village* (Penguin, 1972) and *Shenfan* (Secker and Warburg, 1983), which continues this detailed 'documentary' up to 1971.

Beverley Hooper, *Inside Peking* (Macdonald and Janes, 1979). A vivid account of the political U-turn after Mao's death by an Australian student whose stay in Peking happened to bridge that event.

Mao Tse-tung, *Four Essays on Philosophy* (Foreign Language Press, Peking, from SACU and other suppliers).

Stuart Schram, *The Political Thought of Mao Tse-tung* (Penguin, 1968), *Mao Tse-tung* (Penguin, 1966).

F. Schurmann and O. Schell (eds.), *China Readings*: Vol. 2, Republican China (1911–49); Vol. 3, Communist China (1949–1960) (Penguin, 1967).

A useful collection of documents from various sources, on various topics, with commentary by the editors.

Ruth Sidel, *Women and Child Care in China* (Penguin, 1982).

Han Suyin, *The Morning Deluge*, 2 Vols (Panther, 1976), and *Wind in the Tower* (Cape, 1976). Biography of Mao Tse-tung.

D. J. Waller, *The Government and Politics of Communist China* (Hutchinson, 2nd ed., 1981).

E. L. Wheelwright and B. McFarlane, *The Chinese Road to Socialism: Economics of the Cultural Revolution* (Monthly Review Press, 1971). The authors' sympathy with the Maoist view in the political debate of the 1960s helps to make clear the principles at stake in that controversy.

Peter Worsley, *Inside China* (Allen Lane, 1975).

The following booklets in the *Modern China* series published by the Anglo-Chinese Educational Institute mostly describe Maoist policies of the 'Eleven Years' period and are especially relevant to Chapter 19. Nos. 5 and 7 are easily comprehensible to younger readers. Available from SACU.

No. 3: Isaac Ascher, *China's Social Policy* (1972)

No. 4: Joan Robinson, *Economic Management – China 1972* (1973)

No. 5: P. and S. Mauger and others, *Education in China* (1974)

No. 7: Innes Herden, *Introduction to China* (1976)

History of the Twentieth Century magazine series (see Notes on Resources, page xi for full information); the issues particularly relevant to this Part of the book are:

Chapters 15 and 16: No. 36 (May 4th Movement).

Chapter 16: No. 75.

Chapters 17, 18 and 19: No. 89 (China under Mao, and the Sino-Soviet split).

GLOSSARY OF OLD AND NEW FORMS OF CHINESE SPELLING

Old spelling	New spelling (adopted in 1978)	Old spelling	New spelling (adopted in 1978)
Chiang Ching	Jiang Qing	Teng Hsiao-ping	Deng Xiaoping
Chou En-lai	Zhou Enlai	Kuomintang	Guomindang
Hua Kuo-feng	Hua Guofeng	Sinkiang	Xinjiang
Lin Piao	Lin Biao	Yenan	Yan'an
Liu Shao-chi	Liu Shaoqi	Peking	Beijing
Mao Tse-tung	Mao Zedong		

Part IV

The World Powers' Relations
since 1945

A Russian soldier raises the Soviet flag over war-shattered Berlin, 1945.

Confrontation or Coexistence?

At this point we suggest a pause for revision. Look at the chart on the inside front cover to remind yourself of the main events in each World Power's history and the sideways connections between them. Notice, for example, that McCarthyism was a reaction to events in Europe and China as well as the product of American circumstances. It is also important to remember the relative position of each country on the ladder of economic development. By 1950 the United States could afford costly weapons *and* an affluent society for her citizens – whereas Russia, after the steep climb through the Plans to an industrial economy, was now repairing the damage of a terrible war. China did not even begin to develop her industrial muscles until the mid-1950s.

You have already seen how each power became involved in the Second World War, and the effect of the war on its history and outlook. Before we plunge into the events after 1945 it may be helpful to sketch out the route ahead.

The Cold War

Outwardly the wartime Grand Alliance, now including liberated France and China, seemed unshakable and permanent in 1945. With all the 'big boys' on the same side and all their enemies defeated, most people were looking forward to a long period of peace. Yet by 1949 citizens of Western countries had come to feel that their gallant Soviet ally was now their most dangerous enemy. The Cold War was under way.

With the longer view of historians, you will not be surprised that the wartime unity of East and West did not last. The hostility between Russia and the West which began in 1917 was only temporarily buried in 1941. The extension of Soviet power in Eastern Europe after 1945 alarmed American statesmen: was this the first step in Moscow's well-known plan to conquer the world? The continued American presence in Western Europe was equally worrying to Stalin: why were they rebuilding Germany, and distributing the almighty dollar so freely? The Cold War in Europe soon became a world conflict, both sides interpreting later events as 'evidence' to justify their suspicions of each other.

Peaceful Coexistence

If the roots of the Cold War go back to 1917, we can also see in the 1920s the germ of another post-war theme: Peaceful Coexistence. Lenin in 1921 did not intend his coexistence with Capitalism to be permanent – but Lenin did not foresee nuclear weapons. For Khrushchev in the 1950s this was the most important fact of the post-war world: H-bomb war was impossible, so East and West must learn to coexist peacefully. His new foreign policies tried to bring this about, while at the same time defining the frontiers of the 'Soviet camp' (and if possible extending them) by any means short of war.

By 1960 we can see two overlapping themes in East–West relations: the 'old' Cold War theme (shown, for example, in the war in Vietnam), and the 'new' theme of Peaceful Coexistence which began with the untying of smaller knots in Korea and Austria and then moved towards more complicated tangles like Germany. This warmer atmosphere was suddenly shattered by the Cuba missile crisis in 1962.

Détente ... and a New Cold War

In spite of Cuba – in fact to some extent because of it – the new theme eventually became the dominant one: by the early 1970s Peaceful Coexistence had evolved into *détente*. Another important influence on this development was the Sino–Soviet split: by 1970 Russia and China had moved so far apart that each feared the other more than their former common enemy the United States.

But East–West *détente* was no more than the word itself means: a relaxation of tension. Both sides still held to their conflicting ideologies, their military alliances and nuclear weapons. *Détente* was soon replaced by a new Cold War between the USA and the USSR, while China now stood on the sidelines maintaining 'friendly' relations with America and 'less friendly' (but no longer dangerously hostile) relations with Russia.

What to include, what to leave out?

Part IV is not a history of the world since 1945, but only of the relations between the three World Powers. Even this limited story could lead almost anywhere, for there is scarcely a corner of the globe where their interests have not clashed. The short cut we have chosen is to emphasize the World Powers' *policies* rather than present a full narrative of the past thirty years. We shall give most attention to key events in Europe and the Far East to see how the attitudes of the Cold War were established, and what they led to – ultimately, to the brink of nuclear war over Cuba and a dead-end street in Vietnam. On the way we shall glance only briefly at other danger areas – the Middle East, for example – where existing conflicts were greatly intensified by Cold War rivalries.

The Cold War has dominated world politics since 1945. Often the intervention of the World Powers into an area of conflict so obscured other issues – Jew against Arab, Black against White, Nationalist against Imperialist – that the war of Capitalism against Communism seemed to be the only issue that counted. Vietnam was one unlucky victim of this over-simple view of the world. To the people of that country the ideological argument was always less important than their nationalist revolution which, because it was led by Communists, turned Vietnam into a Cold War frontier. The tragic war in Vietnam made many other people question whether the issues of the Cold War were so important after all. Who could support a cause which brought such suffering to a small country caught in the cross-fire?

Unhappily the new Cold War of the early 1980s continued to involve Vietnam, and also spread into other Third World areas— notably the Middle East and Central America—where once again the national interests of small countries were subordinated to the strategic rivalry of the three World Powers. The last chapter of this book starkly demonstrates the tragedy and danger of a 'Cold War mentality' on both sides of the USA–USSR confrontation.

Nuclear weapons

Most of the Study Topics in this book are optional extras for those who have time and interest to study them. But Study Topic 14, about nuclear weapons, is *essential reading* for every student of this period. To make it easier to understand, we have gathered the basic information into one connected story and have deliberately placed it centrally in the period 1945–83, following an account of the Cuba missile crisis. It was that event above all which made *everyone* realize the horrific danger presented by the new doomsday weapons, which still threaten us all today.

21

The Second World War and the Post-War Settlement

This chapter considers briefly the Second World War and the Big Three discussions of post-war problems. The events of the war are not dealt with in detail, but the problems it raised, and the plans of the wartime Allies to solve them, are an essential introduction to the Cold War of propaganda and diplomatic manoeuvre which began to divide the Allies even before they had finished the shooting war against Germany and Japan.

THE SECOND WORLD WAR

Some people regard the Japanese invasion of

China in 1937 as the real beginning of the Second World War. But it was German aggression in Europe which made it a world conflict, so we shall start there. We take up the story where we left it in Chapter 12.

Phase 1 – The Axis Powers sweep the board

Western Europe (Figure 21.1)

September 1939 The war began in Poland. Britain and France, having tried unsuccess-

Figure 21.1 Blitzkrieg, 1939–40.

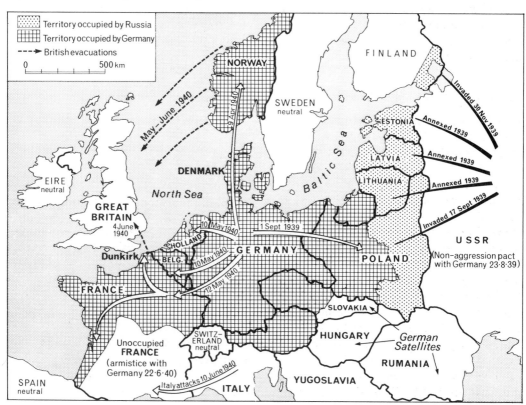

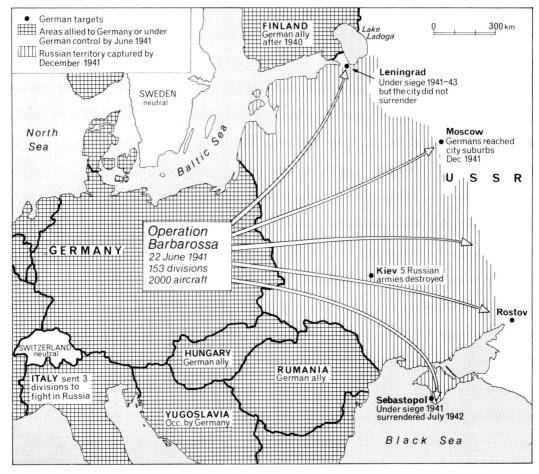

Figure 21.2 Operation Barbarossa.

fully to appease Hitler at Munich in 1938, decided to resist any further German aggression. Hitler invaded Poland from the West on 1 September and Britain and France then declared war on Germany. Russia – in accordance with the Nazi–Soviet Pact signed in August – invaded Poland from the East on 17 September. Poland was defeated by the end of the month and its government fled to exile in London (these were the London Poles, one of the groups which contested the right to rule Poland after the war).

Winter 1939–40: the Phoney War   For many months after the defeat of Poland there was no other fighting on land while the Allies waited expectantly for Hitler's next move. At sea the Battle of the Atlantic was under way: it was vital to keep open the sea-lanes for supply ships to Britain through areas patrolled by German U-boats (submarines). In a separate conflict Russia defeated Finland and took some of her territory.

April–May 1940   German troops overran Denmark, Norway, the Netherlands and Belgium. The British Expeditionary Force, surrounded and cut off from the French forces, was evacuated from Dunkirk, 27 May– 4 June. Churchill replaced Chamberlain as British Prime Minister in May.

June 1940   France sued for peace. The Germans allowed the puppet French Vichy Government to rule southern France and French North Africa until they imposed direct German control in November 1942. General de Gaulle formed the Free French forces in London.

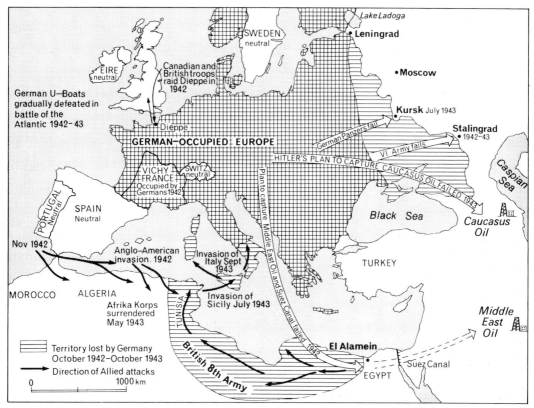

Figure 21.3   Turning points, 1942–3.

Late summer 1940: the Battle of Britain   The RAF successfully beat off the Luftwaffe's attempt to destroy it in preparation for an invasion of Britain. The invasion did not take place, and the Luftwaffe turned to the night bombing of British cities.

East Europe–Russia (Figure 21.2)

Hungary, Rumania, Bulgaria and Finland became allies of Germany. Yugoslavia, Albania and Greece (where troops of Germany's ally Italy were being defeated) were overrun and occupied by German forces.

22 June 1941: Operation Barbarossa   The German invasion of Russia. The Red Army made a 'scorched earth' retreat eastwards, blowing up bridges and dams and burning crops to hinder the German advance.

North Africa

British troops were doing well against Italian

troops until a German army under Rommel reinforced the weak Italian forces. The Germans advanced, retreated, then advanced to El Alamein in early 1942.

The Pacific (Figure 21.6, page 230)

From March 1941 the USA aided the European Allies and China with Lend-Lease (China had been continuously at war with Japan since 1937). Pearl Harbor enrolled America's full strength for the Allied cause, but it took her some time to mobilize efficient forces for overseas combat.

December 1941–June 1942   Japan 'swept the board' in Asia as Germany had done in Europe, taking British, French, Dutch and American colonies and American bases in the Pacific.

Phase 2–Turning points (Figure 21.3)

The Battle of El Alamein, October 1942

This was the first major German defeat.

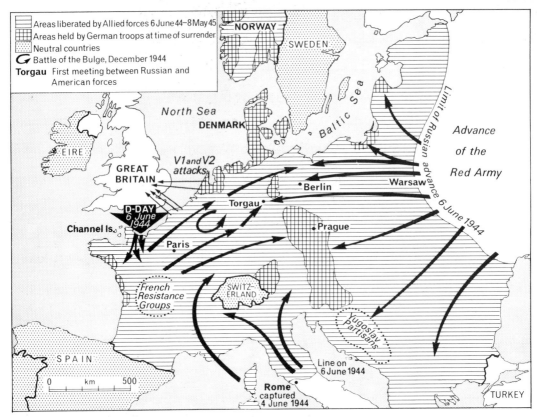

The legend on the map reads:

Areas liberated by Allied forces 6 June 44–8 May 45
Areas held by German troops at time of surrender
Neutral countries
G Battle of the Bulge, December 1944
Torgau First meeting between Russian and American forces

Labels on the map: NORWAY, SWEDEN, North Sea, DENMARK, Baltic Sea, EIRE, GREAT BRITAIN, V1 and V2 attacks, Berlin, Warsaw, Advance of the Red Army, Limit of Russian advance 6 June 1944, D-DAY 6 June 1944, Channel Is., Torgau, Prague, Paris, French Resistance Groups, SWITZERLAND, Yugoslav Partisans, SPAIN, 0 km 500, Line on 6 June 1944, Rome captured 4 June 1944, TURKEY

Figure 21.4 The defeat of Germany, 1944–5.

British troops routed Rommel and then advanced along the North African coast to join an Anglo-American force which had invaded Morocco and Algeria, to defeat the Germans in Tunisia in May 1943. From there the Allies invaded Sicily in July, and then Italy, which surrendered and joined the Allies. Allied forces advanced slowly up Italy fighting German troops sent in from the north.

Battle of Stalingrad, winter 1942–3

This titanic five-month struggle was eventually won by the Red Army. It was followed by the defeat of another German army at Kursk in July 1943. The Red Army then began a steady advance westward.

Battles of the Coral Sea and Midway Island, May and June 1942 (Figure 21.6, page 230)

American naval victories turned the tide in the Pacific theatre. US forces began their island-hopping counter-attack to recover the Philippines and lost bases.

Phase 3 – The Axis Powers in retreat

Western Europe (Figure 21.4)

6 June 1944: D-Day The Allied invasion of Normandy in northern France opened the Second Front. By mid-September most of France was liberated. V1 and V2 rocket attacks on South-East England continued until their launching sites were taken. The 'broad front' Allied advance was temporarily checked by a German counter-attack in December 1944 – the Battle of the Bulge – and then continued on into Germany.

Meanwhile the Red Army was advancing steadily through eastern and central Europe to link up with American troops in Germany. The Red Army reached Berlin in April 1945 (Figure 21.5). Hitler committed suicide on 30 April and early in May, the German army surrendered.

VE (Victory in Europe) Day was 8 May 1945.

The Far East

1944–5 American forces were now winning

Figure 21.5 Refugees in Berlin, 1945.

steadily, and British and Commonwealth troops re-opened the Burma Road supply route to China. But the Allies met fanatical Japanese resistance everywhere. It was estimated that the invasion and conquest of Japan might cost 1 million Allied lives.

President Roosevelt died in April 1945 and was replaced by President Truman – up to then little known in American politics, and with little experience or knowledge of foreign affairs. His first major decision as President was to use the Atom bomb to end the war (Figure 21.6). Two bombs were dropped on Japan: on Hiroshima (6 August) and Nagasaki (9 August).

VJ (Victory over Japan) Day was 14 August 1945.

BIG THREE WARTIME CONFERENCES

Military discussions

Several important Big Three meetings were held during the war to discuss military tactics and, later, the solution of post-war problems. On the whole Stalin, FDR and Churchill worked well together in their common cause to defeat the Axis powers, but there was one sore point in their military discussions.

From 1941 Stalin called impatiently for a Second Front in Europe to relieve the pressure on the Red Army. But the Anglo-American generals wanted their expeditionary force to be invincible, and took a long time to prepare the D-Day landings which finally opened the Second Front in June 1944. The full weight of the German armies in Europe pressed down on Russia alone for three long years, causing terrible human and material losses. This was the nightmare that Stalin had tried to avoid by his pact with Hitler in 1939. It increased his determination to prevent any future attack from the west at all costs.

Different aims and interests of the Big Three

By 1943 the Allies could begin to make plans for after the war. To understand their wartime agreements – and, more important, why those agreements were broken in the years that followed – you must bear in mind their differing aims.

Stalin was concerned, above all, with the future strength and security of the Soviet Union. He wanted to protect her against attack from the west (which had already happened three times in the twentieth century: 1914, 1918, and 1941) and to strengthen her position in the Far East when her historic rival Japan was defeated. This self-protective aim was consistent with Stalin's whole foreign policy since 1928, and was reinforced by Russia's experience of war from 1941–5.

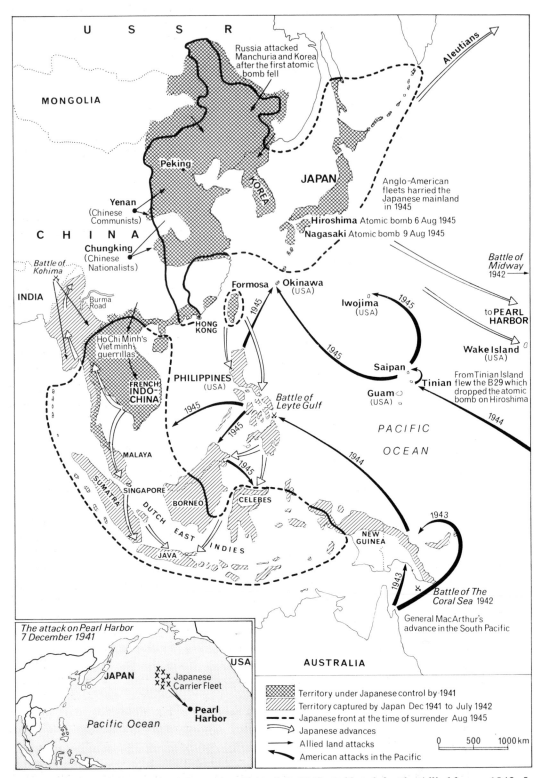

Figure 21.6   Japanese advances, December 1941–July 1942, and her defeat by Allied forces, 1942–5.

Roosevelt was an internationalist: he did not want America to slide back into isolationism after the Second World War as she had done after the First. He saw that the United States, with other major powers, would have to take some responsibility for keeping world order and to guarantee what he considered the basic rights of mankind. In a speech in 1941, FDR had defined these rights as the Four Freedoms: Freedom from Want, Freedom of Speech, Freedom of Religious Belief and Freedom from Fear. America thus had idealistic aims for the post-war world, and in later years her leaders naturally emphasized these in their Cold War propaganda.

But American post-war policy was also self-interested. You saw in Part I that the Great Depression of the 1930s was 'cured' only by the economic boom of wartime production. To prevent another depression after the war it would be necessary for America to keep on making and selling things at home and overseas – if not arms, then other more useful consumer goods. The famous remark of President Coolidge in the 1920s – 'the business of America is business' – is a solemn truth about the style of life America has developed: without ever-increasing production and consumption, the affluent society would collapse. FDR and his successors therefore wanted a world in which there would be 'free trade' for American ideas *and* American goods.

At the same time FDR recognized that the USSR needed to feel secure in a world which had been hostile towards it since 1917. He did not want to frighten Stalin by 'ganging-up' with Churchill against him; indeed he wanted to prevent, if possible, what he guessed would be one of Churchill's post-war aims – to re-establish the British Empire.

Churchill was aware of two uncomfortable facts as the war neared its end: the increased strength and bargaining power of the Soviet Union, and the decreased strength and influence of Great Britain. He wanted to check both these trends as soon as possible, and to do so he would have welcomed a joint Anglo-American stand in discussions with Stalin, and American sympathy, at least, for British imperial interests. Without this, he felt that Russia would get too much of her own way.

In spite of FDR's internationalism, Churchill feared an American withdrawal after the war (President Wilson in 1919 was also an internationalist, but that did not prevent America's return to isolationism). Churchill wanted democratic friends to help Britain against Soviet strength, so he insisted, for example, that France should be given great-power privileges in the United Nations, and should help to administer defeated Germany.

THE POST-WAR SETTLEMENT

The Big Three readily agreed on certain matters, while other questions, particularly the post-war arrangements for Europe, presented sticky problems. Like all statesmen, they found it easier to issue high-minded declarations than to work out the details for putting them into practice – or to abide by the declarations later, when their own national interests seemed to be threatened.

The United Nations

The Big Three all recognized the need for a new, revised international organization to replace the ill-fated League of Nations. In June 1945, at San Francisco, the representatives of fifty states met to found the United Nations.

The UN was based on the League's general principle of collective security: if any dispute between nations threatened the peace of the world, the UN would sort out the quarrel and if necessary go to the aid of a victim of aggression. The job of peace-keeping was assigned to the Security Council, in which the Big Five (the USA, USSR, Britain, France and China) had the special privilege of a permanent seat and the power of veto: any major decision must be agreed by all five, or it would not pass. The veto system may seem unfair, but it was a recognition that no decision which might involve going to war could be enforced without great-power support – and that a

231

resolution which *did* have their unanimous backing would be obeyed by smaller nations.

The economic and social work begun by the League was to be greatly expanded in the UN mainly through its Specialized Agencies – for example FAO (Food and Agriculture Organization), WHO (World Health Organization), UNESCO (UN Educational, Scientific and Cultural Organization) – and other bodies like the UN High Commission for Refugees and the UN Children's Fund (UNICEF). New York was chosen as the Headquarters of the UN, where meetings are held and the Secretariat (the administration) does its work. By placing the headquarters within the United States the founders hoped to counteract any post-war American desire to withdraw from the UN as America had withdrawn from the League of Nations in 1919.

By the 1980s we must record, regrettably, the UN had not fulfilled the high hopes invested in it in 1945. Except for the Korean War (discussed in Chapter 23) the UN gets scarcely a mention in our account of the post-war relations of the World Powers – a period of many international disputes, several serious wars and more than one 'near miss' which could have set off a Third World War. As the founders had foreseen, the UN could not work effectively as a peace-keeping force without great-power agreement. Under its first Secretary-General Trygve Lie of Norway the Soviet Union came to feel that the UN was just another vehicle of American policy against her, and in the early years the Russian contribution to Security Council debates was just one word: *Niet* (No). The United States could always round up a majority both in the Security Council and the General Assembly (where every nation has one vote and no veto) because so many nations depended on American aid and goodwill. In this way Communist China was excluded from membership until 1971, which undermined the UN's claim to speak for all the peoples of the world.

Under later Secretaries–General (who have all been nationals of small countries) the UN earned a reputation for greater impartiality. Moreover by the 1960s the admission to UN membership of many newly-independent states allowed blocs of smaller states to out-vote the larger ones in the General Assembly. But by this time the great powers were used to conducting their serious business outside the UN, and they continued to do so.

Nevertheless the UN was (and still is) at least a necessary meeting-place and forum for the quarrelling great powers, and it has played an essential role in smaller disputes by interposing a neutral military force between growling opponents: Israelis and Egyptians, Indians and Pakistanis, Greeks and Turks in Cyprus. The UN's contribution in economic and social fields – food, health, education – is undisputed, and in the long run these efforts to remove the causes of misery and inequality may do something 'to save succeeding generations from the scourge of war', as the UN Charter hoped.

New frontiers and governments

1. The Far East

In 1943 it was agreed that Japan, when defeated, would be stripped of all her imperialist gains since 1894, including some rights in China won from Russia in 1905: the use of two ports and a railway in Manchuria. Later the Big Three agreed to recognize the 'independence' of Mongolia from China (which in fact had been a Soviet satellite since 1921), and that Russian rights in Manchuria would revert to the USSR rather than to China. In return, Stalin promised to join the war against Japan three months after the defeat of Germany.

The post-war fate of Japan will not concern us further in our study of the relations between the World Powers. American troops under General MacArthur occupied Japan in 1945, and her post-war reconstruction was supervised and aided by the Americans. The new Japan was therefore politically in the 'American camp' and did not become, like Germany, a victim of direct Cold War conflict. But one of Japan's former possessions –

Korea – was to be the scene of bitter confrontation, as you will see later.

At their conferences in 1945, the Big Three were much more concerned with the future of territory in Europe than the Far East.

2. Eastern Europe

Before the war all the countries of East Europe except Czechoslovakia had had right-wing or near-Fascist governments, and three of them (Hungary, Bulgaria and Rumania), as well as Finland, had assisted Hitler's war against Russia. The Western Allies were therefore sympathetic in a general way to Stalin's concern that the post-war governments of these countries should be friendly towards the Soviet Union. Churchill acknowledged this when in 1944 he and Stalin agreed to share out future spheres of influence in Eastern Europe – by which, for example, Bulgaria and Rumania would be mainly in the Russian sphere and Yugoslavia and Greece in the British sphere. But this Anglo-Soviet bargain was not taken any further because FDR disliked the idea of great powers assuming rights of influence over other countries.

Poland presented the greatest problems. At the Yalta Conference in February 1945 it was agreed that the USSR should keep the territory she had taken in 1939, including eastern Poland. The new Poland would be compensated with territory in the west taken from Germany (see Figure 21.7). The future government of Poland, however, was a thorny question. Britain sponsored the London Poles, the pre-war government which had fled to England in 1939, while the USSR wanted the Communist-dominated Lublin Committee in Poland to form the post-war government. The London Poles were too right-wing and anti-Soviet for Stalin's liking; he was determined that the historic invasion route to Russia should be a safe neighbour in the future. Eventually the Western Allies recognized the Lublin Committee, on Stalin's promise that its government would include representatives of the London Poles and other groups. The Big Three signed a 'Declaration for Liberated Europe' pledging

their support for democratic governments based on free elections in *all* European countries.

3. Germany (Figure 21.7)

In the heat of the war, the Allies were united in their desire to punish Germany and to make sure that she would never again be a military threat. At one stage there was an Anglo-American plan to de-industrialize Germany and turn it into an agricultural state, but this was soon dropped. In 1945 it was agreed to divide Germany into four Occupation Zones – Soviet, American, British and French – which would nevertheless be administered as one economic unit, run by a joint Allied Control Council. The capital city, which was an 'island' in the heart of the Eastern (Soviet) Zone, was similarly divided into four.

This division of Germany and Berlin was intended to be temporary until the reunification of a new, 'safe' Germany could be arranged. The Allies hoped to create a new, safe Germany during the period of military government through the Allied Control Council's general policy of the Four Ds: DeNazification, Demilitarization, Disarmament and Democratization.

DeNazification was begun at once when the surviving Nazi leaders were brought before the Allied Tribunal at Nuremberg in November 1945 (some, like Hitler, had escaped Allied justice by committing suicide). The German leaders were accused of waging aggressive war and of 'crimes against humanity'. Three were acquitted, seven were sentenced to long prison terms and the rest were hanged. Similar trials of lesser-known Nazis took place later, and for some years it was impossible for a known former Nazi to take part in political life. Another aspect of deNazification was the provision of new school textbooks which, it was hoped, would instil democratic values of tolerance and freedom in the younger generation. But ideas are not so easily killed as people! After a while, especially as anti-Communist feeling grew in Western Germany, Nazi-type organizations

233

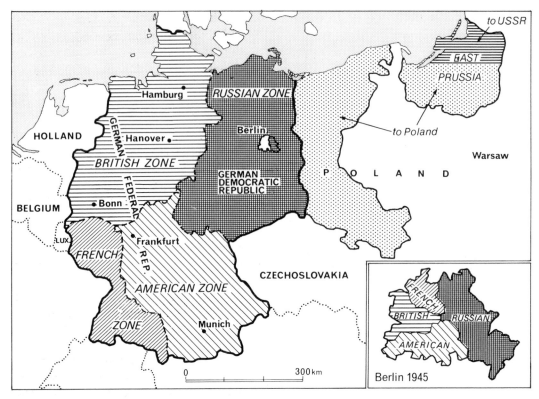

Figure 21.7   The occupation zones of Germany and Berlin, 1945.

began to reappear and a pro-Nazi record did not necessarily disqualify a would-be politician or official.†

The rights and wrongs of the Nuremberg trials have often been debated since 1945. Does the victor have the right to try his defeated enemy for 'crimes against humanity' without considering his own possible 'crimes'? Hitler was responsible for terrible deeds, but what about the Atom bombs which killed at least 114,000 Japanese civilians? Or the Anglo-American 'saturation bombing' of the historic German city of Dresden which killed 135,000? In 1945, however, with the revelation of concentration camps in which

the Nazis had put to death 6 million Jews and other 'inferior races', the peoples of Allied countries were not in a mood to question their own leaders' methods of winning the war before punishing the top Nazis.

4. Other matters

Austria, like Germany, had been liberated by Russian and Western Allied troops and in 1945 it too was divided into four Occupation Zones on the pattern of Germany.

In 1947 a series of peace treaties were signed with Germany's other allies (Italy, Finland, Rumania, Hungary, Bulgaria) which made minor territorial changes and fixed reparations to be paid to the victors. It was intended to make final settlements with Germany and Austria later, and a peace treaty was eventually signed with Austria in 1955. But the future of Germany was to be more complicated.

---

†The case of Nazism in Germany illustrates a familiar problem for any liberal democracy. A truly democratic system has to take the risk of allowing the free circulation of extreme Right *or* Left ideas which might destroy Democracy itself if they attracted enough support. This is in fact what happened when the Nazi party came to power in Germany in 1933 by democratic means and then established a one-party state. In post-war Germany Nazi ideas have fortunately gained little support.

Were the Western Allies 'fooled' by Stalin?

The vital questions about Europe and historic Russian rights in China were mainly dealt with at the Yalta and Potsdam Conferences in 1945. The Western leaders at Yalta (especially FDR) were later criticized for giving way to Stalin's ambitions in Europe and for 'selling China down the river' (that is, selling out the interests of the Kuomintang Government to Communism).

To suggest that FDR and his Democratic party were 'soft on Communism' was of course a good vote-catcher for the Republican party in American elections; as we saw in Chapter 5, the extreme right-wing McCarthyites made very effective use of this tactic. But these accusations were also part of a wider debate in the West about whether the Cold War might have been prevented if the West had been 'tougher' with the Russians in 1945. Truman and some other Western politicians thought that Stalin had a long-standing plan for world conquest, and that the West's 'weakness' at Yalta had encouraged him to think he could put it into action after the war.

This point of view about how the Cold War started ignores two important military facts of the last phase of the war:

1. The Red Army's triumph

At the time of the Yalta Conference (February 1945), the Red Army had already liberated most of Eastern Europe and was fast approaching Berlin, while the Anglo-American forces in the West had not yet crossed the Rhine into Germany. Victory in Europe was in sight, and the commanding position of the Red Army was plain for all to see. FDR and Churchill had little choice but to acknowledge Soviet influence in the eastern half of Europe.

On the other hand, victory over Japan still seemed a long way off (the Atom bomb was not yet ready), and the Western Allies thought they would need Russian help to achieve it. They were therefore ready to allow Russia greater post-war influence in the Far East (especially as that would be China's loss, not theirs) in exchange for Soviet help to defeat Japan.

2. America's Atom bomb

By the time of the Potsdam meeting (July 1945), several East European countries already had Communist-dominated provisional governments. But the West's bargaining position had also improved, and the new American member of the Big Three – President Truman – wanted to advertise that new strength in a dramatic way. During the conference Truman heard of the successful testing of the Atom bomb and gave the word for it to be used on Japan. He discussed this momentous development with Churchill but was not so frank with Stalin, to whom he merely remarked casually that America had a new weapon 'of unusual destructive force'. Truman's later statements make it clear that he intended the bomb on Hiroshima on 6 August not only to end the war but to begin the 'peace' with a warning to the Russians, whose every move and motive he regarded with deep suspicion.

As the victory bells clanged all over the world, most ordinary people looked forward to a long and genuine peace, maintained by the continued co-operation of the Big Three and the revived great powers France and China. Few people realized that East–West unity was already beginning to crack. Russia, still weak from the effort to defeat Germany, now faced another possible enemy with a terrible new weapon. America, eager to spread her influence in parts of the world which up to now had not much interested her, found that certain areas were already reserved – or soon to be seized – for the hated doctrine of Communism. Russian fears and American frustrations soon brought them into head-on collision.

Questions

Did you notice?

1. Which of these was not one of the Big Three? (a) Churchill (b) de Gaulle (c) FDR
2. Which power does *not* have a veto in the United Nations? (a) Britain (b) India (c) France
3. In 1945 Poland gained territory from (a) Germany (b) Russia (c) Czechoslovakia
4. The 'Four Ds' refers to (a) the occupation zones of Germany (b) Allied policy towards Germany (c) the Big Three plus France
5. The decision to use the Atom bomb was made by (a) the Big Three (b) all the Western Allies (c) Truman
6. True or false?
   (i) The Four Freedoms were agreed by the Big Three at Yalta
   (ii) The headquarters of the UN is in Switzerland
   (iii) Korea was ruled by Japan until 1945
   (iv) The London Poles were pro-Communist
   (v) Senator McCarthy commanded US occupation forces in Japan
   (vi) France was given an Occupation Zone in Germany
7. Which statement is *more* accurate?
   (i) At Big Three wartime conferences
     (a) Churchill and FDR 'ganged-up' against Stalin
     (b) Churchill wanted a joint Anglo-American policy
   (ii) At the Nuremberg trials of 1945
     (a) the legality of the Atom bombs was discussed
     (b) the surviving Nazi leaders were tried
   (iii) (a) Berlin was part of the Soviet zone of Germany
     (b) Berlin was surrounded by the Soviet zone of Germany

Can you explain?

8. In what way was Stalin's post-war foreign policy consistent with his pre-war policy?
9. 'The business of America is business.' What does this phrase have to do with America's post-war foreign policy?
10. What was the reason behind the veto system in the United Nations Security Council?
11. Briefly describe these aspects of the post-war settlement in Europe:
    (a) the 'temporary' partition of Germany
    (b) the change in Poland's frontiers
12. Some people in the West thought Churchill and FDR had encouraged Stalin to think he could expand Soviet influence in Europe after the war, and that his determination to do so started the Cold War after 1945.
    (a) How far did Churchill and FDR accept Soviet influence in Eastern Europe at the Yalta conference, and why did they do so?
    (b) What new reason did Stalin have to fear Western attitudes towards Russia in 1945?

What's your view?

13. Do you think the Allies acted correctly in trying the Nazi leaders at Nuremberg?
14. Truman defended his decision to use the Atom bomb on the grounds that it would 'shorten the agony of war' and save the lives of Allied soldiers. Was he right to use it for that reason? Should any weapons of war be 'outlawed'? If so, how could this be done?
15. One reason for the weakness of the United Nations and other international organizations is that national governments are reluctant to give up national sovereignty (that is, their own powers of decision) to any outside body. Why do they insist on national sovereignty in all matters? Are they right to do so?

22

The Cold War in Europe, 1945–9

This chapter deals with a short but very important period: the four years between the end of the war and the setting up of the North Atlantic Treaty Organization (NATO). In these years the foundations of the *Cold War* (k) were laid and its European frontier drawn: the Iron Curtain which separates the two Europes, the two Germanys and the two Berlins of today. The events of 1945–9 created attitudes and policies on both sides of the Iron Curtain which, once they were established, made a reconciliation between East and West almost impossible. From this point onwards, the Cold War conflict seemed to follow an inevitable course. We must therefore ask *why* certain actions were taken, and consider how they looked to the other side.

Here there is a difficulty which must be explained before we go further. There is general agreement about *what* happened in the Cold War, but when we ask *why* Russia or America did this or that, there are different answers.

DIFFERENT INTERPRETATIONS OF HISTORY

Discovering the 'why' of history is always more difficult than just describing the events. The historian's job is to arrange the facts and statements of the past into a coherent story, and there is always more than one way to do this. His interpretation may be disputed by others, or up-dated later by a reappraisal of the evidence.

The history of the Cold War is an example of this. The Russian view of who started it, whose 'fault' it was, is certainly different from the Western view†. But even Western historians disagree in their interpretations of events. They offer two main versions of the story:

The *conventional* view starts from the belief that Stalin set out in 1945 to conquer the world for Communism. The West (in effect the United States) was forced to defend itself and other free nations from Soviet expansionism which threatened to engulf Western Europe and the world.

The *revisionist* view suggests that Stalin was not interested in world conquest but only, as all statesmen are, in the safety of his country. American policies which Truman claimed were defensive not only continually provoked him, but were in fact trying to establish American domination of Western Europe and other parts of the world.

The *conventional* view was generally accepted in the West until recently – and this is not surprising, since we have been living through the Cold War all these years. At least until the Cuba missile crisis in 1962, there was firm support in the United States (and the West generally) for America's Cold War policies, and the belief that '*they* started it' was a necessary part of this. For if Communism *didn't* threaten us all, then what was the Cold War all about?

The *revisionist* school of thought began in the 1960s. You will see in Chapter 25 that the Vietnam War and other events of that period led many Americans to question their own

---

† You can get an idea of Soviet teaching about the history of this period from *The Russian Version of the Second World War* (Leo Cooper, 1976), compiled by its editor, Graham Lyons, from the two main textbooks used in Russian secondary schools today.

country's foreign policy and propaganda of the previous twenty years. Some historians asked, 'Did the Cold War *really* start in the way we have all been taught?' and began to re-examine the evidence. Their conclusion was that Truman and others on 'our side' should share the blame with Stalin, and that American motives were not so 'innocent' as she had pretended.

In the 1980s it is even harder to accept the 'cops and robbers' view of the Cold War which was current in the West for many years (in fact such a simple-minded view of history should always be challenged). Later events and revelations have shown that American foreign policy is just as self-interested as that of any other great power, past or present.

Nevertheless many Western history books still lay most of the blame for the Cold War on Stalin. Is this an honest appraisal of the facts, or the result of national and political bias? It is hard to be sure while we are still so close to the events described. The Cold War is an underlying theme of all East–West relations since 1945; it affects judgements on both sides of the Iron Curtain. So you must make your own assessment of any account you read: what interpretation does it offer, and how convincing is it?

Our own account of the early phase of the Cold War avoids the choice between a straight conventional or revisionist version by treating the events of 1945–9 in a different way. You don't really need to decide whether Stalin *did* intend to conquer the world in 1945; what matters is the fact that many people in the West *thought* he did – or were persuaded to think so – and were ready to support the West's policies of counter-attack. In other words, what actually happened was less important than what people *thought* had happened, and (as in all wars!) actions by one side which may have been genuinely defensive looked aggressive to the other.

SIX STEPS TO NATO

There are six major events or developments to describe and explain. We can call them the

Six Steps to NATO, although you should note that they were not strictly consecutive: developments in different parts of Europe were going on at the same time. Once again it is more important for you to recognize and understand the main trends over a period of years than to memorize every detail of what happened.

Step 1   The Soviet 'take-over' of Eastern Europe, 1945–7.

Step 2   Churchill's 'Iron Curtain' Speech, March 1946.

Step 3   The Truman Doctrine and Marshall Plan, March and June 1947.

Step 4   The setting up of the Cominform, October 1947.

Step 5   The Communist *coup** in Czechoslovakia, February 1948.

Step 6   The Berlin Blockade, June 1948– May 1949.

1949   In April the North Atlantic Treaty set up NATO.
In August the German Federal Republic (West Germany) was established.
In September the German Democratic Republic (East Germany) was established.

To explain the reason behind a policy, or the reaction to it, our description of each 'step' is followed by a summary of the Soviet and the American view of it. These contrasting views are borne out by facts and statements of the time, but of course our summaries oversimplify complex issues. Their purpose is only to show you that the same problem or event could look quite different from each side of the Iron Curtain.

To set the scene we must first consider the general political climate in Europe at the end of the war.

The post-war mood in Europe

In 1945, Communism and other left-wing views were attractive to many Europeans. Communists had often led partisan resistance groups which had helped the advancing Allied armies or, in some cases, had carried out the liberation themselves. Moreover, in every country involved in the war, hopes had been stirred for a better world after it. In Britain, for example, the war effort had shaken up society and revealed to everyone the shocking poverty of working-class victims of the 1930s depression. Social reform was long overdue.

These factors led to a large left-wing vote in post-war elections all over Europe. To the great disappointment of Churchill and the Conservative Party, in July 1945 the Labour Party took power in Britain with a landslide victory. Left-wing coalition governments were formed in most other European countries. In Eastern Europe the key posts in these governments were all held by Communists.

Step 1: The Soviet 'take-over' of Eastern Europe, 1945–7

We saw in Chapter 21 that as the Red Army advanced through Eastern Europe, pro-Communist temporary governments were set up. Post-war elections in these countries were held under the watchful eyes of the Red Army, which had not yet withdrawn. The West did not regard then as free elections, and disliked even more the subsequent Communization of the coalition governments which were elected.

In Poland, for example, the pro-Communist National Front coalition party controlled the police and could prevent the opposition Peasant Party from freely canvassing its views. In the 1946 elections the National Front won 90 per cent of the vote and formed a government which was Communist in fact if not yet in name. In 1947 the Peasant Party's leader fled to the West and eventually the National Front absorbed the Peasant Party and became the Polish Communist Party.

By 1947 every East European government except that of Czechoslovakia had been 'Communized' in a similar way. Opposition parties had been outlawed or squeezed out by other means. It is open to argument whether Stalin intended *from the beginning* to do this, as we have explained above. The dismantling

of coalition governments and the Stalinization of the whole area came *after* the announcement of the Truman Doctrine and the Marshall Plan, as Step 4 (page 241) explains further.

Starting Point (see Chapter 21)

THE SOVIET VIEW
Starting point
The West has got The Bomb, and Truman is not afraid to use it. We *must* protect ourselves.

The only way to *ensure* friendly neighbours in East Europe is to have Communist-controlled governments in the area acknowledged by the Big Three as the Soviet sphere. There is nothing wrong in helping our European comrades to achieve this.

THE AMERICAN VIEW
Starting point
Beware those cunning Russians! Marxism aims to conquer us all, and Stalin will try to do so.

This is a clear case of Soviet imperialist expansion. Stalin has broken his Yalta promise of free elections. With large Communist parties in Italy and France, Western Europe may suffer the same fate. We must stop this from happening.

Step 2: Churchill's 'Iron Curtain' speech, March 1946

Churchill was now only Leader of the Opposition in Britain, but he still enjoyed great prestige because of his wartime leadership. In March 1946 he made a speech in Fulton, Missouri (USA), in which he warned that an Iron Curtain had descended across Europe and that the USSR wanted 'indefinite expansion of their power and doctrines'. He proposed an Anglo-American military alliance to prevent this.

THE SOVIET VIEW
This was a deliberately provocative and aggressive speech designed to stir up hatred of the USSR. It shows that the West is working up to an anti-Soviet crusade – with A-bombs held behind its back.

THE AMERICAN VIEW
This speech may upset the Reds – but he's right, after all, so let's have it out in the open! It's time our own people woke up to what's happening over there – we shall need their backing for any action we take.

239

Step 3: The Truman Doctrine and the Marshall Plan, March and June 1947

Before the Second World War Greece had a right-wing monarchy and was under British influence. When British troops arrived in Greece in 1944 they found a civil war in progress between Communist and Royalist forces. They restored the monarchy, and for a time all was quiet. But in 1946 the Greek Communists again rebelled and now they were aided by neighbouring Communist governments in Yugoslavia, Albania and Bulgaria. Stalin made vague promises of aid, but did not actually send any. In fact he tried to discourage Yugoslavia's leader, Tito, from helping the Greek rebels, for fear of provoking Western reaction.

Britain, weakened by the war, told the American Government she could no longer assist the governments of Greece and Turkey (also under threat). The United States responded with the Truman Doctrine: in March 1947 Truman announced that America would aid 'free peoples' to resist threats 'by armed minorities or by outside pressure'. He carefully did not name Communism as the enemy, but no one had any doubt as to what he meant.

American aid of $400 million was sent at once to Greece and Turkey and in later years the Truman Doctrine was applied (and American aid sent) to any government which

could prove itself anti-Communist, no matter how right-wing and oppressive its own régime might be. The Truman Doctrine of 1947 thus became the cornerstone of America's entire Cold War policy.

In June 1947 came the Marshall Plan, a vast programme of American economic aid to Europe (Figure 22.1). Over the next few years $15,000 million was made available for post-war reconstruction to sixteen 'free world' nations. The Marshall Plan was the economic arm of the Truman Doctrine in Europe: in Truman's phrase, they were 'two halves of the same walnut'. Marshall Aid had two aims: first, to create economic stability which it was hoped would prevent the growth of Communism; and secondly, to help the American economy by enabling Europeans to buy American goods. You can see these aims, and the link between the Truman Doctrine and the Marshall Plan, in the extracts from Truman's and Marshall's speeches in Study Topic 13. At a personal level there was warm approval of Marshall Aid in the United States. Many Americans were deeply concerned by the plight of post-war Europe and conscious of their own lucky escape from the devastation others had suffered.

Marshall Aid was officially open to *any* European country (including the USSR), but it is doubtful if the American Government seriously expected any Communist country to apply for it – or could have got Congress to

Figure 22.1   Dollar aid to Europe under the Marshall Plan.

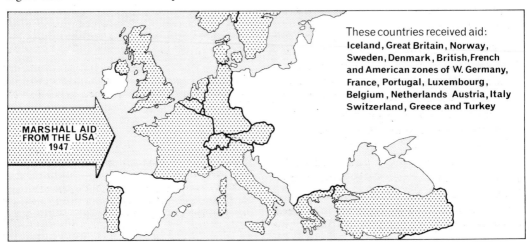

These countries received aid:
Iceland, Great Britain, Norway, Sweden, Denmark, British, French and American zones of W. Germany, France, Portugal, Luxembourg, Belgium, Netherlands Austria, Italy Switzerland, Greece and Turkey

MARSHALL AID FROM THE USA 1947

approve aid to a Communist government if it had been asked for. In any case the problem did not arise: the Soviet Government spurned the American offer and instructed their 'satellite' states (as they were now coming to be called in the West) not to take part in the Plan.

THE SOVIET VIEW

The right-wing monarchy in Greece is certainly unwelcome, but our 1944 bargain with Churchill agreed that Greece was in the British sphere. Therefore we did not aid Greek Communists in 1944 or 1946, though we had to support their cause 'officially' to East European comrades.

The Truman Doctrine and the Marshall Plan are a blatant attempt by America to gain economic and political domination, especially of Western Europe. The American offer of aid to anyone is only a propaganda device to wean the USSR's friends away from Communism. To ensure their loyalty, they must now be bound more firmly to the Soviet Union.

THE AMERICAN VIEW

Aid to the Greek Communists *must* have come from the USSR, or at Stalin's direction. The Greek rebellion was part of Moscow's plan for world conquest – as are Communist threats anywhere. The USA must now take firm action: 'The British are getting out of Turkey and Greece and if we don't go in the Russians will.'

(These views led to the Truman Doctrine, later expanded 'to defend free peoples anywhere'.)

The free world must be defended both militarily and economically. By relieving poverty and hunger, which might make Communism seem attractive, we can also save ourselves from depression and be sure of future trading partners (hence the Marshall Plan).

Step 4: The setting up of the Cominform, October 1947

The Communization of Eastern Europe after 1945 went forward without much difficulty in most cases. Hungary, Rumania, Bulgaria and Poland had all been hostile towards the Soviet Union before the war, but most of the surviving anti-Russian groups, seeing no future in a Soviet-dominated homeland, had left it. Land reform was usually welcomed by the peasantry, and Soviet-style industrialization brought a taste of 'progress' to poor societies which badly needed it. Democratic government was hardly missed, since they had never

had any. All this was also true of Yugoslavia, where the Communist Government had the added strength of strong popular support. Communist partisans under Tito had liberated the country from the Germans without the Red Army's help, and Tito himself was a strong and much-admired leader.

Whether as a reaction to the Truman Doctrine and Marshall Plan or as part of a preconceived strategy, in October 1947 the above-named countries were gathered into a new organization: the Cominform. In effect this was a new version of the Comintern, which had been dissolved in 1943. By linking together all the European Communist parties (including those of France and Italy), the USSR intended that the 'Socialist camp' should speak with one voice – the voice of Moscow.

Tito at once began to resent the new arrangement. He had plans for a Balkan Pact with Rumania and Bulgaria, and had also been aiding the Greek Communists against Stalin's wishes. In June 1948, after trying unsuccessfully to bring Tito to heel, Stalin expelled Yugoslavia from the Cominform, confidently expecting Tito's régime to collapse without Soviet support. But it didn't – and from that time onwards, Yugoslavia has followed its own brand of 'national Communism', with its own national features and owing no special allegiance to the USSR. Soviet–Yugoslav relations were now frozen, and so they remained while Stalin lived.

THE SOVIET VIEW

With East–West relations deteriorating, nothing less than absolute obedience to Moscow is safe in Eastern Europe.

Tito is far too cocky – look how he upset the West over Greece! He must be taught who is master: 'We will shake our little finger and there will be no more Tito.'

THE AMERICAN VIEW

The Cominform, with its tentacles spreading into Western Europe, is further proof of Stalin's aggressive intentions.

Tito's overtures for trade and other contacts with the West are very welcome. We can overlook his aid to the (now-defeated) Greek Communists now that he has taken a step towards 'our side.'

Step 5: The Communist *coup* in Czechoslovakia, February 1948

Looking westwards from Moscow in 1948, there was another possible chink in the Iron Curtain: Czechoslovakia. Up to now its democratically elected coalition government, under a Communist Prime Minister, had survived. In the elections of 1946 the Communists had received 38 per cent of the vote, but by 1948 they were losing popularity and would probably lose votes in elections due in March. Rather than take that risk, the Czech Communists took power by force, watched approvingly by Soviet troops over the border in Austria. In May a single-party election confirmed Czechoslovakia as a Communist country.

Thus by May 1948 the Communization of Eastern Europe (Figure 22.2) was complete – except for troublesome Yugoslavia. Now, just

Figure 22.2   Soviet advances in Eastern Europe by 1948. (Austria was neutralized in 1955, thus withdrawing the Iron Curtain to the Czech–Hungarian border.)

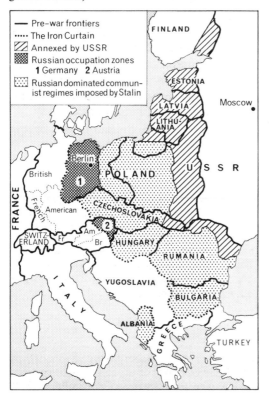

to make sure of the other satellites' loyalty, Stalin ordered a purge of any 'national Communists' who might be tempted to go Tito's way. Between 1948 and 1950 they were weeded out of East European governments and replaced by reliable Moscow Communists who would do Stalin's bidding. Eastern Europe fell silent under a blanket of Stalinism all too familiar from the history of the Soviet Union itself.

THE SOVIET VIEW
Czechoslovakia has not yet given any trouble – but she may. She has many trade connections with the West and has shown an interest in the Marshall Plan. The *coup* by Czech comrades is therefore very welcome.

Like it or not, we are 'at war' again, and from now on Moscow alone must give the orders.

THE AMERICAN VIEW
This is the last straw! Not content with Bulgaria, Hungary, Poland, etc. Stalin must have poor little Czechoslovakia under his boot. Of course Moscow carried out that take-over.

(The West felt especially sensitive about Czechoslovakia. Pre-war, it was the only democratic country in East Europe – and the one which they had sacrificed to Hitler in 1938.)

Step 6: The Berlin Blockade, June 1948–May 1949

The division of Germany into Communist East and Democratic West was complicated by the awkward question of Berlin. The West's refusal to allow it to be absorbed into East Germany led to the first major crisis of the Cold War – the Berlin blockade – and to the geographical oddity we see today: an island of Capitalism in the heart of Communist East Germany.

In 1945, as we saw in Chapter 21, Germany was divided into four Occupation Zones, with four-power joint control of Berlin. The Allied Control Council was not a unified government of Germany: its job was to co-ordinate the separate policies administered in each zone by the occupying power. But in practice this arrangement never worked.

Arguments began almost at once over reparations. France and the USSR, whose

" IF WE DON'T LET HIM WORK, WHO'S GOING TO KEEP HIM ? "

Figure 22.3   A British view of the problem which faced the occupying powers.

zones could support themselves in food, both took what the British and Americans regarded as excessive reparations to compensate for German devastation of their own countries. The British and Americans expected the other two zones to make up the food deficit in their own more industrial areas of Germany. Instead, they had to import food to starving Germans – an obligation especially resented in Britain, which itself had little enough to eat. The British and Americans therefore decided to make their zones self-supporting as soon as possible (Figure 22.3). By 1948 they had persuaded France to merge her zone with theirs in a unified Western zone, and were pumping in Marshall Aid.

By this time, fear of Soviet hostility had increased in Western Europe – but fear of a German revival was equally strong. In March 1948 the Brussels Treaty was signed, by which Britain, France and the Benelux countries undertook to aid each other in case of attack. The Americans (who had no doubt that the possible enemy was not Germany but the USSR) said they would provide military backing for the pact. In June the Brussels Pact countries approved the proposed formation of a West German government.

All these developments looked grim through Russian eyes. In March 1948 they

had withdrawn from the Control Council, seeing no way to prevent the formation of a non-Communist, self-governing Western Germany. But they feared it greatly. Bolstered with American aid, West Germany would soon become strong – and then, no doubt, it would be incorporated into the Western military alliance which had just been formed. The best they could do now was to cling on to 'their' part of Germany, at least to ensure that the West's Germany would be smaller and weaker than Hitler's. But what about Berlin?

In June 1948 a dispute over currency reform brought matters to a head: both the Western and Soviet authorities introduced new, separate currencies into their zones. How could Berlin – one city – have two sorts of money? The Russians took this excuse to try to tidy up the situation by driving the West out of Berlin altogether. They blockaded West Berlin by closing the road, rail, and canal routes from Western Germany to the city, presumably hoping to starve the West Berliners into amalgamation with the Soviet Zone.

The West's reply to the Berlin blockade was the Berlin airlift: an amazing Anglo-American feat by which, for ten months, all the essentials of life were flown in to the $2\frac{1}{2}$ million West Berliners. In May 1949 the USSR gave in and lifted the blockade.

POST-WAR ATTITUDES TO GERMANY
In the bitter mood of 1945 everyone felt that the Germans should be kept down for several years until they had learned to behave themselves. But after 1945, as the Americans became *less* harsh towards Germany, the Russians became *more* scared of a German revival. And so did some West Europeans! To reassure them, the Americans made it clear from 1946 onwards that they were going to stay in Europe – which only increased Russian fears.

THE SOVIET VIEW
1945–6: Germany deserves no mercy; reparations for devastated Russia are perfectly just. The Americans have plenty of money (though they

243

won't lend *us* any)† – why shouldn't they feed the Western zones?

1947–8: The rebuilding of the Western zones looks ominous – what are the Americans up to? There can certainly be no reunification (and therefore no peace treaty) unless Germany is Communist dominated or permanently neutral.

June 1948: They are determined to have *their* Germany (and whatever they say now, they will soon start rearming it) so we must have *ours*. But first let's try to winkle them out of Berlin – it's rightfully ours anyway, as anyone can see on the map.

(*So the Berlin Blockade was enforced . . . and the West replied with the airlift . . .*)

We dare not provoke an incident – who knows where it might lead?

May 1949: O.K., you win. For the time being we'll have to suffer this 'fish-bone in our gullet'.

THE AMERICAN VIEW

By 1946: We are not prepared to carry 75 million people indefinitely – they must stand on their own feet. This will mean self-government before long – but why not? The Germans are not such bad guys after all.

1947–8: As reunification seems impossible for the moment, at least the West Germans must have their own government and become part of Western Europe – especially now that the menace in the East is becoming serious. (See Steps 3, 4, 5 above.)

June 1948: Our West European friends have sensibly signed a defence pact, though some of them still seem to think the enemy is Germany! (we must put them right on that). They're going to need help to rearm, and we must give it.

(*Then came the Soviet blockade of West Berlin . . .*)

Hey, what's this? A bid for Western Europe already? Now, shall we: (a) evacuate West Berlin? – no, too weak; (b) send tanks in? – no, too risky. So let's *fly* in – they'll never dare to shoot us down.

(*So the Anglo-American airlift was mounted . . . and after eleven months the blockade was lifted.*)

---

†Lend-Lease aid to the USSR ended as soon as the war was over. In 1945 the USSR had asked for a large loan from the USA but could not get acceptable terms. This made her all the more determined to loot Germany for post-war reconstruction in Russia. By the time Marshall Aid was offered, Stalin's suspicions of the Americans had increased and he would not humble the USSR – or reveal her economic weakness – by asking for it (see page 240).

THE BATTLE-LINES ARE DRAWN

Not surprisingly, the Berlin blockade hardened Western attitudes. America's promised backing of the Brussels Pact was enlarged into a full-scale military alliance of twelve nations, centred on the colossal strength of the United States. The North Atlantic Treaty was signed in April 1949 by the USA, Canada, Britain, France, the Benelux nations, Denmark, Norway, Iceland, Italy and Portugal. Greece and Turkey joined the North Atlantic Treaty Organization in 1952. In 1955 the USSR's fears of a rearmed Germany were realized when, after six years of American persuasion, the countries of Western Europe agreed to let West Germany join NATO. The USSR replied by organizing its East European allies into the Warsaw Pact (Figure 22.4).

These two alliances still confront each other across the Iron Curtain today, but there are fundamental differences between them. Members of the Warsaw Pact are more closely tied to their 'big brother' than members of NATO, who have a say in running the Organization and are free to leave it if they wish (as France did in 1966). Warsaw Pact ground forces throughout Eastern Europe are directed from Moscow and its air support provided by the Soviet National Air Defence Command; moreover, the USSR demonstrated in regard to Hungary in 1956 and Czechoslovakia in 1968 that membership of the pact is compulsory for the states in her East European 'empire' (see Chapter 24).

The North Atlantic Treaty was the first 'entangling alliance' in America's history: she now committed herself *in advance* to go to war on another country's behalf. In 1949 there was some opposition in Congress to this departure from her traditional foreign policy of non-commitment, while some people in Western Europe (and even in America) thought that the setting up of NATO was a provocative move which would only increase Soviet hostility. But the rising tension and propaganda of the previous four years had given most Americans a sense of moral duty

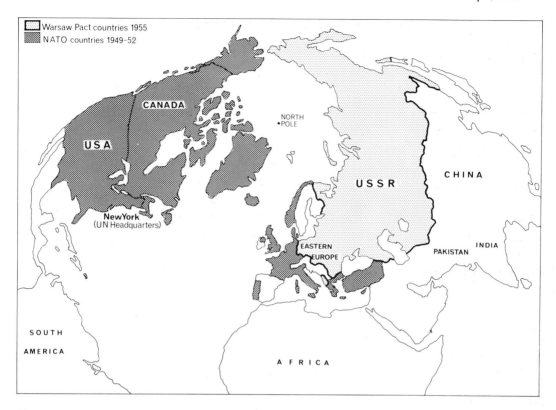

Figure 22.4   East–West military confrontation by 1955.

to undertake new responsibilities throughout the world, and had made most people in countries which felt threatened by the Soviet Union only too glad to take refuge in an American-sponsored military alliance.

The Berlin blockade also sealed the fate of divided Germany. In August 1949 the German Federal Republic (West Germany) came into being, with its capital at Bonn and the right-wing Dr Adenauer as its first Chancellor (Prime Minister). In September the German Democratic Republic (East Germany) was formed with East Berlin as its capital. In 1949 these arrangements were still 'temporary': as yet, neither side recognized the other side's protégé state, and Germany (especially Berlin) was to be a sore point in

East–West relations for many years to come. But as things have turned out, those lines drawn for military occupation in 1945 have become permanent European frontiers. In the 1980s it looks as though there will be two Germanys and two Berlins for as far ahead as anyone can see.

Almost before the ink was dry on the North Atlantic Treaty, two other events of 1949 seemed to justify every word of it. Late in August the USSR exploded its first Atom bomb – much earlier than the West had expected. And in October came another unwelcome blow – the victory of Mao Tse-tung in China. In the next chapter you will see the significance of that event in the developing Cold War.

245

Study Topic 13

Cold War Documents

1. Extracts from President Truman's speech announcing the Truman Doctrine, 12 March 1947.

... One of the primary objectives of the foreign policy of the United States is the creation of conditions in which we and other nations will be able to work out a way of life free from coercion. This was a fundamental issue in the war with Germany and Japan. Our victory was won over countries which sought to impose their will and their way of life upon other nations. ...

The peoples of a number of countries of the world have recently had totalitarian régimes forced upon them against their will. The Government of the United States has made frequent protest against coercion and intimidation in violation of the Yalta Agreement, in Poland, Rumania and Bulgaria. ...

At the present moment in world history nearly every nation must choose between alternative ways of life. The choice is too often not a free one. One way of life is based upon the will of the majority, and is distinguished by free institutions, representative government, free elections, guarantees of individual liberty, freedom of speech and religion, and freedom from political oppression. The second way of life is based upon the will of a minority, forcibly imposed upon the majority. It relies upon terror and oppression, a controlled press and radio, fixed elections, and the suppression of personal freedoms.

I believe it must be the policy of the United States to support free peoples who are resisting attempted subjugation by armed minorities or by outside pressure. ...

I believe that our help should be primarily through economic and financial aid, which is essential to economic stability and orderly political processes. ...

The seeds of totalitarian régimes are nurtured by misery and want. They spread and grow in the evil soil of poverty and strife. They reach their full growth when the hope of a people for a better life has died. We must keep that hope alive. The free peoples of the world look to us for support in maintaining their freedoms. If we falter in our leadership, we may endanger the peace of the world – and we shall surely endanger the welfare of our own nation. ...

2. Extracts from a speech by Secretary of State George C. Marshall announcing the Marshall Plan, 5 June 1947.

The truth of the matter is that Europe's requirements for the next three or four years of foreign food and other essential products – principally from America – are so much greater than her present ability to pay that she must have substantial additional help, or face economic, social and political deterioration of a very grave character.

The remedy lies in breaking the vicious circle and restoring the confidence of the European people in the economic future of their own countries and of Europe as a whole. The manufacturer and the farmer throughout wide areas must be able and willing to exchange their products for currencies, the continuing value of which is not open to question.

Aside from the demoralizing effect on the world at large and the possibilities of disturbances arising as a result of the desperation of the people concerned, the consequences to the economy of the United States should be apparent to all. It is logical that the United States should do whatever it is able to do to assist in the return of normal economic health to the world, without which there can be no political stability and no assured peace.

Our policy is directed not against any country or doctrine but against hunger, poverty, desperation and chaos. Its purpose should be the revival of a working economy in the world so as to permit the emergence of political and social conditions in which free institutions can exist. Such assistance, I am convinced, must not be on a piecemeal basis as various crises develop. Any assistance that this government may develop in the future should provide a cure rather than a mere palliative.

Any government that is willing to assist in the task of recovery will find full co-operation, I am sure, on the part of the United States Government. Any governments, political parties, or groups which seek to perpetuate human misery in order to profit therefrom politically or otherwise will encounter the opposition of the United States.

*GLOSSARY

***coup**, short for *coup d'état* (French): a forcible seizure of power.

KEYWORD

Cold War has been defined as 'a state of tension between countries in which each side adopts policies designed to strengthen itself and weaken the other, but falling short of actual "hot" war.'[†] This description doesn't quite fit the Cold War we are concerned with, for there have been two 'hot' wars – Korea and Vietnam – which were partly, at least, battlefields of the larger East–West Cold War. American and other Western troops were involved in both these conflicts, and in Korea they met Chinese soldiers face to face. But the efforts of the World Powers to contain these wars – to prevent them from escalating into all-out fighting between themselves – bears out the general rule of 'Cold Warfare': 'no holds barred *except* armed conflict'.

[†]Florence Elliott and Michael Summerskill, *A Dictionary of Politics* (Penguin, 1964 ed.) p. 77.

Questions

Did you notice?

1. Whom does the *conventional* view of the Cold War blame for starting it? (a) Stalin (b) Truman (c) Stalin and Truman

2. The National Front party in Poland was (a) very right-wing (b) pro-Communist (c) a peasant party

3. The 'corner-stone' of America's Cold War policy was (a) the Marshall Plan (b) NATO (c) the Truman Doctrine

4. Before the Second World War, the Greek Government was under the influence of (a) Britain (b) the USA (c) the USSR

5. The Berlin Blockade was sparked off by an argument over (a) currency reform (b) reparations (c) boundary lines

6. True or false?
   (i) Churchill's 'Iron Curtain' speech was delivered in America
   (ii) The USSR aided the Communists in the Greek Civil War
   (iii) Tito abandoned Communism in 1948
   (iv) At first the Allied Control Council ruled Germany effectively
   (v) NATO membership was open only to North Atlantic countries

7. Which statement is *more* accurate?
   (i) Marshall Plan funds were used
      (a) on both sides of the Iron Curtain
      (b) only 'west' of the Iron Curtain
   (ii) (a) Yugoslavia joined the Western camp in 1948
      (b) Yugoslavia left the Soviet camp in 1948
   (iii) The Western zones of Germany were unified in 1948 so that
      (a) they could become economically self-sufficient
      (b) they could join NATO

Can you explain?

8. What is the 'cops and robbers' view of the Cold War? When, and why, did some Western historians begin to take a different view of it?

9. Briefly recount, as a connected story, *either* the American View *or* the Soviet View of events in Eastern Europe from 1945 to May 1948 – that is, Steps 1, 4 and 5 (pages 239–42).

10. What was the Soviet attitude towards:
    (a) taking reparations from Germany?
    (b) the economic revival of Western Germany?

11. In what way was NATO 'a new departure' for the United States? Why did most Americans support it?

12. Why did Truman think economic (as well as military) aid was necessary to prevent the spread of Communism?

What's your view?

13. What is the essential difference between the *conventional* and the *revisionist* view of Stalin's post-war foreign policy? Does the account in this book favour one view more than the other? If so, what statements in Chapter 22, or previously, show this interpretation?

14. Imagine yourself as a completely impartial observer of the events described in this chapter. Can you identify any serious mistakes of either side which worsened East–West conflict?

15. Immediately after the war some people felt so bitter towards Germany that they opposed sending aid of any kind, even to starving civilians. Would you have agreed with them, do you think? How far should ordinary people be held responsible for the actions of their government?

23

American Policy in Asia, 1950–54

This chapter describes the extension of the Cold War into Asia, and the centre-piece of that development is the Korean War of 1950–53. But for several reasons it is helpful to place this event in the context of American foreign policy. American reaction to the Korean War led her to undertake other commitments in Asia and to assume the costly and controversial role of 'world policeman' against Communist threats anywhere. This task would be carried out by the *containment* (k) of Communism, a policy which rested on the *Domino Theory* (k), but some Americans were tempted to pursue a more aggressive (and therefore more dangerous) policy of *liberation* (k). These keywords are defined at the end of this chapter (pp. 257–8); their meaning in practice will become very clear in the discussion of Cold War events after 1950.

The United States undertook her world role without fully considering what it might lead to, or whether her aim could be achieved. Like other momentous decisions of history, this one was taken in the heat of the moment. The 'heat' was the pressure of right-wing opinion in the United States, and the moment was the invasion of South Korea in June 1950 by Communist troops from the North. We shall briefly interrupt the narrative of the Cold War to look at the political scene in Washington at that dramatic moment.

AMERICAN FOREIGN POLICY DISCUSSIONS, 1949–50

In April 1949, when the North Atlantic Treaty was signed, the United States Government could be reasonably optimistic about the world situation. The march of Russian

Communism in Europe had been contained by the Truman Doctrine and NATO. So far the cost of NATO was relatively low: it rested on America's monopoly of the Atom bomb. (After the Second World War the United States had demobilized its army rapidly, whereas the Russians had not. But one Atom bomb outweighed millions of Red Army soldiers.)

By the autumn of 1949 the Soviet A-bomb and the Communist victory in China had clouded the skies again. In military terms, the Russians now had two trumps – the A-bomb *and* a large army – to the West's one. The defeat of the Kuomintang was another bitter blow. But most Americans did not yet see Mao as a dangerous 'Moscow puppet', and the first instinct of American policy-makers was to swallow their disappointment and come to terms with Communist China.

The China White Paper of 1949–'Limited Commitment'

In mid-1949 it was obvious that the Communists were on the verge of winning the Chinese Civil War. Regretfully but realistically, the American Government now recognized that in supporting the KMT they had backed a lame horse – as their own China experts had been saying for several years – and that the imminent Communist victory was beyond American control. In August came the China White Paper (a statement of intended policy) in which Secretary of State Acheson said:

> Nothing that this country did or could have done within the reasonable limits of its capabilities could have changed that result; nothing that was left undone by this country has contributed to it. It was the product of internal Chinese forces,

forces which this country tried to influence but could not. A decision was arrived at within China, if only a decision by default.

Acheson acknowledged that America's proven enemy Russia would gain strength by having a large Communist neighbour, but he did not think their friendship would last. Historic Sino–Soviet rivalry over territory would soon cause quarrels, and America could exploit those differences by remaining the 'friend of China' she had always claimed to be. Before long China would follow the example of Yugoslavia, and the United States would be ready to welcome 'Mao Tse-Tito'. Accordingly, the US Government stopped its aid to the KMT in the last stages of the civil war and prepared to adjust to the new situation. This would mean withdrawing official recognition from the KMT government as the rulers of China, which by September had fled the mainland and set itself up in the island province of Taiwan, recently restored to China after many years of Japanese occupation.

The American attitude to China had to be fitted into the context of her policy in the Far East as a whole. By 1945 she had recovered her own Pacific possessions and had even acquired some new ones: the administration of several groups of islands near Japan, including Okinawa. She had also occupied the southern half of Japan's former colony Korea (the northern half being occupied by Russian troops), and an American military government was supervising the post-war democratization of Japan. By 1949, as we shall explain in more detail later, both Russia and America had withdrawn from Korea, apparently to avoid the face-to-face confrontation which had entangled them in Germany.

Early in 1950 Washington was considering its defence policy in the Far Eastern sphere. The intended withdrawal of support from the KMT in Taiwan would invite the Communists to overrun the island (which was expected to happen soon anyway) and the USA could then recognize the Peking government as the rulers of *all* China. The same 'inevitable' fate might befall South Korea if the Communist North invaded, but this too would be no great loss to American interests. The dictatorial methods of South Korea's right-wing government were an embarrassment to its democratic sponsor, and in military terms both Taiwan and South Korea were *outside* America's 'defence perimeter' running from Japan through Okinawa to the former US colony the Philippines, granted independence in 1946 (see map, Figure 23.4, on page 256).

These views were expressed by Acheson and other foreign policy spokesmen during the spring of 1950. They did not affect America's policy in Europe, where her pledges to contain Soviet expansionism would stand. The important point to note is that so far, American policy-makers did *not* see Mao's victory in China as part of the already established Cold War with Russia. In global and military terms, they proposed a policy of 'limited commitment' for the United States.

McCarthyism in the United States

Meanwhile the 1949 White Paper had set off a howl of protest from right-wing Republicans in the United States – especially those who accepted the McCarthyite analysis of how China had been 'lost' to Communism. According to the China Lobby (as the Washington supporters of the KMT were called), Chiang Kai-shek could have been saved by more American aid, and even now he could be helped to recover the mainland with renewed American support. Instead, Truman's traitorous Government was throwing him to the Red wolves!

The hysteria of McCarthyism was now at its height in America, and Truman's Democratic Government was feeling the heat. In 1947 Truman had brought in the loyalty oath for government servants, in his own words to 'take the smear off the Democratic Party'. The Truman Doctrine of the same year was also to some extent a response to the

McCarthyites. Now, with his back to the wall on the China question, Acheson turned somersaults to appease them. He could not of course admit that the CCP's victory in China was 'America's fault'†, but he did now agree that it was a cunning Moscow plot! In February 1950 he said:

> ... The Communists took over China at a ridiculously small cost. What they did was to invite some Chinese leaders who were dissatisfied with the way things were going in their country to come to Moscow. There they thoroughly indoctrinated them so that they returned to China prepared to resort to any means whatsoever to establish Communist control. They were completely subservient to the Moscow régime.... These agents then mingled among the people and sold them on the personal material advantages of Communism....

Our own study of China shows you the absurdity of this statement. But the McCarthyites had got Truman's Government on the run: to come to terms with Communist China *now* would be political suicide for the Democratic Party.

Meanwhile, Truman was worrying about that other Moscow victory of 1949: the Soviet Atom bomb. In January 1950 he had called for a much more far-reaching review of *all* America's foreign and defence policy 'in the light of the loss of China, the Soviet mastery of atomic energy, and the prospect of the fusion bomb [H-bomb].'

National Security Council Paper No. 68 – 'Total Commitment'

In April 1950 Truman's State and Defence Department advisers submitted their report. National Security Council Paper No. 68 (NSC 68) saw the Soviet threat in Europe, their recent Atom bomb and Mao's victory in China as one global theme: *the rising strength of Russia*. It foresaw 'an indefinite period of tension and danger' and advised

†But behind the scenes he *did* admit it: all but two of those State Department China experts who thought the KMT was not worth saving lost their jobs. They were among the best-known victims of McCarthyism.

that America must be ready to meet each fresh challenge promptly. To do so, she must undertake 'an immediate and large-scale build-up in our military and general strength and that of our allies with the intention of righting the power balance and in the hope that through some means other than all-out war we could induce a change in the nature of the Soviet system'. The estimated yearly cost of this policy would be $35 to $50 billion.

We can see that by now Truman's Government was ready to shift its ground. American officials were moving towards the so-called 'monolithic view' of Communism: the idea that every Communist country, present or future, is part of one vast and threatening bloc with its nerve-centre in Moscow. America must prevent the further enlargement of this global bloc with military and economic aid to *any* country under threat.

But Truman did not immediately adopt the policy of 'total commitment' recommended by NSC 68. Whatever he and his advisers thought, he knew that Congress and the American taxpayer would not consider a military budget of wartime size, especially in an election year. So he shelved the whole uncomfortable question of American commitment – and the recognition of Communist China – until after Congressional elections due in November.

Then occurred the event which left no more time for sober consideration of whether 'total commitment' was a wise and realistic policy, and whether America could afford it. On 25 June Communist troops from North Korea crossed the border into the 'democratic' South.

THE KOREAN WAR

The background

In 1945 Korea was occupied by Russian troops north of the 38th parallel and by American troops south of that line. Like the military occupation of Germany, this was to be a temporary arrangement, but the two provisional governments set up by the occupying forces at once began to develop their parts of Korea along different lines.

In 1948 attempts were made to reunify the country through nationwide elections supervised by the UN, but the Russians (who regarded the UN as an American-dominated agency) would not give UN officials access to the North. The Communist Government elected there in 1946 had won its support by putting through land reform. The right-wing government elected under UN auspices in the South was popular at first, but began to lose ground when it ruthlessly suppressed left-wing opposition.

In 1949 the US Army left the South, where the Republic of Korea had been proclaimed independent under Syngman Rhee. The Soviet Red Army soon left the North, whose new state, the Korean Democratic People's Republic, was led by Kim Il Sung. Both these leaders were Korean patriots, each wanting a unified Korea under his own rule and resenting the artificial division which had been forced upon the country. They began a propaganda war against each other and there were frequent border incidents.

The outbreak of war

On 25 June 1950 North Korea invaded the South with a modern, Russian-equipped army. It is still not known for certain who ordered this attack and why. Was it a show of strength by Stalin towards the United States? – or even, as one American strategist has suggested, to show China his power over some Asian Communists? Did Kim Il Sung alone decide to launch the attack, thinking that America's back was turned? Did Syngman Rhee, feeling abandoned by the United States, deliberately provoke an attack to bring his powerful protector rushing back?

Evidence has been cited to support *all* these theories! But as with other unanswered questions of this period, it is not our job to decide the correct answer. North Korean troops were certainly the first to cross the border, and at the time the West assumed that Moscow (or possibly Peking) had ordered

them to do so. For Truman this was the final proof of what he already half believed: that there was a vast Moscow-directed Communist conspiracy, ready to strike *anywhere* the West showed weakness. As we have already noted, another influence on his behaviour was the pressure of domestic politics: he now had to prove that the Democrats were just as anti-Communist as the Republicans.

So Truman reacted like a scalded cat. He ordered US forces to give sea and air cover to the South Koreans and sent the US 7th Fleet to patrol the Taiwan Straits, lest the Chinese Communists should take this chance to attack Taiwan. From that moment forward, America's former policy of 'limited commitment' in the Far East was a dead letter.

United Nations intervention

The North Korean army had soon driven the South Koreans to the far south-east corner of their country (the maps, Figures 23.1 and 23.2, show you this and later stages of the war). But meanwhile, the United States had organized full-scale military support for South Korea under the umbrella of the United Nations. On 27 June the UN passed a resolution calling on its members 'to furnish such assistance to the Republic of Korea as may be necessary to repel the armed attack and to restore international peace and security in the area'.

In September the UN forces, under their American commander General MacArthur, made a landing up the coast at Inchon and before long had driven the North Koreans back over the border. On the face of it, the purpose of the UN resolution had now been fulfilled: the armed attack had been repelled, and the way was open for a negotiated peace. But on 1 October MacArthur crossed the 38th Parallel and six days later, the UN approved this further step. The objective of UN action was now to reunify the country under a non-Communist government. UN forces drove far into North Korea and soon were approaching the Yalu River border with China.

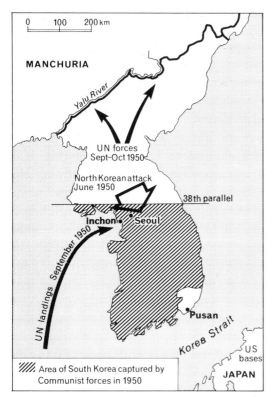

Figure 23.1   War in Korea to October 1950.

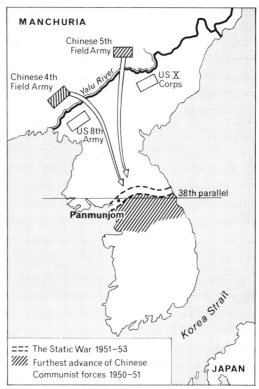

Figure 23.2   War in Korea, October 1950–53.

Chinese intervention

China regarded the extension of the war into North Korea as a threat to her own security. Less than a year after the defeat of the American-backed KMT, here was another American-backed army on her doorstep. After two warnings (transmitted to Washington through neutral India), in November 1950 Chinese troops entered the war in massive numbers. Once again the military situation was reversed. By January 1951 the Chinese/North Korean forces had reconquered about one-third of South Korea, and the UN had passed a resolution denouncing China as a 'wilful aggressor'.

Containment or liberation?

The war now entered its most dangerous phase. General MacArthur argued that it could not be won 'with hands tied behind our backs'. He wanted a free hand to extend the war against China – and if his advice were followed, there was a real danger that the A-bomb would be used. America's allies and the rest of the world trembled at this awful prospect. Britain's Prime Minister, Attlee, flew to Washington to advise caution.

MacArthur argued his case in military terms, but to step up the war against China would have been a political decision – and one which only the McCarthyites would have applauded. For them, the *containment* of Communism was not enough: they hoped for a policy of *liberation* to save its victims behind existing Cold War frontiers. But they had not seen a way to achieve this – until now. General MacArthur (who, as a soldier, should not have argued publicly with his President anyway) was the spokesman for their point of view. Luckily, President Truman settled for containment. In April 1951 he relieved MacArthur of his command for the simple reason that what he proposed was far too dangerous.

This moment of tension was the second 'near miss' of the Cold War. Significantly, when General MacArthur returned to the United States he was greeted as a national hero. The row over his dismissal, and the further progress of the war, won the American people to a firm policy of containment (if not yet quite one of liberation) – no matter what the cost!

Back to the old frontier

The Korean War (Figure 23.3) was a sickening and fruitless struggle which cost 5 million casualties and made millions more homeless. China's main strength was in men: hundreds of thousands were killed in suicidal mass attacks. America's main strength was technology – a foretaste of what was to come in Vietnam – but she was unpleasantly surprised by some Russian-made weapons such as MIG-15 aircraft. Naturally all this intensified the hostile atmosphere of the Cold War, especially the new sphere of that conflict: Sino–American relations.

The war dragged on until an armistice was arranged in 1953, roughly along the original line of the 38th Parallel. By that time Stalin

had died and Eisenhower had replaced Truman; the truce was in fact an early sign of the slight warming-up of East–West relations which began in the mid-1950s. But to this day the Korean question has not been finally settled: there is still a 'temporary' border separating a Communist state in the North from a repressive but nominally democratic state in the South.

AMERICA – WORLD POLICEMAN

The West's involvement in the Korean War was officially the UN *v.* North Korea (and later China), but it was in fact almost entirely an American operation. Many Western countries (including Britain) sent troops or token military aid to the UN forces, but 90 per cent of the war effort was American.

We can be certain that the United States would have been prepared to 'go it alone' in Korea even without UN participation. The vital UN resolution calling for aid to South Korea came *after* Truman had ordered American forces to provide it; UN approval for crossing into North Korea came *after* the step was taken. In fact UN action was only possible at all because the USSR – who would

Figure 23.3 Korean refugees watch an American convoy moving up to the front.

otherwise have vetoed it – was boycotting the UN in protest against its refusal to hand over China's seat to the new Communist Government in Peking.

Some historians have claimed that the Korean conflict was essentially a civil war and that the Koreans should have been left alone to settle it for themselves. But whatever the real causes and issues of that war, it *could* be seen as the first sabre-thrust of Communism against Democracy – and that's how America interpreted it.

'Total Commitment'

Truman's reply to the 'proven' world-wide Communist threat was now inevitable – NSC 68 and all it stood for. Without difficulty he got a huge military budget through Congress. After 1950 the United States increased its military strength around the globe, urged on the re-militarization of Germany and Japan (against strong pacifist feeling in those countries) and was ready to aid *any* anti-Communist government or cause anywhere. The adoption of NSC 68 extended the Truman Doctrine to the whole world.

The isolation of China

China's 'aggression' in Korea, and American policies thereafter, put her out in the cold for twenty years. Her government could not take its seat in the UN until America's attitude softened sufficiently to allow it (in 1971). Meanwhile the United States operated a trade embargo against her and within a few years had encircled her with military bases and alliances.

Military alliances

Since China was now Enemy No. 2 after Russia, every enemy of China was a friend of the United States. Syngman Rhee and Chiang Kai-shek were back under her protective wing, and in the next few years the United States made defence pacts with Japan, Australia, New Zealand, the Philippines, Thailand, South Korea and Taiwan; and in 1954

set up the South-East Asia Treaty Organization (SEATO) to contain the Far Eastern front of the Cold War as NATO contained it in Europe. An attempt to fill the gap with a third major alliance – CENTO, centred on the Middle East – was less successful, but SEATO lived on until 1977, and NATO is still with us today.

Aid to the French in Indo-China

Yet another new commitment of 1950 was the start of United States involvement in Indo-China. In Chapter 25 we shall look more closely into the complicated background of what later became an American war in Vietnam. Here we are concerned with an earlier phase of that struggle: the effort by France to recover her pre-war colonial empire.

French Indo-China included the countries of Laos, Cambodia† and three areas (Tonkin, Annam and Cochin-China) later collected together as Vietnam (see map, Figure 23.4). During the Second World War the whole area had been ruled by the puppet French Vichy régime in collaboration with Japan, which had similarly taken over other South-East Asian colonies of European powers. Resistance to Vichy French/Japanese rule was organized by the Communist-led League for Vietnamese Independence (Vietminh) under Ho Chi Minh. Ho had spent his life working for his Marxist beliefs and for Vietnamese independence from all foreign rulers – French, Japanese or anyone else.

In the general upheaval of Japan's defeat in 1945, Ho Chi Minh declared a shaky independence (Figure 23.5) for the newly-liberated and united Vietnam. But the post-war French Government now wanted its overseas colonies back, and after the failure of a kind of half-independence for Vietnam, in 1946 war broke out between the French and the Vietminh. After 1949 the Vietminh received aid from Communist China for their 'war of national liberation'.

The French army and government became increasingly demoralized by the strength of its

† Now re-named Kampuchea.

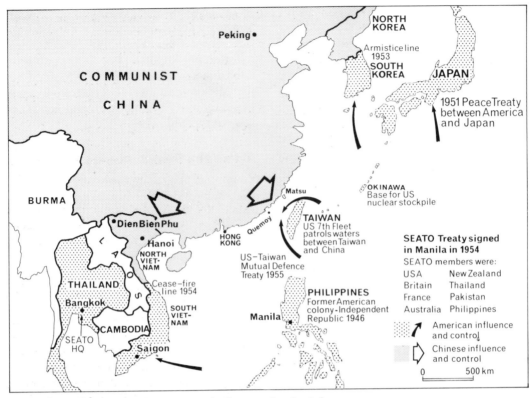

Figure 23.4 American efforts to contain Communism in Asia.

Figure 23.5 Ho Chi Minh reading the Declaration of Independence for Vietnam, 1945.

foe (General Giap followed Mao Tse-tung's rules for guerilla warfare with great success) and the lack of support for the war at home in France. Colonialism was not a popular cause in the post-war world – but anti-Communism was. The Vietminh leaders were Communist, and were getting aid from Communist China, so why not take advantage of America's public offer of aid to fight Communism? As one historian puts it, by 1950 the French Government had discovered that 'to fight for French supremacy brought neither sympathy nor success, and the only way to continue the fight was to call it a fight against Communism and invoke the aid of anti-Communist friends'.†

So what had begun as a colonial war became, in American eyes at least, an anti-Communist war, and by 1954 the United States was financing 80 per cent of it. But all to no avail! In May 1954 the French were decisively beaten at Dien Bien Phu in North Vietnam, and had no heart to continue the struggle further.

The Geneva Agreement

The calamity at Dien Bien Phu coincided with an international conference at Geneva where France, Britain, the USA, the USSR and Communist China had gathered to discuss Korea and Indo-China. The French came to the conference looking for a way to get off the hook in Indo-China and found it in an armistice agreement with the Vietminh which became known as the Geneva Agreement of 1954. It recognized Ho Chi Minh's independent government in North Vietnam but for the time being 'saved' the South (where the Vietminh had far less support) with the device already used elsewhere: a 'temporary' division by a demilitarized zone (DMZ) along the 17th Parallel. National elections were to be held within two years to decide the question of reunification. In the meantime there was to be free movement across the border, and neither part was to accept military help

from outside. Laos and Cambodia were set aside from the Vietnam dispute: it was agreed that they would be independent and neutral countries.

Ho Chi Minh was very reluctant to give up the unity of Vietnam, but in the end he agreed to it because he expected to win the promised elections: the North had a majority of Vietnam's population, and the 'temporary' régime in the South was tainted by its French connections. Britain, the USSR and China all approved the Agreement – but the United States (and the government in the South) did not. Nevertheless, the United States undertook not to upset it by force or the threat of force.

Of course the Geneva Agreement did not 'settle' the Vietnam question; in Chapter 25 we shall return to the story at this point to see what happened next and why. But the clue which explains later American intervention is already here: the US Government saw the Geneva Agreement as a *failure* of the policy of containment because it had surrendered North Vietnam to Communism. Earlier, when the French faced military defeat, the United States had tried to organize a joint Western force to help them, but could find no support for this plan. So she had to stand aside while a compromise solution was worked out at Geneva.

By 1954 American foreign policy – now in the hands of a Republican hard-liner, John Foster Dulles – was beginning to move from the defensive concept of containment into a more offensive phase. In January Dulles had made a famous speech in which he used the term which became the keynote of his period of office: he threatened 'massive retaliation' (meaning of course nuclear weapons) against further Communist aggression. In the next chapter you will learn more about Dulles' Cold War strategy, and the Russian reaction to it.

KEYWORDS

containment, the American policy of confining Communism to the areas it already occupied, while resisting any further

†Peter Calvocoressi, *World Politics Since 1945* (Longman, 1968) pp. 288–9.

expansion. Its main instrument was the Truman Doctrine and the military alliances – especially regional defence pacts like NATO – which the United States made with non-Communist countries. Containment was seen as a defensive policy compared to the more offensive policy of liberation described below.

Domino Theory, the belief that the fall of one country to Communism would knock down its neighbour, which in turn would knock down *its* neighbour, and so on. It was therefore imperative to keep the first domino in the line standing. The idea was mainly used to justify America's efforts to prevent South Vietnam from being taken over by Communist forces from the North, as Figure 23.6 shows.

liberation, the American policy (several times discussed but never fully undertaken) by which it was hoped to free people already under Communist rule. This did not necessarily mean going to war, but it did imply firm pressure against the Communist world to try to bring about changes within it – for example, by keeping up a propaganda barrage and encouraging rebellious movements behind the Iron Curtain. The idea of liberation was mainly associated with John Foster Dulles, American Secretary of State 1953–9, but the United States came closest to a military version of the policy during the Korean War, and with the American-sponsored Bay of Pigs invasion of Cuba in 1961 (see page 265).

Figure 23.6   The Domino Theory.
SOURCE: Brian Catchpole, *A Map History of the Modern World* (Heinemann Educational Books, 3rd ed. 1982) p. 127.

Questions

Did you notice?

1. In the spring of 1950 American policy-makers intended to defend (a) Japan (b) South Korea (c) Taiwan
2. The China Lobby wanted the US Government (a) to recognize Communist China (b) to give more help to the KMT (c) to adopt the China White Paper
3. NSC 68 recommended (a) crossing the 38th Parallel (b) a low defence budget (c) increased military aid to America's allies
4. The McCarthyites saw Mao Tse-tung as (a) 'Mao Tse-Tito' (b) a Moscow puppet (c) the rightful ruler of China
5. Dien Bien Phu was a defeat for (a) France (b) General MacArthur (c) the Vietminh
6. True or false?
   (i) Syngman Rhee was Japanese
   (ii) General MacArthur wanted to extend the Korean War
   (iii) Cambodia was part of French Indo-China
   (iv) Ho Chi Minh fought the Japanese during the Second World War
   (v) In 1954 Vietnam was divided at the 38th Parallel
   (vi) Britain approved the Geneva Agreement of 1954
7. Which statement is *more* accurate?
   (i) According to the 'monolithic view' of Communism
      (a) all Communist countries are controlled from Moscow
      (b) Communist governments may follow independent policies
   (ii) United Nations forces in the Korean War were
      (a) entirely American
      (b) mainly American
   (iii) Chinese troops entered the Korean War
      (a) to defend North Korea
      (b) to conquer Taiwan
   (iv) The Americans aided the French in Indo-China because

   (a) Indo-China was within their 'defence perimeter'
   (b) The Vietminh was led by Communists

Can you explain?

8. In 1950 the McCarthyites seemed to think that Mao Tse-tung owed his victory in China to Stalin. From your study of China, what evidence can you recall:
   (a) about Moscow's influence on the CCP before 1949
   (b) about Soviet policy towards China at the end of the Second World War
   which suggests that was a mistaken view?
9. Why did Truman react 'like a scalded cat' to the outbreak of the Korean War?
10. When and why did China enter the Korean War? How did that intervention affect her future relations with the United States and other Western countries?
11. What was the effect of the Korean War on American Cold War policy?
12. By the Geneva Agreement of 1954 Vietnam was temporarily divided.
   (a) Why did Ho Chi Minh agree to that division?
   (b) Why did the United States refuse to approve the Geneva Agreement?

What's your view?

13. List all the points you can think of to *support* the 'monolithic view' of Communism held by many people in the West in the early 1950s. Was it a reasonable view to hold at that time?
14. Both the United States and China condemned each other for 'aggression' in Korea. Do you agree with either of these views?
15. In the 1950s there was considerable opposition to the rearmament of Germany and Japan, both within those countries and among their recent enemies of the Second World War. Was the United States justified in overriding that opposition?

24

The Global Chess Game

The previous two chapters have dealt with a few years in considerable detail to explain the origins of the Cold War and the attitudes behind it. Now we can quicken the pace of the story. This chapter sweeps through a complicated period of Soviet–American relations from 1953 to the late 1960s, with the focus on their eyeball-to-eyeball confrontation over Cuba in 1962. China was excluded from this two-power global struggle while it was centred on areas far from her borders – Europe, the Middle East, Latin America – but she comes back into the picture when we consider Vietnam separately in Chapter 25. We shall also see later that the Soviet move towards Peaceful Coexistence with the West – a main theme of this chapter – was an important factor in the Sino–Soviet split.

Earlier we explained how the United States arrived at her decision to 'defend freedom' around the globe. For obvious reasons we cannot analyse Soviet policy decisions in the same way: we can only guess at what the Soviet Government thought about certain events (as we did in Chapter 22) from rather fragmentary evidence. Nevertheless, Soviet actions and public statements after 1945 can be pieced together into an overall Cold War strategy. Essentially it was the well-known international game of marking out spheres of influence. By the early 1950s the United States, having undertaken to protect other people from Soviet influence, was ready to play the same game. But at first her government didn't seem to understand the rules: Secretary of State Dulles was unwilling to exclude areas *already* in the Soviet sphere, and moreover he was waving that Bomb around as though he really intended to use it.

NEW LEADERS, NEW WEAPONS, NEW POLICIES

The foreign policy of Dulles

By 1953 the United States had a Republican President (the first since Herbert Hoover!). Eisenhower's Secretary of State, John Foster Dulles, at once made clear his basic Cold War outlook. His first official speech in January 1953 made this promise: 'To all those suffering under Communist slavery . . . Let us say: you can count on us.'

Dulles thought that the people of Eastern Europe would be encouraged to throw off their chains themselves if they knew what life was like in the West, if they were confident of America's support, and if their Soviet masters were firmly told that no further repression or expansion would be tolerated. So Western propaganda was stepped up (especially by radio broadcasts to Eastern Europe) and the ring of encircling military alliances was created. Dulles threatened 'massive retaliation' if any Communist boot stepped beyond the territory already held, and declared that America must be prepared to 'go to the brink' of war. Apparently he was ready to run the risk of a nuclear holocaust to make the Communist empire 'crumble from within' – and especially to 'roll it back' in Eastern Europe (Figure 24.1).

But 'roll-back', 'massive retaliation' and 'brinkmanship' were policies of bluff – and the bluff was soon called. The rebellions of the East Germans (in 1953) and the Hungarians (in 1956) were crushed by Soviet tanks – and America did not intervene. Thus it was shown that a policy which relied on the

Figure 24.1

bomb was unworkable, because nuclear war was unthinkable.

Or was it? Dulles and his successors had to decide which parts of the world (other than America) were 'worth' defending with the only weapon that now counted against the USSR. Budapest? West Berlin? South Vietnam? Only in 1962, when President Kennedy faced that question over Cuba, was the American Government ready to go *over* the brink if necessary. Cuba was different from Budapest or Berlin: it was on America's own doorstep.

The power of H-bombs

By 1953 both the USA and the USSR had exploded H-bombs, which were very much more powerful than the primitive A-bombs dropped on Japan. In the next ten years, as Study Topic 14 shows, both the power of

these bombs and techniques to deliver them rapidly progressed. Americans gradually realized what Dulles had overlooked – that Soviet technology had caught up with American technology, and was perhaps even ahead of it. And since an H-bomb war could destroy humanity, it became obvious that Soviet–American manoeuvres must exclude the use of these doomsday weapons. Cuba above all made this fact crystal clear.

The foreign policy of Khrushchev

In 1956 it seemed that Khrushchev understood these nuclear realities very well. Before his death in 1953, Stalin had hinted at forthcoming changes in Soviet foreign policy by suggesting that war between Capitalism and Socialism was not 'inevitable', and Khrushchev confirmed this in a dramatic way at the Twentieth Congress of the Soviet Communist

Figure 24.2

Party in 1956. Alongside de-Stalinization at home he announced that 'Peaceful Coexistence' was to be the new theme of Soviet relations with the Capitalist West. To Khrushchev, the need for peaceful coexistence was self-evident. 'There are only two ways: either peaceful coexistence, or the most destructive war in history. There is no third way.' (Figure 24.2.)

There were three different aspects of the new Soviet foreign policy:

1. Socialism v. Capitalism

'Peaceful Coexistence' seemed to set aside the Marxist–Leninist idea of continuing conflict between Communism and Capitalism. But Khrushchev did not abandon the ultimate aim of a Socialist world – he merely proposed new ways to reach that goal. The superiority of Socialism would be proved not through war but by peaceful economic competition. The economic successes of the USSR, its ability to provide a high standard of living, its feats of advanced technology, would win converts to Socialism all over the world, especially when the West was plunged into another 'inevitable' depression. At home he hastened to fulfil that boast, as we saw in our study of the USSR, with a new accent on consumer goods and by efforts to increase productivity.

2. Policy towards uncommitted nations

In the competition for friends among the uncommitted nations of Asia, Africa and Latin America, the Soviet Union would offer economic and military aid to rival America's aid programmes. But its support for national liberation movements would be carefully controlled to avoid provoking the West too far. (In practice, Soviet support for such movements reinforced the American belief that they were *nothing more than* vehicles for Communist expansion. Vietnam is an example of this—see Chapter 25.)

3. Policy towards Soviet satellites

Thirdly, the USSR's policy towards its satellites and foreign Communist parties was 'de-Stalinized' by Khrushchev's new concept of

'different roads to Socialism'. There were two ideas here: (1) that the road to power for a Communist party need not be violent revolution, but could be a 'parliamentary road' (thus the Communist party in Italy or France might be voted into power); and (2) that a Socialist state need not be an exact copy of the Soviet model (thus making Tito's 'national Communism' acceptable). 'Different roads to Socialism' was an important break from Stalin's policy of 'Cominformism' established in 1947 (see p. 241, Step 4).

Khrushchev demonstrated the USSR's new tolerance by visiting Yugoslavia in 1955 and re-establishing friendly relations with Tito. But the Hungarian Revolution of 1956 called the bluff of Moscow's de-Stalinization as it called Washington's bluff of 'roll-back': Soviet tanks quickly brought breakaway Hungary to heel. It was clear that the reins of Soviet control in Eastern Europe were only to be slackened, not broken.

In other ways, however, Khrushchev *did* seem to mean what he said. In the face of several 'provocations' by the West, and despite the indignant protest of his ally China (for reasons we shall explain in Chapter 26), Khrushchev carefully avoided confrontation with the United States. *Or did he?* In 1958 and again in 1961 he seemed to be asking for a show-down over Berlin – and in 1962, when he planted Soviet nuclear missiles in Cuba, he had apparently forgotten altogether his own words of 1956.

The conflicting ambitions of strong leaders, and above all the devastating power of new weapons: these are the background themes of the international chess game we shall now describe. Only in the course of the game – and most dramatically, when they reached 'checkmate' over Cuba – did the players discover the rules which would govern their future relations:

Rule 1   H-bombs were too dangerous to use, to threaten to use, or even to be freely tested. From now on the superpowers would try to control their use, and prevent them spreading.

Rule 2　Each super-power had a recognized sphere, and the other had better stay out of it...*or else!*

Rule 3　In other parts of the world each power could continue to look for recruits, but they would avoid confrontation with each other.

The brief chronological account which follows inevitably skims over the details of each event and leaves out some altogether. Once again you should look for *themes* rather than try to memorize all the facts and dates. What signs can you see of more conciliatory policies by each side towards the other? In what ways do the leaders still show the 'hawkish'† attitudes of the early Cold War years?

SOVIET–AMERICAN RELATIONS, 1953–61

1953　● USA and USSR explode H-bombs.
　　　● Workers' rising in East Germany suppressed by Soviet tanks.
　　　● Settlement of the Korean War (see Chapter 23).

1954　● Geneva Agreement on Indo-China (see Chapter 23).

1955　● West Germany joined NATO, which renewed Soviet fears of German military strength. In reply the USSR set up the Warsaw Pact. Nevertheless the thaw continued: the USSR gave up military bases in Finland, agreed to an Austrian peace treaty (on condition that Austria would be neutral) and attended the first Summit meeting of heads of state in Geneva.
　　　● Khrushchev visited Yugoslavia to re-establish friendly relations.

1956　● Khrushchev announced the policy of Peaceful Coexistence at the Twentieth Congress of the CPSU. The Cominform was dissolved. De-Stalinization immediately sparked off reactions in Eastern Europe:

---

†It is customary to speak of 'hawks' and 'doves' in Washington and Moscow: those who advocate an aggressive policy, and those who want a more peaceful one.

(i)　In Poland the Communist leader Gomulka, previously imprisoned for 'Titoism', came to power and introduced reforms. The USSR agreed to this limited form of 'national Communism'.

(ii)　In Hungary the revolt was far more radical. Popular demand brought Nagy to power; he abolished the one-party system and proposed that Hungary would leave the Warsaw Pact. US propaganda radio encouraged the Hungarians to rebel, promising American help – though not saying exactly what help – and in the end, none came. While the world's attention was diverted by the Suez Crisis in Egypt, the Red Army brutally 'restored order' in Hungary: 30,000 Hungarians were killed and 180,000 fled to the West. Nagy was shot.

Why did the USSR react so ruthlessly? Because the Hungarian Revolution was a direct threat to the USSR: first to her military security, and secondly because Nagy's proposed reforms would have set an example for other countries in Eastern Europe and for the USSR itself.

● The Suez Crisis. The USA refused to back the Anglo-French invasion of Egypt (which it regarded as a foolish imperialist adventure) even though the Anglo–French forces were helping America's protégé Israel, whereas Egypt was a prospective recruit to the Soviet camp (see pages 268–70 for a fuller discussion of this topic).

1957　● The Soviet Sputnik demonstrated the USSR's ability to deliver nuclear missiles to the USA.

1958　● US military intervention in Lebanon and Britain's in Jordan to support right-wing, pro-West governments. This was a response to a left-wing *coup* in Iraq, and to Egypt's growing friendship with the USSR after her quarrel with the West over Suez. Khrushchev protested at these interventions, but took no action.

- For fear of provoking the United States, the USSR refused to back China's bombardment of offshore islands between China and Taiwan which were held by the Kuomintang.
- Khrushchev provoked a Berlin crisis by his threat to hand over East Berlin to the GDR (East Germany), which would probably then hamper Western access to West Berlin. He demanded a final settlement of German frontiers which would oblige Western troops to withdraw from West Berlin and again expose the half-city to absorption by East Germany. This put the USA on the spot: was their presence in West Berlin worth an H-bomb? Talks began in 1959, but the crisis grumbled on....

1959 • Friendly and successful visit by Khrushchev to the USA for his Camp David meeting with Eisenhower. They agreed to hold another Summit.

1960 • Paris Summit failed: Khrushchev walked out because the Russians had shot down an American U-2 spy plane over the Soviet Union. Eisenhower first denied spying, then admitted it when the American pilot was produced, and declared America's 'right' to such 'reconnaissance flights'.

1961 • John F. Kennedy became President. He re-asserted the Truman Doctrine with his promise to 'defend liberty wherever it was threatened'.

- Khrushchev again raised the Berlin question at a Summit meeting with JFK – with no result. Tanks faced each other across the border dividing East and West Germany. The GDR built the Berlin Wall (Figure 24.3) to close off the escape route for refugees (over 3 million since 1945) and because West Berlin was a 'shop window' of Capital-

Figure 24.3   The Berlin Wall, erected in 1961.

ist affluence and a centre for Western espionage activities. Western authorities in Berlin could have taken action over the Wall – but didn't. General indignation in the West was soon overshadowed by the Cuba Missile Crisis.

THE CUBA MISSILE CRISIS, 1962

Here we must pause to look at the background to the events of 1962.

The Cuban revolution

Cuba, an island 90 miles off the shores of Florida, was a prime example of traditional American overlordship in her 'back yard'. In 1898 the USA helped the Cubans to overthrow Spanish rule because she considered Cuba to be in the American sphere, from which she had banned the influence of European powers. But 'independent' Cuba then became, in all but name, an American colony. Its constitution gave America the right to intervene in Cuban affairs (waived in 1934), a naval base at Guantanamo (still held today), and allowed American investment in the Cuban economy to the point where in the 1950s, 'U.S. citizens controlled 80 per cent of Cuba's utilities, 90 per cent of the mines, 90 per cent of the cattle ranches, almost 100 per cent of the oil refining industry, 50 per cent of the public railways, 40 per cent of the sugar industry and 25 per cent of all bank deposits'.† Cuba was a poor country whose livelihood depended on the sale of her sugar harvest to the United States.

In 1959 the brutal dictatorship of Batista was overthrown by a band of Cuban guerillas led by Fidel Castro. Unlike Mao's Communist army in China, Castro's guerilla force had spent only a few years 'in the hills'; they came to power inexperienced in government but full of reforming zeal. At this stage Castro was not a convinced Marxist, but some of his comrades were. At any rate his proposed reforms – including a take-over of land – looked Communist enough to the American Government. When he applied for loans, first to the United States and then to the American-dominated Organization of American States (OAS), he was refused. America threatened to cut Cuba's life-line – her guaranteed quota of US sugar imports – whereupon Cuba signed a trade pact with the USSR in February 1960. In July the US Government carried out its threat, the USSR undertook to buy Cuba's sugar, and US – Cuban relations rapidly deteriorated until diplomatic ties were cut in January 1961.

The Bay of Pigs invasion

Meanwhile a group of Cuban exiles in the United States (Batista supporters and other middle-class people who disliked the radical tone of Castro's reforms) had been planning a counter-revolution. They were helped and equipped by the American Central Intelligence Agency (CIA), a project approved by President Eisenhower and inherited by Kennedy when he took office in January 1961. In April 1961, 1,400 men of the Cuban Brigade 2506 invaded Cuba from US bases in Guatemala, landing at the Bay of Pigs. The invasion was a fiasco: the hoped-for popular rising did not occur, the exiles' force was easily defeated and its survivors captured. The whole episode was an embarrassment to the Cuban exile organization and its American sponsors.

†David Horowitz, *From Yalta to Vietnam* (Penguin 1971) p. 198.

Soviet–American confrontation

In December 1961 Castro publicly declared himself a Marxist, which confirmed to Americans that Cuba was now a Soviet satellite. Early in 1962 Cuba was expelled from the Organization of American States, and she now had to depend on Soviet protection.

Events moved rapidly to a crisis. In June 1962 Cuba received huge shipments of Soviet arms – patrol boats, ground-to-air missiles, MIG-21 fighter planes. These weapons could be regarded as defensive, but by September medium-range offensive missiles and IL-28 bombers had arrived. All this was observed by American U-2 reconnaissance planes, and by 14 October the United States had photographic proof that Soviet missile bases were being built in Cuba. They would bring all the main cities of North America within range of a Soviet 'finger on the trigger' (Figure 24.4).

Was Khrushchev trying to force concessions on Berlin, or to get rid of NATO missile bases close to the Soviet Union? To this day the real motives for his provocation are not known. But the American reaction was sure enough. Kennedy put US troops on alert and on 22 October he proclaimed to the world that:

(i) the USA would consider an attack by Cuba anywhere in the Western hemisphere as an attack by the USSR on the United States; and

(ii) the United States would enforce a naval 'quarantine'* around Cuba until the missiles were removed (in other words, any ship in the area might be stopped and searched by the US Navy).

After recent American 'failures' – the Bay of Pigs, the Berlin Wall – Kennedy needed a victory to boost US prestige. Perhaps he welcomed a chance to gamble for one. At any rate, since twenty-five Soviet ships were en route to Cuba, his ultimatum put Khrushchev on the spot. Should he stand firm and perhaps cause a Third World War? Or give way and lose face? Kennedy and Khrushchev exchanged ten letters in the next seven days and the UN Secretary-General, U Thant, tried

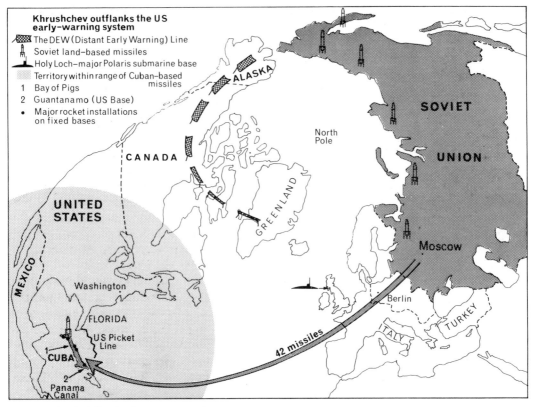

Khrushchev outflanks the US early-warning system

- The DEW (Distant Early Warning) Line
- Soviet land-based missiles
- Holy Loch—major Polaris submarine base
- Territory within range of Cuban-based missiles
- 1 Bay of Pigs
- 2 Guantanamo (US Base)
- • Major rocket installations on fixed bases

Figure 24.4   Cuba, 1962.

to mediate between them. Khrushchev tried to strike a bargain by offering to remove Soviet missiles from Cuba if the United States removed theirs from Turkey,† but this was ignored. On 28 October he promised to withdraw the missiles if the United States would undertake not to invade Cuba. Kennedy accepted, and the withdrawal began on 3 November. The American naval blockade was called off on 20 November.

Results of the missile crisis

For six days from 22–28 October the whole world held its breath. Whatever the issues of the Soviet–American power struggle, there was understandable rage that everyone's safety should be put at risk by it. Fortunately the Soviet and American leaders themselves

†Progress in nuclear weapons since these bases were installed in the 1950s had made them obsolete by 1961. In fact the United States had planned to remove them before the Cuba crisis, and soon after it they were dismantled.

realized that there must be no more near misses like Cuba! After the crisis their relations thawed considerably at the diplomatic level:

(i) In June 1963 they set up a Washington–Moscow 'hot line' telephone link to avoid the awful possibility that a nervous finger might press the nuclear button through a misunderstanding.

(ii) In August 1963, after ten years of deadlock, they were able to agree on the partial Nuclear Test-Ban Treaty which forbade above-ground nuclear tests.

(iii) In 1968 the Nuclear Non-Proliferation Treaty tried to stop the spread of weapons beyond the existing 'nuclear club'.

But these agreements have by no means eliminated the danger of nuclear war, as Study Topic 14 shows.

For Khrushchev, accused of 'adventurism' by his colleagues, Cuba was a personal disaster. Together with failures in his domestic policy, the Soviet defeat of 1962 contributed to his downfall in October 1964.

The missile crisis also had sad results for Cuba itself. The outcome of her struggle for independence was only to exchange American domination for Soviet domination. Nevertheless, within these limits, her form of Socialism is Cuban: a mixture of Chinese, Russian and purely Castroite ideas.

The events of 1960–62 did not improve the image of the USSR or the United States in Latin America generally. Castroism struck a sympathetic chord among many left-wing movements, but direct help from Cuba always risked provoking America (see ahead, Chapter 27).

Predictably, right-wing forces still looked to the United States to keep them in power or get them into power, either openly by sending troops (as in the Dominican Republic in 1965) or through under-cover help from the CIA. The best-known example of CIA 'de-stabilization' was in Chile: having failed to prevent the election of President Allende's Marxist government there in 1970, the CIA supported a military *coup* to overthrow it in 1973. But the Soviet leaders now trod very warily in Uncle Sam's back yard: against the wishes of some Moscow hawks, they gave little help to Allende's government and did not interfere when it was crushed.

Meanwhile the Soviet–American chess game was not yet over! But after 1962, as you will see, it was played strictly according to the rules.

SOVIET–AMERICAN RELATIONS, 1963–9

1963 • Hot-line phone link set up (see p. 266).
  • Nuclear Test-Ban Treaty (see Study Topic 14).
1964 • US escalation in Vietnam meant
on   greatly increased American aid to the South, while the USSR and China aided the North. Throughout, the World Powers avoided direct confrontation.
1967 • Israel–Arab Six-Day War. The West aided Israel and the USSR aided the Arabs, but again the super-powers avoided direct confrontation (see below).

1968 • Invasion of Czechoslovakia by a combined force of Warsaw Pact countries. The Czech leader, Dubček, and his proposals for 'Socialism with a human face' were overthrown. Czech patriots threw jeers and insults at their 'Socialist brothers' in tanks, but did not risk the fate of Hungarian rebels in 1956 by armed resistance. Western public opinion was outraged by Soviet action – as it was over Hungary – but Western intervention was never a possibility. This event gave rise to what the West calls the Brezhnev Doctrine (in fact only a reiteration of the earlier lesson of Hungary) – that 'different roads to Socialism' in Eastern Europe did *not* include roads away from Soviet domination.
  • Nuclear Non-Proliferation Treaty (see Study Topic 14).
1969 • Recognition of post-war German frontiers was finally achieved by the *Ostpolitik* (East policy) of West German Chancellor Willy Brandt. Whereas previous West German governments had clung to the hope of reunification (and even the recovery of land in the East lost to Poland in 1945), Brandt was willing to recognize the GDR as a *de facto** separate state. Exchanges across the border – and the Berlin Wall – could then take place. The official status of West Berlin remained unresolved (but since 1949 it has always been in practice a kind of 'island province' of West Germany).

Thus by 1969 the terms for Peaceful Coexistence in Europe were clear: there was to be no 'liberation' in the East, but civilized relations across the Iron Curtain would be possible. In terms of the chess game, the USA and the USSR had been forced to accept 'stalemate' rather than outright victory, and were content to leave it at that. So were the nations

267

of East and West Europe, which had been pawns in the game for more than twenty years. As Soviet–American relations thawed, they began to develop East–West links among themselves which set the stage for European *détente* in the early 1970s.

Nevertheless Eastern Europe remained a very sensitive area for the USSR. In the 1960s Albania took China's side in the Sino-Soviet quarrel and for many years complained loudly about Soviet 'revisionism'. As other states forged links with Western Europe, e.g. Rumania's with France, they became less obedient to Moscow in foreign policy. But the most intractable problem for the USSR, as you will see in Chapter 27, was the emergence in the 1980s of a new form of resistance to the Soviet model of Socialism, and to Soviet domination, in Poland.

THE COLD WAR IN THE MIDDLE EAST

The Middle East is a special case in the Soviet–American chess game which requires further explanation. The region inevitably became a theatre of the Cold War because of its vital importance to both the USSR and the West. Russia has strategic interests (which preoccupied the Tsars just as much as the Soviet leaders) in her long frontier with Turkey, Iran and Afghanistan, and her access to the Mediterranean through the Dardanelles Straits, bordered by Turkey. The West has an obvious interest in the region as the main source of our economic life-blood, oil. In the 1950s the United States tried to marshal 'friendly' Arab states into a regional defence pact with the same aim as NATO in Western Europe and SEATO in the Far East: to prevent the expansion of Soviet influence. The USSR was equally anxious to break out of this encirclement on her southern flank by finding friends in the Arab world. The Middle Eastern states, though little interested in the Cold War objectives of their protectors, were happy to accept arms and aid for their own national purposes.

The founding of Israel

In the hey-day of nineteenth-century Western imperialism Britain and France became the main colonial powers in North Africa and the Middle East. The peace settlement of the First World War gave large areas of Middle Eastern 'Arabia' to these two powers as 'mandates', to guide towards self-government. Up to the Second World War, and for some years after it, these two states therefore had colonial interests in the region.

The central conflict in the Middle East today arises from the creation of Israel as a 'national home for the Jewish people' in 1948 from the British mandate of Palestine. This was furiously resented by the surrounding Arab states and especially by the Palestinians, whose country was partitioned to provide it. The Arab world refused to recognize the new state, and the four Arab–Israeli wars which followed – in 1948–9, 1956, 1967 and 1973 – were therefore a fight for survival for Israel. These wars also created, and then worsened, the two main problems which are still unsolved today:

1. *The occupied territories* In the first war with her Arab neighbours Israel 'rationalized' her borders by absorbing some areas originally designated as part of the parallel 'national home' for the Palestinians (see Figure 24.5). In the 1956 Suez War (fought in collusion with France and Britain, who were interested in the Suez Canal) Israel occupied the Sinai peninsula and the Gaza Strip of Egypt, but withdrew her forces after the war. In the Six Day War of 1967 Israel again occupied these Egyptian territories and also the West Bank of the Jordan river and East Jerusalem (up to then ruled by Jordan), and the Golan Heights of Syria (see Figure 24.6).

Following this war, UN Security Resolution 242, backed by both super-powers and later accepted by most of the Arab states, called for Israeli withdrawal to her pre-1967 borders in return for guaranteed peace and security for 'every state in the area'. Israel,

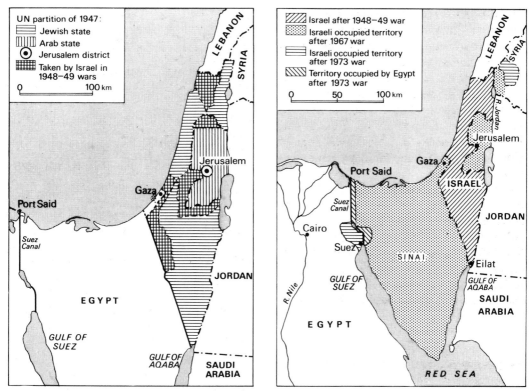

Figures 24.5 and 24.6   The Arab–Israeli conflict, 1947–73.

however, preferred to guarantee her own security by retaining her military conquests. Resolution 242 still has international support as the basis for a negotiated settlement, but Israel's later actions have disregarded it (see pages 309–10).

2. *The Palestinian problem*   Israel's military successes left the displaced Palestinians bitterly determined to recover their homeland. Now numbering some 3½ million altogether, nearly 500,000 Palestinians live in Israel as Israeli citizens and over a million more under Israeli rule in the West Bank and Gaza (all that now remained of the 1948 'Palestine homeland'). The rest are scattered far and wide, but mostly in the surrounding Arab lands. Exactly where or when, and in what form, an eventual Palestinian homeland could be set up remains a matter of continuing dispute.

The Palestine Liberation Organization (PLO), under its leader Yassir Arafat, was founded in 1964. It was originally based in Jordan but after a clash with the conservative government of King Hussein it was forced into Lebanon in 1970. In its role as a left-wing 'national liberation movement' it launched frequent raids on Israel or within the occupied territories, and was therefore regarded by Israel as a terrorist organization, unfit to be negotiated with or 'recognized' by other states. Over the years, however, the PLO gained the support of all the Arab states, which vary from feudal kingdoms like Saudi Arabia to Socialist republics like South Yemen, and are united *only* in their support of the Palestinian cause against Israel. After 1974 the PLO was regarded by the Arab world as the official spokesman of a sort of Palestinian 'government in exile'.

Arms from the super-powers

The birth of Israel in 1948 was supervised by the UN and recognized by the Western world *and* the USSR. From the outset the USA had a special commitment to the survival and prosperity of the new state because of strong pressure from Jewish Americans (more Jews live in New York City than in Israel!). But after the first Arab–Israeli war the West agreed to limit arms sales to the Middle East, to discourage further armed conflict. This policy later broke down: during and after the Suez War of 1956 Britain and France increased their arms supplies to Israel, which at that time was a useful 'tool' in their mutual hostility to Egypt, while after 1956 the USSR became the chief supplier to Egypt, Syria and Iraq (who had all overthrown their feudal rulers and become Arab Socialist republics). The Soviet leaders were ready to overlook the periodic persecution of Communists in these states–these were the Arab 'friends' they had been looking for to prevent Western dominance of the Middle East. And for the same reason in reverse, the United States quickly stepped in to arm and support Israel as Britain and France gradually relinquished their imperial role in the region.

By the 1960s, therefore, any explosion between the two super-powers' client states carried the danger of a wider conflict–a danger so widely recognized that the 1967 and 1973 wars were quickly stopped by UN action in which both the USA and USSR took part. But the 1973 Yom Kippur War led to an important adjustment of US policy. First, the OPEC oil embargo imposed on America as 'punishment' for arms supplies to Israel (see page 76) made Washington aware for the first time that a solution of 'the Palestinian problem' must be part of any general peace settlement. Secondly, the war had so *nearly* become a general conflagration (Nixon declared a nuclear alert when he thought the USSR might intervene directly to stop the fighting) that Washington now seemed ready to acknowledge the USSR's rightful interest in the region and to co-operate with Moscow in supervising a per-manent settlement there. Thus by 1973 there was hope of *détente* even in this tortured area of the Cold War.

We have carried through the Middle East story to a convenient 'pause' (unfortunately it was no more than that, as you will see later). But in the late 1960s, with *détente* on the horizon in Europe and other areas of East–West tension, the most important unre-solved conflict between Democracy and Communism was in Vietnam.

Nuclear Weapons

This Study Topic discusses three aspects of nuclear weapons development:

1. What the Nuclear Age means.
2. Attempts by the nuclear states to achieve a nuclear 'balance of power'.
3. Efforts to control the development and spread of these weapons.

We have summarized the nuclear story from 1945 to the 1980s in one place so that you can follow it more easily. But since nuclear weapons development is the backdrop to *all* the World Powers' relations with each other since 1945, you will need to relate what follows *back* to the events and policies described in Chapters 22–4, and *forward* to the interplay of the USA and the USSR, especially, which is taken up in Chapters 26 and 27. Notice, for example, that Dulles's threats of 'massive retaliation' derived from his belief in American nuclear superiority, and that efforts to control H-bombs were only considered *essential* by the nuclear super-powers once they had achieved a rough equality in weaponry and had narrowly escaped a show-down over Cuba. But when a new phase of strategic thinking and a new generation of weapons had made nuclear war 'thinkable' again, we find the super-powers resuming the deadly chess game they had apparently given up for *détente*. No longer content with 'stalemate', once again they seemed ready to risk the safety of the world for an outright 'win'.

THE NUCLEAR AGE

In the nuclear age, political leaders face the prospect that to go to war no longer risks thousands of lives but tens of millions; not merely the loss of a province but the survival of human society. Any 'little war' *may* escalate to a nuclear level, especially if a nuclear state has an interest in it.

While there are limits to the size of explosion from an Atom bomb, Hydrogen bombs opened up the possibility of *unlimited* explosive power. In addition to the immediate effects of heat and blast, the long-term effects of radioactive fall-out resulting from a nuclear explosion can cause death and chronic disease over a wide area, and for many years. No relief service yet devised could cope with these widespread after-effects.

In fact man has the power to destroy himself. Any place on earth can be destroyed from any other in a matter of minutes. Even a defence which is 90 per cent effective may not be able to prevent crippling damage from missiles which penetrate the 10 per cent gap in the fence.

Because it seemed that the certain losses of a nuclear war now outweighed any possible gain from such a conflict, the major powers recoiled from the direct use of force against each other. Instead they sought safety in the idea of a balance of power.

THE NUCLEAR BALANCE OF POWER

In the past when one nation became supremely powerful it usually set out to conquer others, as did Ancient Rome or France under Napoleon. So the idea evolved that if there was a 'balance of power', peace would be preserved. The search for a *nuclear* balance of power to prevent a *nuclear* war led to three developments:

1. The build-up of huge nuclear strength by the USA and the USSR meant that since

1945 these two super-powers have dominated the world. Only recently has their dominance been challenged by the emergence of China as a nuclear power and of other 'power centres', such as Japan and the Middle East, with *economic* strength.

2. In the early Cold War period, most European states (and some in other parts of the world) took shelter under the nuclear umbrella of one or other super-power, thus dividing the world into two hostile armed camps.

3. The main aim of the super-powers has been to avoid a nuclear conflict. They have had to recognize that:
   (i) adequate defence can no longer be achieved by building overwhelming military superiority;
   (ii) national defence must be based on *deterring* aggression rather than preparing to resist it;
   (iii) the super-powers have something in common – the wish to survive! So their room to manoeuvre against each other is limited.

With the gradual recognition of a revolutionary change in *the nature of war*, there was a corresponding development in military thinking. For some, war became 'unthinkable'. But those prepared to 'think about the unthinkable' put forward the idea that a full-scale war between the super-powers would be avoided by the knowledge of 'assured destruction' – the 'unacceptable level of destruction' which each could inflict on the other would prevent either side from starting a war. This position of nuclear balance was achieved by the end of the 1960s with the concept of Mutual Assured Destruction, known as MAD.

We can follow the development of military thinking since 1945 through several periods:

(a) 1945 to the mid-1950s: American superiority

The West's nuclear strategy grew up in the context of the Cold War, the military confrontation in Europe and the belief that the Soviet take-over of Eastern Europe was the beginning of world-wide Communist expansion.

In the early years, Western military thinking was based on the American nuclear monopoly (which was expected to last much longer than it did). Even after the Russian A-bomb in 1949 and H-bomb in 1953, America had an immense superiority and was invulnerable to direct nuclear attack. The USSR had far more ground forces, but America's nuclear power more than compensated for that. So here was the desired balance – our Bomb against their soldiers and tanks (Figure ST 14.1).

The West's strategy in this period was the

Figure ST 14.1

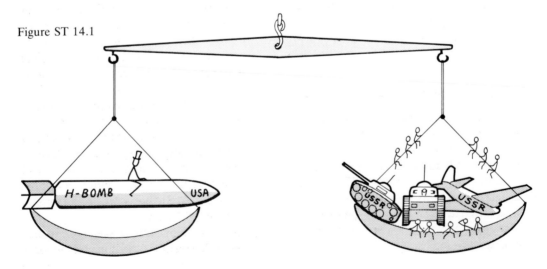

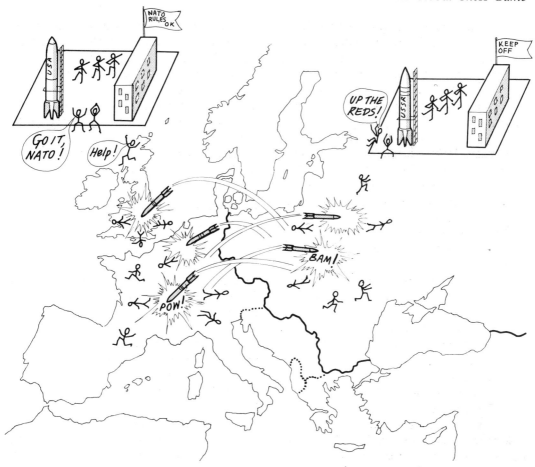

Figure ST 14.2 Late 1950s: an exchange of tactical weapons in Europe need not spread to the super-powers.

idea of meeting any local aggression with 'massive retaliation' by American nuclear bombers against the Soviet homeland. The most important question raised by this strategy was its credibility. Would the other side believe it? Would they be bluffed by the bluff?

(b) 1957–61 : are the Russians ahead?

In 1957 America was shaken by the Russian launching of Sputnik I (the first space satellite), which demonstrated that Russia was within reach of being able to launch nuclear missiles on the United States. This ended American invulnerability to nuclear attack and seemed to destroy the pre-Sputnik balance. The USA now began a new tack in its strategic thinking:

(i) To make credible the threat to use nuclear weapons, a theory was developed of a 'stepped down' or *graduated nuclear exchange* to give the super-powers some option other than having to strike directly at each other's homelands. It was possible to imagine an exchange of tactical, short-range nuclear weapons across the Cold War frontiers in Europe which would not escalate into a face-to-face super-power conflict. (Not surprisingly, America's European allies now became alarmed that the United States would not defend them because to do so would provoke the 'step up' to a Russian attack on America.) (Figure ST 14.2.)

(ii) As Russia seemed to be ahead in missiles (what President Kennedy called the 'mis-

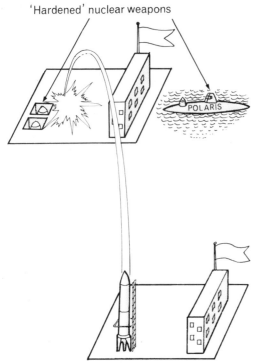

'Hardened' nuclear weapons

POLARIS

Figure ST 14.3

capacity, i.e. to be able to retaliate *after* being hit. She did this by 'hardening' her nuclear weapons, which meant putting them underground or undersea (e.g. in Polaris submarines) where they would survive a first-strike attack. If a Russian missile hit the United States in a surprise attack, these 'buried' missiles would whizz off to Moscow as a second-strike. (Figure ST 14.3.)

(c) The 1960s: 'the balance of terror'

As the two sides moved towards parity (equality) in warheads and delivery systems, it became obvious that neither had the means of effective defence. Both could launch a second-strike, so now both had to rely on the idea of 'deterring by threat of retaliation'. *Deterrence* then became the most significant factor in the super-powers' relationship (Figure ST 14.4).

Once again we are back to balance – what is often called 'the balance of terror'. Since the consequences of nuclear war would be Mutual Assured Destruction, neither side would be 'mad' enough to start one (Figure ST 14.5). And now that nuclear war was again 'unthinkable', the super-powers were ready to limit the production of some of their weapons and even to consider reducing the stockpiles. This was the military logic leading to Soviet–American *détente* in the early 1970s.

sile gap') – and missiles could not at that time be stopped in flight – there was now the possibility of a successful 'first-strike' attack by the USSR (that is, one which could knock out the United States with one blow). America was faced with the need to develop a 'second-strike'

Figure ST 14.4 Deterrence became the only possible nuclear defence.

GRRR! NIET!

USA USSR

(d) The 1970s: 'flexible response'

For military strategists, however, the MAD concept was always unsatisfactory because it left *no option* in a crisis. Any world leader would shrink from pressing a button to 'blow up the world' – but must America stand by while the USSR took it over piece by piece? And could Russia risk a disabling attack by new American weapons she could not match? Alongside their negotiations to limit the 'big bang' weapons both super-powers continued to develop a variety of 'smaller bang' missiles which would be *accurate*

Figure ST 14.5   By the 1960s the world's safety depended on this idea: no one could be 'mad' enough to provoke Mutual Assured Destruction.

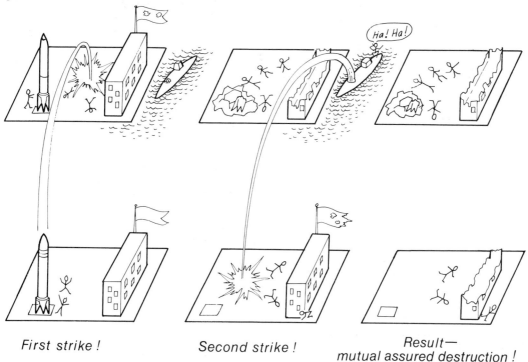

First strike !   *Second strike !*   *Result—*
mutual assured destruction !

enough to be aimed at purely military targets and as nearly as possible *invulnerable* to equally accurate missiles from the other side. By the mid-1970s a new generation of these smaller weapons provided American defence planners with 'a flexible range of strategic options' to meet any circumstances which might arise. The MAD option could now be supplemented by a more credible defence policy of 'flexible response'.

One significant event of the new 'flexible response' phase was NATO's decision in 1979 to deploy American Cruise and Pershing II missiles. These intermediate-range missiles are theoretically invulnerable because they are *mobile*, and are NATO's 'reply' to Soviet SS 20 missiles targeted on Western Europe.† Although placed in

† The Soviet justification for these missiles, which began to be deployed after 1976 as an upgraded replacement of earlier types, was that they balanced the combined strength of NATO plus the independent nuclear forces of France and Britain. Since these French and British weapons are not part of *NATO*'s armoury, the United States refused to count them as part of the East–West European nuclear balance.

Europe, Cruise and Pershing are *American* weapons and can reach far into European Russia. Thus they give the USA a new 'forward base' in its confrontation with the USSR, and are perceived by the USSR as 'first strike' rather than defensive weapons.

The political context of NATO's decision is explained in Chapter 27. The military thinking behind it harks back to a point we explained earlier: the fear that America might not come to the rescue of Western Europe under a Russian attack, to avoid an all-out 'big bang' conflict. By inviting American-operated missiles onto their own territory the NATO states wanted to 'couple' American defence strategy to their own, an idea called 'extended deterrence'. (On the other hand it could be argued, as some people did, that the new, accurate missiles in Europe gave the United States *greater* freedom to 'stand off' in the event of a European conflict, without risking the American homeland.)

The new concept and the new weapons of

'flexible response' have made the balance of terror even more dangerous. Once again it is 'thinkable' to launch a small, accurate missile against military targets of the other side, either in response to an attack by conventional forces – or, in a serious crisis, as a preemptive first strike. Both sides *say* that these weapons (along with all their others) will never be used to start a war, *but can we be sure of that*? Renewed nuclear instability, and the mutual distrust it has generated, are the military reality of the New Cold War of the 1980s.

EFFORTS TO CONTROL NUCLEAR WEAPONS

Unfortunately the nuclear super-powers have not shown the same determination to control the new weapons as they have in developing them. But the 'near miss' of the Cuba crisis, and the acceptance of the MAD concept by both sides, did lead to some achievements in this area. The most important successes, and failures, are indicated below.

1. *The Partial Nuclear Test-Ban Treaty* of 1963 forbade all nuclear tests except underground ones (which, it is hoped, do not cause serious environmental damage). But France and China, wanting freedom to develop their own H-bombs, did not sign the treaty. Methods of detecting small tests are not perfect, and several states, including Britain, are known to have conducted above-ground tests since 1963.

2. *The Nuclear Non-Proliferation Treaty* of 1968 tried to prevent the spread of nuclear weapons. Existing nuclear states agreed not to help other states to make them, and non-nuclear states agreed not to develop them on their own. By 1975, 94 countries had signed and ratified this treaty, but two 'suspected nuclear states' (Israel and South Africa) and three other 'non-nuclear' ones (Argentina, Brazil and Egypt) have not yet done so. In 1974

India joined the nuclear club by exploding a device, and in 1981 her old enemy Pakistan moved into the 'near-nuclear' group.†

3. *Arms limitation* We cannot enter into the complexities of the many weapons and control agreements here.‡ But a few basic points will help you to understand what follows, and what you may read elsewhere. First there is the difference between *strategic* weapons (long-range inter-continental missiles), medium or *intermediate-range* weapons, and tactical or *battlefield* weapons with a short range and a limited purpose, e.g. to stop an oncoming tank attack. Secondly, we have to think in terms of *warheads* rather than missiles, since many missiles now have several warheads, some of which can be independently targeted, i.e. sent to different places. Thirdly, the number and type of *launching devices* is critically important in the 'flexible response' era – that is, the range and detectability of aircraft and submarines, and the vulnerability of silos or carriers of ground-launched missiles.

(a) *strategic weapons*

In 1972 the USA and USSR at last reached an 'interim agreement' at their Strategic Arms Limitation Talks (SALT). SALT I placed a five-year 'freeze' on their intercontinental and anti-ballistic missiles (ICBMs and ABMs), but did not hinder their efforts to improve and develop smaller 'Salt free' weapons, as explained earlier. In 1974 negotiations began to replace SALT I with SALT II. This was eventually signed in 1979, but in the worsening political

---

† The 'suspected' category are those which are believed to have built a device already; the 'near-nuclear' group are those technically within reach of doing so.

‡ More detailed information can be found in Bown and Mooney, *Cold War to Détente*, Chapters 18–20. *Over Our Dead Bodies*, edited by Dorothy Thompson, contains a useful political-military chronology from 1945–81, and a glossary of terms and acronyms. See Further Reading list.

climate of that time, the US Congress refused to ratify it.

The SALT agreements only placed a ceiling (a rather high one) on the numbers of strategic weapons, but SALT II included a future commitment to *reduce* the stockpiles. When the third round of these talks began in 1982, President Reagan changed their name to Strategic Arms *Reduction* Talks (START). These negotiations are at a very early stage; a successful outcome will depend on an improvement in Soviet–American relations, which were at a very low ebb in 1983.

(b) *lower-range weapons*

Another result of the warmer climate of *détente* was the beginning of discussions to reduce the level of military forces in Europe. This was the 'military side' of West Germany's *Ostpolitik* and the several East–West agreements which followed it (see page 267). The Mutual and Balanced Force Reduction Talks (MBFR) began in Vienna in 1973, but had reached no agreement ten years later. This lack of success was partly due to the complexity of the problems, but also to the worsening of East–West relations after the brief respite of *détente*.

The plain fact is that *no arms agreements can be reached without the political will to do so*. This was shown by the collapse of the Intermediate-range Nuclear Forces talks (INF) in November 1983, followed a few weeks later by the suspension of the START and MBFR talks. Chapter 27 explains the political lead-up to this new nuclear deadlock; the point we wish to emphasize here is that political and military policies are inextricably linked.

Anti-nuclear protest

Anti-nuclear protest movements, such as

Britain's Campaign for Nuclear Disarmament, began in Western Europe in the 1950s. At that time they helped to arouse public concern about the dangers of unrestricted nuclear testing (which eventually led to the Test-Ban Treaty of 1963), but few politicians were won over to CND's view that Britain should give up her own H-bomb as an example to the rest of the world and to make Britain less of a target in a super-power conflict. During the 1960s and early 1970s CND fell into decline, while most ordinary people either closed their minds to the danger of nuclear war or believed that the West's defence strategies would prevent it.

The New Cold War of the 1980s, with its perilous nuclear dimension, brought increased support for CND and similar organizations elsewhere–now including America, where in 1982 several states passed a special referendum calling for a 'freeze' in the nuclear arms race. In Western Europe many politicians were opposed to the deployment of Cruise and Pershing missiles, but the right-wing governments of Britain and West Germany, and the moderate-left one in Italy, went ahead with the policy. Mounting public protest kept the debate in the news, and now included threats of civil disobedience by militant groups like the 'Greenham Common women' (who could make Cruise missiles at that base inoperable by preventing their necessary dispersal exercises round the countryside).† But despite the efforts of the Campaign for European Disarmament (END), founded in 1980, no comparable protest was allowed on the other side of the Iron Curtain. This fact, coupled with the sympathy in Moscow for anti-nuclear protests in the West, allowed opponents of CND to dismiss it as 'a dupe of Soviet propaganda' (or worse), and thus pre-

† Perhaps appropriately, the technique of non-violent 'civil disobedience' against unjust or immoral laws was first advocated by the nineteenth-century American writer Thoreau and the Russian writer Tolstoy. These methods were used in the Civil Rights campaign of Martin Luther King, who learned it from their writings and the example of the Indian nationalist leader Gandhi against British rule in India.

vented a calm consideration of the anti-nuclear arguments.

In fact many sober and 'responsible' voices have also questioned the West's reliance on a nuclear defence system. In 1979 Lord Mountbatten, a retired Admiral and a member of the British royal family, stated his view that nuclear weapons serve 'no military purpose' and that their existence 'only adds to our perils because of the illusions they have generated'. One of these 'illusions' was the idea that nuclear war is survivable – as suggested, for example, in the Home Office pamphlet *Protect and Survive*, describing do-it-yourself bomb shelters and other pre-cautions for ordinary citizens to take in the event of a nuclear alert. This document was greeted with ridicule by the protest move-ment and caused alarm among scientists and doctors who consider that official predictions vastly underestimate the after-effects of a nuclear explosion (which in their view could *not* be coped with by existing rescue ser-vices). There is also an unanswerable military argument that NATO's dependence on nuc-lear weapons would force the West to use

them at a very early stage in any European conflict. Many strategists have proposed an alternative defence system based on a higher level of conventional forces, keeping nuclear weapons as a last resort.

So far, however, neither cogent argument from many expert sources nor the moral out-rage and sheer terror of ordinary citizens has succeeded in changing Western defence strategy, or in checking the dangerous prolif-eration of nuclear weapons both within and beyond the original 'nuclear club'.

*GLOSSARY

de facto (Latin), in fact. In diplomatic lan-guage a distinction is made between a *de facto* government which has power 'in fact' and a *de jure* government which has power 'by right'.

quarantine, literally, the deliberate isolation of someone who has a contagious disease. President Kennedy probably chose this word to avoid the more aggressive 'block-ade' – but that's what his 'quarantine' of Cuba was.

Figure ST 14.6   From the late 1950s the Campaign for Nuclear Disarmament campaigned continuously in the West – but with little success – against the developing nuclear arms race.

Questions

Did you notice?

1. In 1955 Khrushchev renewed Soviet friendship with (a) Poland (b) Yugoslavia (c) East Germany
2. The U-2 was (a) the first earth satellite (b) an American spy plane (c) a nuclear missile
3. A 'hardened' nuclear missile is one which (a) has gone rusty and cannot be used (b) moves faster than others (c) is carried in a Polaris submarine
4. In 1961 Cuba was invaded at the Bay of Pigs by (a) American marines (b) the Soviet navy (c) Cuban exiles
5. The 'hot line' refers to (a) the Iron Curtain (b) the Berlin Wall (c) a telephone link
6. True or false?
   (i) In 1956 Hungary wanted to leave the Warsaw Pact
   (ii) In 1959 Khrushchev visited the United States
   (iii) Britain invaded Egypt in 1956
   (iv) Castro was overthrown in 1973
   (v) Willy Brandt was Chancellor of West Germany
7. Which statement is *more* accurate?
   (i) Khrushchev thought Peaceful Co-existence was necessary because
       (a) nuclear war was too dangerous
       (b) he no longer disliked the Capitalist system
   (ii) In 1962 Kennedy placed a 'quarantine' round Cuba
       (a) to prevent Cuba from becoming a Soviet satellite
       (b) to prevent Soviet missiles from being installed there
   (iii) In 1968 the Nuclear Non-Proliferation Treaty
       (a) tried to keep nuclear weapons within the 'nuclear club'
       (b) succeeded in preventing the further spread of nuclear weapons

Can you explain?

8. Why did the West step up propaganda broadcasts to Eastern Europe in the early 1950s?
9. What did 'different roads to Socialism' mean in relation to:
   (a) the Italian Communist party?
   (b) Yugoslavia?
10. In what way did the Hungarian Revolution of 1956 call the bluff of 'roll-back' *and* 'de-Stalinization' in Eastern Europe? What was the connection between this event and the Warsaw Pact invasion of Czechoslovakia in 1968?
11. Why was the Cuba missile crisis of 1962 such a dangerous moment for the whole world?
12. What is meant by the following terms as used in Study Topic 14: (a) Mutual Assured Destruction? (b) 'flexible response'?

What's your view?

13. Why do you think Khrushchev wanted the removal of NATO missile bases from Turkey to be part of a package settlement of the Cuba crisis? Why do you think Kennedy refused to agree to this – although in fact the redundant Turkish bases were later removed?
14. By the late 1960s the *Ostpolitik* of West Germany enabled her to recognize East Germany as a *de facto* state. What do you think were the reasons behind this policy? Why had it not been possible earlier? What results might follow from it?
15. Consider carefully the events of 1955–68 covered in this chapter. On balance, which super-power was more generally aggressive towards the other, in your opinion?

25

The American War in Vietnam

Alongside the Cuba missile crisis, the most significant turning point in the East–West Cold War was the failure of American policy in Indo-China. Already the Vietnam War is a historical legend like the biblical one of David and Goliath: 'fearless Vietnamese peasant slays Almighty America with home-made catapult'. There is some truth in this picture, but it is not the whole story by any means:

> In the end, the North Vietnamese victory was a triumph for Russian military hardware as well as for Vietnamese courage and determination.... The final offensive was made possible by Russian long-range artillery, and the skies above it cleared by Russian-built anti-aircraft missiles. In the end, symbolically, the gate of the palace in Saigon was broken down by a Russian tank.†

The final result of the war which ended in 1975 was therefore a major victory for Communism in the Cold War. But oddly enough the Soviet Government did not use the occasion to rub America's nose in the dirt. On the contrary, although American blunders and Vietnamese suffering had given them plenty of ammunition, in the previous few years both Russia and China had deliberately soft-pedalled Vietnam in their anti-American propaganda. Continued American involvement there was an inconvenient barrier on the road to *détente* which both the Communist World Powers, each for its own reasons, were anxious to develop at that time.

This is one reason for the importance of Vietnam in our survey of the World Powers' mutual relations. But Vietnam is also a reminder, as we follow the footprints of the

†Edmund Stevens, 'The New Four-Power Game', *The Sunday Times* 4 May 1975.

World Powers round the globe, that every smaller country where they trod had its own history, its own society and the wish to decide its own future. President Johnson seemed to have forgotten that when he said of Vietnam, 'I want to leave the footprints of America there. We're going to turn the Mekong into a Tennessee Valley.' Whatever the intentions behind that promise, America's big feet brought disaster to Vietnam.

AMERICAN MISTAKES IN INDO-CHINA

To understand 'what went wrong in Vietnam' we need first to consider the assumptions on which American policy there was based. In this respect the history of China recounted in Part III is especially relevant. There you saw the hatred of imperialism in a country which had been dominated for so long by foreigners; there too a corrupt government, whose reforms benefited only a few people, could not survive against a revolutionary tide of Nationalist–Communism which offered far more radical change to a backward, peasant country. But many Americans believed that the tide could have been held back in China if they had sent more arms and money – in other words, that America could have influenced the course of events if only she had tried harder.

In applying these lessons to Vietnam, America's main mistakes can be summarized as follows.

1. 'Communism is the enemy'

From 1950 onwards, America always mis-judged the nature of the opposition in Indo-

China. At first she thought there must be 'something bigger' behind Ho Chi Minh than a few million Vietnamese peasants. Perhaps Moscow was pulling the strings? Or was it Peking? As the years went by the exact source of the Communist threat became more vague – but all American governments from Truman's onwards assumed that 'the enemy' in Indo-China was the red tide of Communism.

In fact the strength of the Vietminh force which defeated the French in 1954 – as of its successor the National Liberation Front in South Vietnam – rested far more on nationalism than on the doctrines of Marx. Was Ho Chi Minh a Communist masquerading as a Nationalist, or a Nationalist who also happened to be a Communist? As with Mao Tsetung, the answer to this question doesn't really matter. What *did* matter was that Ho Chi Minh's Government in Hanoi came to symbolize 'Vietnam for the Vietnamese' – and a rather better Vietnam for the majority of her peasant population – whereas the government in Saigon (like the KMT in China) came to mean corruption, too little social change, and foreign influence. For behind it, the United States had taken the place of France as the big white shadow saying 'We know what is best for you.'

2. 'We can win if we try hard enough'

In 1954 it was already clear that the struggle to control Vietnam could not be won by a conventional army, and that foreigners could not dictate a political solution to it. France had recognized this when she bargained herself 'off the hook' with the Geneva Agreement. But Americans 'simply could not bring themselves to believe that the United States could be defeated by a bunch of Asian guerillas in black pyjamas. France, yes; but not the United States.'†

Underlying every new move of successive American governments was the unshakable belief that South Vietnam could be saved from Communism *somehow* – it was just a

†Louis Heren, 'How it Began for the U.S. . . .', *The Times*, 25 April 1975.

matter of finding the right technique. So one ploy after another was tried out, both to win the war and 'the hearts and minds' of the Vietnamese people. And for a policy of 'total commitment' there could be only one result: total victory. No bargain, no compromise – there were several chances to make one – was acceptable to the American Government. The eventual result of this blinkered attitude was total defeat.

3. 'Victory is worth any sacrifice'

To this aspect of American policy we might cynically add, 'especially when Vietnam is making the sacrifice – not us'. This seems unfair when we remember the extent of American sacrifice in Vietnam – more than 57,000 American lives, for a start. But both before and after the period when American combat troops took over the full management of the war, it was always America's policy, as President Johnson said, 'not . . . to send American boys nine or ten thousand miles away from home to do what Asian boys ought to be doing for themselves'. By 1975 more than 2 million Asian boys had died in a conflict prolonged beyond all reason by America's refusal to give it up. Add to this more than 1½ million civilian casualties in South Vietnam (the country that was being 'protected'!), and perhaps an equal number in the North, and you will see why people questioned whether an American victory in Vietnam was 'worth the sacrifice'.

The chronicle of events after 1954 shows the consequences of these policies.

THE STRUGGLE FOR THE SOUTH, 1954–75

Two Vietnams

You saw in Chapter 23 that the Geneva Agreement of 1954 had concluded the eight-year French Indo-China War with a compromise solution. This ended the French phase of a twenty-nine-year armed struggle in Vietnam; the American phase was about to begin. The Geneva Agreement had recognized Ho Chi Minh's rule over the Democratic Republic of Vietnam with its capital at Hanoi, while the Southern zone was ruled by a French nominee, Bao Dai. In 1955 Ngo Dinh Diem, who had American support, pushed aside Bao Dai and established the Republic of Vietnam south of the 17th Parallel, with its capital at Saigon. Diem and his American backers ignored the requirement of the 1954 Agreement to hold elections on reunification, despite loud protests from Ho Chi Minh. France also took no responsibility for enforcing the Geneva Settlement after it was signed.

The United States extended the South-East Asia Treaty Organization (SEATO) to include the new state in South Vietnam, and began to pump in aid. By 1956 this amounted to $250 million a year, and later climbed much higher. The North meanwhile began to build up its economy with Russian and Chinese aid (see Figure 25.3, page 285, for a comparison of the amount of economic aid each part of Vietnam was receiving in the 1960s).

The Republic of Vietnam

In the twenty years of its separate life, the Republic of Vietnam never had a truly democratic government. Its first President, Diem, had a good anti-French record – but he was a rich Catholic ruling a country in which the majority ($12\frac{1}{2}$ out of $16\frac{1}{2}$ million) were poor Buddhists. Diem's Government was dominated by his own family; it soon became notorious for corruption, discrimination against non-Catholics, and harsh repression of all opposition.

In 1963, after government troops killed nine demonstrators at a Buddhist rally, Buddhist monks staged a protest by burning themselves to death in the street. The world was shocked – and the United States was understandably embarrassed by the obvious unpopularity of its protégé government. In November 1963 American advisers 'looked the other way' when a group of army officers

Figure 25.1 'If there's an election tomorrow, which general would you vote for?' – a British cartoon of 1966.

overthrew Diem, killing him and one of his brothers.

After Diem came a succession of military leaders (Figure 25.1) ending with President Thieu, who served from 1967–75. None of these governments was quite as corrupt as Diem's, but neither did any of them achieve much popular support. None of them carried out effective reforms, despite American pressure to do so. Nor could they suppress the tide of internal rebellion, even with American help.

The growth of resistance in the South

By 1958–9 the opposition to Diem's Government came from all sides: from right-wing rivals for power, from poorer peasants wanting land reform, from nationalists who disliked the American influence in Saigon, and from Buddhist victims of discrimination. One element in this resistance was a guerilla movement in the countryside, led by former members of the Vietminh (the force which had defeated the French). They began to assassinate unpopular government officials in the villages.

In 1960, delegates from a dozen or so nationalist groups (ranging from ex-Vietminh guerillas to Buddhist leaders) formed the National Liberation Front (NLF) (Figure 25.2)–'the Vietminh reborn'. The NLF issued a Ten-Point Programme which called for a coalition government to replace the 'disguised colonial régime' in Saigon. This government would provide democratic

Figure 25.2   A meeting of the Central Committee of the South Vietnam National Liberation Front.

liberties for all, carry out reforms, follow a neutralist foreign policy (with no foreign bases) and work for 'peaceful reunification of the Fatherland' through negotiations.

The Communist connections of the NLF made it easy for Diem to dismiss the Ten-Point Programme as a cloak for a Communist take-over (Diem blamed 'Communist agitators' for all opposition to his government). Similarly Diem's successors and their American advisers always insisted that the NLF was a Communist organization – and thereby actually encouraged the growth of 'Communism' in South Vietnam! As a Nationalist priest said (in an American TV interview): 'It is the Saigon government which gives validity to being a Communist, because *they* say that the people who work for national liberation are Communist.'

The issues of the war

Denied any political expression in the South, nationalist feeling found a violent outlet in guerilla warfare. Saigon labelled all the guerillas Vietcong (Vietnamese Communist) – which indeed most of them were – and so the necessary stereotype was created for the bitter war which was to last for fifteen years.

The issue was presented to the world in simple terms: the Vietcong (Bad) was trying to overthrow a democratic government (Good). The Saigon Government was being helped by America (well-known champion of Freedom and Democracy) to put down an illegal revolt. All Good People should support this noble cause.

The war which began as a rebellion against the Saigon Government later became one between the United States and North Vietnam (although neither side ever declared war on the other). It was always Washington's belief that the rebellion in the South was started by 'agents from the North', and that without aid from the North it would fizzle out. Beginning in 1964, North Vietnam was heavily bombed by the US Air Force. Far from quelling the guerilla activity in the South, this onslaught only provoked more direct military intervention by the North, and increased Russian and Chinese backing for Vietnam's 'struggle for national liberation', as they termed it. After 1964 increasing numbers of North Vietnamese regular troops were sent to assist the 240,000 guerillas in the South.

From the beginning, the North certainly encouraged armed rebellion in the South with weapons and supplies. Since the elections promised at Geneva were never held, and negotiations would not be considered by Saigon and Washington, there seemed to be no choice but warfare to achieve its long-standing aim of national unity. Gradually 'moderate' nationalists in the South were driven to the same view. After 1960 the NLF's guerilla arm, the Vietcong, won increasing support as the only tool to rid South Vietnam of the corrupt American-backed régimes in Saigon.

American intervention

For convenience we can follow the story of American involvement in Vietnam under the successive Presidents who directed it.

Eisenhower, 1952-60

In 1952 Eisenhower inherited the commitment to aid the French war in Indo-China which Truman had undertaken in 1950 (see page 255). It was his Secretary of State, Dulles, who rescued South Vietnam from the French collapse of 1954 and steered it into the safe waters of American protection. You will recognize the Domino Theory (page 258) in this statement by the National Security Council in 1954: the Geneva Agreement had 'completed a major forward stride of Communism which might lead to the loss of South-East Asia'. Now it was essential to hold up the South Vietnam domino to prevent disaster in the whole area.

Along with economic aid, the first American advisers to the Saigon Government arrived in 1954: a self-styled 'Cold War combat team' which undertook various undercover measures in the South – and, incidentally, against the new-born state of North Vietnam. But they were not able to prevent the growing resistance to Diem's Government, and by the time Kennedy replaced Eisenhower in 1961, the membership of the NLF was reckoned at 15,000, of whom perhaps half were armed.

Kennedy, 1961–3

Kennedy's conduct of American foreign policy was a mixture of 'hard' and 'soft'. His speeches were 'hawkish', but privately he wanted to be more reasonable than Dulles, whose threats of 'massive retaliation' had scared many people stiff. Yet it was Kennedy who 'went to the brink' over Cuba, and who saw Vietnam as a similar trial of strength which America *must* win, or be disgraced. All later American policy there was based on this inflexible stand.

During Kennedy's three years in office, American advisers in Vietnam were increased from 800 to 17,000. His administration believed that China was behind the trouble in Vietnam, and that it could be countered by Chinese methods. After reading Mao and Che Guevara on guerilla warfare, JFK produced his own version: the so-called Green Berets or Special Forces, who were trained to 'melt into the countryside' and fight the enemy in his own style. But what use were guerillas from Texas in South Vietnam? They might wear jungle-coloured denims and learn unarmed combat – but the Green Berets missed the main point about guerilla warfare: its success depends on the support of the local people (as Study Topic 15 illustrates).

Another ineffective tactic was the 'strategic hamlets' policy begun in Kennedy's time. Here the idea was to 'separate the Vietcong from the people' by herding the peasants into fortified areas where they could not be terrorized into giving food and shelter to the night visitors. This and later efforts to pacify the countryside cruelly demoralized the peasants by separating them from their villages and fields; it also failed to keep the Vietcong (who were indistinguishable from 'real peasants') out of the safe areas, where they continued their work of subversion.

When JFK was killed in 1963 (two weeks after Diem's overthrow and death in Saigon), American advisers in South Vietnam estimated that about half the population supported the NLF. This was the depressing picture that Johnson faced when he suddenly found himself President.

Johnson, 1963–8

Johnson's administration was the period of

American escalation in Vietnam. He transformed it from a relatively quiet counter-insurgency campaign into a fierce war which led to a moral crisis in America as well as untold cruelty and hardship in Vietnam.

LBJ's anti-Communist strategy was 'the quick kill'. Like all his predecessors he believed it was America's rightful job to put down 'Communist threats' to 'democratic governments' anywhere in the world – and without enquiring too closely into the real rights and wrongs of the case. In 1965 he achieved a 'quick kill' in the Dominican Republic, where American marines were in and out almost before Congress and world opinion noticed. So why not in Vietnam? And why not strike at the head of the snake – North Vietnam – instead of flailing uselessly at its wriggling tail in the South?

This was the reasoning behind Operation Rolling Thunder, the first massive bombing of the North. The excuse was an alleged attack in August 1964 on American ships patrolling the North Vietnamese coast. After this, Congress passed – with only two dissenting votes – the Gulf of Tonkin Resolution giving their President a 'blank cheque' to do whatever was necessary to prosecute the war (Figure 25.3). With this power in his hands, Johnson began the 'carpet bombing' of the North (carried to greater extremes by Nixon), and steadily increased US ground troops in the South until by 1968 there were more than half a million. He also obtained token support from SEATO allies ('token' except for 50,000 South Korean troops) which made the Vietnam War look like a general commitment undertaken by the whole 'free world'.

The Tonkin Resolution was even more important than it seemed at the time. It later turned out (when in 1971 the *Pentagon Papers* were deliberately leaked to the *New York Times* by a former State Department official) that Johnson's Government had made plans to 'retaliate' against North Vietnam before the 'provocation' had even taken place, and that Congress was deliberately deceived about the supposed attack on American ships so that Johnson would get the free hand he

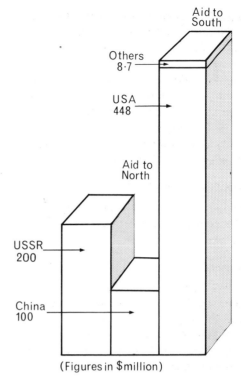

(Figures in $million)

Figure 25.3   Economic aid to Vietnam, 1967.

wanted. When Nixon later used Presidential powers even more freely, it led to a crisis within the American Government which ended with Congress tying the President's hands firmly behind his back.

Try, try, and try again

The White House *v.* Congress confrontation – and perhaps even the outcry in America to stop the war – might never have happened if Johnson's 'quick kill' strategy had worked. But it didn't. At first, however, the generals confidently predicted that each new tactic – or the *next* contingent of GIs* – would do the trick.

In the years after 1964 the full horror of American technological warfare broke upon Vietnam. Not only the North – inevitably including civilian areas – but South Vietnam was subjected to the heaviest bombing the world has ever seen. By 1969, over 70 tons of bombs for every square mile of Vietnam – that is, about 500 lb for every person in the

285

country! – had been dropped. At the same time the ground warfare of men and helicopters was stepped up with a variety of 'sure' techniques: 'free fire zones' (spaces in between the barbed-wire villages, where spare bombs could be dropped and napalm or bullets thrown at anything that moved); chemical defoliation of the countryside to deprive the Vietcong of cover; 'search and destroy' missions in which villagers suspected of aiding the guerillas were liable to be destroyed regardless of evidence against them. (The shocking massacre of more than 500 men, women and children by American troops at My Lai in March 1968 was one such mission.) Yet still the Vietcong crept through the countryside, and their supplies from the North came bumping down the Ho Chi Minh Trail through neighbouring Laos and Cambodia *on bicycles*! (Laos and Cambodia, officially 'neutral' since the Geneva Agreement of 1954, both had growing Communist movements of their own which allowed the passage of supplies to South Vietnam through areas they controlled – see map, Figure 25.4.)

The bravery and daring of the Vietcong and their peasant supporters was certainly one reason for the Americans' lack of success against them. But the GIs now had more than 'a bunch of Asian guerillas in black pyjamas' to defeat. The Vietcong forces in the South were strengthened by an increasing flow of regular troops from the North (an estimated 55,000 by 1967), and of Russian and Chinese aid. For both the Communist World Powers it was just as much a matter of principle to *prevent* an American victory in Vietnam as it was for the United States to achieve it. Sophisticated Soviet arms, in particular, were formidable:

> By 1968 the Russians were shipping some remarkable weapons to both the North Vietnamese Army and the Viet Cong: the superb AK–47 rifle, so effective for guerila combat; the SA–2 heat-seeking missiles that could destroy the high-flying B–52s; and the tiny missiles fired from hand-launchers which enabled a solitary Viet Cong to bring a US helicopter tumbling from the sky.†

Figure 25.4   The war in Vietnam.

In 1965 Washington had curtly dismissed Hanoi's offer to negotiate Four Points which rested on the provisions of the Geneva Agreement and the NLF's Ten-Point Programme. Johnson had decided on a military solution to the conflict, and for some years he continued to believe it would work. Then came the dramatic Tet offensive in January 1968 when the Vietcong surged into the cities of the South, holding the important city of Hué for two months and even, in a symbolic gesture, capturing the American Embassy in Saigon for a few hours. Despite this impressive display of Vietcong strength, General Westmoreland ('Waste-more-land', he was mockingly called by a hostile journalist) still insisted that 'the enemy was on the ropes' and

†Brian Catchpole, *A Map History of Russia* (Heinemann Educational Books, 1974) p. 96.

that 200,000 more GIs would finish him off. But some people in LBJ's government now began to doubt it, and (more decisively in the long run) so did millions of American citizens.

The effect of Vietnam in the United States

So far the American critics of her Vietnam policy had been a few voices in the wilderness. By the mid-1960s, however, several factors made Vietnam an important political issue: the growing number of American casualties (from 78 in 1963 to 14,500 in 1968); the horror of the war itself (relayed to the world on colour television); the draining of funds from LBJ's 1964 election pledge to build a Great Society in the USA; and the unpleasant racial overtones of the war in South-East Asia. Civil Rights protesters were quick to notice (and to exploit in their own campaigns) the fact that 'gooks' and 'dinks' could be slaughtered without a qualm in Vietnam because, as their own generals publicly stated, 'life is cheap for the Oriental'.

Thus the Vietnam War became part of a huge crisis of confidence in American society itself. Was there not something rotten in a nation which could lay waste 'a raggedy-ass little fourth-rate country' (as LBJ once described North Vietnam) just because it was

Communist? And whose government had so little concern for the future of 'free' South Vietnam that it too could be casually destroyed in the very process of 'saving' it? And whose soldiers (as one of them later confessed) could mow down women and children 'because like I said I lost buddies'?

At first the Vietnam objectors were mainly students, blacks or well-known 'Lefties' whose protest could be dismissed by the simple mental trick we saw at the time of McCarthyism: they were 'unpatriotic' or 'Communist' (which was really the same thing anyway). But gradually the anti-war movement (Figure 25.5) gathered 'respectable' support which Washington could not ignore:

> What finally altered American policy was not the protests of the intellectuals and the radicals, the growing opposition in Congress, the steady deterioration of relations with the news media, or the anxiety of the Allies. It was the revolt of the American Establishment, the university presidents, the lawyers, the bankers, the corporation heads who are the articulate élite of 'middle America'. By the spring of 1968 they were convinced that victory in Vietnam was not worth the immense social cost (300 American dead a week) and the immense financial drain ($30,000 million a year).†

†Alastair Buchan in *The Observer*, 28 January 1973.

Figure 25.5   A draft-card burning ceremony at a rally against the Vietnam War in Central Park, New York, April 1967.

It was more these pressures at home than the situation in Vietnam itself which made 1968 a turning point. In March Johnson called a partial halt to the bombing of the North and in May peace talks with North Vietnam began in Paris. Meanwhile LBJ, seeing the way the wind was blowing at home, had withdrawn from the Presidential election. In November Nixon became President with a vague promise to end the war.

Nixon, 1969–74

The special characteristic of Nixon's Vietnam War – as of his whole Presidency – was deceit. His problem was that it was now politically impossible to send any more American boys to Vietnam – but neither he nor Kissinger, his foreign policy adviser, could bear to lose Vietnam and thereby, as they saw it, destroy the credibility of America's whole foreign policy. To resolve this dilemma in Vietnam, they developed to a fine art that old political game: say one thing, do another.

Officially the policy was now Vietnamization: the re-arming and training of the South Vietnamese army to take over the war from American ground troops. The first contingent of GIs left for home in 1969... But meanwhile, efforts to win the war were stepped up. A further mountain of bombs was dropped on Vietnam (in the next two years, more than America's total tonnage in the Second World War); new methods of rooting out the Vietcong were applied in the South; and the 'quick kill' technique of in-and-out invasions (of Cambodia in 1970 and Laos in 1969 and 1971) tried to stop the flow of arms and men down the Ho Chi Minh Trail (see Figure 25.4). At the end of three years, 15,000 more Americans had been killed. The invasion of Cambodia and other acts of escalation had sparked off further angry protest in the United States; at one student demonstration four students were shot dead by the National Guard.

Yet by now, under the pressure of world opinion and strong public disapproval of the war in America, the peace talks in Paris were moving inexorably towards a negotiated settlement. As the 1972 Presidential election approached, Nixon had a double-edged task: how to be re-elected (for which he had to appear a peace-maker) while still saving the great United States from defeat by that 'little fourth-rate country'. In October, draft peace terms from Hanoi were agreed (but not signed); in November Nixon was re-elected; in December new, unacceptable conditions for signing were delivered to Hanoi, and when they were refused, a further terrible rain of bombs came down on North Vietnam. Thus Nixon showed that only a 'firm hand' forced Hanoi, in January 1973, to sign a Peace Agreement almost identical to their own offer of the previous October which Nixon had rejected.

'Peace with honour'

The 'peace' of 1973 was remarkably like the Geneva Agreement of 1954. It called for American withdrawal, the neutrality of Laos and Cambodia, and eventual reunification of Vietnam 'step by step through peaceful means'. But all parties knew that in reality, military action was bound to continue; both the Saigon Government and its enemies soon began to prepare for it. By now the strategy of Kissinger was to find a face-saving formula for American withdrawal (the 1973 peace terms) and then, after a 'decent interval', to accept regretfully the 'inevitable' collapse of the Saigon Government.

The year 1973 was one of triumphant victory parades in America for 'peace with honour' and the return of American prisoners of war. Meanwhile the world watched the cease-fire in Vietnam being openly violated by both sides.... In the next two years of 'peace', a further 100,000 people were killed in Vietnam and Cambodia (where an American-backed government installed in 1970 was fighting another losing battle against Communist forces).

In 1973 also, the American Congress began to re-assert its powers over the White House. Enraged by Johnson's and Nixon's deception and conduct of the war, Congress passed the War Powers Act, over Nixon's veto, limiting the President's power to make war without step-by-step Congressional approval. Then it tied his hands with purse strings: thereafter every request to Congress for money to aid Indo-China was severely cut or refused.

Ford, 1974–5

Nixon's behaviour over Vietnam was one factor in the spreading scandal of Watergate which forced him to resign in August 1974. When North Vietnamese troops and the Vietcong began their final assault in the spring of 1975, President Ford asked Congress in vain for money to help the failing régime of Saigon. Without American support, it collapsed like a popped balloon. The South Vietnamese army rapidly fell back and on 20 April 1975 Saigon was occupied and re-named Ho Chi Minh City. (Ho Chi Minh himself did not live to see this triumph; he had died in September 1969.) The NLF's Provisional Revolutionary Government, which had been waiting in the wings since 1969, now took over the administration of the southern zone of Vietnam.

Despite America's efforts to save her own face, the final days of 'free' South Vietnam were bitterly humiliating for her. In his speech of resignation, President Thieu said he had only agreed to the 1973 peace on Nixon's secret promise 'to respond with full force' if it was broken by the other side. In the open discussion of American policy which took place after Watergate, this secret promise was recognized as part of the Nixon–Kissinger 'decent interval' ploy: America's desperate effort to get herself off the hook regardless of the fate of her friends in South Vietnam. Kissinger, unlike Nixon, was still in office. Weakly he asked that there should be 'no recriminations' about Vietnam – to which an American commentator replied, 'That's like a burglar saying to the police when he's caught, "Hey, fellas, don't let's get into any arguments about who was in the wrong."'†

This remark seems a suitable point at which to end the story of American involvement in Vietnam.

†Richard Holbrooke, a former State Department official, then editor of the journal *Foreign Policy*, quoted in *The Sunday Times*, 4 May 1975.

This is not a complete account of Vietnam's history after 1954 – or even of America's contribution to it, which included many acts of generosity as well as destruction. For years the American war in Vietnam was hotly discussed in the West as a balance sheet of rights and wrongs – Vietcong atrocities to match GIs' brutality, Hanoi's stubbornness against Washington's blindness, and so on. We have avoided this catalogue to present the story as *a failure of American policy*. And there is no dispute about that! By the end of 1975 not only South Vietnam but Laos and Cambodia (where America had also intervened, though not on the scale of Vietnam) had Communist governments. Beyond this 'local' failure, America's world reputation was badly damaged. Vietnam was the classic lesson in how *not* to win friends and influence the world.

Finally, however, it is fair to point out that the strongest critics of American policy in Vietnam were Americans themselves. Not all were critical, even when the truth about massacres and Washington's deception came out. But in the words of Daniel Ellsberg (the man who leaked the *Pentagon Papers* to the press): 'It is a tribute to the American people that its government saw they had to be lied to, to carry on the war.'

Figure 25.6   An American cartoon of 1969.

Study Topic 15

Guerilla Warfare

The defeat of the Kuomintang in China, and of the French and then the Americans in Vietnam, all show the strength of guerilla warfare against larger and better-equipped 'conventional' forces. What is the secret of its success?

Guerilla warfare as a method of military and political struggle is not new in history. Spanish resisters against Napoleon's conquest of Spain in 1808 were the original *guerilleros* (little-war makers) who gave rise to the term, but the technique was used in the American revolutionary war of the 1770s and in other conflicts where natives fought foreign invaders unfamiliar with the terrain and hated by the local population. Local knowledge was the key weapon against superior arms and numbers.

In China and Vietnam guerilla warfare was the road to power for 'national liberation movements' which had a political as well as a military war to win. They had to recruit the local people to their cause as well as defeat 'the oppressors'. Both Mao Tse-tung and Ho Chi Minh understood this very well and trained their men to gain the confidence of the peasants wherever they went. Remember the Eight-Point Code of the Red Army in China in the 1930s? The Vietminh had a similar code in the Twelve Recommendations issued to them by Ho Chi Minh in April 1948. Although it belongs to the earlier period of the war against France, we include it here to illustrate the grass-roots approach which is the main strength of a successful national liberation movement anywhere.

Twelve recommendations†

Six Forbiddances

1. Not to do what is likely to damage the land

†Quoted in Felix Greene, *Vietnam! Vietnam!* (Penguin, 1967).

and crops or spoil the houses and belongings of the people.
2. Not to insist on buying or borrowing what the people are not willing to sell or lend.
3. Not to bring hens into mountainous people's houses.
4. Never to break our word.
5. Not to give offence to people's faith and customs (such as to lie down before the altar, to raise feet over the hearth, to play music in the house, etc.)
6. Not to do or speak what is likely to make people believe that we hold them in contempt.

Six permissibles

1. To help the people in their daily work (harvesting, fetching firewood, carrying wood, sewing, etc.)
2. Whenever possible to buy commodities from those who live from markets (knife, salt, needle, thread, paper, pen, etc.)
3. In spare time to tell amusing, simple, and short stories useful to the Resistance, but not to betray secrets.
4. To teach the people the national script and elementary hygiene.
5. To study the customs of each region so as to be acquainted with them in order to create an atmosphere of sympathy, then gradually to explain to the people to abate their superstitions.
6. To show to the people that you are correct, diligent, and disciplined.

*GLOSSARY

GIs, a slang term for ordinary soldiers in the US army which derives from the words 'Government Issue' stamped on their kit.

290

Questions

Did you notice?

1. Diem's régime was overthrown by (a) Buddhists (b) the Vietcong (c) army officers
2. The Ten-Point Programme was (a) the policy of the NLF (b) peace terms from Hanoi (c) America's plan of escalation
3. My Lai was the scene of (a) a Vietcong defeat (b) a massacre (c) 'carpet bombing'
4. Vietnamization of the war was a policy of (a) Nixon (b) Kennedy (c) Johnson
5. In 1975 President Ford wanted to (a) abandon the Saigon Government (b) make peace with Hanoi (c) send more aid to Saigon
6. True or false?
   (i) Members of the NLF were all Communists
   (ii) North Vietnam received aid from China
   (iii) LBJ expected a long-drawn-out war in Vietnam
   (iv) The Ho Chi Minh Trail went through Laos
   (v) Saigon changed its name in 1975
7. Which statement is *more* accurate?
   (i) The US Air Force bombed North Vietnam
      (a) to stop the flow of supplies to the South
      (b) to liberate North Vietnam from Communism
   (ii) The Green Berets were not very successful mainly because
      (a) they were not well trained
      (b) they were not Vietnamese
   (iii) The *Pentagon Papers* revealed that
      (a) LBJ's Government had misinformed Congress
      (b) American ships were not in the Gulf of Tonkin

Can you explain?

8. In what way did the United States 'misjudge the nature of the opposition' in Indo-China?
9. One of Sun Yat-sen's Three People's Principles in China was 'Nationalism: to expel foreign influence and unite the country'. How did the NLF's Ten-Point Programme show similar nationalist aims?
10. It could be said that the American bombing of North Vietnam in the 1960s was a logical development of the policy she had maintained for the previous twenty years. See if you can follow the thread of American policy along this path, briefly explaining each step on the way:

    | 1947 | The Truman Doctrine |
    | 1950 | NSC 68 |
    | | The 38th Parallel |
    | 1954 | The Geneva Agreement |
    | | The Domino Theory |
    | 1960 | The NLF |
    | 1965 | The Ho Chi Minh Trail |
    | | The bombing of North Vietnam |

11. In what way did (a) Johnson, and (b) Nixon, deceive Congress and the American people about the Vietnam War? How did Congress show its displeasure in 1973 and afterwards?

What's your view?

12. During the Vietnam War some young Americans burned their draft cards (call-up papers) as a form of protest. This meant that others had to go to Vietnam in their place. Were the protesters right to burn their draft cards?
13. In the 1970s the American Government was urged to grant an amnesty (that is, a free pardon) to 'draft dodgers' who had taken refuge abroad during the Vietnam War. Do you think their 'crime' should have been forgiven after the war? What difficulties might this present for the American Government?
14. Anti-Vietnam protesters in Britain frequently asked the British Government to dissociate itself publicly from American policy in Vietnam. Why do you think the British Government did not do this? Should it have done so?

From Cold War to Détente

In 1950 the World Powers were lined up in a simple 'two against one' confrontation: America *v.* Russia and China. By 1975 there was a serious split between the two Communist powers, while a measure of *détente* had been achieved between America and each of them. In 1983 the scene had shifted again: Russia and America were into a new Cold War, while Russia and China were cautiously trying to mend their rift. An attempt to represent these changes in diagram form might look like this:

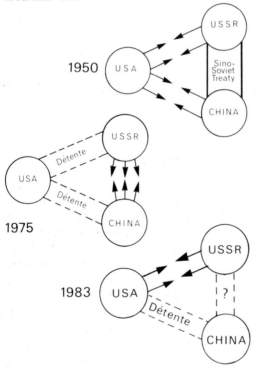

Figure 26.1 Shifting relations of the World Powers, 1950–83.

This chapter and the next deal with three overlapping topics: the Sino–Soviet Split, East–West *Détente*, and the New Cold War between the USA and the USSR. For the sake of clarity, and to keep the story roughly chronological, the Sino–Soviet Split and East–West *Détente* are treated as separate topics here, while the New Cold War needs a chapter to itself. But of course all these developments influenced each other: no state likes being the 'one' in a 'two against one' situation, and when the opportunity arose they all exploited differences between the other two. To follow this series of manoeuvres you will need to recall the internal history of each country, and the earlier chapters in this Part of the book. Use the chart on the inside front cover for a quick reminder when necessary.

THE SINO–SOVIET SPLIT

In retrospect we can see that the Sino–Soviet Treaty of 1950 was more a marriage of convenience than a love-match. Even the shared Marxist ideology of the alliance was soon a cause of friction within it. There were also historical causes of tension between China and Russia which were set aside for the wedding–but not forgotten.

Disputes over territory

During periods of weakness in her history, China frequently came under pressure from her strong northern neighbour. Sizeable areas were signed away to Tsarist Russia by unequal treaties during the nineteenth century, and Mongolia broke away to become a Soviet satellite in 1921 (Figure 26.2). China does not lay claim to these regions today, but she has often asked for negotiations to draw exact frontiers in certain border areas. In 1921 Lenin pledged the new Soviet Government to do this, but the promise has never been carried out.

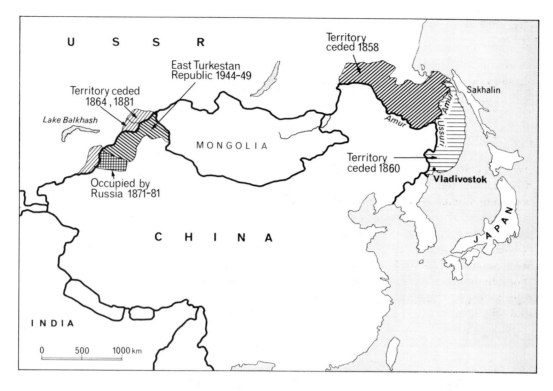

Figure 26.2 The China–Russia border. In the nineteenth century Russia absorbed large areas of nominal Chinese territory, while in border areas the two powers have competed for economic influence.

Figure 26.3 The Sino–Soviet 'honeymoon': Khrushchev with Mao during a visit to Peking.

Stalin and the CCP

You will remember from Part III on China that the Soviet Union did little to assist the CCP into power. The Comintern's 'help' in the 1930s was nearly disastrous, and in 1945 Stalin was more concerned to secure Soviet interests in China than to help Mao defeat the KMT. But these differences were forgotten in the glow of the CCP's victory in 1949. Both states felt menaced by Western hostility in the early 1950s, and took comfort from their own friendship. Nevertheless, Stalin did not carry out his promise to give up Russian rights in Manchuria; it took a further agreement with Khrushchev in 1955 before they were finally surrendered.

The years 1953–6, after Stalin's death, were the honeymoon of Sino–Soviet friendship (Figure 26.3). But like other honeymoons, this one was soon over.

The split over global policy

Whatever resentment and irritation there had been in earlier periods, the real break between China and the USSR occurred in the years 1956–9 over global policy. Once the quarrel had begun, old grievances and new ones fed the flames.

Khrushchev's new policies

At the Twentieth Congress of the Soviet Communist Party in 1956, in addition to de-Stalinization Khrushchev put forward important new foreign policies: Peaceful Co-existence and the idea of 'different roads to Socialism'. In the nuclear age, said Khrushchev, a major war was impossible. To fit the new historical circumstances, the Marxist idea of continuous conflict between Socialism and Capitalism must be adjusted. This was a change of methods, not aims: the USSR would now set out to 'prove' the superiority of Socialism by providing a standard of living equal to the West's.

Elsewhere, the road to power for Communist parties need not be the classic Marxist route of revolution and civil war. Large Communist parties in Italy or France, for example, might achieve power by a 'parliamentary road'. In the Third World, wars of national liberation should not be encouraged to the point of provoking a world conflict.

China's reaction

As you know, Mao took his Marxism very seriously. Though critical of Stalin's 'mistakes', he disliked the abrupt way in which Khrushchev had de-throned him, encouraging revolt in the Socialist camp (Poland and Hungary), and jubilation in the Capitalist camp. Stalin was, after all, a great Socialist leader; who was this upstart Khrushchev to dismiss so lightly his contribution?

Even more important was Khrushchev's revision of Marxism–Leninism. Lenin had said that there could be no peaceful coexistence while Imperialist–Capitalist oppres-

sion existed – yet now the advanced Communist countries (the Soviet bloc) were ready to abandon their millions of comrades still struggling to free themselves. What other hope for liberation existed in the Third World, except the proven method of revolutionary war?

At a Congress of Communist parties in Moscow in 1957, a compromise declaration took account of both the 'parliamentary' and the 'revolutionary' road to power. At this Congress Mao's famous phrases 'US imperialism is a paper tiger' and 'the East wind is prevailing over the West wind' were a salute to the strength of the Communist world which had just been demonstrated by the Soviet Sputnik. Mao thought that the Soviet Union should use its vast strength for hard bargaining with the West to benefit the whole Socialist camp, but just at the moment when Mao called for a tough line, Khrushchev was embarking on a softer line in pursuit of Peaceful Coexistence with the United States. Moreover he was mainly interested in matters of Soviet concern (Berlin, for instance) and was not going to upset Washington by making claims on behalf of America's arch-enemy, China.

It was inevitable that as Soviet–American relations became friendlier, Sino–Soviet friendship rapidly cooled. This can be seen happening in events touched upon briefly in Chapter 24:

1958   In July, the United States and Britain sent troops to the Middle East to prop up right-wing régimes there. China said that if the aggressors would not withdraw, they should be 'hit on the head'. But Russia reacted calmly.

In August, China began to shell some off-shore islands still occupied by the KMT. The USA growled its continued support for the KMT, but the USSR made clear it would not support this 'adventurism' of its Chinese ally. Without Russian backing, the bombardment ceased.

1959   In June the USSR cancelled its agreement to help China develop nuclear weapons, apparently as a peace offering to the USA before Khrushchev's forthcoming visit. China was highly suspicious of this meeting of the super-powers, especially when she found that Taiwan was not on their agenda.

1960 In May the U-2 incident 'proved' that the USA could not be trusted. Khrushchev made a show of indignation but in Mao's opinion he should have exploited the incident further to win concessions from the USA. In June the Sino–Soviet relationship was further weakened by the sudden withdrawal of Soviet aid and personnel from China, causing great economic hardship there.

This last event was the Sino–Soviet 'divorce'. Thereafter the two Communist powers loudly criticized each other's policies on every possible occasion. At meetings with Western statesmen Khrushchev dropped hints about his troublesome ally to make clear the contrast between 'fanatical' China and the 'reasonable' attitude of the Soviet Union.

This view of China suited Russia *and* America – for naturally Washington was glad to widen the split between her enemies. And 'What better way . . . than to show willingness to talk meaningfully with Moscow but not with Peking?'† While Americans were ready to talk over Soviet–American differences, Washington maintained a stony silence towards Peking.

Revisionism *v.* dogmatism

By the early 1960s China felt increasingly isolated and fearful. But there was little she could do except *argue*. In 1963 Mao Tse-tung initiated an exchange of open letters between the Chinese and Soviet Communist parties which exposed their quarrel to the world. This was bound to bring comfort and joy to the Capitalist camp (which it did), but Mao

†John Gittings, *The World and China, 1922–1972* (Eyre Methuen, 1974) p. 201.

now believed that the whole future of Communism was at stake. The world must know (and especially the Communist world must know) that the Soviet Union was selling out!

From the CCP–CPSU letters, and statements by Russian and Chinese leaders, we can construct a summary of their argument. In Marxist language, China charged the USSR with *revisionism*, i.e. revising the hallowed doctrine of Marxism–Leninism, while the USSR accused China of *dogmatism*, i.e. sticking rigidly to Marxist–Leninist dogma without taking account of changing historical circumstances.

1. China's point of view

(a) A new ruling class in Soviet society The 'revisionist Khrushchev clique' denies the continuing class struggle during the period of transition towards Communism and 'is spreading the tale that there are no longer antagonistic classes and class struggle in the Soviet Union'. On the contrary, a 'privileged stratum' has developed there, which lives 'the parasitical and decadent life of the bourgeoisie', dominating the masses instead of serving them. By promoting material incentives they are 'turning all human relations into money relations and encouraging individualism and selfishness'.

(b) Foreign policy To achieve world-wide Communism is *still* the first duty of a true Marxist – and the Third World is the area for urgent attention, where revolutionary war is the proven route. Chairman Mao has always said that 'revolution cannot be exported', but Marxists must *support* national liberation movements when they spring up. China is now the natural leader of these movements in the Third World, for the 'corrupting influence of material progress' has seduced the Russian and European Communist parties away from their Marxist duty. Those 'traitors' think the oppressed peoples and nations of the world must now 'serve the private interests of the Khrushchev clique' and not disturb its 'sweet dream of partner-

ship with imperialism for the division of the world'.

2. Russia's point of view

(a) The state of Soviet society Khrushchev said that the USSR was now 'a state of the whole society' where everyone shares equally in the practice of democracy and material progress. China's 'leaps forward' were a rash and misguided attempt to 'skip historical stages' in the achievement of Communism. The USSR has shown the correct path by developing modern technology and schemes of 'Socialist competition' to increase production. Only when material abundance is achieved can Socialism merge into Communism and each man be rewarded 'according to his need'.

Khrushchev mocked Mao's emphasis on equality as the first principle of Communism. 'It transpires that if a people walks in rope sandals and eats watery soup out of a common bowl, that is Communism, and if a working man lives well and wants to live even better tomorrow, that is almost tantamount to the restoration of Capitalism.'

(b) Foreign policy Khrushchev condemned Mao's 'adventurism' towards the West as far too risky. 'As for US imperialism being "a paper tiger", those who used the phrase knew quite well that it was equipped with atomic teeth.'

Under Khrushchev and later Brezhnev the USSR moved slowly towards *détente* with the West. In competition with China for the leadership of world Communism, she was always ready to aid national liberation movements (for example in Vietnam), and in her power struggle with the USA also tried to win friends through aid to non-Communist governments (for example, Egypt) – but never to the point of direct confrontation with the US. As we saw in Chapter 24, this was one of the rules established during the Soviet–American 'chess game' of the 1950s and '60s.

In the revisionism *v.* dogmatism argument you will recognize some of the issues of China's internal split in the 1960s, the Cultural Revolution. You may remember that the Rightists, fearful of the escalating war in Vietnam, wanted to make up the quarrel with the USSR, whereas the Maoists said that China must stick to the 'Socialist road', and be ready to travel alone if necessary. After three years of 'struggle' the Maoists won the argument, and in foreign policy this made the USSR China's Enemy No. 1.

In the international Communist movement the Maoist point of view was not so successful. About 65 out of 86 national Communist parties took Russia's side in the Sino–Soviet dispute; in many cases a Maoist fragment broke away to form a separate party.

Border incidents

Sino–Soviet relations steadily deteriorated during the 1960s. In 1964 there had been border clashes on the Sinkiang frontier, and in 1969 more serious fighting broke out on the Ussuri River frontier between Manchuria and the USSR. In parallel with their own quarrel the two states supported opposite sides in other conflicts – notably on the Indian subcontinent, where China, itself disputing border areas with India, lined up with the 'reactionary' Moslem government of Pakistan while the USSR supported and armed India. All these developments seemed to suggest that Sino–Soviet hostility really had little to do with 'revisionism' and 'dogmatism'. Wasn't it just the normal rivalry of two powerful neighbours whose long common frontier had often caused trouble in the past?

While Mao lived, ideology was central to domestic *and* foreign policy: Chinese border guards on the Ussuri river shook *Little Red Books* as well as guns at the Russians on the other side! But after those heady days of the Cultural Revolution it was the revival of age-old differences and mutual fear that kept Sino–Soviet relations cool, even into a period when China had become more 'revisionist' than the USSR had ever been.

In regard to America, China naturally did not enjoy the uncomfortable 'freeze' imposed on her by American policy in the 1950s; she had waited patiently to be recognized as a power with legitimate world interests, especially in South-East Asia. As soon as America, for her own reasons, seemed ready to 'normalize' her relations with China, Peking diplomats eagerly stepped forward.

This leads us to Phase 2 of the slowly changing relationship of the three World Powers.

EAST–WEST DÉTENTE

In French there is one word–*détente*–to mean 'a relaxation of tension between states', so we all use it to describe the lessening of East–West hostility which developed in the 1970s. The outward signs of this were several much-publicized journeys by the World Powers' leaders: Nixon to Peking and then Moscow in 1972, Brezhnev to the USA in 1973, Nixon again to Moscow in 1974 (Figure 26.4) and Ford to Peking in 1975. Deng Xiaoping visited the USA in 1979, and further summit exchanges between America and China are scheduled for 1984.

Figure 26.4   Sweet talk: Nixon and Brezhnev meet in Russia, June 1974.

To continue where we left off, let us take Sino–American relations first before we consider the briefer period of Soviet–American *détente*.

The United States and China

At one level, the first American moves towards Peking were part of the Nixon–Kissinger strategy to defeat North Vietnam, which for many years had been sustained by aid from China and the USSR. 'If Communist China and the Soviet Union should clash, for whatever reason, Hanoi would be finished ...' said Kissinger hopefully in 1970.† If that didn't work, a rapprochement with China would at least divert attention from America's humiliating defeat in Indo-China.

Step one towards the normalization of US–China relations was their 'ping-pong diplomacy' of 1971 when, in response to hints from Washington, Peking invited an American table-tennis team to visit China. This led to Nixon's visit to Peking in February 1972, which in turn led to the easing of trade and diplomatic restraints between the two countries.

Equally important was the decision by the United Nations in October 1971 to allow Peking to take China's seat in the Organization, which had been occupied by the KMT government since the UN's formation in 1945. The United States had refused to give even diplomatic recognition to the Communist Government, and in the UN had always rounded up enough votes to prevent the admission of 'Red China' (Figure 26.5). Even now the Americans did not want to see the Nationalist Government in Taiwan expelled: they hoped for a compromise whereby 'two Chinas' could be represented at the UN. But this was not accepted, and the delegates from Taiwan therefore had to withdraw (this is the only case of expulsion from the UN).

The long overdue admission of China to the UN showed that many uncommitted

†Quoted in D. Landau, *Kissinger–The Uses of Power* (Robson Books, 1974), p. 212.

297

nations were no longer willing to follow the American lead automatically. China, 'respectable' at last, began to develop trade links with Japan and the West, and to welcome foreign visitors. The 'modernizing faction' in the CCP, who would later take power after Mao's death, were keen to import Western technology and waited impatiently for full 'normalization' with the USA to open the American supermarket to Chinese buyers.

On the American side, Kissinger's tactics did not 'finish Hanoi', as we know: China and Russia continued to aid North Vietnam until its final victory in 1975. But the opening to China allowed Kissinger to pursue a more

Figure 26.5 'Mao's regime does not represent the Chinese people'–a banner in New York's Chinatown. Not all Americans welcomed the admission of 'Red China' to the UN in 1971.

flexible and devious global policy, where the central aim was now to achieve *détente* with the USSR–but without conceding too much to the Russian bear. Hand-shakes between Mao and Nixon in Peking, a few months before Nixon's first visit to Moscow in May 1972, were a clear signal to Brezhnev that *détente* was now a *three*-handed game.

By 1975 Washington had achieved *détente* with Moscow, which we shall presently describe. But the warm-up with China was still hopelessly hooked on the question of Taiwan. America had abandoned the 'two Chinas' idea but continued to sell arms to her old ally the KMT, while China insisted that American support must be withdrawn and would not rule out the use of force to recover her long-lost island if a peaceful solution could not eventually achieve that aim. On a visit to Peking in 1975 President Ford and Kissinger still could not resolve the issue. Carter took over in Washington and Deng Xiaoping in Peking, but there the matter rested...

Suddenly both sides reached agreement, and full diplomatic relations between the USA and China were resumed in January 1979. Deng Xiaoping at once made a friendly visit to the United States, and American businessmen, like their predecessors in the nineteenth century, eagerly tripped off to China to get a foot in the vast market of the mainland. Liberal opinion in the United States was equally pleased to think that China would be 'liberalized' through the contacts of trade and tourism.

The US–China agreement of 1978 merely shelved the question of Taiwan with a vague compromise statement which led to further arguments later. Under the Reagan administration after 1980, the Sino–American friendship repeatedly trembled over the issue of arms sales to the KMT, while the problem of when and how Peking would reassert her acknowledged right of sovereignty over the island remained unsolved. So too did the future of Hong Kong after 1997, when Britain's 99-year lease of the colony runs out (the subject of Sino–British talks during

1983).† Peking will not jeopardize her new ties with the West–or Hong Kong's economic prosperity, from which the mainland also benefits–by 'getting tough' about either of these territories, but neither will she ever renounce her legal *right* to rule them, or the long-term aim to reabsorb them into China.

Since they had not solved the Taiwan issue, it is clear that the *real* reason for the sudden breakthrough in Sino–American negotiations during 1978 was their shared hostility to the third World Power: it was now in both their interests to look like a 'united opposition' against the growing power and influence of the Soviet Union. For China, apart

†The future of the tiny Portuguese colony of Macao is also tied to the fate of Hong Kong. In 1977 a new government in Portugal offered to return it to China, but the offer was refused for fear of panicking Western business interests in Hong Kong!

from the Soviet forces massed on her borders since the 1960s, the threat was most obvious in adjacent Indo-China. Despite the end of direct American intervention there in 1973, Indo-China remained helplessly entangled in super-power politics.

China and Vietnam

China's aid to North Vietnam during its long anti-Western struggle was another case of self-interest (plus Communist solidarity) overcoming an even longer history of suspicion and dislike between these two neighbours. China was determined to preserve the North, at least, as a buffer against hostile Western powers, as her intervention in the Korean war had preserved a Communist buffer on that border of China. At the approach of North Vietnam's victory, however, Peking

Figure 26.6 Refugees from Vietnam arriving in Hong Kong after seventy days' journey in small fishing boats.

feared that a strong and united Vietnam would soon dominate the whole peninsula, and therefore tried to ensure a pro-China counterweight to Vietnamese influence in next-door Cambodia (now Kampuchea). This manoeuvre was foiled by American intervention in the area in the last stages of her Vietnam war, but China supported the Pol Pot Communist régime which came to power in Kampuchea in 1975, purely for its anti-Vietnam stand.

After 1975 China's relations with Vietnam deteriorated over several issues. The Communization of South Vietnam caused a mass exodus of refugees (many of them ethnic Chinese) across the border into China or as 'boat people' (Figure 26.6) to Hong Kong and elsewhere, while China and Vietnam also disputed the ownership of several islands and sea areas of potential interest for oil exploitation. Vietnam soon exerted her influence over the new Communist government of Laos, and in 1978 invaded Kampuchea to replace the anti-Hanoi Pol Pot government with another pro-Hanoi one.† Worst of all, in 1978 Vietnam signed a Treaty of Friendship with the USSR and thus became a Soviet 'pawn' as irritating to China as the Soviet 'pawn' of Cuba is to the United States.‡

During his visit to America in 1979 Deng Xiaoping talked about 'teaching Vietnam a lesson' and when he got home the lesson was duly delivered with a short-lived Chinese

---

†Few people regretted Vietnam's overthrow of the brutal Pol Pot régime, which killed an estimated 3 million of its own people in its short period of rule. But Peking, in a display of naked self-interest, continued to uphold Pol Pot's claim to be the legal government of Kampuchea. In 1983 the factional war still continued, and as usual the saddest victims were the thousands of refugees camped on the border of Kampuchea and Thailand.

‡It is worth a sideways glance to explain Vietnam's situation at that time. Before surrendering her 'independence' to the USSR she had hoped to use Western aid, and reparations from the United States, to rebuild her shattered economy. But in 1978 the USA broke off discussions to facilitate Western aid to Vietnam, apparently as a concession to Peking in their normalization negotiations. Vietnam was thus forced into the Soviet embrace in the same way that Cuba had become a client of Soviet aid, and then the unwilling site of the missile crisis, in the 1960s–see page 265.

invasion of Vietnam, in which Chinese troops fared badly against the experienced Soviet-armed Vietnamese army. In the same fateful year of 1979, the Soviet Union invaded its neighbour to the south, Afghanistan. This event naturally alarmed China, the USSR's south-eastern neighbour, and made her more anxious to cling to her new American friend despite the 'little differences' between them.

But the Soviet invasion of Afghanistan was even more significant in the collapse of *détente* between the USA and the USSR. We must now go back a few years to plot the course of events in that relationship.

The United States and the Soviet Union

The starting-point here is the gradual improvement in Soviet–American relations, and between East and West Europe, in the late 1960s (see page 267). The Cuba missile crisis had forced both super-powers to recognize the brake of nuclear weapons on their policies towards each other, while the *Ostpolitik* of West Germany had acknowledged the existence of 'two Germanys' and the 'new Poland' (which incorporated areas of pre-war Germany–see page 233). All this was confirmed by East–West treaties signed in the early 1970s, which cleared the way for trade and other links across the Iron Curtain to develop.

By 1975 Soviet–American *détente* could be summarized as follows:

1. A series of *nuclear agreements* now restricted the testing of nuclear weapons, tried to prevent their spread, and had begun to limit their future development (see page 276). Arms control was still at a very early stage, but in 1973 Nixon and Brezhnev had signed an Agreement on the Prevention of Nuclear War, accompanied by a joint pledge to 'turn the development of friendship and co-operation between their peoples into a permanent factor for world-wide peace.'

2. Alongside *détente* in the vital nuclear area, a number of *trade agreements* established mutually beneficial commerce

(notably to guarantee sales of surplus American grain to the USSR), while *technical co-operation* was developed in many fields of shared interest, from space exploration to cancer research.

3. *Recognition of frontiers* was achieved at the European Security Conference in Helsinki, Finland, in 1975. In carefully-chosen general phrases the Final Act, signed by all the European states except Albania,† together with the USA, Canada and the USSR, recognized the permanence of post-war European frontiers. In effect this was the long overdue peace settlement of the Second World War.

In return the West extracted from the Soviet bloc nations a formal promise to guarantee free East–West contacts and to 'respect human rights and fundamental freedoms'. Dissident groups behind the Iron Curtain saw this as a chance to win greater personal liberty from their Marxist rulers; committees were set up in the USSR and several Eastern bloc states to press their governments to adhere to 'Basket Three' (as it was called) of the Helsinki accords.

Apart from these specific agreements, the 'rules' of *détente* were not written down anywhere. But statesmen on both sides spoke of creating a 'web of relationships' which would bind them together–not in friendship, exactly, but in that 'peaceful coexistence' which had been so much talked about for the past twenty years. Both governments welcomed the chance to limit their huge arms spending, while both their populations were apparently ready to give up their nation's world mission–Russia's to turn the whole world Communist, and America's to prevent it.

For a few years in the mid-1970s–only a pause in historical terms–the awful prospect of a nuclear holocaust had receded into the background and East–West relations seemed less important than other deep-rooted international problems like the North–South divide: the ever-widening gap between the rich, developed countries and the poverty-stricken Third World. But all too soon, these issues were again overshadowed by the global struggle for supremacy between the nuclear super-powers, the United States and the Soviet Union.

---

†Albania at that time was the 'voice of China' in Europe. China was bitterly opposed to *détente*, and castigated the USA and Western Europe for this policy. By making the USSR 'safe' in the West, *détente* freed Moscow to be more aggressive in the East, and of course the Soviet–American partnership also threatened China's not yet 'normalized' relations with America.

Questions

Did you notice?

1. The Sino–Soviet 'divorce' was marked by (a) the withdrawal of Soviet aid (b) the U-2 incident (c) better relations between China and the USA
2. In the Sino–Soviet quarrel, dogmatism meant (a) developing a privileged élite (b) exporting revolution (c) sticking to Marxist principles
3. The Helsinki conference in 1975 was mainly concerned with (a) nuclear weapons (b) European frontiers (c) Taiwan
4. Who went to Peking in 1975? (a) Ford (b) Brezhnev (c) Nixon
5. 'Red China' was admitted to the UN in 1971 because (a) America now recognized the Peking government (b) a majority of UN members wanted it (c) the KMT had lost American support
6. True or false?
   (i) Russia lost territory to China by 'unequal treaties'
   (ii) Mao thought Khrushchev had encouraged revolt in East Europe
   (iii) China and Vietnam signed a Treaty of Friendship in 1978
   (iv) China invaded Kampuchea in 1979
   (v) West Germany's *Ostpolitik* paved the way for *détente* in Europe
7. Which statement is *more* accurate?
   (i) Mao disapproved of de-throning Stalin because
      (a) Stalin was a great Socialist leader
      (b) Khrushchev's accusations against him were untrue
   (ii) Khrushchev thought Mao's attitude towards the West was reckless because
      (a) the 'Socialist camp' was not strong enough yet
      (b) 'the paper tiger had atomic teeth'
   (iii) In 1979 the USA and China normalized their relations because
      (a) they had settled all their differences
      (b) they feared Soviet strength

Can you explain?

8. What is the origin of border disputes between the USSR and China?
9. After 1956 the USSR was hoping to establish Peaceful Coexistence with the USA.
   (a) Why did Khrushchev embark on this policy?
   (b) What was China's attitude towards this development?
10. Following up the references to Taiwan in this chapter,
   (a) Why did China cease bombarding the offshore islands in 1958?
   (b) Why was the KMT delegation expelled from the UN in 1971?
   (c) Why was Taiwan still a cause of dispute between Peking and Washington after 1979?
11. How and why did China's relations with Vietnam change after 1975?
12. What were the main features of US–Soviet *détente* in regard to
   (a) nuclear weapons?
   (b) post-war European frontiers?

What's your view?

13. In 1946 Mao Tse-tung called the Atom bomb 'a paper tiger' and he later said the same thing about 'US imperialism'. What do you think he meant? Do you agree with him?
14. Some people think that in the long run, the North–South divide between rich and poor countries is more dangerous to world peace and stability than East–West relations. Do you agree?
15. Do you think that the Helsinki agreements of 1975 – in effect, a 'permanent' Iron Curtain in exchange for 'Basket Three' – was a fair bargain for both East and West?

The New Cold War

Undoubtedly the Soviet Union had a bigger stake in *détente* than the United States. We saw in Chapter 13 that the Soviet Government had great difficulty in providing both guns *and* butter,† whereas America, at a pinch, could afford both. Soviet citizens (who are not much interested in world affairs anyway) readily accepted their government's explanation that *détente* with the arch-Capitalist USA was not a *failure* but a demonstration of their own nation's new-found strength. Americans, on the other hand, although suffering from 'the Vietnam syndrome' in the mid-1970s (a reluctance to get involved in anything like *that* again), have become accustomed to being an imperial power‡–they would prefer the phrase 'a nation with global interests'–and are sensitized to any threats to American influence abroad by ample news coverage of world events, especially at election times. And their opinion, when shouted loud enough and expressed at the ballot-box, *does* have an effect on the policies of their government.

The changing national mood in America in the late 1970s (see Chapter 7) certainly weakened Washington's commitment to

---

†This phrase derives from the 1930s, when Nazi Germany embarked on a rearmament programme of 'guns, not butter'.

‡By the early 1970s '. . . America had established an empire of its own. It had military commitments to 47 nations; 375 major bases and 3,000 minor facilities in foreign lands; 1 million troops stationed abroad; 2.5 million more troops under arms at home. It had spent more than $1 trillion for its own military programs and $150 billion for foreign aid. American business also controlled more than half of all direct foreign private investment, produced more than half the world's manufactured products, and consumed a disproportionate quantity of the world's raw materials.' John M. Blum and others, *The National Experience*, Part 2, 5th ed. (Harcourt Brace Jovanovich, 1981), p. 848.

détente. But how did we come to be caught up, just a few years later, in another crusade against that 'evil empire' centred in Moscow?

As we pointed out in Chapter 22, it is difficult to analyse the causes of a Cold War while it's actually happening, especially when you are embedded in one side of the conflict (as all Britons are). Were the actions and attitudes of Western statesmen a *reaction* to new transgressions by the USSR (as they claim)–or did the West, in reverting to a 'Cold War mentality', simply interpret every Soviet move to fit into it? Without access to the records of meetings in the Kremlin, we can only report that sometime around 1976, the West's *perception* of the Soviet Union began to shift, from that of a strong power whose understandable fears about its own security deserved recognition, to one of a ruthless, expansionist empire causing 'trouble' all over the globe.

Adapting the method we used to describe the first Cold War, we shall first try to explain, in simplified form, the general 'view' of each of the super-powers, and then see how they applied to particular issues and events.

The original source of misunderstanding was the different interpretations of *détente* in Washington and Moscow.

What were the rules of *détente*?

1. *The Soviet view*

The Soviet leaders saw *détente* as a matter of practical state-to-state relations which allowed both sides to pursue their own interests by the 'rules' they thought were established in the late 1960s and early '70s. There would be no meddling in each other's internal affairs, nor in their respective spheres of influence, but 'ideological competition' would continue in the no man's land of Africa, Asia and the Middle East. Wasn't that the message of Czechoslovakia in 1968, of Chile in 1970–3–and even of Vietnam, where the USA and USSR continued to aid their client states even as Nixon and Brezhnev signed the first SALT agreement?

The USSR was a powerful state–as the West had now acknowledged–but she had not yet achieved the global stature enjoyed by the United States, and which the USSR also deserved. Accordingly the USSR would continue to develop her conventional arms and 'Salt free' nuclear weapons, increase her fleet of long-range aircraft and expand her navy from a coastal defence force to a world-wide Red Navy which could exercise 'gunboat diplomacy' as the US Navy already could (and just as the British Navy did in the days when Britannia ruled the waves). By the late 1970s the USSR was approaching *overall* military parity with the USA, not just in nuclear weapons, and now had the global 'reach' Moscow wanted.

Increased military strength would be useful in spreading Soviet influence in the uncommitted world through assistance to 'national liberation struggles' and by selling arms to all willing buyers.† Moreover the USSR must keep up its guard in the East (where Peking was still bitterly anti-Soviet, even after the death of Mao); in the West (where NATO's strength could not be ignored, and grumbling East Europeans were unreliable); and above all on its sensitive southern flank, where the new force of Moslem fundamentalism threatened unpredictable dangers, while the Arab–Israeli conflict got steadily worse and worse...

† Of course the arms trade was nothing new: for many years weapons had been an important export for the USSR and other technically advanced states. Today the Third World spends about $103 billion per year on arms, of which 70 per cent are supplied by the USA and USSR, 10 per cent by France and 4 per cent by Britain.

2. The American view

For most Americans the real pay-off for *détente* was the chance it offered to liberalize the repressive Soviet system. In the language of the earlier Cold War, they had given up hope of 'rolling back' Communism, and had realized that it couldn't even be 'contained' in certain areas, but there was new hope that it would 'crumble from within' since the Soviet bloc states had promised at the Helsinki conference to increase personal freedoms for their citizens. It might also be possible to bargain with Moscow on this issue: in 1974 the US Congress amended a Soviet–American trade treaty to make it conditional on the guarantee of a certain number of exit permits for Soviet Jews (but this so affronted Moscow's pride that Brezhnev indignantly cancelled the treaty).

Washington had originally seen military *détente* as conditional on 'responsible behaviour' by Moscow in other areas. This was the Nixon–Kissinger concept of 'linkage', neatly stated by Nixon in a letter to his Cabinet in 1969: he would not proceed with arms talks unless Soviet leaders were 'brought to understand that they cannot expect to reap the benefits of cooperation in one area while seeking to take advantage of tension or confrontation elsewhere'.

Presumably believing that they *were* ready to 'show restraint' in the world, in 1972 Nixon signed SALT I and Washington committed itself to *détente* ... But not for long! While ready to concede a 'rough equivalence' in *nuclear* arms, American military chiefs soon became alarmed by the Soviet build-up of other weaponry 'under the cover of *détente*'. What could they possibly need it for? A senior American general had no doubts: 'The Russians are going for superiority. They want to dominate, to get a war-winning capability.'‡

So it seemed that the West had 'given something for nothing' with SALT agree-

‡ This unnamed military spokesman was quoted by Kim Willenson and Lloyd H. Norman, 'Is America No. 2?', *Newsweek* magazine, 1 March 1976.

ments, Helsinki declarations, and all those trade treaties. Moscow was just using the East–West truce to further its aim of world domination, and *possibly* to prepare for World War Three . . .

NEW SOURCES OF CONFLICT

Human rights

President Carter's 'absolute commitment to human rights' became the main theme of his foreign policy. This refreshing change from the wheeler-dealing of the Nixon era appealed to liberals as well as anti-Communists, since it seemed that American pressure would be used to liberalize repressive régimes in the 'free world'–South Africa, Argentina or South Korea, for example–as well as the notorious tyrannies of Communism. But it soon became a one-sided campaign: while pressure against the Soviet empire steadily increased, no equal pressure was applied to equally brutal governments of states strategically important to the United States, such as Nicaragua or Iran.

Whatever the original intentions behind Carter's campaign, Moscow saw it as an anti-Soviet weapon. The Soviet leaders greatly resented this 'interference' in Soviet internal affairs, which occasionally forced them to release particular victims to a triumphant welcome in the West. The only effective liberalization resulting from Soviet promises at Helsinki was increased emigration (see Chapter 13). By 1980 dissident groups in the USSR had been harassed into silence, while those in Eastern Europe suffered a similar fate. Thus the human rights issue only confirmed the West's view that Helsinki's 'Basket Three' was 'a waste of time' and Moscow's view that it was 'another trick to undermine the Socialist system'.

Soviet influence in Africa

During the 1950s and 1960s most of the white-ruled colonies of Africa had become independent–some by a peaceful transition to African rule, others through bitter and bloody warfare. In the early 1970s the notable exceptions were Rhodesia (which *just* escaped massive bloodshed to become independent Zimbabwe in 1979); Namibia (still illegally ruled by South Africa today);† and the Portuguese colonies of Angola and Mozambique, where a relentless guerilla war against white rule contributed to the fall of the Salazar government of Portugal in 1974. Mozambique then moved smoothly to independence under a left-wing government which took up a 'non-aligned' stand, but in Angola a complicated factional war ended in 1975 with the victory of a Marxist group assisted by massive Soviet aid and 20,000 Cuban troops (South Africa and the USA had both backed losers). Cuban forces and East European personnel remained in Angola to strengthen the weak Marxist government, and thus the USSR acquired, through its 'surrogates',‡ a toe-hold in a continent where up to now its influence had been confined to arms sales and other forms of aid.

The Soviet–Cuban partnership again went into action in a war between Ethiopia and

---

†Namibia was originally the German colony of South-West Africa which in 1919 became a mandate of the League of Nations–and subsequently a 'trust territory' of the UN–to be guided to self-government by South Africa. Considering that South Africa had broken its trust, in 1966 the UN cancelled the mandate and in 1973, in the face of South Africa's virtual annexation of the territory, recognized the South-West African People's Organization (SWAPO) as 'the sole representative of the people of Namibia'. Since 1975 South African forces have made incursions deep into Angola against SWAPO guerilla bases there. The major Western powers have tried to mediate between South Africa and SWAPO, while black African states and the Communist world have provided military assistance to SWAPO for the continuing war.

‡'Surrogate' (which literally means a deputy or substitute) is the term currently used in the West for Cubans or East Europeans who are seen as 'tools' of Soviet policy. This is an over-simple view, at least in regard to Cuba: Castro has an idealistic commitment to 'national liberation movements' anywhere in the world. Help from foreign Communists is welcomed by the Angolan government, which still faces internal rebellion from another faction and is also backing SWAPO's guerilla war to liberate Namibia from South Africa (see footnote above)–a cause which attracts considerable sympathy in the West as well as the Communist world.

Somalia in the Horn of Africa in 1977–8. Here the West saw with apprehension that new Soviet global 'reach': a massive airlift of tanks, rocket-launchers and other military hardware such as only the USA could have organized a few years previously. Equally alarming was the fact that by 1978 the USSR had a naval base in Ethiopia, opposite an existing one in the left-wing state of South Yemen. The Red Navy now patrolled the Red Sea, dangerously near the Persian Gulf and the sources of the West's oil.†

The Horn of Africa is the southern tip of what is now sometimes called an 'arc of crisis' which curves north through the Middle East and then turns south-east to include Iran, Afghanistan and Pakistan (see Figure 27.1).

†Soviet interest in this area is strategic. By 1970 the USA had Polaris missiles of sufficient range to reach Soviet cities if fired from the Indian Ocean. But with the Red Navy able to threaten oil tankers en route from the Gulf states to the West, would Washington ever dare to fire them?

In the minds of American strategists at least, all these countries now merged into one critical sphere of Soviet–American confrontation.

The 'arc of crisis'

1. Iran

In January 1979 America's 'police chief' in the Persian Gulf region, the Shah of Iran (who ran an internal police state of his own), was overthrown by the fiercely anti-Western (and especially anti-American) Islamic fundamentalist revolution led by the Ayatollah Khomeini. This event, entirely unforeseen by the watchful CIA, seriously undermined American power and prestige in the region. A series of incidents later in the year kept Washington's nerves jangling: a brief skirmish between Communist South Yemen and non-Communist North Yemen, a sudden

Figure 27.1   The Horn of Africa and the 'arc of crisis'.

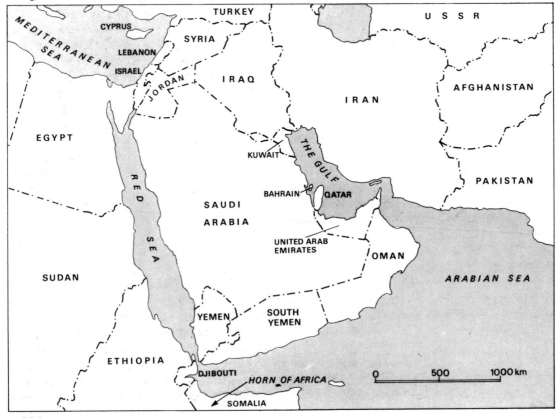

threat to the stability of Saudi Arabia, America's main Arab ally, from another group of Moslem fanatics, and the seizure of American hostages in Iran in November (see pages 76–7). And on top of all *that*, in December the USSR invaded Afghanistan.

2. *Afghanistan*

Ironically, the threat to Soviet interests in Afghanistan was yet another brand of Moslem fundamentalism. In 1973 this feudal kingdom had become a republic, taken over in 1978 by a left-wing régime which signed a Treaty of Friendship with the USSR. This city-based, 'modernizing' government soon antagonized traditionalist Afghans as the 'Westernizing' Shah had provoked traditionalist Iranians. As a resistance movement gained ground on the faltering government, 80,000 Soviet troops moved in to install a new leader, Babrak Karmal, and 'restore order' in the country (according to Moscow, at the Afghan government's request).†

For the first time since 1945, the USSR had intervened directly in a country *beyond* its own sphere. Like Khrushchev's missiles in Cuba in 1962, this move had painful consequences for the Soviet Union (probably underestimated by its leaders). The invasion was roundly condemned by the UN and the Moslem world and provoked sharp punishment from the United States: the suspension of grain supplies and other Soviet–American trade, the refusal to ratify SALT II (signed by Carter and Brezhnev earlier in the year), and an American boycott of the Moscow Olympic Games in 1980.

While the whole Western world deplored this Soviet 'adventurism', opinions differed as to the motives behind it. Recalling the nineteenth-century rivalry between British India and Tsarist Russia in this craggy buffer

---

†In 1983 Soviet control was still confined to the cities, while a sporadic and unwinnable war continued against Afghan tribesmen in the hills. For *them* it was a 'holy war' against the government lodged in the capital, Kabul; for the USSR, Afghanistan had become a kind of 'Soviet Vietnam'.

state, many Europeans saw it as an ill-judged attempt to deal with 'a little local difficulty' on a sensitive border. But to Washington strategists it looked much more ominous. Still smarting from the loss of Iran, and fearing that the Soviet aim might be a drive towards the Persian Gulf, President Carter proclaimed that region as a zone of 'vital interest' to the United States which would be protected 'by military force if necessary'. To reinforce this Carter Doctrine America increased her defence budget, upgraded her arms supplies to Middle East allies (now including Pakistan, which had hitherto failed to get sophisticated arms from the West for fear they would be used against India), looked around for new bases in the region, and built up a Rapid Deployment Force to deal with any future crisis. And there was no doubt who might cause such a crisis: Washington was now beginning to 'see red' in every international trouble spot.

America's resumption of her role as world policeman–at least in this area of 'vital interest'–alarmed the Gulf states and India, who feared they might now become a Soviet–American battlefield. Carter was by temperament a dove and up to this time had made an effort to lower international tension rather than raise it: against the advice of some hawks in his administration he had pursued SALT II to the point of signature, had cancelled the development of some 'provocative' new nuclear weapons (though at the same time giving the go-ahead for Cruise missiles), and had pulled off two creditable feats of peace-making, the Panama Canal treaties (see page 77) and the 'miracle' of an Egypt–Israel peace treaty (see ahead, page 309). If his view of the 'Soviet threat' now seemed a little exaggerated, it was the rising tide of right-wing opinion in America which caused the distortion–and which swept Ronald Reagan into the White House in 1980. Within days of taking office he made clear *his* vision of the USSR by describing its leaders as 'liars and cheats', and brushed aside *détente* as 'a one-way street which the Soviet Union has used to pursue its own aims'. This was the first taste of the 'Reagan rhetoric' (his rather insulting language about the USSR) which further soured the atmosphere of Soviet–American relations after 1980.

We must now examine the central conflict of the Middle East in more detail than other areas of tension in the early 1980s, since this is–as it has been for years–*the most dangerous area of Soviet–American confrontation.* You will soon see why.

3. The Arab–Israeli conflict

Since 1973 the Arab–Israeli dispute has worsened in almost every respect. The super-powers' involvement in it cannot be understood without reference to events at ground level, so you will have to look back at

Figures 24.5 and 24.6 on page 269 and remind yourself of the story up to 1973 before you venture into the new complexities of the past decade.

For a brief moment after the Yom Kippur War there seemed hope of a general Middle East peace settlement supervised by a Geneva Peace Conference under the joint chairmanship of the USA and USSR. But Kissinger soon broke away from this partnership for two reasons: first, to keep the peace-making process firmly under *American* control, and secondly to pursue the 'step by step' approach favoured by Washington, i.e. settling one issue at a time between different pairs of antagonists rather than a general conference to discuss *all* the problems with *all* the parties concerned. The United States seemed well qualified as a

Figure 27.2   Israel and the occupied territories in the early 1980s. East Jerusalem was annexed in 1978 and the Golan Heights in 1981. The evacuation of the Sinai peninsula (Zones A, B and C consecutively) was completed in April 1982. The future status of the Gaza Strip and the West Bank remained unresolved.

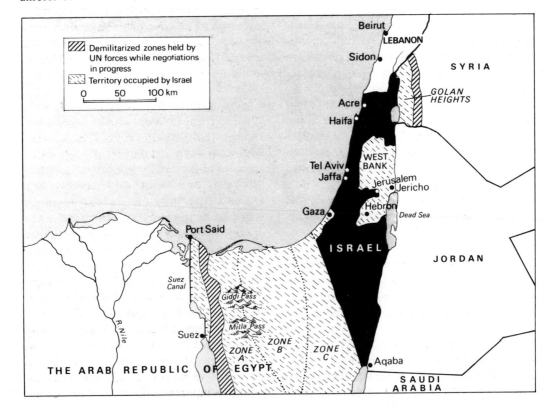

mediator, having good relations with moderate Arab states like Jordan and Saudi Arabia, and as the only state which could 'deliver Israel to the conference table' by putting pressure on her headstrong client. But could Washington be a fair referee towards the Palestinians?

The Egypt–Israel Treaty Before Kissinger left office he had achieved a disengagement between Israeli and Egyptian forces in the Sinai, which at once aroused the suspicions of the other Arab states and the Palestine Liberation Organization (PLO) that a sell-out of *their* interests was under way. Their apprehension increased when, following the conciliatory visit of Egypt's President Sadat to Israel in 1977, President Carter negotiated with these two states the 'Camp David peace framework' which led to the Egypt–Israel Treaty of 1979 providing for the staged withdrawal of Israeli troops and settlers from Egyptian territory (see Figure 27.2). Earlier Carter had tried to reassure the Arabs by openly supporting a Palestinian homeland, and had even backtracked on Kissinger by trying to re-involve the USSR in mediating the conflict. But under pressure from Israel, and with Egyptian–Israeli reconciliation almost within his grasp, he now reverted to a 'step by step' and purely *American*-sponsored settlement.

The original Camp David 'framework' agreed in 1978 was that after the Egypt–Israel Treaty, a 'second step' would draw in other Arab states to arrange with Israel a form of self-rule for the Palestinians in the West Bank and the Gaza Strip. But that hopeful 'first step' turned out to be the *only* step towards a lasting peace in the Middle East. All the other Arab parties rejected what they saw as a sell-out to Israel by the 'untrustworthy' United States and the 'traitor' President Sadat. Egypt now became a black sheep in the Arab world and also dependent on the United States for arms, having earlier broken her ties with the USSR, leaving the more radical Syria and Iraq (still backed by Moscow) to confront the

'US–Israeli partnership' from the north and east. President Sadat's reward for his peace effort was his assassination by Moslem fanatics in 1981.

By 1981 President Reagan was in office and had set aside peace-making between Israel and the Arabs for a more urgent priority: the Soviet threat in the 'arc of crisis'. Israel was now seen as 'a major strategic asset to America' and would be the king-pin of a 'strategic consensus' of well-armed American allies (Egypt–Israel–Saudi Arabia) which would also provide bases for the American Rapid Deployment Force. To this end the USA began to supply Saudi Arabia and Israel with her latest fighter planes and other high-grade weapons, seemingly unsuspecting that they might be used for other purposes than to defend *American* interests in the Middle East. In the summer of 1981 Washington was startled and embarrassed to see Israel using US-supplied jets to bomb Palestinian civilians in Beirut, and overflying two American allies (Jordan and Saudi Arabia) to destroy a nuclear reactor in Iraq. Reagan now had to lower his binoculars from a strategic overview of the 'arc of crisis' and focus on that little Arab–Israeli squabble at ground level.

Israeli settlement policy By this time Israel's increasingly aggressive stance under the right-wing government of Menachem Begin had further alienated moderate Arab states and was causing international concern. The 1979 treaty with Egypt had secured Israel's western border, freeing her to concentrate on the confrontation with Syria and the PLO in the Lebanon, and to deal with the other occupied territories in her own way. Regardless of Begin's 'second step' promises at Camp David, Israel wanted no advice from Arab states on the future of the West Bank and Gaza. The Begin government's idea of self-rule for Palestinians there was something like the 'self-rule' that Wales enjoys in Britain today. From the early 1970s Israeli policy in these areas had been moving steadily from 'temporary military rule' to 'permanent sovereignty'–or to put it more bluntly, outright annexation. To facilitate this aim, Jewish settlements sprang up all over the West Bank, vital water and electricity supplies were linked to those of Israel, Palestinian civic leaders were deported and their schools and colleges supervised to prevent 'nationalistic' teaching. By the early 1980s the West Bank and Gaza were, in all but name, Israeli colonies. East Jerusalem and the Syrian Golan Heights were formally annexed in 1978 and 1981 respectively.

As the Palestinian dream of an independent homeland disappeared over the horizon, the murderous eye-for-an-eye PLO–Israel vendetta intensified. For every Israeli schoolbus or settlement blasted by an Arab shell, an Israeli airstrike on a Palestinian refugee camp; for a car-bomb in Jerusalem, a West Bank Arab mayor's legs blown off ... and so on, and so on.

Lebanon By 1975 the overspill of this conflict, and the presence of a Palestinian 'state within a state' in Lebanon, had shattered the fragile political-religious cohesion of that country. In the ensuing nineteen-month Lebanese civil war more people were killed than in the four previous Arab–Israeli wars, and the country was literally wrecked as a political entity. Israel and five other Arab states supported various Lebanese or Palestinian factions on this convenient battleground, until Syrian forces ended the inter-Arab fighting in 1976. Thereafter Israel continued her fierce retaliatory attacks on Palestinian settlements in Lebanon, culminating in the occupation of the southern half of the country in 1982 to evict the PLO from areas up to and including Beirut, while Syria now controlled other large areas.

Several times during this dangerous escalation Washington showed disapproval of Israeli transgressions, even to the point of withholding a few super-jets and supporting a UN resolution condemning the airstrike on Iraq's nuclear plant. State department officials now realized *privately* that 'the Palestinian problem' must eventually be resolved, but Washington was still under pledge to Israel never to negotiate with the 'terrorist' PLO.

In the rest of the world, however, despite the PLO's many acts of terrorism over the years, there was now widespread sympathy for the plight of the Palestinians. Israel's settlement policy and her trigger-happy treatment of her Arab foes were strongly condemned. The Begin government, however, relying on Israel's military superiority and confident that Uncle Sam would always forgive her trespasses, seemed as indifferent to outside opinion as to the pleas for moderation from a few Israeli politicians and many of her citizens. While Israel's image abroad was changing from 'gallant little nation fighting for its life' to 'expansionist bandit', the PLO had been making diplomatic contacts with many Western governments and was increasingly recognized as the respectable spokesman of a just cause–but not, of course, in Washington.

Other issues By 1980 Lebanon was not the only scene of 'hot war' in the Middle East. In that year Iraq invaded Iran, partly to settle a border dispute but mainly out of fear that Iran's Islamic revolution would spread into Iraq–a fear shared by several other states with Moslem fundamentalist minorities. Iraq had hoped for a quick victory with Iran in revolutionary disarray, but the Ayatollah's government was well equipped with religious zeal (and Western arms previously supplied to the Shah) for the war of attrition which still continued in 1983. Potentially, the Gulf War could threaten oil traffic through the Gulf, which would upset major oil producers like Saudi Arabia just as much as the Western recipients.

Religious extremism, in various forms, is another ingredient in the cauldron of Middle East politics which may have an unpredictable influence on future developments. Some ultra-Orthodox Jews would like to extend 'greater Israel' into *all* the biblical lands of the Jews; there was bitter resistance from settlers in the Sinai when their own government evicted them in 1982 to comply with the Egypt–Israel treaty. On the Arab side, Islamic terrorists, reportedly directed from Iran, were responsible for suicide truck bombs late in 1983 which killed 241 American marines and a smaller number of French soldiers in Lebanon, and for a series of bombs in Kuwait, a tiny oil-rich state with many Western connections.

Multi-national peace-keeping efforts Those American and French victims were part of a multi-national force now trying to keep the warring factions apart so that a Lebanese government could reassert its authority over the country. As a first step the PLO fighters loyal to Yassir Arafat were evacuated to seek refuge elsewhere in the Arab world, leaving Lebanon in a state of utter chaos: Israel occupying the south, Syrians in the north and east, and a no man's land of factional conflict in the middle (including extreme fragments of the PLO who consider Yassir Arafat's group too 'soft' on Israel).

The fact that *Americans* were the largest contingent of the mediating force cast doubts on its usefulness, especially when Washington signed a new strategic agreement with Israel in December 1983 and American forces came into direct conflict with Syria, losing two aircraft to Soviet-supplied missiles. In a bid to rally support for a 'moderate' Arab viewpoint, King Hussein urged that the Soviet Union must be given a role in the peace-making process so that 'the danger of mounting polarisation may be prevented and a new disastrous eruption averted'.†

The Soviet role What part has the USSR played so far in this Middle East tangle? In fact Moscow's political influence in the area has declined since 1973: rejected by Egypt in 1974 in favour of the USA, condemned by the whole Moslem world for invading Afghanistan, and with even less influence over its main arms clients, Syria and Iraq, than the United States has been able to exer-

†In a speech to the European parliament reported in *The Guardian*, 16 December 1983.

cise over Israel. But Moscow must of course take a share of the blame for the hair-raising arms race in the area.‡

The Soviet desire for Middle East peace is obvious–no sane statesman wants a festering problem like *that* on his nation's doorstep–but in Moscow's view it must be a *general* settlement which includes justice for the Palestinians as well as for Israel. After 1973 the USA deliberately excluded the USSR from the 'peace process'– in the Soviet view unjustly, since the Middle East is of 'vital interest' to Moscow too–and every time American arms supplies to Israel were jacked up, the USSR followed suit on the Arab/PLO side. Thus the half-formulated 'rules' which both super-powers had obeyed up to 1973 (*joint* peace-making through the UN, and a voluntary restraint on top-grade arms to their allies) were cast aside in a 'free for all' contest.

The interlocking disputes of the Middle East have nothing to do with Democracy *v.* Communism, but it is easy to see how any incident there could escalate into a wider conflict. High-performance weapons in the hands of uncontrollable users in an area where both nuclear super-powers have declared their 'vital national interest'–what a recipe for disaster!

‡One recent study of the Middle East warns us that the arms race there is now 'out of control'. More than a third of all the world's arms exports go to the Middle East, of which 48 per cent come from the USA, 26 per cent from the USSR and the rest from Britain, France and a few others. By 1981 the super-powers were supplying their main clients with top-grade conventional weapons hitherto reserved for their own use (in 1983 France was also criticized for supplying super-jets to Iraq for use against Iran). Israel now produces (and exports) her own lower-grade weapons, while Egypt and Saudi Arabia are also developing their own arms industries with American help. Israel has not signed the Nuclear Non-Proliferation Treaty and is believed to have a small stock of nuclear weapons. Since Iraq's nuclear reactor was destroyed by Israel in 1981, only Pakistan is now within reach of an 'Islamic nuclear bomb' and has also not signed the Non-Proliferation Treaty. (Iraq's nuclear reactor *had* been regularly inspected by the International Atomic Energy Agency under the terms of that treaty, but Israel thought Iraq might evade that inspection to make bombs, which is technically possible.) Most of this information comes from Everett Mendelsohn, *A Compassionate Peace* (Penguin, 1982), an excellent short analysis of the deepening Middle East crisis.

By contrast the super-powers' acknowledged 'spheres' were not a likely arena for direct Soviet–American conflict–*that* much of the 'rules of the game' was still agreed between them. But both the USA and the USSR had cause to be nervous about recent developments uncomfortably close to home, and their anxieties further contributed to the tensions of the New Cold War.

Tremors in the spheres of influence

1. America's 'back yard'–Central America

The USA's desire for 'stability' in Latin America and the Caribbean–and her determination to enforce it in her own way–is a long-running theme of her foreign policy (see Chapter 4). At times America has tried to encourage political and economic reforms to benefit the millions of repressed and poverty-stricken peasants–President Kennedy's Alliance for Progress in the 1960s and Carter's more recent human rights campaign were supposed to achieve this aim–but a far greater priority has always been to protect US strategic and economic interests by supporting right-wing governments, in recent years through military aid often used by the recipients to suppress their own people.

The emergence of Cuba in the 1960s as a Soviet-assisted Marxist state challenged traditional American overlordship in the region. Whatever the extent of subsequent Cuban and/or Soviet penetration elsewhere in Latin America (which we cannot investigate here), the *example* of Cuba has certainly encouraged left-wing reformers in other countries to try to break the mould of brutal right-wing rule and introduce ground-level reforms which American 'assistance' has signally failed to achieve. The scandalous contrast between the poverty and despair at the bottom of society and the affluence of a few bejewelled plutocrats at the top has 'radicalized' many intellectuals and churchmen, who follow a breakaway Catholic philosophy of 'liberation theology'† and are

prepared to co-operate with local or foreign reformers of any political creed, including Marxists. As a Mexican priest told a group of conservative American Protestants on a 'consciousness-raising' tour of Honduras and Nicaragua, 'In Latin America, in order to be a Christian, you *can't* be anti-Communist.'‡

The current focus of American concern in her traditional sphere of influence is Central America and the Caribbean (see Figure 27.3). Washington's lop-sided view of 'problems' in this area can be seen in the fact that US military aid to the government of Nicaragua in the early 1960s provided every soldier with $930 worth of equipment, in a country where the annual *per capita* income was $205.

Three examples will serve to illustrate America's anxieties and actions in her back yard in the New Cold War period:

Nicaragua Since 1936 the Somoza family dictatorship (two sons following their father) had provided a centre-point of stability for Washington, and also served as a base for American operations against left-wing eruptions in the area (Guatemala in 1954, Cuba in 1961, the Dominican Republic in 1965). In 1979, despite last-minute efforts by President Carter to press reforms on the Somoza régime, it was driven out by a revolution led by the left-wing Sandinista movement. The Sandinista government (which was far too 'left' for Washington's liking and also formed strong links with Cuba) then came under economic and military siege by the United States, which now saw Nicaragua as a centre-point of *in*stability in a region seething with discontent and impatience for *real reform* after centuries of feudalism. The Americans armed and trained a guerilla opposition to the Sandinista régime in neighbouring Honduras, where vast US Army and Navy manoeuvres were launched in 1983 with the secondary purpose of building a new American base to replace the 'loss' of

†Priests who believe in this idea call themselves 'the church of the poor'.

‡Quoted in an article by Judith Moore, 'The Road to Managua', in the San Francisco journal, *Express*, 2 December 1983.

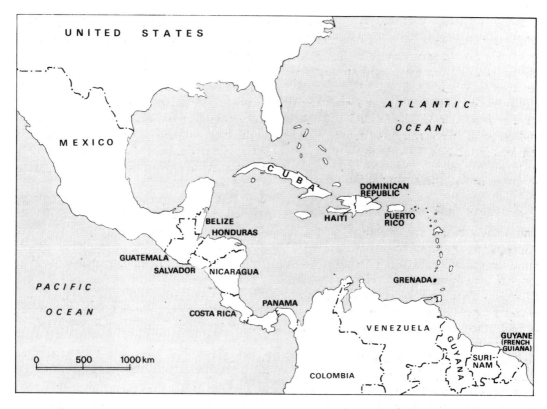

Figure 27.3 Central America and the Caribbean: the United States' back yard.

Nicaragua. There was general apprehension that America was on the verge of intervening directly to reverse the Sandinista revolution.

El Salvador Here the extreme-right government set up in 1977 was replaced by a middle-right military régime in 1979, pledged to begin modest land reform (the most explosive issue in countries of this area, where most of the land is owned by a few rich families). In 1982 this government 'legitimized' itself with elections under the eye of invited outside observers. Meanwhile a left-wing guerilla revolution was under way, while at the other end of the political spectrum right-wing 'death squads' continued to roam the country killing thousands of left-wing sympathizers or 'collaborators' (including, in 1980, the archbishop of San Salvador). Were these assassins directed or encouraged by the government, or simply 'uncontrollable'? No one knew for sure, but

the statistics were shocking: late in 1983 the Catholic Church in El Salvador reported November's total of 534 murders, apparently carried out by off-duty National Guardsmen paid by absentee landowners living in Florida. This information caused concern in the United States, but Washington remained committed to the elected government, hoping it would check right-wing terrorism and bring in genuine land reform soon enough to prevent mass defections of peasants to the guerillas.

Grenada In this tiny Caribbean island, population 110,000, Maurice Bishop's New Jewel Movement (Joint Endeavour for Welfare, Education and Liberation) ousted the notoriously corrupt Eric Gairy in 1979 and launched social and economic programmes with Cuban help, including a large new airport supposedly to develop the tourist trade – but in Washington's eyes a potential

313

airstrip for Soviet use. In 1983 an internal *coup* within the New Jewel Movement gave Washington the excuse to make sure it *wouldn't* be–in October American troops and some from Grenada's Caribbean neighbours invaded the island, evicted the Cuban construction workers (or soldiers in disguise?) and set up an interim government under the British-appointed Governor Sir Paul Scoon, up to then a mere symbol of Grenada's status as a member of the British Commonwealth.†

Critics of the Grenada invasion pointed out that Reagan's defence of his action was the same as the Soviet justification for invading Afghanistan–to prevent a perceived 'threat' from getting worse. By now Washington's policy towards Central America and the Caribbean was beginning to be seen as an undeclared 'Reagan Doctrine' with the same message as the Brezhnev Doctrine in Eastern Europe: 'Do things our way–or take the consequences!'

Meanwhile, since 1980 Brezhnev had been facing a new challenge to *his* Doctrine, which still plagued his successors after Brezhnev's death in 1982.

2. Russia's 'front gate'–Poland

As the pathway for previous invasions of Russia from the West, Poland has always been the most sensitive spot in the USSR's buffer zone created by the Red Army's occupation of Eastern Europe in 1945 (see Figure 22.2 on page 242). With a population of 35 million, it is also the largest state in the Eastern bloc and the largest contributor to the Warsaw Pact. In *Polish* history, however, Soviet control since 1945 is only the latest chapter in a centuries-old struggle against Russian domination of their homeland–or rather, of *the Polish nation*, since territory is

†According to a right-wing American interviewed by a BBC reporter (Radio 4, 'Pax Americana', 14 December 1983) '90 per cent' of Americans didn't know of Grenada's British connection, which may explain why President Reagan felt confident in ignoring Mrs Thatcher's advice not to invade it. The invasion was loudly applauded by most Americans and welcomed by many Grenadians.

less important in this context than the bonds of culture, language, history and devout Roman Catholicism which make up the Polish 'national soul'. Under Soviet rule Poland has submitted to Communism–at least superficially–but never to *Russia*. The Polish 'national soul' lives on.

In 1980 a succession of events led to the founding of the Polish free trade union, Solidarity. Since the strike of 1956 which brought the 'reformer' Gomulka to power (see page 263), there had been other serious strikes which were crushed by the Polish government, including one in 1970 when many shipyard workers were killed in the 'Gdansk massacre'. The USSR had tried unsuccessfully to appease the people's grievances by 'strengthening' the Polish government with economic aid and two more changes of leadership: from Gomulka to Gierek in 1970, from Gierek to Kania in 1980.

In that year the visit of the new *Polish* Pope John Paul II was the occasion for an ecstatic display of love and worship from his countrymen. The visit was followed by a national strike in which the Gdansk shipyard workers, under their leader Lech Walesa, forced an unprecedented bargain from their government: in return for their acceptance of the Socialist system and Poland's membership of the Soviet bloc, the workers won a free trade union, a free press, and the promise of reforms to end the chronic shortages of food and goods. But the government became alarmed as Solidarity gathered support like a snowball rolling downhill. Within months the new trade union had become a 'total social movement' embodying that inextinguishable Polish 'national soul', and thus presented an undefined but serious threat to the government's authority and its Soviet backers. In December 1981 General Jaruzelski imposed martial law and imprisoned Lech Walesa and his main supporters.

For the next eighteen months Poland was under strict military rule (although Walesa was released in 1982), until in the summer of

1983 the government felt 'safe' enough to lift martial law and to allow another visit from the Pope. Although more subdued than in 1980, the acclamation he received on every processional route, watched with a stony glare by the government, was another chance to demonstrate that Solidarity might be officially dead, but in the hearts of the Polish people, 'Solidarity lives!' By now the Solidarity movement had become a pervasive underground society, still 'visible' through its *samizdat* publications and occasional symbolic gestures like Walesa's appearance in August 1983 to lay a wreath to the Gdansk martyrs of 1970. The trial of strength between the Polish government and the Polish people had reached a position of 'stand off': both sides knew that neither could defeat the other, and their contest had become a waiting game.

For the USSR, Poland in the 1980s presented a much more difficult problem than Hungary in 1956 or Czechoslovakia in 1968 – and one which could not be solved with soldiers and tanks or massive economic aid (which might well be necessary, however, to bail Poland out of economic chaos). And there was always the unnerving possibility that Poland's Solidarity might inspire similar unconquerable passive resistance among the many other non-Russian peoples ruled directly or indirectly from Moscow...

Poland brings us back to Europe, a suitable place to end this survey of the New Cold War since that is where the first one began. In the early 1980s Europe was also the focus of the most serious international problem since 1945: the failure of world statesmen to control the nuclear arms race.

The nuclear arms race

The year 1979 was a particularly tense moment in deteriorating East–West relations. To those who see the whole world as a theatre of the Cold War (and not everyone does, we should remember!) events in Indo-China, Iran, Afghanistan and Central America all seemed to indicate an increasing 'Soviet threat' and a corresponding decline in American influence. In the USA a mini-crisis had also been set off by the sudden 'discovery' of a Soviet brigade in Cuba (which in fact had been there since 1962). The fuss over this, and Afghanistan soon afterwards, contributed to the decision of Congress not to ratify SALT II, which Carter and Brezhnev had signed in June.

It was also in 1979 that NATO agreed to deploy in Western Europe a new generation of American nuclear weapons: Cruise and Pershing II missiles. The new phase of strategic thinking which led to this decision is explained in Study Topic 14, which you should reread alongside the next few paragraphs. What concerns us here is the contribution of the 'Cruise and Pershing issue' to the rising tension of the New Cold War.

NATO's decision set off a debate in Western Europe which became increasingly heated as the planned date for deployment of the new missiles approached. At parliamentary level there was bitter controversy between doves who saw it as a provocative and unnecessary escalation of the nuclear arms race and hawks who considered it an overdue upgrading of the West's defences against a hostile USSR. At citizen level public opinion divided along similar lines: while the nuclear protest movement grew rapidly, especially in Britain and West Germany (Figure 27.4), the election of 'pro Cruise and Pershing' right-wing governments in 1983 in both these countries confirmed that deployment *would* go ahead. In December the missiles began to arrive in Britain, West Germany and Italy. As yet it was undecided whether Belgium and the Netherlands would accept their quota of missiles, due to be deployed at a later stage.

NATO and its American spokesmen had been following a 'twin track' policy of announcing the date of the intended deployment of their new missiles while at the same time trying to persuade the USSR, through Soviet–American Intermediate-range Nuclear Forces talks (INF) begun at Geneva in November 1981, to remove its SS 20 missiles

Figure 27.4 Anti-nuclear demonstration at Marburg, West Germany, Easter 1983. The banner reads 'Euroshima thanks to Pershing–stop the NATO arms race'.

targeted on Western Europe. If the USSR complied, the deployment of Cruise and Pershing would be cancelled. On the other hand the Russians made it clear that *if* deployment took place they would withdraw from the INF talks. For two jittery years there were proposals, counter-proposals and more proposals ... but neither side would accept the compromises offered by the other. When a 'last hope' debate in the West German parliament in November 1983 ended with a vote *for* deployment, the Russians angrily walked out of the INF talks. A few weeks later two other sets of East–West arms negotiations were 'indefinitely suspended' by Soviet withdrawal from them, leaving no channel for East–West dialogue except the periodic 'review conferences' provided for at Helsinki in 1975 (the next of these was scheduled for 1984 in Stockholm).

On this side of the Iron Curtain, however, the argument raged on. As the anti-Cruise and anti-Pershing campaigns in Britain and West Germany gathered strength, some people questioned whether the Reagan government was 'serious' about arms talks, seeing Cruise and Pershing–and yet more lethal missiles in the offing–as part of a long-term American aim to regain nuclear *superiority* over the USSR. Others thought that Moscow was following a similar strategy by developing new block-buster nuclear submarines which could get as close to the heartland of America as NATO's new missiles were to the heartland of Russia. Both the super-powers were accused of deliberate 'threat inflation', i.e. exaggerating the military might of the other side to justify increasing *theirs*.

We must leave the technical details of these arguments to political hot-heads and defence analysts, who seem able to produce a convincing case for *any* point of view. The tragedy and the danger of the New Cold War atmosphere was the apparent lack of political will–and for the time being, even a conference table–for *any* progress towards nuclear arms control. Such a high degree of international tension also increased the risk of accidental conflict, as we were reminded in September 1983 when a straying South

Korean airliner was shot down by a Soviet jet which mistook it for an American spy plane (only the latest of many instances over the years when a false alarm has set off a military reaction by one side or the other).

Meanwhile the nuclear 'overkill' statistics† would be laughable if we didn't know what these weapons *mean*. (Has the world forgotten that 'little bomb' at Hiroshima in 1945?) Any history book which touches on this subject cannot be optimistic, especially at the depressing moment when this one goes to press: 'All previous arms races in history have ended in war. If the nuclear arms race continues, sooner or later, by accident or design, there will be a nuclear war.'‡

To complete this account of the New Cold War between the USA and the USSR, we need a postscript to summarize China's relations with the Soviet Union during the period, and to explain that question-mark in Figure 26.1 on page 292.

SINO–SOVIET RELATIONS

After the death of Mao Tse-tung in 1976 Moscow soon began to make friendly overtures to Peking but was disappointed to find them coolly received. Soviet 'revisionism' was no longer an issue between them, since China's new leaders had buried Maoist 'dogmatism' along with Mao, as we know— but Soviet 'hegemonism'†† was still a problem. In the 1970s China was just as fearful as the West of Soviet influence beyond its own

borders, particularly in areas of interest to China: Indo-China and Afghanistan. And there was still the direct threat of Soviet forces on China's northern border with the USSR and its satellite, Mongolia. Peking therefore welcomed the re-emergence of America as world policeman, now that the thrust of American policy was directed towards the USSR and not China, and for the same reason was eager to normalize Sino–American relations in 1979.

Diplomatic visits and negotiations between Moscow and Peking continued, but China made it clear that these 'three obstacles' prevented full Sino–Soviet normalization: the Soviet military threat, Soviet occupation of Afghanistan, and Soviet support of Vietnam in Indo-China. Of these, Vietnam was Peking's first priority, since it represented a Soviet presence in China's age-old 'sphere of influence' which was nibbled away by Western, Russian and Japanese imperialism at a time when China was too weak to resist. And in *that* connection, the Reagan government's increased support for Taiwan infuriated China almost as much as Soviet aid to Vietnam.

In the New Cold War of the 1980s, both the USA and the USSR hoped for some kind of alliance with China to tip the balance in their confrontation with each other. But it was now China's turn to play 'hard to get' towards both of these suitors, smiling first at one, and then the other, according to the circumstances of the moment. Meanwhile Peking was busily expanding trade links with America *and* Russia–and increasingly with Japan, since her 1978 Treaty of Friendship with that former enemy. China's new leaders were well aware that only *modernization*, the overriding theme of their policy, would give China the economic and military 'clout' (including, of course, nuclear weapons) to compete on equal terms with the other two World Powers. It remains to be seen whether China will also be impelled, as they do today, to threaten the whole world with a nuclear holocaust in pursuit of alleged 'national interests'.

---

†One recent book points out that at the time when the concept of 'mutual assured destruction' was arrived at in the 1960s, the estimated minimum nuclear arsenal required to achieve 'assured destruction' of the enemy was about 400 one-megaton warheads; yet by 1979 the USSR already had more than ten times, and the USA plus NATO more than twenty times, that number. Hugh Higgins, *The Cold War* (Heinemann Educational Books, 1984), p. 139.

‡John Cox, *Overkill: The Story of Modern Weapons* (Penguin, 1977), p. 113.

††Marxists often use the word 'hegemonism'–meaning the attempt to exert hegemony or dominance over other countries–instead of the more general term 'imperialism'.

Questions

Did you notice?

1. The Soviet–American trade treaty of 1974 (a) ensured exit permits for Soviet Jews (b) guaranteed grain supplies from the USA (c) was cancelled by Brezhnev

2. The Carter Doctrine applied to (a) Eastern Europe (b) the Persian Gulf region (c) Central America

3. President Reagan hoped to include in his 'strategic consensus' (a) Israel and Saudi Arabia (b) Iran and Iraq (c) Jordan and Lebanon

4. 'Liberation theology' means (a) the Pope's support of Solidarity (b) Reagan's crusade against the 'evil empire' of Moscow (c) the 'church of the poor' in Latin America

5. To Peking the most important 'obstacle' preventing normal relations with Moscow was (a) Soviet aid to Vietnam (b) US aid to the KMT (c) Soviet military strength

6. True or false?
   (i) Rhodesia became Angola in 1979
   (ii) Ethiopia is in the Horn of Africa
   (iii) The 1980 Olympic Games in Moscow were cancelled
   (iv) NATO decided to deploy SS20 missiles in 1979
   (v) In 1983 the USSR shot down a South Korean plane

7. Which statement is *more* accurate?
   (i) Carter's human rights campaign was 'one-sided' in the sense that
       (a) it was never intended to apply to the 'free world'
       (b) it was not firmly applied to America's right-wing allies
   (ii) The Camp David 'peace framework' did not settle the Arab–Israeli conflict because
       (a) Israel did not abide by her 1979 treaty with Egypt
       (b) it did not solve the Palestinian problem
   (iii) Cruise and Pershing II missiles
       (a) were American weapons which no Europeans wanted
       (b) caused a Russian walk-out of East–West arms talks

Can you explain?

8. What was (a) the Soviet view and (b) the American view of the build-up of Soviet military strength in the 1970s?

9. What was the Carter Doctrine, and what led up to it?

10. Why is the Middle East described as 'the most dangerous area of Soviet–American confrontation'?

11. Using information in this chapter and Study Topic 14, in what ways has the nuclear arms balance between the super-powers become more unstable since the period of *détente*?

12. What is the nationality of each of the following, and how do their countries fit into the history of the New Cold War? (a) Ayatollah Khomeini (b) Menachem Begin (c) Maurice Bishop (d) Lech Walesa.

What's your view?

13. In November 1983 the former West German Chancellor, Herr Schmidt, complained that the 'ignorant, bellicose-sounding speeches' of some Western leaders had contributed to East–West tensions. Why are public speeches (which usually do not contain specific proposals) so important in international relations?

14. Most people in the West would like to see the Soviet empire 'liberalized' eventually. Is there anything we can do, short of nuclear war, to accomplish this aim?

15. Are the anti-nuclear protesters justified in opposing the defence policies of democratically-elected governments? Have they any hope of changing those policies? If so, how?

Further Reading

There are few simple accounts of the whole period other than world history textbooks, to which students could refer for a different approach from the one presented here. A few of these are mentioned in Notes on Resources, page xii. The *Map Histories* by Brian Catchpole, also listed on page xii, are a useful back-up to this part of the book. Two other map treatments of world problems are:

Michael Kidron and Dan Smith, *The War Atlas: Armed Conflict–Armed Peace* (Heinemann Educational Books, 1983).
Michael Kidron and Ronald Segal, *The State of the World Atlas* (Heinemann Educational Books, 1981).

Most of the books listed below are for the general reader or students beyond 'O' level, but younger students can use many of them for reference by means of the index.

SUPPLEMENTARY READING

Christopher Barlow, *Islam* (Batsford, 1983).
R. Beggs, *The Cuban Missile Crisis* (Longman, 1971).
John Cox, *On the Warpath* (OUP 'Standpoints' Series, 1976). The moral and practical problems of modern warfare. Very easy text, copiously illustrated.
M. N. Duffy, *In Your Lifetime* (Basil Blackwell, 1969). General Studies treatment of the Cold War.
Charles Freeman, *Defence* (Batsford, 1983). This book won a TES Senior Information Book Award for its lucid and balanced coverage of 'war in the twentieth century', super-power conflict and policies, and the 'nuclear debate'.
S. R. Gibbons and P. Morican, *The League of Nations and U.N.O.* (Longman, 1970).
P. Hastings, *The Cold War* (Benn, 1969).
D. Heater, *The Cold War* (OUP, 1969).
W. P. Rae and N. C. Coutts, *Contemporary Files: Book 2, The World* (Heinemann Educational Books, 1980). Many relevant subjects are examined in this 'topic book': Vietnam, the Middle East, world power conflicts, nuclear weapons.
Rius, *Cuba for Beginners* (Writers and Readers Publishing Co-operative (Society Ltd.), 14 Talacre Road, London NW5 3PE. Published 1976.) A light-hearted treatment by a Mexican cartoonist. Strong 'anti-Yankee' flavour.

There are a few novels set in the period of the Cold War:

Len Deighton, *Funeral in Berlin* (Cape, 1964).
P. George, *Dr. Strangelove* (Corgi, 1963).
Grahame Greene, *The Quiet American* (Penguin, 1969).
John Le Carré, *The Spy Who Came in from the Cold* (Pan, 1964).
William J. Lederer and Eugene Burdick, *The Ugly American* (Gollancz, 1959).

MORE ADVANCED

Colin Bown and Peter Mooney, *Cold War to Détente* (Heinemann Educational Books, 2nd ed. 1981).
A. Boyd, *An Atlas of World Affairs* (Methuen, 6th revised ed. 1970). Useful quick reference: terse factual text.
P. Calvocoressi, *World Politics Since 1945* (Longman, 4th ed. 1982).
Noam Chomsky, Jonathan Steele, John Gittings, *Superpowers in Collision–The New Cold War* (Penguin, 1982). An essay on each World Power's foreign policy and attitudes in the transition from *détente* to the 'new Cold War'.
I. Deutscher, *Russia, China and the West* (Penguin, 1970).
R. Palme Dutt, *Problems of Contemporary History* (Lawrence and Wishart, 1963). Contains a section on the Soviet point of view in the Cold War.
André Fontaine, *History of the Cold War* (Secker and Warburg, 1970). From a West European viewpoint.
Norman Graebner (ed.), *The Cold War* (Heath, 1963). A collection of extracts giving different points of view.
Louis J. Halle, *The Cold War as History* (Chatto and Windus, 1967). From the American viewpoint.
Hugh Higgins, *The Cold War* (Heinemann Educational Books, 2nd ed. 1984).
D. Horowitz, *Imperialism and Revolution* (Penguin, 1971).
Walter La Feber, *America, Russia and the Cold War, 1945–80* (John Wiley, 4th ed. 1980).
Roger Morgan, *The Unsettled Peace* (BBC Publications, 1974). Detailed treatment of the Cold War in Europe.
D. Rees, *The Age of Containment: The Cold War* (Macmillan, 1967).
Daniel Yergin, *Shattered Peace: The Origins of the Cold War and the National Security State* (Penguin, 1977). Early Cold War period.

American foreign policy—general

Here are some of the many books analysing American Cold War policy:

S. E. Ambrose, *Rise to Globalism – American Foreign Policy Since 1938* (Penguin, 2nd ed. 1983). This is vol. 8 of *The Pelican History of the United States of America.*

D. Horowitz, *From Yalta to Vietnam* (Penguin, 1971).

D. Landau, *Kissinger: The Uses of Power* (Robson Books, 1974).

J. W. Spanier, *American Foreign Policy Since World War Two* (Holt, Rinehart & Winston, 8th ed. 1980).

American policy in Vietnam

H. Brandon, *Anatomy of Error: The Secret History of the Vietnam War* (Deutsch, 1970).

N. Chomsky, *The Backroom Boys* (Fontana, 1973).

F. Fitzgerald, *The Fire in the Lake* (Macmillan, 1973).

P. A. French (ed.), *The Pentagon Papers* (General Learning Press, 1974).

A. Schlesinger, *The Bitter Heritage: Vietnam and American Democracy, 1941–1966* (Sphere Books, 1969).

Soviet foreign policy

N. S. Khrushchev, *Khrushchev Remembers* (Little, Brown, 1970).

R. W. Pethybridge, *A History of Post-War Russia* (Allen and Unwin, 1966).

Jonathan Steele, *World Power: Soviet Foreign Policy under Brezhnev and Andropov* (Michael Joseph, 1983).

Chinese foreign policy

G. Clark, *In Fear of China* (Humanities Press, 1967).

J. Gittings, *The World and China, 1922–1972* (Eyre Methuen, 1974).

A. Huck, *The Security of China* (Chatto and Windus, 1970).

Nuclear weapons

John Cox, *Overkill: The Story of Modern Weapons* (Penguin, 1977). A fuller treatment than his *On the Warpath* listed above.

Peter Goodwin, *Nuclear War: The Facts* (Macmillan, 1982).

Robert Jungk, *Brighter Than a Thousand Suns* (Penguin, 1970). An influential book in awakening public opinion to the perils of the nuclear age.

Adam Suddaby, *The Nuclear War Game* (Longman, 1983).

Dorothy Thompson (ed.), *Over Our Dead Bodies – Women Against the Bomb* (Virago, 1983). Includes a useful 'Chronology of the Nuclear Age' and a Glossary of terms.

E. P. Thompson and Dan Smith (eds), *Protest and Survive* (Penguin, 1980). A plea for nuclear disarmament, taking its title from the Civil Defence pamphlet *Protect and Survive.*

Other special topics

In most cases the title indicates the subject-matter.

Neal Ascherson, *The Polish August* (Penguin, 1981).

Phillip Benjamin, *What's Wrong in Central America and What to do About it* (American Friends Service Council, 1983). Available from Friends Book Centre, Friends House, Euston Road, London NW1 2BJ.

Arthur Gavshon, *Crisis in Africa: Battleground of East and West* (Penguin, 1981).

Felix Greene, *Vietnam! Vietnam!* (Penguin, 1967).

Fred Halliday, *Threat From the East? – Soviet Policy from Afghanistan and Iran to the Horn of Africa* (Penguin, 1982).

Hugh Higgins, *Vietnam* (Heinemann Educational Books, 2nd ed. 1982).

Keesings Research Report, *The Sino–Soviet Dispute* (Keesings Publications Ltd, 1970).

Robert F. Kennedy, *Thirteen Days* (Macmillan, 1969). White House discussions during the Cuba missile crisis.

J. Lacouture, *Ho Chi Minh* (Penguin, 1969).

H. L. Matthews, *Castro* (Allen Lane, 1969).

Mary McCarthy, *Vietnam* (Penguin, 1968).

Everett Mendelsohn, *A Compassionate Peace* (Penguin, 1982). A very fair-minded analysis of Middle East conflicts. Appendices contain texts of UN Resolutions and other peace proposals.

Jenny Pearce, *Under The Eagle* (Latin America Bureau, London, 1982). Detailed examination of US interests and policies in Latin America.

R. Scheer and M. Zeitlin, *Cuba: An American Tragedy* (Penguin, 1976).

History of the Twentieth Century magazine series (see Notes on Resources, page xii for full information); the issues particularly relevant to this Part of the book are:

Chapter 19: Nos. 73, 74
Chapters 20 and 21: Nos. 77, 80
Chapter 22: Nos. 84, 88
Chapter 23: Nos. 93, 99
Chapter 24: No. 89 (Sino–Soviet split).

	PART I: THE USA SINCE 1920		PART II: THE USSR SINCE 1917	
	home	foreign	home	foreign
1914				enters First World War
1915				
1916				
1917		enters First World War	Fall of Tsar . . . October Revolution	
1918			CIVIL WAR	Treaty of Brest-Litovsk
1919	Red		1918-21	Comintern set up
1920	President Harding Scare			
1921			Kronstadt revolt New Economic Policy	
1922		High		
1923	President Coolidge	tariff		Treaty of Rapallo
1924	PROHIBITION	policy	Lenin dies	
1925	1920-33			
1926				
1927				
1928	President Hoover		Stalin rules: First Five-Year plan begins	
1929	Wall Street Crash		Trotsky exiled	
1930			Liquidation of the Kulaks	
1931				
1932	President Roosevelt			
1933	New Deal emergency laws			
1934			Party famine	Popular Front
1935	New Deal reforms	Neutrality	purges	policy
1936		Acts		
1937		1935-39		
1938				
1939				Nazi-Soviet Pact
1940		Lend-Lease		
1941		Atlantic Charter SECOND		SECOND
1942		WORLD		WORLD
1943		WAR		WAR
1944		1941-45		1941-45
1945	President Truman	A-bomb		
1946				Communization of
1947		Truman Doctrine		Eastern Europe
1948		Marshall Plan		
1949				A-bomb
1950	McCarran Internal Security Act	KOREAN WAR		Sino-Soviet Treaty
1951	McCARTHYISM	1950-53		
1952	President Eisenhower			
1953		H-bomb	Stalin dies	H-bomb
1954	Supreme Court bans segregation	begins aid to S. Vietnam		
1955	Alabama bus boycott		Khrushchev rules	
1956			20th Party Congress	invades Hungary
1957	Little Rock confrontation			sputnik
1958	CIVIL			'Peaceful Coexistence'
1959	RIGHTS		DE-STALINIZATION	
1960	President Kennedy MOVEMENT			trade pact with Cuba
1961		Bay of Pigs invasion		
1962		Cuba missile crisis		Cuba missile crisis
1963	President Johnson			Sino-Soviet
1964	'War city Civil Rights Act		Khrushchev ousted	dispute
1965	on riots Voting Rights Act	'escalation'	Brezhnev rules	
1966	Poverty'	in Vietnam		
1967	student ANTI-			
1968	President Nixon revolt VIETNAM			invades Czechoslovakia
1969	PROTEST			border clashes with China
1970				
1971				
1972		Nixon visits China and USSR		
1973	'energy crisis'	withdrawal from Vietnam		Brezhnev visits USA
1974	President Ford (after Nixon resigns)			
1975		Ford visits China		trade with USA
1976	President Carter		suppression	and other Western states
1977		Panama Canal treaties	Brezhnev Constitution of	intervenes in
1978		mediates Egypt–Israel treaty	dissidents	wars in Africa
1979	Iranian hostage crisis	normalizes relations with China		invades Afghanistan
1980	President Reagan Miami race riots	Carter Doctrine		
1981				
1982			Brezhnev dies: Andropov rules	
1983		invades Grenada		withdraws from arms talks

Vertical labels (left to right, spanning years):

USA home column: ECONOMIC BOOM (1921–1928) · DEPRESSION (1933–1939) · WAR BOOM (1941–1944) · AFFLUENT SOCIETY (1954–1966) · INFLATION AND HIGH UNEMPLOYMENT (1966–1980)

USSR home column: COLLECTIVIZATION · INDUSTRIALIZATION (1928–1941) · ECONOMIC RECOVERY (1946–1956) · NEW ECONOMIC POLICIES RAISE LIVING STANDARDS (1957–1980)

home	foreign	PART IV: THE WORLD POWERS' RELATIONS SINCE 1945	
(Fall of Manchu government in 1911)		FIRST	1914
	Japan's Twenty-One Demands	WORLD	1915
WARLORD RULE		WAR	1916
1916-28	enters First World War	1914-18	1917
		Foreign	1918
May 4th movement		intervention in	1919
		Russian Civil War	1920
Sun Yat-sen: Three People's Principles			1921
		Fascist government formed in Italy	1922
KMT/CCP united front	aid from USSR		1923
			1924
Sun Yat-sen dies; Chiang Kai-shek leads KMT			1925
			1926
'White terror' against CCP			1927
KMT government at Nanking			1928
			1929
KMT attacks			1930
Communist Red bases	Japan occupies Manchuria		1931
			1932
		Hitler comes to power in Germany	1933
CCP's Long March, 1934-35			1934
Mao Tse-tung becomes Chairman of CCP			1935
Sian incident: KMT/CCP united front			1936
	SINO-	Japan invades China	1937
	JAPANESE		1938
	WAR	Germany attacks Poland ... SECOND	1939
	and	WORLD	1940
	SECOND	Germany attacks Russia WAR Japan attacks USA	1941
	WORLD	1939-45	1942
	WAR		1943
	1937-45		1944
		Yalta and Potsdam conferences	1945
KMT/CCP		COLD	1946
CIVIL WAR 1946-49		Truman Doctrine-Marshall Plan WAR	1947
		Berlin Blockade, 1948-49 Israel founded	1948
People's Republic declared		NATO set up Soviet A-bomb	1949
social and	Sino-Soviet Treaty	KOREAN	1950
economic reforms	KOREAN	WAR, 1950-53	1951
	WAR 1950-53		1952
First Five-Year Plan begins			1953
		Geneva Conference on Indo-China	1954
		First Summit meeting THAW	1955
Hundred Flowers campaign		Hungarian Revolution Suez War	1956
		Soviet sputnik	1957
Great Leap Forward: communes formed		Berlin crisis	1958
three		Khrushchev visits USA	1959
'Rightist' 'hard		U-2 crisis	1960
economic years'		Berlin Wall built Bay of Pigs invasion	1961
policies		Cuba missile crisis	1962
	Sino-Soviet	Nuclear Test-Ban treaty Sino-Soviet dispute	1963
	A-bomb dispute	develops	1964
		American escalation	1965
Great		in Vietnam	1966
Proletarian	H-bomb	Six-Day War	1967
Cultural		Nuclear Non-Proliferation Treaty Soviet invasion of Czechoslovakia	1968
Revolution	border clashes with USSR	West German Ostpolitik	1969
			1970
	admitted to UN	UN admits Communist China	1971
	welcomes Nixon	Nixon visits China and USSR DETENTE	1972
Anti-Confucius		Brezhnev visits USA Yom Kippur War	1973
Campaign		Nixon visits USSR India tests nuclear bomb	1974
		Lebanon Vietnam War ends Helsinki Conference	1975
Mao Tse-tung dies 'Gang of Four' disgraced		Civil War Soviet and	1976
Deng Xiaoping 'in charge'		Cuban aid to	1977
'Democracy	border	USSR–Vietnam Treaty wars in Africa	1978
Wall'	Deng visits USA clashes with	US–China normalization Egypt–Israel Treaty USSR in Afghanistan	1979
Gang of Four trial	Vietnam	Carter Doctrine Gulf War begins NEW COLD WAR	1980
Maoist policies condemned	trade with the West and Japan	guerilla martial law in Poland Cruise and Pershing	1981
		wars in Israel invades Lebanon missiles	1982
		Central America fighting continues arms talks break down	1983

Side labels: COLLECTIVIZATION / INDUSTRIALIZATION (1952–1962); MODERNIZATION (1976–1983)

IMPORTANT EVENTS

(see also the date chart on pages 322–3)

Part I   The USA since 1920

1920	18th Amendment (Prohibition) in force; Palmer raids; Sacco and Vanzetti arrested
1921	Immigration Quota Act restricts immigration
1925	Scopes Trial (the 'monkey trial')
1929	Wall Street Crash
1932	Bonus Marchers march on Washington
1933	New Deal begins: 'First Hundred Days'; 21st Amendment abolishes Prohibition
1935–9	Series of Neutrality Acts
1937	FDR's 'court-packing' plan; Chicago strike–'Memorial Day massacre'
1939	Outbreak of Second World War in Europe
1941	March: Lend-Lease Act
	August: Atlantic Charter signed
	December: Japanese attack on Pearl Harbor
1945	End of Second World War
1946	Employment Act
1947	Taft–Hartley Act; Truman orders federal loyalty investigation
1949	Alger Hiss convicted of perjury
1950	February: McCarthy campaign begins
	June: Korean War breaks out
	September: McCarran Internal Security Act
1954	McCarthy–Army Congressional hearings; *Brown v. Topeka Board of Education* decision ends 'separate but equal'
1955	Montgomery, Alabama bus boycott
1957	Little Rock, Arkansas school confrontation
1963	Civil Rights march on Washington; President Kennedy assassinated
1964	Civil Rights Act; 'campus revolt' begins in Berkeley, California; 'War on poverty' begins
1965	Voting Rights Act; Immigration Act alters quota system
1966	National Organization of Women founded
1967	Nationwide city riots
1968	Martin Luther King and Robert Kennedy assassinated
1970	Environmental Protection Agency set up
1972	Congress passes Equal Rights Amendment
1973	OPEC oil embargo leads to US 'energy crisis'; US troops withdrawn from Vietnam
1974	Watergate scandal: Nixon resigns
1979	Iranian hostage crisis; Three Mile Island nuclear scare
1980	Equal Rights Amendment fails to be ratified; Senate ratifies Panama Canal treaties; Miami, Florida, race riots

Part II   The USSR since 1917

1917	October Revolution
1918	Brest–Litovsk Treaty
	Civil war and foreign intervention begin
	'War Communism' economic policy
1919	Comintern established
1921	End of civil war
	Kronstadt rising
	New Economic Policy
1922	Treaty of Rapallo
1924	Death of Lenin
1927	Trotsky expelled from CPSU
1928	First Five-Year Plan begins
1929	Trosky expelled from USSR
1930	Liquidation of kulaks
1932	Second Five-Year Plan begins
1933	Hitler becomes German Chancellor
1934	USSR joins League of Nations
1934–8	Party purges
1935	Soviet alliance with France and Czechoslovakia
1936	Outbreak of Spanish Civil War
	Anti-Comintern Pact
1938	Munich Crisis
1939	Collapse of Anglo-Soviet negotiations
	Nazi–Soviet Pact
	Outbreak of Second World War
1941	German invasion of USSR
1945	End of Second World War
1953	Death of Stalin
1955	Khrushchev emerges as new Soviet leader
1956	Twentieth Party Congress: new policies of de-Stalinization and 'Peaceful Coexistence'; revolution in Hungary
1957	'Sputnik' (first space satellite) launched
1957–	Khrushchev follows new economic policies
1958	New Criminal Code adopted
1964	Khrushchev ousted; Brezhnev emerges as new leader
1964–	Brezhnev follows new domestic policies: suppression of dissidents, emigration for some national minorities, more investment in agriculture and consumer industries
1968	Soviet invasion of Czechoslovakia
1975	European Security Conference at Helsinki; five-year grain treaty with USA (both events symbolic of East–West *détente*)
1977	Promulgation of Brezhnev Constitution
1982	Brezhnev dies, succeeded by Andropov
1984	Andropov dies, succeeded by Chernenko

Part III China since 1911

1911	Fall of Manchu Government
1915	Japan's Twenty-One Demands on China
1916	Yuan Shih-kai dies; warlord rule begins
1919	May 4th Movement
1921	Sun Yat-sen's Three People's Principles
1923	First KMT/CCP 'united front' begins
1925	Sun Yat-sen dies, succeeded by Chiang Kai-shek
1926	KMT/CCP March against warlords
1927	KMT/CCP civil war begins
1928	KMT Government established at Nanking
1931	Japan occupies Manchuria
1934–5	CCP Long March to Yenan
1935	Mao Tse-tung becomes leader of CCP
1936	Second KMT/CCP 'united front' begins
1937	Sino–Japanese war begins; Soviet aid to KMT Government
1941	Japan attacks USA; America aids KMT Government through Second World War
1945	Japan defeated: end of Second World War
1946	KMT/CCP civil war resumes
1949	Communists defeat KMT; People's Republic of China declared
1950	Chinese troops occupy Tibet; Sino–Soviet Friendship Treaty; Korean War begins
1953	Korean War ends; first Five-Year Plan begins
1956	Collectivization of agriculture achieved
1956–7	Hundred Flowers Campaign
1958	Great Leap Forward; communes set up
1964	China tests first A-bomb
1964–5	American escalation in Vietnam War
1966	Cultural Revolution begins
1967	China tests first H-bomb
1969	Cultural Revolution dies away; Sino–Soviet border clashes
1971	UN admits Peking Government; Nixon visits China
1973–4	Anti-Confucius Campaign
1975	Vietnam War ends; Ford visits Peking
1976	Mao Tse-tung dies; Gang of Four arrested
1977	Deng Xiaoping now 'in charge'
1978–9	'Democracy Wall' – short period of free political discussion
1979	Deng Xiaoping visits USA
1980	Trial of the Gang of Four
1981	Maoist policies condemned; new official goal, the Four Modernizations
early 1980s	Deng Xiaoping follows new domestic policies: 'open door' to West and Japan, free enterprise in farming and petty trade, material incentives in industry, one-child population policy

Part IV The World Powers' Relations since 1945

1945	End of Second World War
1946	Churchill's 'Iron Curtain' speech
1947	Truman Doctrine; Marshall Plan; Cominform set up
1948	*Coup* in Czechoslovakia; Berlin Blockade begins; state of Israel founded
1949	Berlin Blockade ends; NATO set up; 'two Germanys' established; USSR tests first A-bomb; CCP victory in China
1950	Sino–Soviet Treaty; Korean War begins
1953	Truce in Korea; USA and USSR test first H-bombs
1954	Geneva Agreement on Indo-China
1955	W. Germany joins NATO; Warsaw Pact set up
1956	Khrushchev's 'Peaceful Coexistence' policy; Hungarian Revolution; Middle East Suez War
1959	Khrushchev–Eisenhower Summit in USA
1960	U-2 crisis; USSR withdraws aid to China
1961	'Bay of Pigs' invasion of Cuba; Berlin Wall built
1962	Cuba Missile Crisis
1963	Partial Nuclear Test-Ban Treaty
1964–5	American escalation in Vietnam War
1967	Middle East Six Day War; China tests H-bomb
1968	Warsaw Pact invades Czechoslovakia; France tests H-bomb; Nuclear Non-Proliferation Treaty
1969	West German *Ostpolitik* recognizes GDR; Sino–Soviet border clashes
1971	Peking Government admitted to UN
1972	Nixon visits Peking and Moscow; USA–USSR SALT I Agreement signed
1973	US troops withdraw from Vietnam; Middle East Yom Kippur War; Brezhnev visits USA
1974	India tests nuclear bomb; Nixon visits Moscow
1975	Communist victories in Indo-China; civil war in Lebanon; Soviets and Cubans in Angola; Helsinki Conference
1977–8	Soviets and Cubans in Horn of Africa
1978	USSR–Vietnam Friendship Treaty
1979	US–China relations normalized; China invades Vietnam; left-wing revolutions in Nicaragua and Grenada; Islamic revolution in Iran; Egypt–Israel Treaty; USSR invades Afghanistan
1980	'Carter Doctrine' on Persian Gulf area; Iraq–Iran Gulf War begins; Polish trade union Solidarity founded
1983	Continued fighting in Lebanon; guerilla wars in Central America; US invasion of Grenada; arms talks break down

Index